Dedication

To my readers who walked with me in
The Edmonds Beacon for six years. You
were a great encouragement to me.
In case you missed a column or two,
they're all here, updated, in the book
A New Look At the News.
For new readers, "Welcome aboard."

Rita Bennett
September 8, 2012
Edmonds, Washington

Table of Contents

Acknowledgements

I write this acknowledgement in thanksgiving for Dr. Connie Rice, English professor and C.S. Lewis expert, at Northwest, University, Kirkland, WA. While having lunch with her, earlier this year, she encouraged me to publish my columns and said she had enjoyed reading a number of them.

Thanks to Crystal Linn, talented writer, who has helped us at Christian Renewal Association Inc. while waiting for a full time job to open. Her help was timely for me with my small but talented staff, where every minute is filled with some important project. Crystal took on the project of organizing the files of *Beacon* columns into a very large notebook. I needed that help to get started to fly down the runway.

Next was finding all the columns stored on three different computers over six years! This is where Patricia Pierson, graphic artist and administrative assistant, stepped on to the tarmac. She had kept most of the master copies in PageMaker and then InDesign. It took time to convert the copies to MS Word and put them in chapters for me. Between all of us, 190 columns were found and ready for me for takeoff. Pat was also the creative photographer of the book cover picture, taken in the CRA home office in 2012. As you see, I'm reading a paper and holding a colorful mug, a gift from friend Casey Muhonen in Tennessee. This picture was tailor made for the book title.

Crystal suggested Mr. Ray Ruppert, of Tex Ware Publishing. I contacted him, and he was interested, so we were ready to fly with the air traffic control tower giving oversight.

Patricia Zulauf stopped the plane to read and give helpful suggestions for the first four Chapters, saying "I love the book."

For months I have burned the midnight oil, checked the flight maps, and now and I'm ready to call the tower for a smooth landing. Fortunately the Lord is in the right seat in His omnipresence so all will be well. Let's fly home.

Love to you all,

Rita Bennett
June 11, 2013

Foreword

by Keith F. Oles, Ph.D.
Professor of Geology

In a prelude to her new book Rita Bennett writes, "When in 2005 Editor Al Hooper asked me to write a column for *The Edmond's Beacon* weekly newspaper, I did not know that I would be involved in the project for a little over six years."

Nor did she know that her endeavors would result in 190 worship columns. Today, looking back at her huge project, I am both amazed and heartened that a newspaper in these unfortunately secular times would reach out and regularly publish columns of Christian witness.

Now, in this inspiring book, *A New Look at the News,* the columns are presented in seven discrete chapters. I have used the term "column" as in newspaper jargon. But they are more. There is a fascinating diversity. Some involve Old Testament history and our Judeo-Christian heritage. Some are about Jesus and his disciples and the spreading of the Gospel. Some are stories; some are lessons; some are contemporary vignettes. All are scripturally relevant, and witness to the scholarly research on which the columns are based.

I look forward to this opportunity to savor all of the columns. Through the years my wife, Lee, and I read many of the columns. But not all – when out of state we missed receiving our copies of *The Beacon,* hence the columns. With this new book, I now have the delightful opportunity to read them all.

Dr. Keith Oles
Geology Professor Emeritus, Oregon State University
Corvallis, Oregon
November 15, 2012

Author's Prelude

When in 2005 editor Al Hooper asked me, to write a column for *The Edmonds Beacon* newspaper, I did not know I would be involved in this project for a little over six years. See what one "yes" can do? Though at this time I was a published author and loved to capture inspiring thoughts on paper, I did not have any idea of how many words that would add up to in six years!

During his years as editor, I loved reading Mr. Hooper's columns. He usually made me laugh. Al is humorous, compassionate, and deep. He was a great online mentor to me, until his retirement at the end of 2009. Earlier that year, he emailed me about my recent column (June 30, 2009) saying, "Very well structured and presented, Rita! And thanks for getting it to me a day early. I think you're becoming a seasoned pro."

"Thank you Al."

At first I wrote my column every two weeks, and the last year or so, every week. When I was researching a subject, at times it might take eight hours to complete a column that week. And yes, I'm a night owl, so that works well for an author and columnist.

A Life Change

Fortunately my part in the paper was in the section called "Worship." This allowed me to glean from Bible wisdom that is tried, tested, and true. The age of the Bible goes back to the days of Moses. The Jewish calendar shows that we're living near the 6,000th year of biblical history.

There are two ways of looking at time. One is from earth's biblical perspective of time looking "forward" each day equaling 24 hours, and the other is the scientific perspective looking "backwards" to the point of creation and the ever expanding universe. Dr. Schroeder, physicist and Hebrew Bible Scholar in *The Science of God*, [1] does a masterful job of explaining how science and the Bible are compatible and interdependent.

During the time of looking back and rereading my news columns for this book, I saw the benefit of updating some of them including the

Breaking News segments. My inner editor could not resist a number of other needed touchups making time inclusive, and adding some major information.

While reading *A New Look at the News,* you'll find that I also enjoy the study of Hebrew. It has enriched my life and writing. So then at times, I am also looking at news through Judeo-Christian eyes. And though my chapters are time related, they still have a timelessness from ancient biblical wisdom.

Heaven Makes the News

Heaven in the News? Quite rare. Here's how it got there. My book *To Heaven and Back* had been published by Zondervan in 1997.[2] The research was fresh in my mind, and books on Heaven were sparse at that time. Probably thinking that we needed a little more Heaven than hell in the media, my fingers started dancing on my computer keyboard and out came a series of eleven Heaven columns!

Early in September 2012, I was happy to see the former Edmond's Mayor, Gary Hawkinson at the local Chanterelle's Restaurant. He graciously came over to my table to say hello. During our visit, I mentioned that my newspaper columns would be published soon. He encouraged me by saying that he had always enjoyed reading my articles. That, of course, made my day.

Throughout my book you will find that within my columns are a series of eighteen studies. This was a happening as week-by-week the writing evolved. Then, in chapter six part 1, came another series, a personal one, where I tell about the early days of my life and how I became interested in the Spirit-led life as a new university graduate. The Bible had all of a sudden become alive, life changing, and nourishing.

English scholar and Christian theologian, C.S. Lewis, wrote many books, including the *Chronicles of Narnia*[3] and his science fiction trilogy. If you look at some of the other books listed under Bibliography, they will add to this list of my favorites.

In the detailed outline you'll find the actual dates when the columns were written. Some have been moved slightly out of date order to make this book more readable for you.

Invitation

Come on the journey with me in the columns I've written. You'll find Holy Spirit breadcrumbs dropped along the pathway to guide you and others. I trust you'll find some answers possibly not thought of before, and that it will be food for hungry hearts and souls.

I didn't know, and maybe others of you did not know either, that we humans are spiritually starving – until we partake heartily of the eternal Bread of God's Word anointed by the oil of the Spirit.

My hope is that you too will pass it on, as living Bread falls upon your own pathway of life.

In gratitude and friendship,
Rita Bennett
Edmonds, Washington,
June 11, 2013

Chapter 1

Treasures of Children Series
Heaven to Gain Series
The Seven Churches Series Begins
Breaking News: The Earth groans & Miracles

Arrival at the Eastern Gate (illustration above) – Approaching the central East Gate of Heaven, the traveler has come through lush Garden of Eden beauty. Glory shines out to welcome the faithful. We've dreamed about this moment of entering Heaven's Gate. God's angel is there to greet us. It's powerful!

Rita Bennett

Children Our National Treasure

Children are our hope. Children are our future. What happens to them happens to our society, to our world.

The treasure of children was emphasized even more to all of us through the December 26, 2004 tsunami tragedy in South Asia.[1] Fifty-five thousand children were swallowed up by the Indian Ocean in a matter of minutes.

Do we truly realize, with such huge losses suffered, that a population's greatest loss is their children? Think what those children would have brought to their communities, nations, to the world as artists, writers, parents, businesspersons, ministers, fishermen, chefs, political leaders, priests, teachers, linguists, professors, scientists, counselors, inventors, computer experts, and on.

It Happened Before

Southeast Asia is not the first time in history when masses of children have been wiped out, this time not by the wildness of nature, but by people. History records that around 4 B.C. in Jerusalem, King Herod the Great, had a visit by three magi from the orient. They asked where does the boy live who was born King of the Jews? We've followed a star to find him and bring him gifts! Herod directed them south to Bethlehem, but God led them in a different direction.

Scripture records this 2,000 year old event in Matthew 2:16-18 "When Herod saw that he had been tricked by the wise men, he was infuriated and he sent and killed all the children in and around Bethlehem who were two years old or under according to the time that he had learned from the wise men" (KJV-MOD). Biblical commentator, Finis Dake, estimates that Herod's Slaughter of the Innocents extended at least ten miles around Bethlehem including Jerusalem.[2] Thousands must have been killed!

But toddler Jesus had been whisked away from Nazareth to Egypt by his parents because they had been warned by an angel in a dream.

Meaning Today

What does this mean to us? We should do all we can to nurture and protect our national treasures. Have you hugged your kid today and told

13

her that you love her? Have you spent time reading to him, listening to him? Have you read stories to your child about children in the Bible? Have you visited with your child's teachers? Are you praying with him or her about the orphaned children and the bereaved parents in South Asia? Have you taught your child that Jesus is their greatest treasure? Consider doing all of these, won't you?

Next I'II tell you more about the loss of children and why we need to know about it.

The Young Moses and Jesus Are Linked for Eternity

My first column reviewed the recent children's tragedy of those drowned in the South Asia tsunami. Then as if in time travel going back 2,000 years, we visited the Death of the Innocents when the narcissistic Herod killed many toddler to infant boys in Bethlehem and Jerusalem, in an unsuccessful attempt to find one boy Jesus (*Yeshua*) and snuff out his life.

Jump in the time machine and let's go back 1,500 more years, when the people of Israel were slaves in Egypt. Here again is the story of a death sentence for hundreds of Israelite boys. When the new pompous conqueror of Egypt, Assyrian ruler Rameses II, saw how the captive children of Israel were growing, he decided they might get too strong and break free from their slavery. He then devised an insidious decree to slow down Israel's progress. Calling the chief women, over 500 to 1,000 midwives, he demanded that all newborn boys be killed at birth. Interesting that at this very time 1520 B.C. Moses was born, whom God would use to deliver the Israelites out of Egyptian bondage.

A Six-Year-Old Heroine

In steps our heroine, a little six-year-old girl Miriam, from the family of Levi. Her brother had been born and hidden by his parents three months, hoping to give him a fighting chance before he had to be "thrown into the river" to die – Rameses' second decree. The parents had built a little boat from a papyrus basket, and placed their son in it. This floating bassinet was carefully placed among the reeds at the riverbank, where the child might be found. His little sister stood close by to watch. The princess of Egypt came to the Nile River to bathe, saw the basket, and had it brought to her. When it was opened, the cry of the beautiful boy moved the princess to compassion.

Moses's sister Miriam may have said to the princess, "Would you like me to find one of the Hebrew women to nurse the baby for you?" The answer was one word, "Go" (Exodus 2:8). During his five formative years he had the joy of being raised by his own family! He was named Moses by his adoptive mother. The name in Hebrew, *Mosheh*, means "drawn out" as from the waters of the Nile.

Two Leaders, Two Callings

We know Moses became and is still the leader of the Jews, whereas, Jesus became and is still leader of the Christians. These two great leaders are connected in numerous other ways. Another one is that an evil power was stirring up ideas in the cauldron minds of both Herod the Great and Rameses II to destroy these boys before they had a chance to grow up and set God's people free. These evil plans were outwitted!

As Passover and Easter are celebrated each spring, consider thanking God for both Moses and Jesus. Moses was called to get God's people out of Egypt and into Israel, the Promised Land. And Jesus was called to get Egypt out of people and take us to the glorious place God promised, Heaven.

Next time: another time when children were victims of dictators, and why we must know about it.

Innocent Children at Risk in Our World

World War II ended in Europe with the surrender of Nazi Germany, May 8, 1945. Adolph Hitler, the occult tyrant, was dead and the world had a celebration.

January 30, 1945, is when we remember the liberation of the largest of forty-two Nazi prison camps, Auschwitz in Poland. Now on January 30th, our world remembers the holocaust of six million Jewish people. We should be shocked to know that 1,500,000 of them were children!

In 2003 I had the privilege of visiting The Children's Holocaust Memorial, at Yad Vashem Museum in Jerusalem. The Israeli Knesset built these memorials to honor the dead and perpetuate the memory and lessons of the holocaust for future generations.

The Children's Holocaust Memorial

I visited this Children's Memorial on Christmas Day with a Jewish tour group from America. It was a special honor that I could walk with my new friends and seek to comfort them as we entered the large white stone building. The dark long corridors inside are lined with mirrors and the flame of a single candle – centrally located is multiplied thousands of times visually. When I came in from the bright sunlight, I had to feel my way along the metal handrail in the sudden darkness. My eyes begin to adjust and I looked over the rail downward several stories below and saw thousands of candles representing the children. Looking up I had a similar effect. The sensation was a vastness of the universe with life going on for eternity!

At intervals, we heard names of the martyred children read softly, solemnly, reverently: Isaac – Sarah – David – Rachel – Jacob – the litany continued. That day I saw the evil fruit of what generational prejudice, hatred, ignorance, and occult beliefs can produce.

What's in a Name?

I wondered what the name Yad Vashem means and why it was chosen. The name is taken directly from Isaiah 56 in the Hebrew Bible. The Lord says, those "who choose what pleases Me and hold fast to my covenant – to them I will give within my temple and its walls a memorial (*yad* or hand) and (*va*) a name (*shem*) better than sons and daughters; I will give them an everlasting name that will not be cut off" (vs. 4b, 5). That is a promise for Israel, and for you.

The promise is in two parts. Your hand represents what you do. Your name is your identity. Consider putting your small hand (*yad*) in God's (*HaShem's*) big Hand (*Yad*) and see what He can do to help you make our world a safer, kinder, and happier place.

Why must there be memorials like Yad Vashem? To remind the world of the holocaust so it will never happen again!

Next time we'll look at how children are exploited and what we can do to help them.

Sexual Abuse of Kids Violates God's law

God's Viewpoint

One day Jesus the Messiah and His disciples were having a discussion about the Kingdom of Heaven. "He called a little child and had him stand among them. And He said, 'I tell you the truth, unless you change and become like little children, you will never enter the Kingdom of Heaven. ... But if anyone causes one of these little ones who believe in me to sin, it would be better for him to have a large millstone hung around his neck and to be drowned in the depths of the sea.'" (Matt 18:2-3,6 NIV).

Jesus was angry! Here he gives a heavy sentence to those men or women, heterosexuals or homosexuals, who would cause one of **these little ones** to sin. Those who do this, even today, will be spiritually donning a millstone necklace.

If you have sinned in this way, listen to the words of the Apostle Peter, "The Lord is ... not willing that any should perish, but that all should come to repentance" (2 Peter 3:9 KJV). With Jesus' warning, one's life must be cleaned up before it is too late.

Next time we will consider what happens to children when they die, and the faith of a child.

Help Protect all Kids from Sexual Abuse

Fatherless children are at risk for sexual abuse. Sometimes we act as though fathers are only necessary for their biological contribution. Mature, wholesome fathers are essential in raising spiritually, emotionally, and physically healthy children. Let's look at some ways to protect our children from sexual abuse.

Helping Children

- Teach your child his phone number and address.
- Give your child healthy love and cuddles so he or she will not be starved for love.
- Teach your child not to talk to strangers nor allow anyone to touch his private places.
- Never allow a stranger to take your child to the rest room.

- Do not leave your child with an adult you do not know well.
- Get acquainted with your child's teacher and visit the classroom to see if your child is happy there.

Protecting Teens

- Guard your teen from a molested mind due to exposure of unprotected internet websites.
- Teen, you are warned not to involve yourself with an unknown chat room person without your parent's permission. If you are lonely, talk with a school counselor, your family members, pastor, or rabbi.
- Do not get in a car with someone you do not know or know only slightly. Double date with a couple you know well rather than going out as a single couple.
- Extreme clothing fads portrayed by models and media are not safe for you in the everyday world. It's fun to be in style but do not push the envelope too far and become unsafe.
- When guys or gals are wearing jeans that are too revealing or are nearly falling off – what message does the opposite sex get? Do you really want to say that?
- Do you know virginity is a gift not to throw away? Why did God choose a virgin named Mary to be the mother of His incarnate Son, Jesus?
- Study the ancient wisdom of the Bible that tells you how to have a lifestyle that pleases God and makes you happy and fulfilled. Wash your mind often with the words in the books of Psalms and Proverbs, for starters.

Parents

If you have children and you are living with a partner, see a counselor for emotional healing and seek marriage counseling. Cohabitation is especially hard on your children.

Scripture says, "A father to the fatherless, a defender … is God in his holy dwelling" (Psalm 68:5 NIV). Become acquainted with this loving God and let Him be a Father to those who have missed the safety that a wholesome father brings into a home.

Next time where do children go when they die?

Heaven Awaits for Children Who Suffer

During my five previous columns, we have time traveled over 3,500 years dipping into historical accounts to review how children have been victims of tyrants, abusers, and even the wildness of nature. The result has been millions upon millions dying before they had a chance to live. What happens to infants and children who die prematurely?

In February 2005, *The Edmonds Beacon* Executive Editor, Al Hooper, wrote a poignant article about the death of two Edmonds sisters. Kelsey and Hayley Byrne, ages 11 and 9, who were put to sleep forever by their biological father giving them an overdose of sleeping pills.[3] Mr. Hooper in his article about this senseless killing wondered aloud – with hope – that there might be a Heaven where these girls are now happy and safe. There are many varying theological opinions to such questions, but rather than debate it, let us see what God Himself tells us from the best-selling book of all time, the Bible.

The Good Shepherd speaks

From the Jewish Bible we see a special promise to children in Isaiah 40:11, "He shall feed His flock like a Shepherd: He shall gather the lambs with His arm, and carry them in His bosom, and shall gently lead those that are with young." Here the Good Shepherd gives special attention to the lambs, an analogy to children, and carries them in His bosom.

For Christians, we particularly love Jesus' words. One written by Matthew, in chapter 18:10 says, "Take heed that you despise not one of these little ones [children]; for I say to you, that in Heaven their angels do always behold the face of my Father who is in Heaven" (KJV-MOD).

Verse 14 follows, "Even so it is not the will of your Father who is in Heaven, that one of these little ones should [eternally] perish" (KJV-MOD).

Be Kind to Children

A third word from Jesus is from Mark 9:37, "Who ever shall receive one of such children in My name, receives Me: and who ever shall receive Me, receives not Me, but Him that sent Me" (KJV-MOD). (There are many more scriptures.)[4]

These verses teach us a lot. Here we see the Lord carries children close to His heart. Children are guarded by angels on earth and in Heaven. Our Father does not want one child to perish. Children are so connected to God that receiving them makes a way for us to receive Him.

Yes, I believe Kelsey and Hayley, as well as the holocaust martyred Jewish children, and all children who would want God when they see Him – are in Heaven.

Next: Breaking News, and Tell Me about Heaven.

Miracles Become a Matter of Record
Breaking News

Once in a while we read about miracles in the news; I have two to add to that treasure chest.

On March 4, 2005 I listened and took notes as David Dolan, Journalist, formerly from the Northwest now Jerusalem-based, spoke at *Beit Tikvah Messianic Congregation* in Newcastle, Washington.

"It might surprise you to know," said David, "that Israel was greatly affected by the South Asia Tsunami, December 26, 2004. Walking down the street in Jerusalem, following a lovely Christmas Eve dinner with friends, I was surprised to feel that the Israeli's were in imminent danger." David thought of the massive Bam (Iran), earthquake that had occurred December 26, 2003.

"Many Israeli's go to the beaches of Thailand for vacation," he explained. "I eventually discovered that 3,000 Israeli's were in Bangkok, the Thai capital, at the time of the disaster. Sadly, yet miraculously, only seven were killed and thirty-five injured."

How the others escaped

"December 26th was the Buddhist Festival. It was the one day of the year that most of the visiting Israeli's had chosen to leave!" David's website ddolan.com said, "Israel's international airport has been the setting for many emotional reunions as hundreds of local survivors of the Asian mega-disaster return to their precious homes …"[5]

Second Treasure

I received the following internet testimony written by Pastor Bill Hekman, Indonesia. Eighty percent of the town of Meulaboh in Aceh was destroyed by the Tsunami waves and eighty percent of the people died. This is one of the towns that was hit the hardest.

The pastor gave this fantastic testimony from Meulaboh, "In that town are about 400 Christians. They wanted to celebrate Christmas but were not allowed to do so by the Muslims of Meulaboh. The Christians were told if they wanted to celebrate it they needed to go outside the city on a high hill. As a result the 400 believers left the city on December 25th and camped out overnight.

"On the morning of, December 26, 2004, there was the earthquake followed by Tsunami waves destroying most of the city of Meulaboh where thousands were killed. The 400 people on the mountain were saved!"[6]

The Lord says, "I will instruct you and teach you in the way that you shall go …" (Psalm 32:8 KJV-MOD). Here we see instances of how both Jews and Christians learned that it pays to listen and to obey God.

Is This Life All There Is?

Do you remember when the afterlife had been top of the news for many weeks with the televised drama of Terri Schindler-Schiavo's slow death? That was followed by Pope John Paul's failing health and then his death April 3, 2005, a few days following Terri's. Television screens changed to St. Peter's Basilica in Rome where millions had gathered for days on end. The world saw an open casket funeral that is rare, at least for Americans.

Radio personality, Rabbi Daniel Lapin said, "Terri Schiavo, clinging to life, alerted all Americans to the real distinction between the culture of death and that of life. Perhaps her final role was to herald on high, the imminent arrival of Karol Wojtyla."[7]

Is this life all there is, or is there an eternal life that follows? This is the question before the world. If you are a believer in the Bible, there are a solid 151 references on Heaven to encourage you. The Apostle Paul was transformed from a destroyer of Christians to a believer, due to his heavenly vision and message he received from the glorified Jesus

Christ. This happened as Paul journeyed on the road to Damascus (Acts 9:1-7; 2 Cor.12:1-4).

Near-death Experiences

It was similar to what we today call a near-death experience. The light and presence of God knocked Paul to the ground, and he was blinded for three days. Paul persecuted Christians but Jesus put it this way, "Paul, Paul why are you persecuting Me?" (Acts 9:3-4 KJV-MOD). Apparently when Christians are mistreated or killed, Jesus feels the pain of it.

You can read the numerous books available by people who have had near-death experiences. "As a result of advancements in resuscitation techniques, more and more people are coming back from the brink of death. In 1989 it was estimated that sixteen million people worldwide were in this category."[8]

To help people who had lost a loved one, including myself in 1991, I wrote a book *To Heaven and Back*[9] that amazed me by selling over 200,000 copies. An exciting moment in my research was when I looked up Heaven in my *Interlinear Hebrew-English Old Testament*.[10]

In my Hebrew studies, I found Genesis chapter one has several references to Heaven, which can be transliterated as *Shamayim.* Research scholars such as Robert Girdleston noticed that the form of the word (*shamayim*) is neither singular nor plural, but dual confirming a real place both physical and spiritual.[11]

Saint Theresa brought both of these dimensions together when it is reported she said, "God gives us a little bit of Heaven to go to Heaven in."

Heaven Heals All

Composer Thomas Moore said, "Earth has no sorrow that Heaven cannot heal."[12]

Saint Terri, Saint John Paul, Saint Dennis Bennett, and Saint Theresa have all had tears wiped from their eyes by Jesus, the healer of souls.

Ask Him to wipe away your tears here on earth. Also ask for a little bit of Heaven to go to Heaven in.

Next time, more on Heaven

Heaven is a Place of Love, Peace, Wisdom

In May of 2005, I heard a talk show host who said something like, "I've gone through about 2,000 theories [on Heaven] in the last 30 years of my life and still have yet to come to one that makes absolute sense to me."

Are you one of those people who believes this is it, that we are just fertilizer?

Andrew Greeley, Roman Catholic Priest and sociologist says, "We are born with two incurable diseases: life, from which we die, and hope, which says maybe death isn't the end."[13]

Science Helps My Faith

What helps me believe in Father Greeley's and Bonnie's hope comes from several things. Science and space exploration helps me believe more in the supernatural. I'm amazed when I see people blasting off into outer space and floating around in a spaceship, or taking gigantic leaps on the moon.

When observing astronauts shown as they peer through space helmets covered with transparent gold to protect their eyes from radiation, it reminds me of Scripture's description of transparent gold streets. On television I saw the Russian spaceship docking at a space station to exchange astronauts who live there six months at a time. Amazing.

It's an incredible world we live in but the possibility of Heaven is even more astonishing. Yet it doesn't seem strange any more to consider that people in Heaven may float or glide instead of walk. Sounds like fun!

Our Ultimate Home

Ancient words from Scripture tell us Heaven is a place called home from where we were created and where we will be totally at peace returning to our Creator God. Heaven is a place of unconditional love, tangible peace, wisdom, beauty, acceptance, history, music, praise, worship, dancing, fun, delicious aromas, friendship, fulfillment, learning, light, preparation, eating, drinking, trust, joy, kindness, and healing, for starters.

About this home Jesus said, "In My Father's house are many mansions: if it were not so, I would have told you. I go to prepare a place for you" (John 14:2). What comforting words. What a promise!

I find it hard when looking at the miracles of science and creation all around me not to believe that there is a higher power, whom I, as does the Bible, call God or *Elohim* (Hebrew), Father, Son, and Holy Spirit.

He is the Designer and the Creator of what Physicist Gerald Schroder calls our expanding universe.[14]

Next time: more on Heaven.

This is an Invitation You Can't Refuse

When is the last time you were invited to a party? You probably did not go unless you had a friend attending or heard of other interesting people who would be there. The question about a final journey to Heaven's party is one people are either consciously or unconsciously contemplating.

As a writer, I think of how much fun it will be to meet great writers on the other side. The two best selling Gospel authors who are also apostles are there: The Apostle Matthew, former tax collector, who wrote with an emphasis to the Jews, and the Apostle John, the one called beloved because he was so devoted to his Teacher, Jesus. John also wrote the greatest book on Heaven, the book of Revelation, the conclusion to the Christian Bible.

And in the front of the Bible, the *Torah* (or *Pentateuch),* we have the five books of Moses the great foundation of the Scriptures. This author wrote down what God spoke to him. That's an exciting way to write. Moses was a mighty prophet and miracle worker, yet a very humble man. (The Jewish Bible ends with Malachi.)

C.S. Lewis

A contemporary author who has made his final journey, is the well-known, Clive Staples Lewis. This former English professor of literature at Oxford and Cambridge Universities wrote more than thirty books. His series of books *The Chronicles of Narnia*[15] have a lot of symbolism of Heaven in them. This book is a must for all children as well as adults.

Another of my favorites is *The Great Divorce.*[16] In Lewis's classic vision of the afterworld, the narrator boards a bus on a drizzly afternoon to unknowingly embark on an incredible voyage through the outskirts of Heaven and hell.

Many people on the bus are very aggressive. Some try to shoot or stab one another but it doesn't work since they're in their spirit bodies. This they find frustrating! A bishop is an interesting passenger. When the bus takes the tour group to the gates of Heaven, he decides to return to the bus because he feels it's more important to go back to his theological discussions with his many admirers. The bishop lacks the wisdom to realize that he'll be returning to his present living quarters, at the outskirts of hell.

Join the Party

God is throwing a party in Heaven. Everyone has been invited, but some have chosen not to come. Incredible guests are there. King Jesus has paid your way. If you haven't done so already, I hope you'll be wise enough to RSVP to your invitation immediately.

Next time: The Door to Heaven.

Seeking and Finding the Door to Heaven

The book of Revelation chapter twenty-one says there are twelve gates, or doorways into Heaven and at each doorway is an angel to welcome the weary travelers. In each angel's hand is a book, guessed by some as The Book of Life.

The most significant of the twelve doorways around Heaven's wall is the one in the center on the east side. Those who have visited Israel and have visited the Mount of Olives have seen the beautiful eastern gate. Perhaps you visualized Messiah upon His future arrival walking through the now closed gateway at the beginning of His millennial reign. The significance of the eastern gate follows the pattern God gave Moses for his tent of meeting in the wilderness, which had only one entrance on the east side. The Gate of Eden where humankind was expelled was east of the garden told about in Genesis 3:24.

If the twelve gateways around Heaven are placed equidistant around the jasper wall of 6,000 miles square, then every 500 or possibly 499.5

miles is a doorway. The width of each gateway might be estimated as one-half mile wide, to accommodate all the people. Fortunately, no one is sick or infirm in Heaven and walking will be more like space walking. Traveling hundreds of miles by foot will be a snap.

For the Jewish Believer

Jewish Congregations have an annual festival called *Yom Kippur* or Day of Atonement. This is 24 hours of fasting and confession for sins of the past year. As the gates to Heaven are opened on *Yom Teruah,* or Day of Trumpets - the previous festival, now they are closed on *Yom Kippur* (Lev 23:27). To signify this at some point in the synagogue you may hear a door slam shut. Jesus, or *Yeshua,* as a Jewish boy then man, celebrated these festivals every year of His life on earth.

For the Christian Believer

For the Christian today we think of Jesus' words recorded in John 10:9, "I am the door by Me if any man enter in, he shall be saved …" (KJV-MOD). Jesus also gave us the parable of the five wise and five foolish virgins (believers) and said, "those who were 'ready' went in with Him to the wedding; and the door was shut."

In the *Torah* of Leviticus and the Gospel of John, both remind us that the doorway into Heaven will someday close. Right now in this day of grace it is wide open.

"*Anee HaDelet,*" "I am the door" said Jesus.

It's not hard to find The Door. Just ask, seek, and knock.

Next time: Heaven's Jasper Wall.

Heaven's Jasper Wall Is Like No Other

During my first trip to Old Jerusalem in 1996, I was impressed with the city's dramatic stone wall. It is eight to fourteen feet thick with what was once a rampart, now a walkway, on top, wide enough for two people to walk shoulder to shoulder.

"The current wall was built by Sultan-Caliph Suleyman between 1520 and 1566. It's on the same lines as the Roman fortifications during Jesus' time. The ramparts are between 39 to 49 feet high and roughly

5,330 yards long. With eight gates, they give the city the shape of an irregular trapezoid. In nearly five centuries, these fortifications have not changed significantly."[17] That wall, the Roman wall, and the wall around the city in King David's day were all built to protect the city from its enemies.

Why the Wall?

So why does Heaven, the New Jerusalem, have a wall encircling it? No protection from enemies will be needed, as at last, there will be none. Why a wall? It is a constant reminder of our security in God. Isaiah describes it: "You will call your walls Salvation ..." (60:18, KJV-MOD). You will be surrounded by walls of salvation as an eternal reminder that you were saved from separation, from your Creator God.

What do the walls of Heaven's holy city look like? In his revelation, the Apostle John wrote: "He [the angel] measured its wall and it was 144 cubits thick, by man's measurement, which the angel was using. The wall was made of jasper ..." (Rev 21:17-18, KJV-MOD). Most biblical scholars believe the Scripture here is speaking of the width of the wall rather than the height. My reading indicates that this would be about 216 feet or 72 yards thick – nearly the length of a football field. The height of the wall is not given but I would guess the height of a three story building on earth.

This 1,500–mile–square wall, is made of jasper – a precious stone. Oriental jasper is a sea-green quartz, its crystal is perfectly clear. John says what he saw in his vision was a "precious jewel, like jasper, clear as crystal" (Rev 21:11 KJV-MOD).

Walking and Dancing

Again on my trip to Old Jerusalem, the group I was with climbed the stairs to the top of its wall as part of a prayer walk. Hundreds of us had donned white robes and walked around part of the city walls praying and singing.

This chapter is about the wall around Heaven, and the wall around Jerusalem on earth is a microcosm of Heaven's wall.

I can foresee being part of a similar march, this time, on Heaven's 72-yards-thick, 6,000-miles-long jasper wall – with us dancing, singing, and rejoicing together from every nation on earth.

We'll get to dance with friends old and new, and probably in Hebraic style, hands clasped in a circle. Will you join me?

Next time: A Message on Heaven's Gate.

A Message For All At Heaven's Gates

I never thought about Heaven's gate having a message for anyone until I interviewed Deborah O'Donnell, an Oregon music teacher. Deborah had nearly choked to death by inhaling debris being swept off her roof. She was unconscious around fifteen minutes, and realized upon awakening that she had a near-death experience (NDE).

During her NDE she had walked around looking at this beautiful, peaceful place that eventually led to a highway. Realizing that she was in Heaven, she thought of seeing family members who had died and wanted to find them. Then she thought, "No the greatest thing of all is that I'm going to see Jesus!" She began to run down a street of gold but though she struggled to stay on the path she was pulled away, up into the air. She saw Heaven as a city with a massive gate at the entrance. In huge golden letters were words arched over the gate saying, *"You will return, but I have a work for you to do."*

This really impressed me that God would write a message to Deborah on the eastern gate into the New Jerusalem! Maybe that is the subconscious reason that I later studied the names of the twelve tribes of Israel that are written over the twelve gates to the City and began to wonder what those Hebrew names meant as I prepared to write a book (Rev 21:12). One day as I looked up the meanings, I was surprised by what emerged!

A great discovery: **Judah**: confession or praise of God. **Reuben**: viewing the son. **Gad** a company. **Asher**: blessed. **Naphtali**: wrestling with. **Manasseh**: forgetfulness. **Simeon**: hearing and obeying. **Levi**: cleaving to. **Issachar**: a reward. **Zebulun**: home. **Joseph**: added to. **Benjamin**: son of the right hand.

Here's the meaning I saw:

"Confessors and praisers of God;
Looking upon the Son.
A band of blessed ones;
Wrestling is over,
Forgetting the pain.

Hearing and obeying His Word.
Cleaving to our Lord, who is our reward.
We are Home!
We are added to the family of Jesus;
Son of the Father's right hand."[18]

Notice how this coded message begins with praise and ends with we are at home in God's family.

When my brother Bill's second wife died, he told me that Kay had a dream about a kind of password that one would speak upon entering Heaven. It is given in Psalm 100:4, "Enter into His gates with thanksgiving, and into His courts with praise ..." When you enter, you will automatically "give thanks and praise." How could you do otherwise? This is the way of entering Heaven the psalmist David predicted over 3,000 years ago.

However, David did not know there would be a Hebrew message awaiting him ahead of time.

But now you know God's, "Welcome home message" in advance, and also how you will enter the Gate!

Next time: The Apostles' names at the gates.

Apostles' Names Await at Heaven's Gates

What group of men could be so important as to have their names **eternally inscribed** at the entryway to Heaven? One day we'll see the names of twelve men, Christ's closest disciples, later ordained His Apostles, engraved on the very foundation stones of those twelve gates. In fact, as you enter, you will walk on the memorial stones of their names. John attests to this in his book of Revelation, chapter 21 and verse 14.

An apostle is "one sent with a special message or commission."[19] In addition, as you enter Heaven, Peter gives the qualifications of "the twelve" as those personally acquainted with Christ from His baptism by John to His ascension (Acts 1:21-22). The twelve were those first chosen by Jesus Christ to assist Him in establishing a beachhead to implant His Kingdom on our fallen planet!

For three years after Jesus' short ministry began "they left all and followed Him." He knew that these men must be with Him constantly to be adequately trained to continue what He had begun. As they traveled, they cast out demons that were making people emotionally ill or mad, they healed the sick, worked miracles, and sometimes they failed in their attempts. But they were learning, just as you and I do, as we try to follow in Jesus steps.

The early church wrote down the essence of what the twelve taught in what is called *The Apostle's Creed*. Why were they so honored? Because they established the faith that billions of people have believed during these past 2,000 years. Eleven of the twelve were martyred as they spread the Gospel throughout the region. Now the message is worldwide and trans-world.

You Will Meet Them!

So if you and I are going to read their names on Heaven's foundations, it seems a good idea to know who they are. It's interesting to find that Jesus chose four sets of brothers, and four individuals.

Brothers:
1. Simon Peter (Cephas - the rock) prominent in the early church, author of I and II Peter; and
2. Andrew who led his brother Peter to the Messiah;
3. James ("the greater") son of Alphaeus; brother to
4. John, (prolific writer) Gospel of John, 3 letters, and Revelation. Peter, James and John were very close with Jesus.
5. Philip, another apostle, who brought his brother,
6. Bartholomew (Nathanael), to Jesus. (Not the Philip of Acts 6:5).
7. James ("the less" – perhaps smaller statue); brother to
8. Judas Thaddaeus (surnamed Thaddaeus) - **not** Iscariot.

Individuals:
1. Simon Zelotes firey advocate of the Mosaic Torah.
2. Matthew (Levi) former tax collector, author of the Gospel of Matthew.
3. Thomas (Didymus) a twin. From doubter to faithful.
4. Matthias, was chosen by the 11 apostles to replace the fallen Judas Iscariot.
5. Judas, who betrayed the Lord Jesus. Eternal esteemed position lost!

There you have the bare bones to get you started in your study. After you walk through the gate, you and I will find out so very much more.

Next time: The pearl gate.

Those Luminescent Gates of Pearl Await

My mother, Loretta, told me that she was amazed at the pearl gate's beauty, which she went through upon entering Heaven. You see, Loretta Reed, had a near-death experience when I was born.

Sally Moser, *Heaven Tours*[20] book illustrator, gave the gate an ancient look in her drawing. The rooftop is pearlized as well as the doorway columns but Sally envisioned the pearl itself in the center of the door. This is the opening you and I will walk through into Heaven. The Scripture simply says, "The twelve gates were twelve pearls: each gate was of one pearl ..." (Rev 21:21 KJV-MOD).

Biblical Symbols of the Pearl

What does the pearl symbolize in the Bible? Jesus is teaching on the Kingdom of God when He says, "Again, the Kingdom of Heaven is like a merchant seeking beautiful pearls, who, when he had found one pearl of great price went and sold all that he had, and bought it" (Matt 13:45-46 KJV-MOD). What extreme value the merchant placed on this one pearl!

I find there are two main interpretations to this parable.

First:
Human beings seek many things that do not satisfy and then discover Jesus, the Pearl of Great Price, and sell all they have to follow Him. In this parable you are the merchant and Jesus is the pearl.

Second:
In the second interpretation, Jesus is the Merchant who came to find you. You are the lost pearl of great price. The huge price He paid for you was His life that He gave willingly.

The pearl is a unique gem that comes **not** from depths of the earth, as with gold, but from abnormal growth within an ocean-grown oyster. My friend, internationally known musician, Merla Watson quotes her

Rabbi friend, "Did you ever know that pearls are not 'kosher'? Certain sea animals are ritually unfit for use according to Jewish law. In Bible times, Jewish women would never have thought to wear pearls. So what is meant by the pearl gates in the Bible? The un-kosher pearls stand for the [believing] Gentiles. It is through the plan of salvation received by the Gentiles that we will all enter into Heaven as the New [or renewed] Covenant people of God."[21]

Gentile Believers & Pearls

This belief may show believing Gentiles as part of the very Jewish gates of Heaven too. Even here at the front gate, our Lord is trying to show each one of us, Jew and Gentile, that we are all of great value and that *we need each other.*

Each gate is one pearl, the form of a circle that is a perfect symbol of unity and eternity. Our Savior, having given Himself for all believers whom He calls pearls of great price is now preparing us for presentation to Himself (Eph 5:25-27).

Next time: A Place of rainbow colors and *shekinah* light.

A Place of Rainbow Colors and Brilliant Light

For those of you who love the beauty of gems, and enjoy buying and wearing them, you will find Heaven awesome.

Revelation 21:14 says, "The wall of the City had twelve foundations, and on them were the names of the twelve Apostles of the Lamb" (KJV-MOD). "The foundations of the city walls were decorated with every kind of precious stone" (Rev 21:19a KJV-MOD). John then lists twelve stones, some familiar to us, some not so common: jasper, sapphire, chalcedony, emerald, sardonyx, chrysolite, beryl, topaz, chrysoprasus (chrysoberyl), jacinth (hyacinth), and amethyst.

Notice that if you compare this list of twelve gems to our beloved 12-month list of birthstones you will find five of them to be the same: amethyst, February; emerald, May; sardonyx (peridot), August; sapphire, September; and topaz, November. A sixth birthstone is not listed as being in the wall but in the gate: the pearl, June (Rev 21:19b-20).

Birthstones in Heaven

Next time you wear one of these birthstones, consider that you're wearing one of the same gems found in the foundation of Heaven's wall or gates. In comparison to our small gems, Heaven's jewels are massive in size.

Viewing this sight, John must have been overwhelmed with the rainbow colors of the precious stones: transparent-sparkling blue-green, rich blue, lustrous blue-gray, bright green, orange-red, deep red, gold, sea green, lemon yellow with browns, yellow-green with bluish hue, deep red-brown, and luxurious purple. There is nothing dull and lifeless about Heaven.

When my artist friend, Sally Moser and I, considered where to put the huge slabs of precious stones, we decided the best location was near the base of the sides of the pearl gates. It's easier to show them at the gates, rather than attempting to show the jewels at the foundations of the walls of the city, equaling 6,000 miles square!

Into the Light

Heaven is not only colorful it is full of light. When Jews and Christians try to describe this light they use the Hebrew word, *shekinah,* which means "dwelling of God." The *Zondervan Pictorial Bible Dictionary* says, "It is alluded to in such places as Isaiah 60:2 by the phrase "his glory" and in Romans 9:4 by the phrase "the glory." Moses calls this the "cloud" in Exodus 14:19." It was frequently seen in connection with Christ's ministry in the New Testament (Matt 17:5; Acts 1:9, Rev 21:23).[22]

The Bible is a book filled with the light of Heaven. The bottom line is; do we choose to fill our lives with the kingdom of darkness, or the Kingdom of light? That light is shinning out of the twelve jeweled gates to draw us into the *shekinah* of Heaven.

Will you come with me, next time, as we begin our journey into the City of Light?

Next time, discovering tunnels of light into the city.

Seeking Confirmation of "Tunnels of Light"

It is possible that you and I will one day enter Heaven by walking or floating through a transparent, sparkling, blue-green jasper tunnel of light.

The physical evidence of these Heaven tunnels came first through many of the 16 million people worldwide who reported near-death experiences.[23] A Gallup poll mentioned 8 million people in America as having NDE's.[24]

Serious biblical students feel they must find evidence in the Scripture before they will believe in such phenomenon as tunnels of light. It was easier for me to believe because of my mother's NDE, but I also do diligently search the Scripture for confirmation for all supernatural experiences.

What a surprise it was to me that through my research on Heaven and following the publication of my first book on Heaven that previously unknown confirmation of tunnels of light would be found! This is important since some in the Church have been in debate on this subject for years.

A Vital Clue

The clue is in Rev 21:17-18. In his revelation, the Apostle John wrote: "Then he [the angel] measured its wall: one hundred and forty-four cubits, according to the measure of man, that is of an angel. The construction of its wall was of jasper ..." (NKJV). I found that some Bible translations such as this one and the earlier KJV had not determined if this verse was speaking of the wall's height or thickness. The NIV Bible gives a better translation.

My studies indicated that the wall's thickness would be about 216 feet or 72 yards, close to the length of a football field! This seemed beyond belief to think that Heaven's wall is that thick but it turned out to be the right decision.

I sent these dimensions and my simple sketch of the eastern gate entrance to my artist friend, Sally Moser. When she sent me the finished picture, I was amazed because I, for the first time, saw that the entrance clearly showed a tunnel of light into Heaven! It took a picture and a Scripture verse to confirm that the tunnel of light reports could be true.

Exciting Biblical Discovery

Sally and I were in awe. Many people have seen this entrance into Heaven portrayed on my website since year 2000 to 2011. The Heaven full color illustrations are now, at this time, only found in the center of my book, *Heaven Tours*. In Pediatrician Dr. Melvin Morse's book, *Transformed by the Light,* he lists nine traits of an NDE. The tunnel of light experience is fourth on his list.[25]

So my friend, realize that there are twelve of these huge tunnels of light entrances into Heaven. It's not just the brain dying in layers that creates a tunnel experience, as some have thought, but it is the real thing.

And guess what, "The Bible Tells Us So."

Next time: A Look Inside Heaven.

Standing at Heaven's Portals - Now What?

The moment has arrived! You are actually standing at the pearl gate entrance and are going to enter Heaven! You wondered and hoped that such a place as this existed and prayed, "Heaven, please be there for me!"

As a child you may have knelt to say, "Now I lay me down to sleep, I pray the Lord my soul to keep ..." Those prayers were not ignored.

One name for Heaven is "The City Foursquare" because the jasper wall surrounding it is a square of 1,500 miles on each side, north, south, east, and west totaling 6,000 square miles. Remember all these dimensions are only one layer of the heavenly city. In times of earth's disasters, there are people coming into all twelve of the gates at the same time.

The luminescent gates are before you. No proportion is given, only they're "great and high." In comparison to the thickness of the walls, the gates could be as high as a several story building. The width of the entrance may be as wide as the wall is thick, that is clearly 216 feet. Guessing the gate's width to be that large, will also allow plenty of space between the twelve gates encircling the city.

I'm not an artist, but in 1995 when I took a year to study the book of Revelation with Kay Arthur's precept course, students were asked to draw pictures of each chapter of that book of the Bible. This was to help us remember the contents of each chapter.

A Glorious Boulevard

When I sketched the word picture from chapter 21 of Revelation, I was amazed as I realized that at Heaven's entrance is a glorious boulevard.

This boulevard is what you will see when you stand at the doorway of Heaven, after having come through the shimmering jasper tunnel of light. In the center of the boulevard is a river of life, as clear as crystal.

The river is 750 miles long "issuing out of the throne of God" which is in the center of Heaven. On each side of the river are twelve fruit trees each producing twelve kinds of fruit. In my picture I reasoned six on each side of the river. To complete the scene is a highway of transparent gold, logically with one highway on each side. This is only one portion of the twelve entrances to Heaven.

Heading for the Throne

In your state of awe, what will you do first? Take a drink from the crystal clear river of life, or take a swim in it? Will you join the picnic in the garden, eating delicious healing fruit of all kinds? Or will you visit with spouse, family, relatives, friends who have come to meet you?

I know you will join the joyful, singing, dancing people on the shining highway going toward the throne. Then greatest of all, meet with the One who gave you saving faith to come here, the Messiah, Jesus. He'll take you to *Abba* Father who is waiting to greet and embrace you. You'll sense the presence of the comforting Holy Spirit who has guided you here. The angels are cheering your arrival, including your guardian angel. What a party! "Gladness will overtake you, and sorrow and sighing will flee away." (Isa 35:10 KJV-MOD).

Next time: Why the earth is in pain.

The Whole Earth Groans in Travail Waiting
Breaking News

Looking back on the disaster in New Orleans - we remember the worst natural disaster in America's history. One million, five hundred thousand people had to be evacuated or were displaced. One thousand, five hundred children have been lost or displaced as reported on CNN September 9th, 2005. In just days, hurricane Katrina brought untold dismay to several states, especially to people living in the wide, below sea level, bowl of New Orleans, Louisiana and environs.

Different questions could be heard in the news media. Did God do this? Could God (if there is a God) have stopped it? If so, why didn't He?

Rabbi Lapin's Approach

In my friend, Rabbi Daniel Lapin's September email he responds, "There are two choices. Either God is all powerful in which case He did this cruel thing, or else He couldn't stop it in which case He's impotent and who needs an impotent deity?" Lapin's own approach is that God allows the laws of nature to work. He says, "God wanted us humans to work together to overcome nature's menace. 'And God said to them, be fruitful, and multiply, populate the earth, and conquer [subdue] it' (Gen 1:28a). "We resist disease with medicine… Similarly those who choose to live in low lying areas are morally obliged to do everything possible in order to minimize flood risk."[26]

He feels that God originally planned the menace of nature to cause humanity to come together to help one another. We have certainly seen this strength of bonding and caring through gifts of money, clothing, and shelter.

A New Testament Approach

Very good thoughts, yet I can also see another viewpoint. When God created the earth it is very good (Gen 1:31). So how did it become malevolent? The answer is known as the fall of man. It happened when humans and the creation came under the dominion of a malevolent fallen being who had been cast out of Heaven for treason against God.

Adam and Eve were deceived big-time by this fallen rebel-angel and the Lord ejected them from the garden.

When man fell, nature fell with him. The Apostle Paul says, "For we know that the whole creation groans and travails in pain together until now. And not only they, but ourselves ..." (Rom 8:22-23 KJV-MOD).

Earth is in pain. We in America also groan in pain and other nations with us. Scripture says "... And upon the earth distress of nations, with perplexity; the sea and the waves roaring; Men's hearts failing them for fear, and for looking after those things coming on the earth ..." (Luke 21:25-26).

Now the Good News, "And when these things begin to come to pass, then look up, and lift up your heads; for your redemption draws near" (Luke 21:28, KJV-MOD).

Let us continue to do our best to love and care for one another on earth, and at the same time look up. We are all **displaced persons** until we are gathered into that better **place**, Heaven our home.

Next time: Care of God's creation.

Pray for Higher Ground – Both Out There and Here
Breaking News

Following hurricane Katrina, August 23, 2005, did you awaken in the morning wondering if the leaders of New Orleans were going to choose to rebuild their City on higher ground? Did you wonder if they would understand the laws of nature enough to realize that water will rush toward its lowest point washing away everything in its path? If their city is rebuilt on its average of nine feet below sea level, what does this tell us about future years and other hurricanes?

"Well that's their problem," you might say, and I said that too, until I suddenly realized that whatever New Orleans chooses to do affects the lives of everyone in America. It affects you and me and our children. Since we will continue to pay for the horrendous disaster, and future disasters, it is our moral obligation to let our viewpoints and our wishes be known. Yes, we want to help but the problem is bigger than just one or two hurricanes. We cannot be like the little Dutch boy who put his finger in the hole in the dike to fix it! We have to repair the dike. We need to build massive dikes as they have in Holland and China.

"Bill Nye the Science Guy®" on *Larry King Live*, King–TV September 25th, that same year reminded the viewers that with the increased global warming trend, serious hurricanes will not only continue but will be more frequent. We human beings are playing a part in the cause of global warming. We are helping to create the warmer water in the oceans, which in turn is increasing the ill weather phenomenon.

So we have a second problem and that is unless we diversify our use of fossil fuels, unless we stop cutting down too many oxygen-producing trees and replacing them with asphalt streets and huge steel buildings, we will seriously damage America. We will harm the inheritance of our children. And what happens to our country affects the adults and children of the world. This not a selfish political party decision, but a One-Nation-under-God decision.

How does this relate to the subject of Heaven about which I've been writing? I, for one, don't want to stand before the Lord of the universe, the Creator of this beautiful blue planet, and have Him ask me: "What have you done to My planet Earth since I was last there? I asked you to tend it, to take care of it. Why haven't you lovingly taken dominion over it?"

It's Also about Us

We too, need to build our lives on higher ground physically if needed, but for sure spiritually. Let us pray in the words of the song, "Lord, plant my feet on higher ground."

Then ask what He will have me do?

News Update:

Seven years after Katrina, on August 29, 2012, hurricane Isaac threatened New Orleans again. Though there was catastrophic flood damage and insured losses up to 2 billion, the new levees held!

Next time: More on Heaven – beginning seven churches.

Heaven Awaits - But What Is It Really Like?

Some time ago, I was visiting with an Edmond's businesswoman I hadn't seen for some months. She told me about attending a women's faith-based convention wherein small breakout groups studied the book of Revelation. My friend, Jami Roberts, had gone to church for years, but like many of us, had no teaching on this particular book. Revelation has a lot to say about Heaven. It's written by one of the four Gospel writers, John, who was also one of the twelve Apostles.

The women took turns sharing about their perceptions of Heaven and how they were looking forward to it. Then Jami's turn came up. She said something like, "I cannot really get too excited about leaving earth since I have so many things to do in my life, family, and work. And what Heaven is like is still quite a mystery to me."

One member of the group responded that she was shocked that Jami could seem complacent about a believer's future home!

Jami Got Excited

Jami left that night rather annoyed with the woman and tried to forgive her confrontational attitude.

The second Bible study took them further into the first three books of Revelation. Jami told me, "I got excited when I saw how God had given a personal message to each church."

I'll try to catch you up with Jami. These chapters show a picture of the seven churches of Asia that have been seen first to represent the churches named in the first 100 years of church history, as well as subsequent generations including ours today. Seven is the biblical number of completeness. An angel showed the Apostle John the seven churches in the form of a seven-branch candlestick. These seven candles, biblical scholars believe, are based on the Jewish temple lampstand or menorah. The Lord gave Moses the design for the original seven-lamp menorah, originally written about in the *Torah*.

In my further review of the chapters, I saw that He first gave a message of affirmation (a good way to begin a confrontation); secondly, He gave each a detailed warning about their behavior; following this He challenged each to repent – make an about face. Then He described the reward that each will receive if that church lives as an overcomer.

40

Four Good Steps

Affirm, warn, repent, reward – four good steps for us from the greatest Teacher of all. Only two of the seven churches did not have our Lord's criticism and those were the churches of Philadelphia (brotherly love) and Smyrna (good works). The angel gave John this special peek into Heaven. He saw Jesus there. "And in the midst of the seven candlesticks one like unto the Son of man, clothed with a garment down to the foot, and girt about the chest with a golden girdle ... and his countenance was as the sun shining in his strength" (Rev 1:13, 16b).

After learning about Revelation's beginning chapters 1–3, Jami says, "I'm much more enthusiastic about Heaven." I'm happy to report, also, that the two women were fully reconciled. Shouldn't we too study these biblical church examples and see if we're measuring up? Even the daily news shows the need to do this.

Next: More on the seven churches of Revelation and Ephesus.

Message from Heaven: God truly Loves You!

In my last column I told you how my friend, Jami, found that the study of the seven churches in Revelation made Heaven more interesting. Many of us have never taken time to investigate this mysterious sixty-sixth book of the Bible.

If God has left a message for the people of God today, shouldn't we try to decipher it? What if it has some important guidelines to help us on our journey?

The small Greek Island of Patmos is where John, the disciple of Jesus, then exiled for his faith, wrote the messages to the seven churches. These church locations were near him in the province of Asia – known today as the coast of Turkey.

First on the list is the church of Ephesus that covered the time period of approximately A.D. 33, the birth of the church, until about A.D. 96 when its believed the Apostle John died. The apostle Paul lived here two years as a missionary and later wrote the great book of Ephesians to them.

Christ's compliment from Heaven to Ephesus is, "I know your works, and your labor, and your patience, and cannot bear them who are evil: and you have tried them who say they are apostles, and are not, and found them to be liars ... You have labored, and not fainted" (Rev 2:2-3 KJV-MOD).

The church of Ephesus began in the purity of bride to the Bridegroom. Yet, when false prophets invaded the flock, many in the church fell away.

His Correction: "I have somewhat against you, because you have left your first love" (Rev 2:4 KJV-MOD). Christ longs for that close relationship with His Church that we had at the beginning.

Repent: "Remember from where you have fallen, and repent, and do the first works or else I will come to you quickly, and will remove your candlestick out of its place ..." (Rev 2:5 KJV-MOD).

For the unrepentant, candlestick removal could mean: a shortened life, or diminished place of leadership, or worst of all – the eternal consequences of apostasy.

Second Compliment from the Lord: "But this you have, that you hate the deeds of the Nicolaitans, which I also hate" (Rev 2:6 KJV-MOD). Nicolaitans were, "Followers of Nicolas, a heretic. They were supposed to have been a sect of Gnostics who practiced and taught impure and immoral doctrines ... that committing adultery and fornication was not sinful ..."[27] This can warn that church leaders are supposed to be good shepherds and examples to the flock, not leading them down a destructive pathway. (1 Peter 5:3)!

Reward: "To him who overcomes will I give to eat of the tree of life" (Rev 2:7b KJV-MOD).

The tree of life represents the gift of eternal life. This gift is free, yet it's worth more than you could ever pay. You can be an overcomer by trusting in the Lamb of God, Jesus, who takes away the sin of the world. Also as an overcomer you can share the word of your testimony as doors open for you. You overcome by making Jesus Lord of your life, and putting Him first (Rev 12:11).

Are you lagging behind on your journey with the Good Shepherd? What steps can you and I take to renew our commitment to our forever, Best Friend? Remember He wants to be your First Love – always.

Next time: Smyrna, the persecuted church, one of the two churches God commended.

Pray For Those Who Use and Persecute You

The second church Christ personally addresses in the book of Revelation is Smyrna, known as the persecuted church. Smyrna has myrrh in its name, an aromatic exudation from a thorny tree, used for holy healing ointment. It well describes a persecuted church.

"And to the angel (pastor) of the church of Smyrna write: These things says the first and the last, which was dead, and is alive" (Rev 2:8 KJV-MOD). Here Christ proclaims His divinity! He is the *Alpha* and *Omega,* Greek translation. (Originally Jesus probably said, *Aleph* and the *Tav,* since His mother tongue was Hebrew.) The Lord also proclaims His redemptive death and resurrection in His dictated letter via John to the church.

These two proclamations were very encouraging for believers in Smyrna who have been so abused. After all, earth isn't giving them much to rejoice about and Christians are taught to look forward to their own resurrection.

Smyrna into Idolatry

The city of Smyrna was heavily into Roman emperor worship. It was compulsory for every citizen to worship openly the emperor by burning incense to Caesar. The consequence for not obeying this edict was death. The famous martyr Polycarp, is one of the pastors, who was burned at the stake for refusing to obey this edict. (This happened around A.D. 169).

Jesus finds no fault with Smyrna. He says, "I know your works, and tribulation, and poverty, (but you are rich) ..." (Rev 2:9 KJV-MOD). They did not have earthly riches but rather a flourishing heavenly bank account. The Apostle Matthew says, "But lay up for yourselves treasures in Heaven, where neither moth or rust corrupts ..." (Matt 6:20 KJV-MOD).

Christ also tells them not to be afraid of the suffering ahead. "Be faithful unto death, and I will give you a crown of life" (Rev 2:10b KJV-MOD). Yes, there is something better than life on this earth. There are people all over this planet being persecuted for their faith probably any day of the year.

It is interesting that Smyrna was called "the crown of Ionia–the ornament of Asia." It is now the chief city of SW Turkey, with a

43

population of more than one-and-a-half million."[28] So life goes on and hopefully the present Smyrnaites have learned from the past, as should we.

Jesus who was the most persecuted person on earth, challenges us with, "Pray for them who despitefully use you, and persecute you" (Matt 5:44b KJV-MOD). That is hard to do!

The reason, I think, He tells us this is that we'll have fewer ulcers and wrinkles, and who knows the persecutors might just repent and join the family of God.

Next time the church of Pergamum.

Forgiveness! - God's Gift in the Giving Season

The last words an individual speaks are unbelievably important. Some of Jesus' last words on earth were "Behold, I send the Promise of My Father upon you; but wait in the city of Jerusalem until you are endued with power from on high" (Luke 24:49 KJV-MOD). These are incredibly important words!

Shortly after our Savior's ascension we hear a reversed message, this time sent from Heaven to earth. In a kind of visionary near-death experience, the Apostle John is sent to Heaven long enough to hear Jesus give a last recordable message for earth.

In this *Seven Churches Series,* we have been looking at these messages Jesus sent to us through His Apostle John. They were originally recorded for the seven churches of Asia Minor (now Turkey), and yet, meant for the church in every age (Rev chapters 1-3).

John sees an amazing sight, "I turned around to see who was speaking to me; and when I had turned, I saw seven gold *menorahs*; and among the *menorahs* someone like a Son of Man, wearing a robe down to his feet and a gold band around his chest" (Rev 1:12-13 CJB). This Bible translation clarifies that there was not just one *menorah* with seven candles to represent the seven churches, but seven *menorahs* each having seven candles. That makes 49 candles ablaze and Jesus the light of earth and Heaven walking among the church *menorahs*! What a picture this is.

You Honored God's Name

We have heard the messages to Ephesus, and Symrna. What then does Jesus say to Pergamum, a town in Mysia? [29] "I know your [good] works, and where you live, where Satan's seat is and you hold fast to My name. You did not deny My faith even in the days in which Antipas was My faithful martyr, who was slain among you ..." (Rev 2:13 KJV-MOD). "He is said to be one of our Savior's first disciples and a bishop of Pergamum ... He lived before A.D. 100."[30]

Yet this church of Pergamum is described, by commentators, as the compromising church because they tolerated immorality, idolatry, and heresies. It was the combination of a pagan cathedral city, a university town, and a royal residence. Jesus said, "I have a few things against you because you have there those who hold the doctrine of Balaam, who taught Balak to put a stumbling block before the children of Israel, to eat things sacrificed to idols, and to commit fornication" (Rev 2:14 KJV-MOD).

Unger's Bible Dictionary[31] explains more details. Namely, Balak appealed to Balaam to curse the Army of Israelites. Balaam also taught Balak to teach the Israelites to commit fornication so God would not keep blessing them and they would be defeated. They were taught by Balak to break God's commandments, specifically the second one: You shall not make unto yourselves any engraved image, you shall not bow down to them nor serve them. And number seven is you shall not commit adultery (Exodus 20:4-5,14).

What is the remedy? "Repent, or else I will come to you quickly and will fight against them with the sword of My mouth" (Rev 2:16 KJV-MOD).

Repent means God wants to show you a better way – one of real joy. He wants to take away: your loneliness, rebellion, and addictions that are killing you. You only need to pray sincerely, "Dear Lord Jesus Help me. I repent. Please forgive me! I will follow where You lead me."

A Star and Candle for the Holiday Season

Sometimes the "church" is taken to God's woodshed. For example, this occurs when pastors get in the news, or are the subjects of local gossip sessions due to: running off with a congregant's spouse, for child abuse, or for dishonesty in finances.

We Christian laity at times are taken to Father's woodshed too. I know what that feels like especially during a period of soft tolerance of worldliness in my college days.

Yet He is patient with us – until for the good of His ultimate plan the Ruler of Heaven and earth has to act.

That leads to the fourth church that Christ speaks to as recorded in the book of Revelation. It is in Thyatira, an ancient city in Asia Minor (located today in West Turkey). It was known as a church of extremely good works, always excelling in them, but was eventually so influenced by the world in the marketplace that it earned the infamous title of "The Corrupt Church."

After commending him, Jesus speaks strongly to the pastor of the church in Thyatira, "Nevertheless I have a few things against you, because you allow that woman Jezebel, who calls herself a prophetess, to teach and seduce My servants to commit sexual immorality and eat things sacrificed to idols" (Rev 2:20 NKJV).

This is not the wicked Jezebel, wife of King Ahab of Israel, but Jesus here is giving this title to the Thyatiran woman who exhibited the same unbiblical character traits.

Thyatiran Jezebel

This Jezebel from Asia Minor taught: idolatry, and adultery, spiritually and physically, which means breaking the Second and Seventh Commandments of God as given to Moses on Mount Sinai (Exodus 20).

Bible scholar, Adam Clarke, believes that she was the wife of the messenger or bishop of the church of Thyatira. That is how she gained such influence. As the bishop he could have restrained her, but he did not.[32]

What was the actual problem? History reveals that Christian workers had to join trade unions led by pagans. They would often meet at a pagan temple and begin with a libation to the gods. Licentious orgies were often connected to worship of erotic Greek idols. (Yes, porn started early!)

Compromise in Business

The central problem for Thyatiran Christians was that they had to belong to a union in order to make a living. It seems Jezebel encouraged the workers to compromise, and taught that it was necessary for business, and perhaps for church finances too.

Jesus said He gave her time to repent, but she would not. This may allude to the first as well as the second Jezebel. Dr. Van Impe's *Prophecy Bible* says "The long-suffering and loving God gave Thyatira approximately 1,000 years to do what was right, but she resisted."[33] Judgment eventually comes.

The good news is that a remnant of Thyatirans remained faithful (Rev 2:24). Jesus said to them "But hold fast what you have till I come" (Rev 2:25 NKJV). The Apostle Paul visited Thyatira at least three times on his missionary journeys and some of this remnant of the church were likely his converts. Jesus' final promise to the overcomer is, "… I will give him the morning star" (Rev 2:28 NKJV). Meaning, He will give you Himself. "I am the bright and Morning Star," He says. (Rev 22:16b NKJV). Let Jesus be your *Christmas* Morning Star and *Hanukkah* Menorah Center Candle always.

Next time: Chapter Two continues with the seven churches, and *Sardis*.

Chapter 2

Seven Churches Continued, Provisions
Armor of God Series
Breaking News: Azusa, and Overcomers
Holidays, Breaking News: Da Vinci Code
Shoes as Weapons, Dead Sea Scrolls

The Rev. Canon Dennis Bennett (photo above 1975) – The Rev. Dr. Bennett in his clerical vestments stands in front of St. Luke's Church, Ballard – known for its world-wide revival. In Heaven since 1991, he fully understands God's healing message to the Seven Churches of Revelation we are studying.

Message for today in Sardinian's Fate

What can make a person who was once alive in his faith change so drastically that he is inwardly dead? To have once known the source of life, God Himself, and then be convinced that there is no God, is to turn out the light that once glowed in one's heart.

This does not happen in a moment of time. Unbelief is a slow, steady process. Just as an individual has to feed his body to live, so it is necessary for him to feed his soul – intellect, emotions and will – with good food, both spiritually and psychologically.

If, like the Sardinians, you are beginning to cool off in your relationship to your Creator, right now would be a good time to change your diet. Let me tell you what happened to them.

The chief city of Lydia, Sardis, was located at the junction of royal highways linking Ephesus, Pergamum, and Smyrna with the interior of Asia Minor. It was situated in a valley among almost impregnable cliffs.

Sardis was famous for its arts and crafts, as well as its dyeing and wool industries. Because of its natural resources, it was the first center to mint gold and silver coins. The earliest reference to Sardis is in the Persae of Aeschylus, 472 B.C. Aeschylus is a dramatist who wrote the oldest surviving Greek tragedy, Oresteia in B.C. 458.[1]

In Jesus Christ's epistle to Sardis, as usual, He addresses it to the pastor (angel) of the church living in that city.

"Sardis is said to be the first city in that part of the world that was converted by the preaching of [the Apostle] John; and, some say, the first that revolted from Christianity.[2]

Warning to Sardinians

In Revelation chapter three, Jesus warns them, "… I know your works, and that you have a name that you are alive … and you are dead" (Rev 3:1 KJV-MOD). Jesus gives these five commands to Sardis: "1. Be watchful, 2. strengthen the things that remain, 3. remember your teaching, 4. hold fast, and 5. repent" (Rev 3:2-3a KJV-MOD).

If they do not do this, He says, "I will come upon you as a thief, and you will not know what hour I will come upon you" (Rev 3:3b KJV-MOD).

Commentator Finis Dake says in the sidebar reference g, "This does not refer to the second advent [coming], but to Christ sending sudden judgment upon Sardis if the church would not repent (v3)." [3]

The Lord goes on to commend the few people – the remnant – who have not defiled their garments, or souls. "... they shall walk with me in white: for they are worthy" (Rev 3:4b KJV). Here He is confirming His gift of eternal life.

Three Rewards Given

Jesus concludes with three rewards for the overcomers. "They will be clothed in white, their names will not be blotted out of the Book of Life, and I will confess their names before My Father in Heaven and before His angels" (Rev 3:5 KJV-MOD). How awesome is that? Can you imagine the Lord Jesus saying to His Father, this is Jane, or John, one of your dear children from earth? How about meeting the Archangels, Michael and Gabriel?

A surprise attack by the Persians came in 549 B.C., and three centuries later the Romans won Sardis. The great earthquake of A.D. 17 ruined Sardis physically and financially. Finally, it was destroyed by Tamerlane, a Mongol conquer, in A.D. 1402. "In 1958 the Fogg Art Museum of Harvard and Cornell University, and the American Schools of Oriental Research began a joint excavation at Sardis." [4]

When a nation walks with God, does that sound like a good way to have His help? America started out that way, but how far have we strayed from the beliefs of our founding Fathers? How spotted are our garments?

Change starts with one person at a time. It begins with me and with you. Could one of our resolutions be to follow Christ's five commands to the church in Sardis? Can we review our nation's history and see why we are great, and where we have begun to go astray? Can we work for Holy Spirit Change?

In doing so, we can have the best years ahead. Now, reach out your hand to touch the Hand that is reaching out to you. Our Lord will guide you through the years ahead. He loves you and wants the best for you.

Next time: The Church of Philadelphia.

Philadelphia, Church of Brotherly Love

Of the seven churches mentioned in Revelation, only Philadelphia and Smyrna (previously discussed) received praise and no correction from Christ. Why was this sixth church honored (Rev 3:7-13)?

The home of the church of Philadelphia was "a city in Lydia of Asia Minor [now Alasehir, Turkey] containing one of the seven churches that are in Asia (Rev 1:4, 11; 3:7)."[5]

The city of Philadelphia was founded by Attalus II of the kingdom of Pergamum, in189 B.C. Because of the founder's love for his brother Eumenes II, the city is called Philadelphia –meaning, city of brotherly love. Alasehir has a population of about 20,000 today.

"The district was an area of vine growing and wine production and, thus, a center for worship of Dionysus, the god of wine and fertility."[6]

A challenging atmosphere in which to grow Christianity!

Letter from Jesus

We begin the letter from the Lord Jesus, spoken to John. In the words given to the pastor of the church of Philadelphia, a powerful fourfold description of the Christ is painted: 1. He that is holy, 2. He that is true, 3. He that has the key (authority) as did King David. (Of this Jesus said, "… I am the root and the offspring of David …" (Rev 22:16). and "… All power is given to Me …" (Matt 28:18 KJV-MOD). "… He that opens, and no man shuts; and shuts and no man opens" (Rev 3:7 KJV-MOD).

To the church of Philadelphia Jesus says, "I know your works: see, I have set before you an open door … For you have a little strength, and have kept my Word, and have not denied My name" (Rev 3:8 KJV-MOD).

They were people of good works in the community and strong students of God's Word. In those early days they studied mainly the books of Moses, and probably portions of the Psalms and John and Paul's writings in the New Testament.

Though weak numerically, they were strong in confessing and not denying the One whom they served (2 Tim 2:12).

News report of Modern Philadelphians

"It's 7 in the evening ... Down by the corner, there's a cluster of young boys hanging out. Everyone else stays inside — and for good reason. Suddenly ... Men United roar up in a caravan of vans and jeeps, a rap song blasting from loudspeakers. Like a group of gang enforcers, nine men in baseball caps and bomber jackets emerge and quickly spread to the various corners – approaching the boys ... They are likely the only ones on the streets without guns. They pack pamphlets instead."

"How you all doing?" says Ray Jones, a sprightly leader of the group, approaching the cluster of boys who peer at him coldly. "We're with *Men United for a Better Philadelphia,* a non-violence group. If you were expecting a drive-by, this is a love-by."

"They've helped thousands. Violence has dropped," says columnist Catherine Porter.[7]

Application

Men United ... have probably never read about the ancient church of Philadelphia, yet in 2006 they were practicing its teachings in the city of Philadelphia, USA. Undoubtedly, their expressions of brotherly love had God's attention!

Let us also go and do the works of the Philadelphians, past and present.

Next time: Brotherly Love. .

Brotherly Love – Do we still have it?

When is the last time you went to church and experienced brotherly or sisterly love?

Since the ancient church of brotherly love was so honored by Jesus' words, it seemed to deserve a second column to evaluate more fully what He said to them. The name of this church reflects their consistent loving behavior and it was so called because it was established in a city by that very same name. Was that a coincidence or a God-incidence?

Then it was located in Asia Minor, but today the name of the city is Alasehir in Turkey. In189 B.C., Attalus ll proclaimed it "City of Brotherly Love" named after his biological brother, Eumenes ll. The origin of this title came from the Greek word *philadelphos,* meaning "brotherly or brother."[8] Who would not want a brother as loving as that?

The Bible sometimes speaks of Jesus as our older Brother. One reference is Romans 8:29 that says, ". . . those whom he knew in advance, he also determined in advance would be conformed into the pattern of his Son, so that he might be the firstborn among many brothers ..." (CJB).

When He rose from the dead and breathed resurrection life into His Apostles, they were the first group to experience spiritual resurrection. A new spiritual race of people began. The family has been growing ever since. What an awesome big Brother we have in Jesus, who came all the way from Heaven to rescue us. He is a friend who "sticks closer than a brother" (Prov 18:24 KJV-MOD).

Jesus says further to the church of Philadelphia, "Because you have kept My command to persevere, I also will keep you from the hour of trial which shall come upon the whole world, to test those who dwell on the earth" (Rev 3:10 (NKJV). This is considered by many biblical scholars to speak of trials that would come upon the seven representative churches, and perhaps others, in John's day. That was about 2,000 years ago.

We have certainly had our set of trials through tsunamis, hurricanes, and earthquakes in 2005 and certainly in more recent times. Global warming is still a concern.

Prophetically, it could speak to our days ahead also. Jesus goes on speaking, "Behold, I am coming quickly! Hold fast to what you have, that no one may take your crown [reward]" (Rev 3:11 NKJV). Commentator Finis Dake says, "... This is a reference to the rapture [from: *raptura* Latin, or *natzal* Heb.], for it is the coming of Christ that the Church will experience, before the second Advent."[9]

Christians look at the "rapture" in different ways. Fortunately, there is no prerequisite on this subject for salvation, and no believer should predict an exact time.

The Nicene Creed repeated by many Christians each week recites words about Christ's second Advent, "He [Christ] will come again in glory to judge the living and the dead, and his Kingdom will have no end."[10]

Every year in Jerusalem, on *Yom Terruah*, The Festival of Trumpets (and *Rosh Hashanah*--their 2nd New Year), it is reported that some Orthodox Jews go through the Market Place shouting, *"Mashiach Bah Ah."* That is translated, "Messiah is Coming."

Orthodox Christians look for *Messiah* (Christ, in Greek) to come a second time, Second Advent. Orthodox Jews are looking for Messiah (*Mashiach,* in Hebrew) to come the very first time.[11]

Whether our Lord comes for us, or we go to Him, it would do us well to follow the example of this early church or synagogue of brotherly love. By the way, have you hugged your brother or your sister lately? Have you talked to your Big Brother, Jesus, about how to be more loving?

Next time: The Church of Laodicea.

An Open Invitation to Lukewarm Laodiceans

We've had an interesting journey to the seven churches of old Asia Minor, through the book of Revelation. The seventh and concluding letter is to the church in wealthy Laodicea. Its location was about 90 miles east of Ephesus and twelve miles from Colossae. The City was renamed Laodicea after the wife of Antiochus II (261-246 B.C.), not a positive family genealogy, historically.

Nevertheless, the Apostle Paul was very instrumental in planting the gospel in the church of Laodicea. He mentions this connection in his epistle to the Colossians in which he greets them as brothers (Col 2:1; 4:13).

Paul wrote the Laodiceans a letter but unfortunately it was lost historically – perhaps in the eventual earthquake ruins of ancient Laodicea.

The message, as in all the Apostle John's previous letters, is from the Lord Jesus Christ. It begins with a threefold description of Himself in Rev 3:14 (NKJV):

1. "These things says the Amen." Earlier in Revelation, He is described as the Alpha and Omega meaning He is the first and last. Jesus, The Amen, to me reveals that, He is the end; He brings finality to all earth's history.
2. "The Faithful and True Witness." The word witness comes from martyr meaning being faithful to speak the truth until

your last breath – even if martyred in doing so. Jesus was the first martyr for Christianity.

3. "The Beginning of the creation of God." The Lord Jesus, who was "eternally begotten of the Father," had no beginning *(Nicene Creed)*. Colossians 1:15-17 contains one of the major scriptures that show He is eternal. Yet when God the Son chose to come to earth as a baby, in that sense He did have a beginning. Jesus, who is presently in Heaven, still has a physical body though it is now glorified.

No Commendation

Sadly, there was nothing to commend in the church of Laodicea. Five points can sum them up.

- Their life's goal was not "Thy Kingdom come" but "my kingdom come."
- This church was neither hot nor cold. That is, they were neither heathens nor Christians. If heathens, they might see their plight and change. Also they were listless and indifferent, not willing to stand and contend for their faith.
- The lukewarm lifestyle they exhibited was nauseating to God.
- Their viewpoint of themselves was full of pride and self-satisfaction: "I am rich. I have material goods. I need nothing." Perhaps this reflects their city that was a wealthy place with a famous medical school that created a special eye salve, was a rich banking center, and producer of famous black wool carpets.
- They were blind to their true spiritual condition. God's correction to them is, "You know not that you are wretched, and miserable, and poor, and blind, and naked" (Rev 3:17b KJV-MOD). Jesus is trying to shock them out of their worldly complacency, just as you might do with a rebellious, self-engrossed youth.

A Call to Repent

His plaintive words as He calls to them are, "As many as I Love, I rebuke and chasten: be zealous therefore, and repent" (Rev 3:19 KJV). These very sad words to those who were once so close to Him are recorded for us. Here we see Jesus at the outside door of the church.

They have closed their door to Him. Instead of Him being invited inside the door of their hearts, He is relegated to stand outside.

He calls to them: "Behold, I stand at the door and knock: if anyone hears My voice, and opens the door, I will come in to him. I will have Communion with him, and he with Me" (Rev 3:20 KJV-MOD). Can't you hear the love in His voice as He calls to them, through their closed door?

Is our own church lukewarm about their former love and zeal for Jesus, the Christ? Can we see ourselves in this church of Laodicea? Do we, too, need to repent? For us individually, He cannot force open the door of our heart and spirit, even though He is greatest of all loves. Neither could He do this for the congregants in the church of Laodicea. Love doesn't force.

At this time, will you check the door and see if the "Lover of your soul" is standing there waiting for an invitation to come in? He will provide for you faith of gold, pure white raiment, and sight-curing eye salve (Rev 3:18).

If you have not done so, seriously consider answering the door? I did.

Next time: Heaven's Award Surpass All Others.

Heaven's Awards Surpass All Others

Let us consider the messages God gives to the churches. In our concluding column on this subject, we considered who in the Church can be considered overcomers.

We've studied the seven churches from the final book of the Bible, Revelation. They are:

- Ephesus the church who left her first love but repented
- Smyrna the church who was persecuted for her strong faith
- Pergamus the compromising church
- Thyatira the church who became corrupt
- Sardis the dead church
- Philadelphia the brotherly, loving church
- Laodicea the lukewarm church

A message to each church was given by the resurrected Jesus, in Heaven, to the beloved Apostle John. John was caught up from earth to the Lord's throne in a visionary or near-death experience (Rev 1:10-11).

These seven ancient churches of Asia Minor can represent our churches today. We have looked at the messages that clearly and emphatically give us information about what God does and does not like!

In each of these seven letters, Jesus ends with a message to those who overcome. Each time He also repeats, "He who has an ear to hear, let him hear what the Spirit says to the churches."

You would think after a repetition of seven times, we human beings might take notice! We learned that there were overcomers as well as unbelievers in the seven churches.

Jesus gives to each Church part of the description of the eternal awards ceremony coming in Heaven. This goes beyond achieving medals in the Olympic Games or the Hollywood Oscar awards, as those only last for this life.

Heaven's awards add up to thirteen prepared for earth's overcomers.
- The tree of life – the first human couple had to be removed from the Garden of Eden to be kept from eating from the Tree of Life while in a fallen state. Now in Heaven, there is no limit to the feast.
- Martyr's crown of life – an unforfeitable possession received at the end of life. Usually it is seen as being given to martyrs for Christ. There are four other crowns: watching for Jesus crown, soul winners crown, crown of purity, shepherd's (pastors) crown.[12]
- Escape from the second death – this is an escape from spiritual death. The overcomer may die physically, but he or she will never die spiritually.
- Hidden manna – biblically, this refers to Israel being fed in the wilderness. A pot of manna was preserved in the Ark of the Covenant. The hidden manna can be food for us from the Ark in Heaven one day.
- A white stone and a new name – in ancient times a white stone was used for admission to all public festivals. Believers will be admitted to Messiah's wedding feast. What is our new name? My guess is Bride of Christ. However, a new name is His surprise.

- Reigning with Christ – this speaks of the defeat of earth's rebelliousness, when Christ will reign. It is also an answer to *The Lord's Prayer,* "Thy Kingdom come."
- The Bright and Morning Star –this is a title for Jesus Christ who is the greatest Gift (Rev 22:16).
- Walking with Christ, in white garments – This is beyond walking with God in the cool of the day in the Garden of Eden, as this time, it is without end.
- Name eternally in the Book of Life – What confidence this gives us!
- Confession of your name before Father God and His angels – is awesome! We also need to confess our Savior's Name before persons on earth to confirm this promise to us (Matt 10:32).
- Pillar of honor in God's temple – this is a symbol of eternal abiding with God.
- Written upon you will be God's name, Heaven's New Jerusalem name, and Christ's new name. – My guess for Christ's new name is *Yishi* (Hebrew) meaning "Husband."
- Christ finally has His bride, the name given for all believers. He had no bride on earth, though we were betrothed (engaged) to Him on earth through faith.
- Seated with Christ on His throne – even now, believers are spiritually seated with Him in heavenly places (Eph 2:6). There is no greater place than this: to be seated with the Son of God, on His throne.

Together we have taken time to study our Lord Jesus' last written message to us from Heaven, until He comes. Let us get ready for *Heaven's Awards Ceremony* – it's the ultimate!

And for a true believer, the winner is … you!

Breaking News
Overcomers: Martin Luther King, Rosa Parks – and You

What does it mean to be an overcomer as a person of faith from Israel, Iraq, Africa, China, or America – to name a few countries?

One thing it does **not** mean is that you are to destroy verbally or physically anyone who has a belief different from yours! No, my friend, you are only responsible to God for judging yourself. That is job enough for each one of us!

God *(Adonai),* alone is the Judge of His people (Deut 32:36). What a relief it is to give up having to be judge for everyone. How liberating!

Martin Luther King, Jr.

The word overcomer brings to mind for most of us the theme song of Martin Luther King Jr., *We Shall Overcome.* Leading his peaceful demonstrations for civil rights for African-Americans, and all people, was a new way of getting things done – without violence. You remember the first verse of Dr. King's theme song:

We shall overcome,
we shall overcome,
we shall overcome some day.
Oh, deep in my heart,
I do believe,
we shall overcome some day.[13]

His most famous speech was "I Have a Dream" given in 1963, five years before his assassination in Memphis, Tennessee on April 4, 1968. It became a symbol of his lifelong effort to end segregation through nonviolent means.

I am thankful for Dr. Martin Luther King Jr., who lived the words of the song and speech.

The Greek word *nikao* means "to overcome, prevail, get the victory."[14]

Rosa Parks

Another person who was a great overcomer is Rosa Parks. She was born Rosa McCauley in Tuskegee, Alabama and was married to Mr. Parks at the age of twenty. She often boycotted public facilities marked "Colored."

On December 1, 1955, Rosa had a particularly tiring day. Employed as a seamstress, she had spent the day pressing numerous pairs of pants. At age 42, she admitted that her back and shoulders ached terribly that day. She caught a bus, entering from the back door after paying at the front door! Rosa settled into the middle section where she found a seat. A white man got on and demanded a seat. The bus driver ordered Parks

and three other black customers to move. The others obeyed but Parks
quietly refused. When the driver threatened to call the police, Parks said
to go ahead and call them.

She was arrested. This event inspired a bus boycott that lasted 381
days. The monumental boycott – watched by the world – triggered the
black freedom movement and made a legend of Mrs. Parks.

October 24, 2005, Rosa died, but she lives on in her lasting legacy
as mother of the civil rights movement.

Jesus Christ

As a Jew, *Yeshua Mashiach* (Jesus Christ), knew about the pain of
prejudice. The Roman government occupying Israel was not friendly to
anyone who became so popular that he drew large crowds of thousands
as Jesus did. He preached a new way of life where we honor and respect
one another. He healed the sick, restored the emotionally wounded, and
fed the hungry. Though martyred two millennia ago, He still lives on by
the Spirit and His Words.

He gives strength to others, like Martin Luther King and Rosa Parks
to keep winning by overcoming without violence. Jesus Christ said, "…
In the world you will have tribulation, but be of good cheer, I have
overcome the world" (John 16:33b KJV-MOD).

Remember my friend, you are not alone. The Overcomer is with
you.

Next time: God in Statistics.

God in Statistics

I never knew that I could like the study of statistics. So, if you are
looking for a miracle – in this column you have one.

Once upon a time, the idea of studying and passing an exam in
statistics made me cautious about venturing into academia for a degree
in psychology and counseling. Possibly some of you have also felt the
same. During my first year of Bastyr/LIOS Graduate School, I studied
the textbook, *Statistics A User Friendly Guide* by Dr. Gerald Swanson.[15]
Yes, I passed the required exam. I found regarding the classes that
followed, I actually looked forward to them.

Dr. Swanson defined statistics as "A simplification of reality." Its
purpose is "to simplify a very complex reality to a few numbers that can

be understood and worked with." He likened it to learning a foreign language.[16]

The first use of statistics occurred early in history. It began with the need for rulers to raise taxes (sound familiar). To facilitate this, a census was taken. Joseph and Mary, with Baby Jesus close to delivery, knew about the crush of people traveling to Judea, the city of David, which is called Bethlehem (Luke 2:4).

In December 2006, I flew to Tampa, Florida to visit my three siblings and their families. During that time I also spent part of my time searching for a statistics tutor in my alma mater, the University of Tampa. It was providential that my sister, Georgia, and I located Dr. Cheri Kitrell a stats professor. I quickly read the chapters as I prepared for each of my three sessions with her.

When I e-mailed her the news that I passed the exam she quipped, "I always knew that I was a fantastic professor, but little did I know that I could communicate an entire semester's worth of statistics in three afternoons with such outstanding results!" Yes, I had the best.

One afternoon Dr. Cheri had been teaching me about the bell curve also called the normal curve. I found that the curve is symmetrical, that is, the right-hand side is a mirror image of the left-hand side. The centerline divides the curve in half and is primarily called the mean. The curve is **infinitely** wide, so the bottom of the curve on each side never actually touches the axis.

Of this Cheri said, it goes on and on into infinity or eternity. I remarked that was an exciting thought as I had not considered statistics as spiritual.

Seattle Science Center

Perhaps you have taken your children or grandchildren to the Seattle Science Center as I have. There you have seen an example of the famous normal curve as black balls continuously and randomly fall into this configuration, 50% on the right and 50% on the left.

The shape of the curve is like the silhouette of a bell, and so the name bell curve. It is often called Gaussian distribution after Carl Frederick Gauss, who discovered many of its properties. He was one of the greatest mathematicians in the world and is honored by Germany on their 10 Deutschmark bill. You can see the bell curve pictured on their money!

Anonymous information on internet from time to time claims that Psalm 118:8 is right in the middle of the 1188 chapters of the KJV Bible. That verse says, "It is better to trust in the LORD than to put confidence in man." I cannot prove this is the center, but someone someday might computerize the original languages of Hebrew, Persian (several chapters in Daniel) and Greek to find this out. At least we can count the chapters.

January 1, 2006, for New Years, I was inspired with the idea that a central passage of the Bible would make it the mean, median, and mode of the Bible! Statistically, the mean is the balance center point that reflects all values of all the data. The median is the exact middle of the data. The mode is the central tendency or value that occurs most frequently. Possibly the middle position would be an honored place in the ancient words of Scripture. Is Jesus the Menorah Servant Candle in the middle of the Bible?

Important update follows: Dr. J. R. Church, Bible scholar states, "Psalm 117 is actually the middle chapter of the Bible, with Psalm 118.8 being the middle verse ... Psalm 117 has 594 chapters before it and 594 chapters after it. There are 1,189 chapters in the Bible, making a total of 1,188 chapters apart from the middle chapter. It is remarkable that the middle verse should be Psalm **118.8**, thus alluding to those **1,188** chapters. This must be a product of Divine inspiration," says Dr. Church. "Maybe that is the secret contained in the Menorah — look for the Servant Lamp. You will find it in the middle of the Bible!" [17]

Until my next column, be looking for evidence of our Lord's signature and presence all around you. My friend, you are not alone.

Next time: Our Bible is the Sum of its Parts.

Our Bible is the Sum of its Parts

In my last column I spoke about my graduate statistics class and how I realized there is a touch of spirituality in this mathematical subject.

The piece concluded by my quoting from an article sent by email from a scholarly friend saying that the middle of the Bible – what I called the statistical mean, median, and mod – is Psalm 118:8.

Then a new friend and Edmond's resident hand-counted the Bible's chapters, guessing Psalm 117 for the center chapter. Another person posted on the internet his computer calculations; by counting verses he believes the center is Psalm 103:1-2.

Just like the subject of statistics itself, I always want to be checking to see which hypothesis is correct. The update by Dr. J.R. Church to the preceding chapter is the best answer yet, using the KJV Bible. I wish I had his quote earlier.

The Center Passover Message

What I am being impacted with at this moment – is that where truth is found in the Bible is not dependent on location. I am sure of this hypothesis.

For instance, two of the most important events in the Bible are celebrated annually. They are Passover and Easter, our major Jewish and Christian celebrations. Leviticus chapter 23 tells about Passover being the first of these festivals. The Gospel of John chapters 19 - 21 tells about Messiah's death, burial, resurrection, and ascension, the foundation of the Christian faith. Passover and Easter were four days apart in 2006. At times I celebrate them both.

What is the story of Passover? It started in Egypt about 3,500 years ago when the children of Israel had been taken into captivity and slavery. Moses was called by God (*Elohim*) to lead the Israelites out of Egypt, through the wilderness, and finally into the Promised Land of Canaan, now called Israel. But how could Moses do this? God gave him a plan in which he is required to confront the Pharaoh and warn him of the plagues that would come upon Egypt if he won't let God's people go.

At the Passover meal, I enjoy the part where we dip a finger in the wine or grape juice to drip it on our plates as we together count and call out the names of the plagues: blood, frogs, lice, flies, boils, hail, locusts, darkness.

Even then – Pharaoh resisted, so God had to use the hardest plague of all. He told the Israelites to prepare a meal for their journey that included bread, wine, bitter herbs, and a lamb whose blood would be used to mark their front door. The death angel would come to destroy the firstborn in all of Egypt, but if the lamb's blood was marked over the doorpost, the firstborn would be saved.

The famous words to both Jews and Christians are these: God said, "When I see the blood, I will pass over you" (Exodus 12:13b). Here the

Lord seems to use a play on words: "pass over you" reminds one of the Feast of Passover.

The firstborn plague was the crushing blow, and Pharaoh released the Children of Israel. The Israelites finally and miraculously went through the Red Sea on foot, and the Egyptian army in hot pursuit of them was drowned.

The Center Easter Message

The Christian's celebration begins on Ash Wednesday forty days before Easter with repentance and Lenten fasts. One year I chose a Daniel fast where I gave up as he did meat, and deserts (Dan 1). I felt there were many situations that need prayer in our world and hundreds of us in the USA chose to fast and pray during the forty days.

For Lent at St. Alban's Church in Edmonds, on Wednesdays, parishioners meet for soup suppers. One year retired priest and scholar, Fr. Fletcher Davis, spoke about his inspiring trip to Israel. I love hearing about Israel, my second home.

I remember the first time I visited the Garden Tomb in 1996. People from all nations met in small groups in the gardens to celebrate Holy Communion. My late husband, Dennis, had said, "Communion is the Passover Feast only without the meal!"

In fact, Jesus Christ celebrated the Passover Feast the night before He was betrayed. From his childhood He had annually celebrated the Passover Festival and meal. The difference at His final Last Supper was that He was to actually become the Passover Lamb who would take away the sins of the world (John 1:29, 36).

It is believed that at the same time the annual Passover lamb was being slain by the High Priest in the temple for Israel's sins, Jesus was being nailed to the cross for the sins of the world. That happened at a famous time, nine o'clock in the morning. The Savior of the world died six hours later.

The good news is that Jesus, our Lord and Savior, is not dead but has arisen. He, the Passover Lamb, chose to be our sacrifice and to pay our penalty for sin. Today spiritually, we may come out of Egypt and by faith enter into the spiritual Promised Land. Jesus the Christ made this provision for the whole world, if we will only believe and receive it. To me, the center message of the Bible is Passover in the Old Testament, and Easter or First Fruits in the New Testament. Let's celebrate both!

Next time: Fear of Death.

Fear of Death Is Normal – but It's Unnecessary

April ninth, 2006, I received an e-mail from a woman named Lauren. She said, "I have a bit of a hang-up on death. However, I know that I am saved and will live eternally with my Lord and Savior.

Lauren continued, "I was told something helpful yesterday by a business friend of mine: 'When we die, we will not be alone because Christ's omnipresence is still with us. Death is a peaceful experience and not anything to be afraid of.'"

She continued, "Well, today I went to google.com and typed the words 'Pictures of Heaven' and your website came up. As I was looking at the pictures, tears streamed down my face. How wonderfully you have depicted what I have read from the Bible.

"So, to make this long story short, thank you for following your calling with your beautiful pictures and beautiful words. May God bless you even more to allow a bigger glimpse of Heaven to shine from your website. You turned words into pictures!"

Lazarus's Death & Return

Perhaps you, or a friend, as with Lauren, have a hang-up on death. Jesus tried to tell His best friends what was soon going to happen to Him after His death. To Lazarus's sister, Mary, He said, "I am the resurrection, and the life: he that believes in Me though he were dead, yet shall he live ..." (John 11:25b KJV-MOD). His words of hope were two-fold, for the sisters Mary and Martha, but also for you and me two millennia later. The sisters were about to have the surprise of their lives when they witnessed the resurrection of their brother. It happened when Jesus, who is the resurrection, commanded, "Lazarus come forth." If Jesus had not first said "Lazarus," He could have raised all the cemeteries in Jerusalem!

Lazarus's death experience was a great witness in the community. It was common knowledge that he had been dead four days."

Of course, the religious leaders did not like seeing the resurrected and healed Lazarus walking around, praising Jesus. It was then that they did their "religious thing" plotting to kill Lazarus (John 12:10). What was the reason? Too many of the people were putting their faith in Jesus due to this great miracle.

These religious unbelievers eventually gave up their plan to destroy Lazarus to concentrate on their major plot to destroy Jesus. As for Lazarus, he would eventually die a second time, perhaps from old age.

There are a number of people in the Bible who died and came back. Today we call this a near-death experience, since they died but did not stay dead. However, Jesus is the first person in the Bible who died and came back from the dead, never to die again.

Jesus' Resurrection Body

He now has a resurrected, glorified body. It has the kind of molecular structure that can flow right through walls. How do I know that? It is shown twice in John, chapter 20. On the eve of the resurrection, the Apostles are gathered together in a special hideout for fear of arrest. Their doors were closed and locked. Jesus is not a ghost but a physical being who no longer needs a door for entrance (vs. 19). Eight days later He does the same thing. Here Christ showed His physical wounds in his hands and side to doubting Thomas who immediately becomes such a believer that he cries out, "My Lord and my God" (vs. 26-28). This is to me, the greatest verbal confession to the divinity of Christ I've found in the Bible.

First Corinthians 15 has been called the Resurrection Chapter of the Bible. In the beginning of this chapter, the Apostle Paul tells how many people were eyewitnesses of Jesus following His resurrection, and before His ascension. "And He [Jesus] was seen by *Cephas* [Peter], then of the twelve: After that, He was seen by above five hundred brethren at once … After that, He was seen by James [half-brother of Jesus]; then of all the Apostles. And last of all He was seen of me also, as of one born out of due time" (1 Cor 15:5-8 KJV-MOD).

All those Paul previously listed were actual eyewitnesses, but Paul's own experience was different. Here he, who had destroyed Christians, is referring to his own conversion some years after Jesus' ascension, when the Lord dramatically confronted Paul in a vision (Acts 9:1-31). Some call Paul the thirteenth apostle because of his strong witness to his faith, extensive missionary travels, and for writing a large portion of the New Testament.

One of the greatest witnesses for Jesus' resurrection being real is that all of His Apostles continued in His ministry and eleven out of the twelve willingly died as martyrs. The twelfth was the Apostle John who remained a prisoner on the Isle of Patmos, where he wrote the Gospel of

John, three epistles of John, and the book of Revelation. He too suffered willingly for his faith before dying as a man full of years.

My friend, do not have a hang-up on death. Give your hang-up to Jesus and just hang on to His hand. He knows the way home.

Next time: Azusa Street Revival.

Azusa Street Revival a Welcome "Happening"

"On the morning of April 19, 1906 readers of the Los Angeles Times were shocked to read the banner headline news of the San Francisco earthquake. At 5:18 A.M. the day before the most powerful earthquake in American history, 8.3 on the Richter scale had destroyed 514 city blocks in the heart of the city. More than 700 people died from the tremor and the firestorm that followed.

"The day before, on April 18, readers of the same paper had seen a curious first-page story of a spiritual earthquake that had hit Los Angeles in a little mission church on Azusa Street.

"This is how the world first heard of the Azusa Street revival that was to shake the spiritual world much as the San Francisco earthquake had shaken northern California. Little did the readers know that the aftershocks of the Los Angeles event in a small black holiness church would continue to shake the world with ever greater force throughout the century."[18]

1906, L.A. Renewal Begins

April 18, 1906 William Seymour, son of slaves, had that day traveled to an abandoned African Methodist Episcopal church in Los Angeles to lead a prayer meeting. I'm sure it was to his utter amazement that a three- year daily revival began.

He taught on not only salvation, but also that Pentecost and the nine supernatural gifts of the Holy Spirit were still available today (Acts 2:1-4, 1 Cor 12:7-11).

People of numerous races and denominations came from countries around the world to hear Rev. Seymour preach and receive his life-changing, miracle-working prayer.

2006, L.A., 60,000 people

A hundred years later, the recent centennial of Holy Spirit outpouring brought 60,000 people to the Los Angeles Convention Center and the Coliseum April 25 - 29, 2006 to sing, praise, and tell their personal stories of the power of the Holy Spirit.

Charisma magazine was there and dedicated their entire April issue to the story of the Azusa Street Revival. It was a pleasant surprise to see my late husband Dennis's *Nine O'clock in the Morning*[19] publicized online as one of their featured books at the Azusa Street Centennial.

Christian television networks, Daystar and Trinity Broadcasting covered the convention. Vincent Synan, one of the speakers, stated that today there are 600 million people around the world who claim a Pentecostal or charismatic experience. Now that's good news.

It was a relief for me to get away from the usual television sad news, this time about the Carnival cruise ship's allowing alcoholic binges on board, and a lovely 25-year old woman mysteriously found dead. Or commentators complaining that the Mexican's are singing their own Spanish version of *Star Spangled Banner*.

What an enriching newsbreak to praise God for an African-American, the Bishop William Seymore, who brought to the world transforming words of eternal truths! And the message continues on.

NextTime: *The DaVinci Code.*

Da Vinci Code: **Fact or Novelistic Fantasy?**
Breaking News

The Last Supper, the fifteen by twenty-nine foot mural by artist Leonardo Da Vinci, took center stage in the news in 2006. The controversial movie about Dan Brown's fictional novel *The Da Vinci Code*[20] opened in theaters May 19th.

I got close to seeing Da Vinci's famous painting when hosting a small tour to Italy in 1998. We flew into Turin (*Turino*) on June 5, 2006 to have a few days viewing and learning about The Shroud of Turin, believed by some to be the burial cloth of Jesus.

On June 9, we rented a van to continue our tour. The plan was to drive less than 50 miles to Milan (*Milano*) to the Church of Santa Maria dele Grazie and view The Last Supper. When we arrived, the door was locked on Sunday – a great disappointment! Wish I could give you an eyewitness account.

What I understand from Dan Brown's controversial novel is that he believes Leonardo painted the disciple sitting to the right of Christ to look slightly feminine, which secretly meant it was a woman. This person was supposedly Mary Magdalene. Brown's Gnostic belief is that Jesus and Mary Magdalene were in fact married, had a daughter, and that the bloodline goes on.

Let's stop here and think about what is wrong with this picture. Most students of art and scripture believe the Apostle John was the disciple to Jesus' right. He is believed to be the youngest disciple, so that would make him look less rugged than the others.

It's John, Not Mary

Also, if the individual to Jesus' right was Mary Magdalene, rather than the John, then the beloved John would be missing in the painting of the Last Supper!

Unique to Da Vinci's painting is the major theme of Jesus' betrayal. The surprise can be seen on the faces of the disciples, with the exception of Judas.

The Last Supper is the beginning of the Eucharistic Feast of The Lord's Supper for the Church, and also represents the continuing Jewish Festival of Passover (Luke 22:11-20; Leviticus 23). This painting establishes a very holy time in a believer's life.

It is sad that through the gospel according to Dan Brown, more arrows are being shot at those who revere the ancient words of canonical Scripture.

Simple Cups Not a Chalice

Another concern about the author, Mr. Brown, is what he considers a missing chalice in The Last Supper. Remembering that the original scene was primarily a Passover Feast should help us clarify.

The cups used in most Jewish Passover Seders that I have attended were simple cups or glasses for grape juice or wine. I do not believe that 2,000 years ago Jesus would have had an expensive silver chalice on hand for the Passover meal.

To me that eliminates Brown's idea that there was also a secret code in the missing chalice. It would be logical that Da Vinci, the artist, carefully studied biblical history so that he would be accurate in depicting what scripture teaches.

The Last Supper, a three-year project painted by Leonardo, was completed in 1498, over 500 years ago. A number of needed restorations to the painting have occurred due to the medium originally used, which was tempera on stone.

We must also allow that it does not look exactly as it did originally. Restoration of the painting has, however, prolonged the life of this work of art for future generations.

Mr. Brown, made a large amount of money on his book and movie, at Jesus' expense. Please remember that *The Da Vinci Code* is fiction and not fact, and can be proven to be so with careful study.

Next time: Did Jesus Marry Mary Magdalene?

Did Jesus Marry Mary Magdalene?

The *Da Vinci Code* fantasy novel continues confusing some of the public with the idea that Jesus secretly married Mary Magdalene. A minister recently being interviewed on TV quipped, "I think if Jesus had chosen a wife, it would not have been one from whom He had cast seven demons!"

So why do you think Jesus, the Christ, came to earth? Did he come as a regular man – to be born, grow up, be educated or learn a trade, find a wife, have children, do good works, and then die from old age?

Jesus answers this question as recorded in the Gospel of Luke, "For the Son of man is come to seek and to save that which was lost" (Luke 19:10).

Lost, what was lost? We were, and paradise was lost. In Genesis we learn that the idyllic life in the Garden of Eden was lost when the first created beings, Adam and Eve, chose to give allegiance to the Luciferian evil spirit, rather than to God. With their decision, this planet, all who would be born, humankind and animals, and nature, came under the control of this "Darth Vaderish" spirit, called in Scripture, Satan.

Jesus did not come to earth to have a wife and children. His infinitely greater plan was to save and rescue, the human race and this planet – from domination and bondage of the most universally cruel of dark spirits. The battle took Jesus to the cross and spilled His last drop of blood in sacrifice for us.

Each one who believes in the triune *Yahweh* will one day have a homecoming celebration with Christ. Then Father God, through the **spiritual and eternal seed** of Christ, will have multitudes of children in His Kingdom.

"... He [Christ] shall see His seed, He shall prolong His days, and the pleasure of the Lord shall prosper in His hand" (Isa 53:10, DAKE). Christ the Lord and Messiah began to see His seed or spiritual offspring for the first time on the evening of His resurrection when He with joy visited His Apostles.

"Then Jesus said to them again, Peace to you! [Just] as the Father has sent Me forth, so I am sending you. And having said this, He breathed on them and said to [them] Receive (admit) the Holy Spirit!" (John 20:21-22 AMP).

The first humans were reborn when the Holy Spirit indwelled the Apostle's spirits, and at that moment, Heaven's flag was planted on earth. One God-step was made for humanity for all time.

Born Again and Indwelt

Jesus never had a wedding on earth, nor was that His intention. He was not a regular man with earthly plans; He was God made flesh with heavenly plans! He came to "seek and to save that which was lost" you and me. His death and resurrection broke the power of darkness over this world for all who have eyes to see.

The Bible begins with the creation miracle, the first couple, and their wedding. The closing miracle, as told in Revelation, takes place at Jesus' own wedding. The bride is made of all believing people – now one body, one in Messiah, races and genders of every color – now one family; now one people.

It is a serious error, a heresy, to believe that Jesus had an earthly wife as Brown's novel portrays.

Mary Magdalene was simply a follower of Jesus while on earth. Now rejoicing in Heaven, Mary will one day be part of the spiritual Bride of Christ, as will all of us who say to the Lord, "I Do!"

Up Date: September 19, 2012 *The Seattle Times* quotes the story about a Harvard professor of divinity who translated a fragment of writing on papyrus about 1.5 by 3 inches, in the Coptic or Egyptian language. The quote recorded was, "Jesus said to them, my wife ..."[21]

71

First of all, Jesus was in Egypt as a small child. If he were being quoted as an adult, He would have been most likely speaking in His native tongue – Hebrew. This was not Jesus speaking but an unknown person saying He said these words. This is not even a first person witness. "Alin Suciu, a papyrologist at the University of Hamburg, called it a "forgery."[22] I appreciate Mr. Suciu's honesty and his willingness to take a stand.

Until Jesus the Messiah returns, unbelievers will continue to attack the thousands of ancient biblical records of Holy Scripture that are our Judeo-Christian foundation. They will continue to insult Jesus' reputation, morality, and purpose for His life.

Before His ascension Jesus spoke to us – His Bride saying, "I am going to prepare a place for you, and after I have gone and prepared you a place, I shall return to take you with me" (John 14:3a JB).

These are the words of Jesus Christ the Lord. Words that I trust.

For those interested in learning more about the Bride of Christ, see Chapter 13, *Your Heavenly Wedding*, in my book, *To Heaven and Back*, which can be found at http://www.emotionallyfree.com/E-store.html

Next time: A Miracle of Unity.

A Miracle of Unity - A Continuing Inspiration

Scripture tells us about the Lord's early followers, that they were all in one accord in one place. This is the first miracle-to have about 120 believers in unity! It took ten days of prayer, scripture (scroll) reading, and sharing in community to get to this point. Soon, the 3,500 year prophesied Day of Pentecost would fully come, beginning from the spiritual center of the world, Jerusalem.

This would be the first empowering of a fairly large group of believers. The Bible says the twelve Apostles were all there; Mary, the earthly mother of Jesus was there; Jesus' stepbrothers and sisters were there (Acts 1:13-14).

It is my guess that Lazarus, who was raised from the dead, was there; Mary and Martha, Lazarus's sisters, were there; Mary Magdalene, out of whom Jesus cast seven demons, was there. Simon of Cyrene, who carried Jesus' cross to Golgotha, was there. Joseph of Arimathea and Nicodemus, who prepared the burial tomb for Jesus, were no doubt there. The one healed leper who had returned to thank Jesus was there. The woman who touched the hem of His garment for healing was there.

These and many more, at least 120 were in the upper room obeying Jesus' command for them not to leave, but wait there for the power of the Holy Spirit.

The strengthening power of the Holy Spirit was sent by Father and Son from Heaven to fill all willing human beings. When the time came, flames of supernatural fire sat upon or hovered over their heads. The rushing, mighty power of the Holy Spirit filled the house and the people. "And they were all filled with the Holy Spirit, and began to speak with other tongues [languages imparted supernaturally] as the Spirit gave them utterance" (Acts 2:4 NKJV).

These were languages of prayer and praise to make the body of Messiah ready to be witnesses to the world. They were also signs that Pentecost (*Shavuot,* Hebrew) had indeed arrived. The early community of believers had to have this power to carry on the work that Jesus had begun. That is why Jesus, the Christ, commanded them to wait (Acts 1:4b). They could not do this clean up job, this redeeming work on the earth, in their own strength. They had to have God-given power filling their speech centers, their minds, their bodies.

Power, Unity, Love

We too must have this empowering experience of the Holy Spirit. There is far too much of the unholy spirit being promoted worldwide. We believers must also ask for the unity of the Holy Spirit so we can build more of God's Kingdom on earth. If we do not walk in one accord and humility we will give away more territory to the unholy kingdom.

Jesus' concluding, heart-touching prayer in the 17th chapter of John is intercession for His Apostles and for all believers past and present. In it Jesus prays for unity, "… That they all may be one; as You, Father, are in me, and I in You, that they also may be one in us. … That the world may believe that You have sent Me and have loved them, as You have loved Me" (John 17:21b, 23b, KJV-MOD).

In this last verse I feel He is saying, "How we Christians treat one another will either cause people to believe in Jesus or not believe in Him." That is serious.

This unity and love needed requires not only salvation, but the power (*dunamis,* Greek) of the Holy Spirit. God never makes a requirement without provision. Have you asked and waited for the power? Dennis Bennett did and tells about it in his book, *Nine O'clock in the Morning.*[23]

The world is waiting. And God waits.

Next time: Our Lives are About Being "Test Ready".

Our Lives are About Being "Test Ready"

Near the end of June, most students have already taken their exams. I remember how it was at exam time at the end of my first year in graduate school. Mid June in 2006, I was getting ready to take my first four-hour oral exam. I had a dozen two or three ended questions, and that equals at least twenty-four questions. The oral exam is for five students. We also had to evaluate three case studies, as well as answer the questions given by two faculty members.

Twenty-one of the questions represented textbooks on psychology and business, plus three were psychological inventories on learning styles, conflict resolution, and fundamental interpersonal relational orientation-behavior.

Many of the students at the university had jobs, so our classes were in monthly modules that lasted from three to five days on campus. When we were home we had employment obligations during which we tried to find time to read, study, and write assignments.

Final Exams

How does this relate to my faith-based beliefs, you may ask? In one way, the Christian faith is studying for finals. When we meet the Lord He might ask, "Did you read My Book?" How sad, if we haven't.

Not only that, the study of God's Textbook tells us how to live our lives well on earth. If we do study it, we'll know what God's will is for our lives, day by day. We can save ourselves a bunch of trouble.

Study Hall with God

One famous verse says, "Study to show yourself approved to God, a workman that needs not to be ashamed, rightly dividing the word of truth" (2 Tim 2:15 KJV-MOD). We work hard for man's approval, me for instance with my exam, but how hard do we work to be approved to

God? Maybe there will be an angelic study hall just inside Heaven's eastern gate to catch people up on the greatest Book in the universe!

There are many ways to begin a thorough study of the greatest Book ever written. Bible Study Fellowship (BSF) has an eight year course (summers off) which I took some years ago. Yes, I enjoyed all eight years. As with all groups we have our biases, but you're free to ignore that and concentrate on the well-prepared teaching provided for students.

Many churches, Messianic fellowships, and synagogues have Bible studies to offer. Online Bible courses in the Judeo-Christian faiths are other options. One year of Bible College before entering a university would give a good balance between spiritual and secular education. No one suggested that to me but I think it would have been a good way to go.

Fuller Theological Seminary would give you a good foundation in both Hebrew and Greek to help enliven your understanding of these foundational, biblical languages.

My Test

I hoped I would do well in my exam. One friend said, "Don't worry, we'll get through it."

Another prayed that I'd have complete recall. What comforting words. All I knew is I'll have done my best.

Greatest Exam

My greatest exam is yet to come at the end of my life. In Heaven there will be no more preparation time for my studies. The good news is that His grace, His unmerited favor, will also be applied to my test results and yours too.

Paul, the Apostle, says, "For by grace you are saved through faith; and that not of yourselves: it is the gift of God: not of works, lest any man should boast" (Eph 2:8-9 KJV-MOD).

To that I say, "Praise be to God," and in Hebrew, "*Baruch HaShem.*" – *Bless the Lord!*

Next time: Failure is Stepping Stone to Success.

Failure is Stepping Stone to Success of the Spirit

It's hard not to succeed the first time you try something new. I had been preparing for a race to succeed in graduate school for eight months. The end of this particular oral exam race was not what I had hoped for. I retook part of that exam a few days later. There is nothing like taking an oral exam on a hot, muggy day. My mouth was dry like cotton, but for more than one reason.

I passed on fourteen points but missed three. I was not yet perfect in my answers; three quarters right on a question will not do. I will have yet another exam.

How would it turn out? Only God knows. What I do know is that when I returned from a trip to Israel in 2003, the Holy Spirit showed me that I was to advance my education in the field of counseling, and psychology.

How does God speak to me? One of the favorite ways is through a specific scripture at a significant moment. It was exactly three days after my trip to Israel, 2003, that Isaiah 11:1-2 was emphasized to me.

"And there shall come forth a rod out of the stem of Jesse [Jesus], and a Branch shall grow out of His roots: And the spirit of the Lord shall rest upon Him, the spirit of wisdom and understanding, the spirit of counsel and might, the spirit of knowledge and of the fear of the Lord;"

God's Language

In my study of Hebrew, I had learned that the seven branch Menorah was spoken of in Isaiah 11:1-2. It therefore should be understood by reading it from right to left as in the Hebrew language. The candles had been snuffed out after the worship service. As we sat at a table eating, my friend Erin said to me, "Look, one of the candles of the Menorah has rekindled itself."

I checked my Bible to see which of God's attributes that candle represented. I began in Isaiah reading verse one with: "spirit of wisdom" (far right) and then "understanding" (far left); and again to the right was the "spirit of counsel." I announced to my friend Aaron, "That is the candle of counsel!" As I spoke those words the candle flame immediately extinguished itself! Several saw it and were surprised, but I was the one most impacted. Driving home that day, I realized that it was somehow a message to me. In time it led me to the university.

You can draw a picture of all seven of the candles in this formation, and when you do put the words mentioned before the six candles then the "Spirit of the Lord" is in the center. It represents the Messiah who is called the Servant Candle, the One who lights all other candles in the Menorah.

How God Speaks

God also speaks to me through circumstances. Before marriage to The Rev. Dennis Bennett, I had been a teacher and a social worker. Then for several decades I did pastoral counseling for and with my husband. Since his death in 1991, Inner Healing through *Emotionally Free® Seminars*[24] had grown, and I had become a registered counselor in Washington State near that time.

God often speaks through people. A friend, Pamela, had phoned to suggest that I consider LIOS Grad School of Counseling at Bastyr University. The classes were organized in 3-5 day modules on campus, and presented every few weeks. I had already spent one year at Edmond's Community College taking required Psychology 101. The schedule, curriculum, and teachers seemed perfect for me so I made the big leap to university graduate school that September in 2005.

Through my life's calling as author of the *Emotionally Free® Course,* it is my joy to train prayer-counselors in several states and nations. To help them grow, I needed to keep upgrading myself. One helpful textbook at Bastyr University was, *Learning as a Way of Being* by Peter Vaill.

Learning is an authentic way of being and living. It may be seen through Dr. Vaill's seven focuses: Continual, Creative, Expressive, Feeling, On-line, Reflexive, and Self-directed Learning."[25]

Try, Try Again

If you have to retake a test to succeed – do your best. After that first year at Bastyr/LIOS University, the Counselor's Candle was shining too brightly in my heart for me not to try again. So I tried and passed my exam leading me into my second year of graduate school at Bastyr/LIOS University. I went on to receive my Master's Degree in Counseling – with a Marriage and Family Therapy major – at the Seattle

77

Center Auditorium, June 2008. (Do I hear applause? I'm quite sure from Heaven.)

In Isaiah 9:6 Jesus is called Wonderful Counselor. He has a plan for you too. You may also choose to look for His seven-fold Menorah lights, lighting your way to your special calling.

Next time: God's Spiritual Armor.

God's Spiritual Armor is There for All

On the 4th of July 2006 on news channels everywhere, we saw missiles being fired from North Korea into the Sea of Japan. Some firecrackers! Next, Israeli Soldiers were kidnapped by Hezbollah in Lebanon and the Gaza Strip. The response from Israel was a shoot out with Hezbollah.

What is a Christian to do? One thing I know is that Heaven is neither Democrat nor Republican. It is not Protestant, Catholic, Jewish, or Muslim.

Scripture does, however, teach us that for our salvation Jesus was born in a Jewish body. Everyone will have to make peace with Him before entering Heaven's gates. The gates, by the way, are decorated on top with the names of the twelve tribes of Israel.

One of the best things to do daily is to follow the example of St. Paul the Apostle. One of his forms of prayer is putting on the whole armor of God. You can do it for yourself, your loved ones, and even for soldiers in battle.

Saint Paul's life really got into warfare after he accepted the call to service for his Lord. In 2 Corinthians 11:23-30, he lists some of his sufferings: a few of them are "… in prisons more frequent, in deaths often … Three times I was beaten with rods, once I was stoned, three times I suffered shipwreck, a night and a day I have been in the deep …" (KJV-MOD).

Visiting Paul's Prison

In 1998, I visited The Mamertine Prison in Rome where Paul was incarcerated. It is a stone dungeon. Originally there were no stairs, as the prisoner was let down through a manhole opening dangling from a rope tied around his waist.

The dungeon was quite small, 14 by 16 feet square. For safe keeping the dangerous evangelist, Paul, was deposited in the lower of two prison cells before he was eventually killed for his faith.

If you wondered why Paul talked about putting on this spiritual armor, this little bit of history makes it easy to understand. He tells us believers to prepare for battle since we too are in a spiritual war, a war against our faith, a war against our freedom.

He says, "Finally, my brothers [and sisters], be strong in the Lord, and in the power of His might. Put on the whole armor of God, that you may be able to stand against the wiles of the devil. For we wrestle not against flesh and blood, but against principalities, against powers, against the rulers of the darkness of this world, against spiritual wickedness in high places" (Eph 6:10-12 KJV-MOD).

Spiritual Armor Wins

In this world, humankind is fighting against flesh and blood, lots of it. Yet most soldiers of the world, as well as soldiers of faith, do not know there is spiritual armor to help them.

We must be strong in the Lord not in our own human strength. Missiles, booby traps, rifles, and drones will not defeat an invisible enemy who is stirring up trouble behind the scenes.

This "Darth Vaderish" spirit got his start as a cherub-angel in Heaven before his treasonous rebellion against God, the Almighty. Though Christ's death totally defeated him, the prince of darkness wants to drag multitudes into his cavernous kingdom before his demise.

The list of spiritual armor is the belt of truth, breastplate of righteousness, shoes of peace, shield of faith, helmet of salvation, sword of the Spirit, and prayer in the Spirit.

We will look at each piece of this armor in subsequent columns. Meanwhile, please read Ephesians 6:10-18 and pray for our government and for leaders of the nations worldwide.

You too can be a healing, praying, powerful soldier.

Next time: War Enrages but God Engages.

War Enrages but God Engages, if We Let Him

The battle of Lebanon and Israel raged on, in June 2006. Scores of political leaders in the media were giving their opinions on what should be done, and certainly what should not be done.

Everybody has an opinion. The question is, "How many of them have been praying and listening to God for direction?"

While Paul, the Apostle was in a Roman prison in A.D. 64, he wrote to the Ephesians about the value of putting on the spiritual armor of God. No wonder he uses the symbolism of the Roman soldier as he is writing to believers in Ephesus directly from a prison in Rome.

"Therefore put on God's complete armor, that you may be able to resist and stand your ground on the evil day [of danger], and having done all [the crisis demands], to stand [firmly in your place]" (Eph 6:13 AMP).

The Complete Armor

Paul says for us to put on God's complete armor. In other words, there are seven parts to the armor mentioned, so we need to appropriate them all.

"Stand therefore – hold your ground – having put on and tightened the belt of truth" (Eph 6:14 AMP).

I think that even the order in which Paul names the armor is important, so I personally like to put it on my soul – in this order.

Here Paul mentions first, the belt of truth. For the Roman soldier, the leather belt gathered his garments together as well as securing his sword. The belt covered his loins protecting his sexuality. This part of his warfare equipment gave him confidence and focus.

Commentators consider the truth of God in several ways. It can refer to Christian doctrines such as the *Nicene Creed*, the *Apostle's Creed*, the *Lord's Prayer*, and Jewish prayers as the *Shama*, and the *Priestly Blessing*, that many have memorized. It can mean truthfulness of our words and hearts. All are important.

80

Truth Sets Free

HaSatan (Hebrew) is called in scripture the father of lies. He is very active in his lie-filled campaigns all around us. We need the ancient words of Scripture to help us know the truth and to win our battles.

When Jesus was first confronted by Satan at the Great Temptation the enemy began with, "... If you are the Son of God, command that these stones be made bread" (Matt 4:3b KJV-MOD).

"But Jesus answered and said, 'It is written, man shall not live by bread alone, but by every word that proceeds from the mouth of God'" (Matt 4:4 (KJV-MOD). Jesus' reply was a quotation from the *Torah* – Deuteronomy 8:3b.

Here our Lord shows us how to deal with the Liar. We win by using God's Word above our own.

The Hebrew word for truth is *emet*. In Hebrew letters, *emet* is spelled beginning with the first of the 22 letters of the Hebrew Alphabet, "*Alef*", the middle letter is *Mem,* and ending with the last letter "*Tav.*" In ancient Hebrew, the first letter:

- *Alef*, speaks of God being number one and being all powerful.
- *Mem* means water or *may-eem* - which satisfies your thirst, the middle letter of the alphabet.
- *Tav* the ending, last letter of 22 is the letter t and considered by some as the ancient form of the cross.

God is the beginning, the middle, and the ending of His alphabet. He empowers His disciples. He's the only one who can satisfy our inner thirst. He took our cross for us, gave His all and died in our place.

Study the Bible

All the Hebrew letters have spiritual meanings so a study of these letters for a Christian can be part of this powerful belt of truth.

Before Jesus' death and ascension He said, "When He the Spirit of truth is come, He will guide you into all truth: for He shall not speak of Himself; but whatsoever He shall hear, that shall He speak: and He will show you things to come. He shall glorify Me" (John 16:13,14a KJV-MOD).

You may think of the belt of truth as the words, letters, and beliefs of the Bible. Put them on daily in one of these forms and see how strong and safe you feel.

Put away the rage of war and engage yourself with His protection for battle.

Next time: Anxiety is Inevitable.

Anxiety is Inevitable, but So is Our Sanctuary

In a fallen world, do you think lasting peace will ever occur?

It seems the human race has always been worried about its home, state, or country being taken over by other nations. Will we always have to stay vigilant to keep the enemy from sneaking in through planes, ships, or vehicles to detonate lethal explosives?

We're used to having some kind of world's challenge looming on the horizon to worry about.

Anxiety disorder "is what health experts call any anxiety that persists to the point that it interferes with one's life . . . ranging from very specific phobias to generalized anxiety disorder, it afflicts 19 million Americans," says psychologist Christine Gorman.[26]

This is where faith comes in. For me, the strength of my life is through faith in the One who paid the debt of my sin.

He died in my place so that I could have happiness now, tomorrow, and for eternity. I learn about Him through the sixty-six books of the Bible. In every book, I find Him there.

I worry sometimes but then I remember Jesus' promises, His love for me, and I take a deep breath.

Breastplate of Righteousness

Last time we saw from the sixth chapter of Ephesians that we have protection in this dangerous world through God's armor. We have put on the belt of truth. This time it is the breastplate of righteousness we don (Eph 6:14).

Righteousness is not a holier than thou attitude. I want to give you a picture of human righteousness. My late husband, Dennis Bennett, hired a company to install storm windows in our house. The workman arrived and began the project. At the end of the day, Dennis walked out on the sundeck to assess the job. He was dismayed to see that the wooden storm-window frames had knots in them and were unevenly cut.

He told the worker, "Tomorrow go and buy some good wood. When you come back, I'll work with you to help you cut straight corners."

Instead of having the young man fired, Dennis spent most of the next day working with him. That is an example of righteousness or upright character.

The 18th letter of the Hebrew alphabet is called *tsadik*. This letter looks as if a person is kneeling with his hands lifted in praise. A righteous person can also be called *tsadik*. Paul, the author of Ephesians and a Jewish scholar, knew this connection.

A spiritual meaning of the breastplate of righteousness is right thinking, speaking and acting. It is right standing with God, through Christ. This conveys God's imputed righteousness, or the righteousness of Jesus transferred to my account.

By His Grace

One day when I stand before my Father God, I will be able to do so through this gift from Jesus Christ, God's Son. Important as it is, my own human good deeds will not earn me rights to the Kingdom above (Eph 2:8).

If we imperfect beings have God's imputed righteousness, we will also choose to live holy lives and do acts of righteousness. This upright, godly character also helps us resist the evil one.

Though righteousness is already in a believer's spirit, where God indwells us, why does the Apostle Paul tell us to put it on daily or often?

I think the place He is reminding us to put the armor on is our souls – intellect, will and emotions. Our psychological natures are where temptation battles most often take place.

Eunice, a dear friend of mine, prayed and her two daughters to put on the Armor of God each morning before they left for school. They also prayed *The Lord's Prayer* together. This is a wise family.

Wars will come and go. Yet fortunately, in the midst of an anxious world, God eagerly waits for you to slip your hand into His – to receive righteousness, truth, and peace. Your personal, inner warfare can be won with these words, "Yes Lord Jesus, where You lead me, I will follow."

Next time: Shoes as Weapons?

Shoes as Weapons? How Cruelly Perverse!
Breaking News

The Apostle Paul tells us that the shoes of peace are part of God's armor, and yet we have to put them on. We human beings do not just automatically walk in peace. We have to choose to walk in God's peace every day of our lives.

Unfortunately, there are far too many people walking in shoes of destruction. Think how shocked St. Paul would be if he were able to hear the following news from earth:

"A shoe bomber planned to detonate his black sneakers during an international flight on December 22, 2001, but the plan was foiled. Since that time, travelers boarding planes in the United States major airports have to take off their shoes before they can get through security to take their flights!"

The Apostle would learn that those living in the dark kingdom had received orders to make shoes into killing instruments – bombs, not instruments of peace!

Shoe Bomber

Shoe bomber Richard Reid, 29, 6-foot-4 British citizen and jihad devotee was the first to accept this assignment of calculated destruction. His hope was to bring down American Airlines jetliner flight 63 with nearly 200 people on board, during its flight from Paris to Miami.

Several brave men and some women, including stewardess Christina Jones who sustained a tooth bite in the struggle, took Reid on before he could detonate his shoe bomb. Later on, in 2003, he was sentenced to 60 years to life.

Paul says to the Ephesians (and to us): "Put on the whole armor of God, that you may be able to stand against the wiles of the devil" (Eph 6:11 NKJV). That's what we are doing in this column, putting on the entire armor of God piece by piece to help us to stand against evil. Last time we put on the breastplate of righteousness.

Shoes of Peace

Third in Paul's army dress code are shoes of the Gospel of peace. These shoes, most likely soldier's boots – not flip-flops – provide us with protection and balance. Without good balance it is hard to fight a successful battle.

Also, if we lose God's peace, we can more easily be thrown off balance. Not walking in chaos is one definition of peace or *shalom*.

The shoes speak of readiness to talk about Christ, our Messiah. Our shoes may carry us to different cities, states, or nations where we can share the Gospel.

The famous scripture found in John 3:16 tells what the Gospel means. You can also find a Bible acrostic in the verse spelling the letters of gospel as you see below.

God so loved the world that He gave His

Only begotten

Son that whosoever believes in Him will not

Perish but have

Everlasting

Life.

Think about it – even if you knew only this one verse in the Bible, you would still have understanding of the central message of the Bible. John 3:16 is like a center bell curve of the Bible. God makes His Gospel message so clear that an elementary school child, as well as an educated Ph.D. can understand it.

The prophet Isaiah says the feet of those who share the Gospel are beautiful. He is speaking of messengers of the good news now, and in the Kingdom to come.

The news of the Kingdom is peace – peace within the human heart and peace on earth. Let your shoes spell peace as you walk.

"How beautiful upon the mountains are the feet of him who brings good tidings, who publishes peace, who brings good tidings of good, who publishes salvation, who says to Zion, Your God reigns!" (Isa 52:7 AMP).

You may not think your feet are the most beautiful part of your body, but share John 3:16 with someone and see what God will say about your feet.

Beautiful upon the mountains and beautiful everywhere you go to be a witness.

Next time: Shield of Faith or Shroud of Fear.

Shield of Faith or Shroud of Fear

It takes faith to live and to keep on living especially as we, through the media, learn daily of fearful happenings around the globe.

Yet on September 20, 2006, I was moved by good news on the news. Photos showed infant Abigale "Abby" Lynn Woods at home in Londell, Missouri after being abducted by a woman who was desperate enough to steal a neighbor's baby following her own miscarriage.

For five days the family was wrapped in fear and grief wondering if they would ever see Abby again. The infant's grandpa, a man of faith, said the police, the media, and prayer to Jesus brought the family through.

The most famous faith defining verse in the Bible is, "Now faith is the substance of things hoped for, the evidence of things not seen," (Heb 11:1). Grandpa and family chose to believe, have assurance day by day without physical proof that Abby would be all right.

They now have the substance of their faith – Abby!

Shield of Faith

In Ephesians 6:16 Paul says, "Above all, take the shield of faith, whereby you shall be able to quench all the fiery darts of the wicked" (Eph 6:16 KJV-MOD).

Our soldier example has already in past columns put on the belt of truth, breastplate of righteousness, shoes of peace, and now the shield of faith, so we know this is a believing warrior.

Another definition of faith is found in this Scripture acrostic:

Forsaking
All others
I
Take
Him.

In one's marriage vow, a promise something like this faith acrostic is made. Faithful followers of Christ are to forsake what offends Him, such as the cults, the occult, and false gods. Forsake all others and follow Him.

In Paul's example he used Roman soldiers. We discover they had two different kinds of shields, a smaller round one for hand-to-hand combat, and an oblong one over four feet tall and two feet wide to use when fighting as a company.

Interestingly, *pistis* the Greek word for shield, is derived from the one meaning door or gate; this second shield was similar in shape to a door that hid the soldier.

This door-like shield is the one spoken of in Paul's letter to the Ephesians. When Roman soldiers advanced in battle along with their comrades, the enemy was faced with a terrifying solid wall of shields!

Fiery Darts Quenched

At times we need to use corporate intercessory prayer as a form of this powerful kind of warfare. The pictorial message Paul gives is to help us to walk in unity, to link up with others of like mind and heart.

The Roman shield was covered with leather that had been water soaked to keep the fiery darts from piercing the soldier. Paul said all the fiery darts of the enemy would be quenched. Not one fear, condemnation, or hate dart can penetrate to you.

Isn't that good news? Lets claim God's protection daily in our armor of God prayers.

Paul began with this message of importance, Above all take the shield of faith. That was high on his value's scale. A verse in Hebrews says "and without faith it is impossible to please God" (Heb 11:6 NIV).

You and I need to practice our faith, feed our faith, live our faith, pray our faith, study our faith, increase our faith, speak our faith, claim our faith, share our faith.

We will fight some battles alone and at times stand with others. Warfare equipment was issued to you at your salvation. Use it, won't you?

Remember this motto: "Fear knocked at the door. Faith answered it. There was no one there."

Next time: Helmet of Salvation.

Helmet of Salvation Protects Mind and Soul

Why does the Bible say that we believers should wear helmets of salvation? Perhaps it's because in warfare the enemy will shoot for the head as well as the heart.

How do our heads get shot at in this 21st Century? Many ways it seems. For example, those seeking higher education will have many challenges to their faith. Solid study of Scripture and having a confirming salvation experience are vital before entering college. Young Life is one example of an excellent organization for high school students to get involved in through their headquarters in Colorado Springs, Colorado.

In the business world as well, protection of the mind is important. The old quote is true: "GIGO – garbage in garbage out."

At the *Emotionally Free®* Seminars, we have a time when attendees pray the *Healing of the Molested Mind Prayer.* We may then go forward in twos and stand in front of a large bowl of blessed water. Placing our fingers in the water we then touch one another's foreheads and pray the *Armor of God Prayer*. It's a moving experience.

1 Corinthians 2:16 says, "We have the mind of Christ." This means we are to integrate Jesus' words, thinking, and acting into our lives. Our purpose is to be an expression of His healing life in the world.

Strong's Concordance defines mind (*nous*) as meaning: The intellect, i.e. mind (in thought, feeling, or will).[27] The words mind and soul are used interchangeably.

Helmet of Salvation

Your fantastic brain is also covered by the helmet of salvation. Brain surgeon Dr. Howard Dueker once told me, "The physical brain is the machinery of the soul. The physical brain is not the soul." Yet, the growing knowledge of the human brain is phenomenal.

The Greek word for salvation is *soteria,* meaning preservation and deliverance. Our minds are treasures and we must be careful what we put into them.

In 1 Thessalonians 5:8 we see Paul speaking about putting on the hope of salvation as a helmet.

"But let us, who are of the day, be sober, putting on the breastplate of faith and love; and for an helmet, the hope of salvation." This goes a step further to consider our ultimate salvation, our destiny beyond our present state. This kind of hope sustains us in battle.

We've studied the soldier's defensive armor given in Ephesians 6:10-18, belt of truth, breastplate of righteousness, shoes of peace, shield of faith, and helmet of salvation. Next we'll look at the offensive battle equipment.

We cannot, however, just stand there dressed for war. We have to move forward. Yes, Christ won victory for all humanity on the cross, but the enemy has had millennia to dig in to this world.

Jesus commissioned us saying, "Behold I give you power to tread on serpents and scorpions, and over all the power of the enemy: and nothing shall by any means hurt you" (Luke 10:19).

Our Lord is counting on us through prayer and action to root out the enemy troops and do the clean up job while we look forward to the glorious hope of His return.

The *Nicene Creed* proclaims, "For He will come again in glory to judge the living and the dead, and His Kingdom will have no end." To this let us say together, "Amen."[28]

Next time: Nuclear Threat or Not.

Nuclear Threat or Not, Sword Will Prevail

Back in October 9, 2006, North Korea detonated her first known nuclear device. The earth shook as if a small earthquake 4.2 had occurred and Kim Jong-Il's angry message reverberated around the earth. Will nuclear warfare capability spread to other countries? Will this become a growing nuclear warfare age? These are common questions, written in bold print, on the world community's mind.

Perhaps, our sixth piece of spiritual warfare, the sword of the Spirit, seems minor in comparison. It may – unless the facts are known. Let me assure you that God-breathed Scripture, which is the sword of the Spirit, will not end, whereas every kind of weapon, nuclear, and otherwise, will eventually pass away.

For 3,500 years those 'God wannabes,' who say there is no God but them, have destroyed millions of Bibles plus innumerable humans – Bible scribes and translators. But the Bible marches on.

Sword of the Spirit

The Apostle Paul through Scripture still admonishes us today, "And take ... the sword of the Spirit, which is the Word of God:" (Eph 6:17). It is something we must do ourselves. The Roman soldier of those days could not fight without his sword. It was his major offensive weapon.

The spiritual sword was Jesus' major offensive weapon when He was confronted, by Satan in the wilderness, following His 40 day fast. On my tour in Israel's desert in 1997, I took a picture of the desolate, desert mountain where this spiritual duel took place 2,000 years ago. How dry and bleak it still is today!

I researched the biblical words Jesus used to defeat Satan's attacks during that famous battle, recorded in Luke 4:1-14. I found the three swords Luke records were all from Deuteronomy, a book of the Hebrew Torah.

Jesus' Swords

1. "Man does not live by bread only, but by every word that proceeds out of the mouth of the LORD does man live" (Deut 8:3b KJV-MOD).
2. "You shall have no other gods before me" (1st commandment), "Do not worship other gods" (Idolatry - 2nd commandment), and "Love the Lord your God and serve Him" (Deut 5:7, 11:16b, 11:13 KJV-MOD).
3. "You shall not tempt the LORD your God" (Deut 6:16 KJV-MOD).

As you probably know, all of the Bible had not been written at the time of Jesus' temptation. Today, when you are battling temptation you can select any of the swords Jesus used, as well as those from all sixty-six books of the Bible. Quite an arsenal!

God's Word is a two-edged sword, "For the word of God is quick, and powerful, and sharper than any two-edged sword piercing even to the dividing between soul and spirit ..." (Heb 4:12a KJV-MOD). First of all, Jesus Himself is the living Word, and secondly, the Scripture is the written Word. These are the two edges to a sword. The Bible shows the way to God and tells you about Him, but it cannot replace a living relationship with Him. You need both.

The Word, living and written, is the most powerful weapon in your life. Learn how to wield it skillfully and teach your children to do so. It's dangerous out there.

Jesus won His battle over Satan's three temptations:

1. to eat, when He needed to fast for power to resist the evil tempter;
2. to jump off a pinnacle to show His power, with the false promise angels would catch Him; and
3. to worship another god, with the big lie that He would then have instant power over the kingdoms of this world.

Jesus, in fact, fought and won His great battle for you, as well as for Himself. Now as your Leader and King, He has shown you how you too can win,

Every Time!

Next is: When All Else Fails, Put on the Armor of Prayer.

When All Else Fails, Put on the Armor of Prayer

The seventh and concluding piece of spiritual armor in Paul's list is, "Praying always with all prayer and supplication in the Spirit" (Eph 6:18a).

Our six pieces of armor were all visible but this seventh piece is invisible. This armor is not what a soldier wears, but what comes out of his mouth.

Prayer in the Spirit to God is a powerful weapon. Look at this verse, "Let the saints be joyful in glory: let them sing aloud upon their beds. Let the high praises of God be in their mouth, and a twoedged sword in their hand" (Psalm 149:5-6).

Like two wings of an eagle, prayer and praise go together. It's another two-edged sword. You can soar above the dark clouds of battle and get refreshed for the next call to duty in God's army.

What is prayer? It is talking to God and listening to God. No, it isn't one way communication, it's two way communication. A lot of times we pray only to give a list of what we need. That's fine, but we miss out when we don't wait for an answer, to hear back from Him. We need to learn to listen and get direction from our Commander in Chief. In our busy lives, we find it hard to find time to pray, which is to our detriment.

Pray in the Spirit

But this verse says to pray always in the Spirit. What does this mean? Your prayer to God is a spirit to Spirit communication with God Almighty.

Psalm 42:7 says deep calls to deep and John 4:24 says, "God is a Spirit: and they that worship Him must worship Him in spirit and in truth." The Apostle Paul says, "What is it then? I will pray with the spirit, and I will pray with my understanding also …" (1 Cor 14:15).

We are shown here that prayer comes from one's spirit or *pneuma;* it does not initially come from one's soul or psyche. That's the only reason you can always be praying – in the spirit.

Your born from above spirit longs to have fellowship with your Creator. Human beings are created with an empty place inside that will only be satisfied when it is filled with God and His love.

Theresa Taught Them the Prayer

Recently Theresa, a young friend of mine, phoned from Florida to say that her church was studying the armor of God. She told them that they not only should study about the armor but to put it on. That was a new thought to them. Theresa taught them the prayer we use in the *Emotionally Free® Seminars* to also put the armor on one another.

This is a prayer that you can also use individually everyday of your life. Some people put the armor on in the morning first thing; some at night. The time makes no difference – just do it like Theresa and thousands of people are.

You who have been with me for these seven sessions have some information on a big subject. You can make up your own prayer on the armor as I've done. Or simply turn to Ephesians 6:10-18 and pray your way through those verses given by the Apostle Paul.

Next week I'll give you an *Armor of God Prayer* to assist you.

Meanwhile fold your hands together and pray, "God's Spirit and my spirit are joined as one through His Son. I want to pray and praise Him in Spirit and in truth. Amen."

Next time: Change the World with the Armor of God.

Change the World with the Armor of God

"More things are wrought by prayer than this world dreams of. Wherefore, let thy voice rise like a fountain for me night and day," wrote the famous poet, Alfred Lord Tennyson.[29]

Did he know something that we do not? Did he change his world? Well, we are still quoting him since his life's end back in 1892!

If we really believed Mr. Tennyson, we would pray more and be activists for prayer. Maybe that's what I'm doing now as we've been studying *The Armor of Prayer* for some time in this column.

I believe the Scripture in Ephesians 6:10-18 is meant not only for Bible reading and study, but that Paul meant it for a prayer outline.

The armor of God is already established in a believer's spirit, where God indwells, but it is valuable to prayerfully put it on your soul (psychological nature: intellect, will and emotions and subconscious) daily. Always remember your strength is in the Lord and His power, not in yourself alone.

I promised to give you my own personal Armor Prayer, so here it is. It will take several columns to complete it. Treated as an outline you may add to it and learn to pray by memory in your own creative way.

Dear Father God, I thank you for the prayer you inspired the Apostle Paul to write. Paul went through many spiritual and physically battles while he was on earth. I also realize that I too need to be battle ready. It is valuable to start the day spiritually prepared.

Belt of Truth: I pick up the belt of truth and secure it around the center of my being. The Letter of Paul to the Ephesians, and to me, says to gird myself with truth. You are the Truth and Your Word is truth. I want to be a student of the tried, tested, and true Holy Scriptures.

I realize it is dangerous to rush into battle without having the great doctrines of the faith firmly in my mind and heart. The truth encircling my loins also goes down over my sexual being to help me make morally right choices daily.

Breastplate of Righteousness: Thank You, God, for taking away my old tattered garment of rebellion and sinfulness and replacing it with Jesus' robe of righteousness. Through faith in Your only begotten Son, I'm becoming righteous; I am learning to think, speak and act like Jesus.

I'm taking the soldier's breastplate and putting it over my heart, the center of my soul to protect this vital area. The Breastplate wraps around to protect my back also. You are also my rearguard. You've got my back.

Shoes of the Gospel of Peace: The shoes, my soldier's boots, provide me not only with protection but with balance. If I lose Your peace, Lord, I'll know that I'm off balance. Dear Holy Counselor; fill me with your peace, and cure anxiety in myself and others around me. Help me to walk in the shelter of Your peace that passes understanding.

May my shoes take me different places where I can share the Gospel crystallized in the heart of the Bible (John 3:16). "For God so loved the world that He gave His only begotten Son, that whosoever believes in Him will not perish but have everlasting life" (KJV-MOD).

May my footprints spell out the Gospel of peace wherever I walk.

Shield of Faith: Thank You, Lord that you put a spark of faith into me with which I could reach out to you for saving faith when I was born again. Unbelief is the opposite of faith. Hebrews 11:6 says, "Without faith it is impossible to please God …" (KJV-MOD). Thank You for giving us the list of the saints of faith who pleased You and you wrote of them in the book of Hebrews chapter eleven. And I'm grateful for receiving the shield of faith from You dear Lord that I hold in my left hand, whereby I can resist all the fiery darts of the enemy. Not one can get through as I keep vigilant in prayer.

Helmet of Salvation: I'm putting on the helmet of salvation that is told about in hundreds of places in the Bible. The greatest gift is salvation, and so as the motorcycle driver has his safety helmet, we have our eternal life safety helmets. This life is not the only life we have; those who ask can receive ever lasting eternal life pictured by this helmet. Believers are headed to the amazing place God the Son has prepared for us, Heaven our home. Salvation speaks of Heaven and eternity. There is more to look forward to than this life alone.

Sword of the Spirit: I'm picking up the sword of the Spirit in my right hand that is first, the living Word of your presence Jesus, and secondly, the written Word – all sixty-six books. "Your Word have I hid in my heart, that I might not sin against You" (Psalm 119:11 (KJV-MOD). The sword of the Spirit is my one offensive weapon in battle. It is the two edged sword of the Lord Jesus Himself and the written Word of God. Jesus used the swords of Scripture when He fought and won the battle against the evil one. I can do likewise.

Praying always in the Spirit: Our spirit comes alive when Jesus is invited in as our Savior. Then, we are able to pray to God the Father in Jesus' Name. We can praise the Lord with our understanding and with our born again spirit also. We are three part beings: spirit, soul and body. Our resurrected spirit is connected to God at salvation and so we can speak to Him at any time. Jesus said, "But the hour comes, and now is, when the true worshippers shall worship the Father in spirit (*pneuma*) and in truth: for the Father seeks such to worship Him" (John 4:23a KJV-MOD). This is armor that is invisible but powerful.

Meditate: Try opening your hands in a receptive position. Sit back in your seat. Take a deep breath of God's healing love, and join me in praise to our one awesome God: Father, Son, and Holy Spirit. Be filled with the Holy Spirit. (Relax and pray. Take some time here.)

When ready say with me, "My world is changing for the good. I claim it by faith. Amen."

Next time: Attitude of Gratitude.

Attitude of Gratitude a Blessing for Everyone

In my 25 years as wife and homemaker, I baked a lot of turkeys.

In November of 2006 my brother, Bob Reed, and Alma, my sister-in-law, visited Dennis and me, arriving from Florida for Thanksgiving. I had done my best for my family and loved ones and the large oval table for twelve had quite a spread. The turkey was hormone-free and purchased fresh, not frozen. I had stuffed it with my favorite Pepperidge Farms stuffing. Dennis had gotten up early with me to help lift the 17-pound-plus freshly stuffed turkey into the hot oven.

The ceremony of carving the turkey began with Dennis doing the honors. When that was accomplished, grace was said as we all joined hands, and the feast began. A special treat for me was when Alma, who had blessed me with many meals during my high school and college years, said following her first bite, "Rita, this is the best turkey I have ever eaten!"

I was wonderfully surprised. Here was a gourmet cook honoring me in front of my northwest family!

Expressing an attitude of gratitude blesses not only the person it's intended for, but everyone else in the room. A good reminder each year is to keep that attitude going for special times such as this.

An example was found in a guide to retirement living. I particularly liked the idea of making a table runner of thanks. A nice family tradition.

Here is the idea that can be added to yearly.

Cut a piece of white canvas or muslin eighteen inches wide and long enough to cover the length of your table and hang off the ends.

Using fabric markers or colored Sharpies, which are meant for drawing on washable materials, let everyone in the family write one thing he or she is thankful for, date and sign it. Young children can draw seasonal pictures. During the meal, take turns reading everyone's contributions aloud, and after the meal, roll up your table runner and save it until next year. You can then add another year's worth of thanks.

Doesn't that sound fun? Wish I had known of that years ago.

One of my favorite thanksgiving Scriptures is, "Enter into His gates with thanksgiving, and into His courts with praise: be thankful unto Him, and bless His name. For the Lord is good; His mercy is everlasting; and His truth endures to all generations" (Psalm 100:4-5 KJV-MOD).

Someone could put that verse on the Thanksgiving table runner. It's a good verse to include in one's prayer at the beginning of the meal (for Christians), or at the end of the meal (for Jewish folks). Maybe you'd like to be ecumenical and pray before and after!

I'll describe for you my favorite holiday festive meal.

Thanksgiving Day is:
- Tables laden with turkey browned to perfection;
- Celery, onion, raisin, molasses, stuffing, white mountains of garlicky mashed potatoes;
- Fragrant gravy to pour on top;
- Freshly cooked cranberry, orange sauce, sweet potatoes drizzled with brown sugar and coconut oil;
- Crispy, nourishing Waldorf salad, tender crusted pumpkin pie, apple cinnamon cobbler with cream, warmed mouth-watering homemade sourdough rolls, hot spiced apple cider, and silver bowls of caramelized pecans and chocolate kisses.

Is your mouth watering yet? Our founding fathers of these United States began the tradition of celebrating Thanksgiving. How thankful I am for them and the hardships they were willing to endure. And I am thankful for a nation where we still have freedom to celebrate, to quote from the Bible, and pray around our tables.

I am thankful too, for the Bread of Life Gospel Mission, Pathway For Women, Meals On Wheels for Seniors, Arnie's Restaurant and others who pour out their love each Thanksgiving to help feed those who need to be honored in our society.

"And let the peace (soul harmony which comes) from the Christ rule (act as umpire continually) in your hearts ... And be thankful and appreciative, giving praise to God always" (Col 3:16 AMP). Amen.

Next: Dead Sea Scrolls.

Breaking News
Dead Sea Scrolls, a Gift to All of Us

One winter in 1947 in the region of Palestine, three shepherds were tending their flocks by night at the northern edge of the Dead Sea. Their Bedouin tribe had been shepherds for centuries – moving herds of goats and sheep between Bethlehem and the Jordan River. This evening, however, was different.

Without much to do there in the desert, Khalil, Jum'a, and Muhammad began to look around. Jum'a discovered two small openings in the side of a rock face. He threw a rock into one of the holes and heard what sounded like pottery breaking.

A few days later when they were able to come back to the cave, the youngest crawled into the larger hole and discovered ten tall jars lining the wall. This discovery was made near the ancient ruins now known as Qumran. American scholar, John Trever was one of the first to interview the Bedouin men, as documented in his book *The Untold Story of Qumran.*[30]

Two Kinds of Shepherds: Ancient and Modern

Now what do these three present day shepherds have to do with the ancient shepherds who followed the star to Bethlehem? The shepherds of two millennia ago were looking for the newborn Savior, Christ the Lord whom the angel had told them about (Luke 2:8-18).

The modern Bedouin shepherds were the first to discover the animal parchment scrolls of the Bible hidden in the desert for 2,000 years. Many scholars have worked on piecing together these fragments from the 1947 discovery, and from later ones, for a total (to date 2006) of eleven caves with 50,000 thousand or more fragments.

Both groups of shepherds found treasures. The earliest ones found the person Jesus, Son of God, Savior of the world, and the latest found scrolls of Scripture that authenticate the validity of the Bible which tell of this Son.

News Stories

Reporter Janet I.TU in her article *Discovering the Dead Sea Scrolls*[31] says, "For Jews, Christians and Muslims, the Seattle exhibit is an opportunity to view ancient manuscripts that lie at the root of their faiths."

My friend, Esther Walker and I, visited the Dead Sea Scroll exhibit at Seattle's Science Center when it was here in Seattle December 10, 2006. We spent about four hours there. It was full of exciting treasures.

I had the advantage of seeing the Scrolls at the Shrine of the Book in Jerusalem in 1996. Also, I saw under glass part of the 2,000-year-old copy of the scroll of Isaiah that was found intact – all sixty-six chapters in one piece! This copy confirms the accuracy of later translations to our present day. There is always more than one can absorb so I appreciated my second dip at Seattle's Pacific Science Center.

Professor Scott Noegel, chairman of the University of Washington's Near Eastern Languages and Civilizations Department said about the display, "The Scrolls pre-date by about a thousand years what was previously the oldest known biblical manuscript and show how accurately the texts were conveyed over the years."[32]

"The Dead Sea Scrolls are the oldest documents of our holy Scriptures (and are) still relevant to our lives today,"[33] said Rabbi Anson Laytner, executive director of the Greater Seattle Chapter of the American Jewish Committee.

I'll quote Isaiah's prophecy about the Messiah, Jesus, "For unto us a child is born, unto us a son is given: and the government shall be upon his shoulder: and his name shall be called Wonderful, Counselor, the mighty God, The Everlasting Father, The Prince of Peace" (Isa 9:6 KJV).

That's a 2,000-year-old quote that Jesus (*Yeshua*) Himself most likely read while on earth.

And Jesus is also spoken of as the Good Shepherd in the Gospel of John chapter 10. Let the Shepherd of the flock guide you each season wherever and whenever you celebrate holy days.

Chapter 3

Armor Series for Adults, Teens, and Babies
Greatest Prayer, Breaking News
The Lord's Prayer Series

Rita Bennett and Alex (photo above) – Rita with her British short-haired cat, Alexander (Alex) Bennett. He was found at McDonald's Restaurant in Lynnwood, Washington (1982). Animals are God's gifts and Alex comforted Rita three years after Fr. Dennis' home going. If animals are in Heaven, then Alex is now there with Dennis.

The Joy of Holy Days is a symbol of Faith

Christmas Day, I especially enjoy the little children dressed as Joseph and Mary the angels and shepherds acting in, *Oh little town of Bethlehem.*

Hanukkah, lighting of the nine menorah candles and prayers, has also passed. I unfortunately missed it, but did pray for the peace of Jerusalem.

This year, 2007, Hollywood came out with a great movie *The Nativity Story.*[1] As movies do out of necessity, there was a telescoping of two events. It was the Shepherds and the three kings arrival times at the Bethlehem cave where the Holy Family was, not exactly factual.

Yet I liked telescoping of two years because it brought the whole cast of primary characters together, achieving a Christmas-card effect. It meant more since I had visited the Bethlehem Basilica of the Nativity in 1996.

In Edmonds the electricity came on at 1:45 p.m. Friday, December the 15th – just in time for me to meet my friend Shirley Wilson at the Edmonds Theater for the 2:15 p.m. matinee, ah warmth!

I was also impressed with CNN's two-hour presentation of, *After Jesus,*[2] which gave an accurate historical presentation of early Christianity.

For this New Year, let's encourage ourselves to keep **Bible study** going so peace and biblical wisdom will flow through our year. There are Bible reading plans on many websites. The Student's Spirit-filled Bible is a favorite of many, edited by my friend Rev. Dr. Jack Hayford.[3] Bible Study Fellowship is an excellent study group. I was with BSF seven years, (now eight) though I have to confess my bias is that I believe in miracles today, as well as the past.

The Book of Common Prayer[4] is useful for all denominations with its daily morning and evening readings of the Old Testament, Psalms, Proverbs, and New Testament. You can also use this book, *A New Look at the News* as it has a variety of seventeen inspiring **Bible studies** on interesting topics. As you're finding, there are Bible series tucked in here and there. Sort of like small books throughout the bigger book.

Now let's look into more meditations on the armor of God as we continue praying it together, throughout the year.

The Shield of Faith Prayer

Dear Father God,
The Apostle Paul says, "Above all, I take the shield of faith …" (Eph 6:16 KJV-MOD).

Lord, I lift the shield of faith with my left hand to resist and quench all the fiery darts of the evil one.

Why above all? Scripture says I must have faith to please God. This is a basic bottom line (Heb 11:6).

"Faith comes by hearing, and hearing by the Word of God," says the book of Romans (10:17 KJV-MOD). Saving faith also comes from trust in Christ.

Please guide me to be a capable teacher of the Scriptures so that my faith will grow daily. When the fiery darts of the wicked are shot at me, cause me to be alert to quickly put up my Word-drenched faith shield to cause fiery darts to fizzle out and fall to the ground.

One dart that has been used against many is the whispered suggestion to doubt God's personal love and one's own identity as His child. Jesus had that dart in the wilderness when Satan's opening shot was, "… **IF** you are the Son of God …" (Luke 4:3 NKJV).

I will resist such fiery doubts as our Lord did.

Help me stay in community, so that at times of intense warfare I can connect with God's army. It's good that the Apostle Paul referred to his warfare experience with the Roman army in his teaching on armor. Something good can be learned even from our opponents. When needed, the soldiers closed ranks, creating a wall of door shaped shields with which to resist the enemy.

I want my faith to cover me so I'm not exposed and that it will link me with others for a united wall of defense. Thank You, Lord, for the weapons of corporate and individual Intercessory Prayer and Bible Study, to keep me victorious.

Take a moment to close your eyes, breathe deeply of God's love. Thank God for providing you with the Shield of Faith and all it includes. Picture that wall of rectangular shields surrounding you and your loved ones.

Next-time: Salvation Is the Greatest Gift.

Of All the Divine Gifts, Salvation Is the Greatest

Since Salvation is the greatest gift we can receive in this life, how can we be sure we have received it?

When I was nine years old I heard the message that God the Father sent His only Son, Jesus the Christ, to rescue me from the broken world I was born into. Jesus was born here too, and grew up, with the purpose of rescuing me and all who would ask Him. Jesus healed the sick, even raised some dead people, helped people forgive. But instead of being happy, the wounded and broken people thought Jesus was too good to be true and nailed Him to a rugged cross.

But I eventually found out that Jesus knew all the time that this would happen, and on the cross He took my sins so that I could be a whole person and bring His healing to many people. He took everybody's sins from the first human being to the last who will yet be born. All people have to do is ask Jesus to be their Redeemer as He has already paid the price for them. But they have to ask and receive this free gift for it to take effect. Because Jesus did this redemptive work, I could by faith ask Him to sign my name on His gift certificate in The Lamb's Book of Life (Rev 21:27). Anyone who believes in Him, and receives Him, can do this.

The purpose was to have the resurrected Lord Jesus come, by the Holy Spirit, to dwell in the spiritual core of my being. I have become a temple of the Holy Spirit. He forgave my sins and presented me to His Father God.

As a result, I am now able to make life-giving decisions leading me on a healthy and wholesome pathway. My life will show others the way to happiness and then they will create a little patch of Heaven wherever they go. At the end of life on earth, all who take this step will join our Triune God in His Kingdom.

Dr. Lewis: Life Changer

C.S. Lewis, famous theologian and author, explains Heaven and reigning with Christ in one long, exciting, creative fiction story presented in a series of seven books. In his concluding book *The Last Battle* he says, "All their life in this world and all their adventures in *Narnia* had only been the cover and the title page: now at last they were beginning Chapter One of the Great Story, which no one on earth has read: which goes on for ever: in which every chapter is better than the one before".[5]

I too believe the next life will be like this. Death is not the end of the salvation story, but rather the beginning of Chapter One of the Greatest Story Ever Told.

It is going to get better.

Now let's put on the fifth piece of the armor of God as we continue praying together.

The Helmet of Salvation

Dear Father God,

Your Word says, "… Take the helmet of salvation" (Eph 6:17).

Father, you are inviting me to reach out to You in order to receive Your gift. Next to the last piece of armor You have issued me, is the helmet representing this greatest Gift.

Through faith in what Christ has done for me in His birth, death, resurrection, and ascension, I put this helmet over my head which also encases my physical brain. Thank You for the awesome gift of salvation!

Lord, You are filling me with the glorious light of Your presence. Let my face be filled with the brightness of your omnipresence shining through me. As the face of Moses on Mount Sinai and of Jesus on the Mount of Transfiguration glowed with your presence, let me shine for you, Lord.

My brain is a wonderful treasure that I must take care of and not allow to be molested, invaded, or infiltrated by the darkness and unbelief around me. Proverbs 4:23 says, "Keep your heart [intellect, will, and emotions] with all diligence. For out of it spring the issues of life" (KJV-MOD). Also help me protect my eye-gates, ear-gates, and mouth-gate, as they are entrances to my soul.

I thank you for signing my name in Your salvation registry under Your Son's name. Your gift, Lord, is free, but yet what it cost You was beyond all price. Salvation preserves and delivers me now, in the present, and in each new year I will ever experience. This hope and vision for the future will sustain me in the battle.

Now my friend, sit back and relax. Take some moments of quiet to absorb what has happened. Sign your name and date in your Bible next to John 3:16. Journal any happy thoughts or feelings that come to you.

Happy New Life!

Next time: Wielding the Sword with Skill and Power.

Wielding the Sword with Skill and Power

The words "Sword of the Spirit, which is the Word of God" found in Ephesians 6:17, remind me of a personal example that I experienced.

In 1981 I wrote a book on how to be emotionally free. Then, as a pastor's wife, I had counseled and prayed with people not only in many parts of America, but England, Germany, Scotland, and Jamaica.

A teacher turned social worker, now a pastor's wife, I had an opportunity to pray and counsel thousands of people from all walks in life, in many different nations, and denominations.

My book, *You Can be Emotionally Free*,[6] took off and amazingly sold 200,000 copies. In it I taught about Inner or Soul Healing prayer. The combination of experiential prayer and counseling brought healing to many.

When you are having success in God's Kingdom, get a prayer team praying for you (which I later learned to do), because you will be greatly challenged. You have now become a threat to the enemy's domain. Soon my husband and I were mentioned in a book that also tried to take down at least 20 other Christian leaders. Such chicanery was dividing to the body of Christ.

One day, during these past stormy years, I was driving along listening to a Christian radio program. The Bible expositor began to read from the great Psalm 91, verse 1: "He that dwells in the secret place of the most High shall abide under the shadow of the Almighty" (CJB).

This is an awesome verse of safety. But what impacted me most that day was when the reader got to verse 3:

"My God whom I trust! He will rescue you from the trap of the **hunter** and from the plague of calamities;" (CJB).

The KJV Bible said the "snare of the fowler" but here it was clearer "the trap of the hunter."

That verse was a spiritual sword proclaiming victory for me. The promise is that during the **hunt** I would be delivered from the **hunter's trap.** It had a double meaning for me.

I drove along praising God for speaking to me personally. Later I put my name and date next to that verse in my Bible.

Be sure to listen. You'll find our Lord speaking to you too.

Now let's put on another piece of God's armor, as we do spiritual warfare in prayer.

The Sword of the Spirit

"And the sword of the Spirit, which is the Word of God" (Eph 6:17b).

Dear Lord, in verse seventeen, You have wisely used *rhema* for the **Word** which I find refers to an appropriate word for a specific situation. Thank You so much for giving me the offensive warfare equipment for each situation based on thousands upon thousands of sword-words found in the Bible.

Your Word quickened and revealed to me by the blessed Holy Spirit has a double-edge of power. The book of Hebrews says, "For the Word of God is quick, and powerful, and sharper than any twoedged sword, piercing even to the dividing asunder of soul and spirit" (Heb 4:12).

Thank You for teaching me the difference between my soul (*psyche*) and spirit (*pneuma*). Help me walk in the Spirit with the Sword of Spirit ready for use in my right hand. This double edge of my sword is first, "You Jesus, the living Word," and second, "the Bible, the written Word."

Help me follow Your example, that a Sword of the Spirit is any Word of God that is quickened to me as appropriate for a particular situation in battle. Teach me to read, study, and memorize your Word to keep it close at hand. I want to wield Your sword with skill. Can we all say, "Amen."

To find more Sword-Words, search as you read through the Bible.

For a plan to read the Bible in 90 days, see website http://www.haventoday.org/schedule.pdf, or email me at rbcounseling@frontier.com.

Next time: Hope of Heaven.

Hope of Heaven Hinges on How you Act Now

You and I are not composed only of body and brain, but we are spirit beings who live in a body. Our spirit will live somewhere after this life. We are choosing with the words we speak and the life we live, what kind of community we will call home.

C.S. Lewis's novel *The Great Divorce* shows[7] people who had recently died, riding on a bus. It was taking them on a tour towards Heaven. The people are in different stages of maturity. One man wants to fight and even tried to stab his seatmate. But alas, the knife went straight through the other spirit person without a sign of injury. All of a sudden the irate man realized he was dead. They were all dead. No more murder was possible!

This book gives the psychology of the ghosts who are unknowingly from the outskirts of Hell and are given an opportunity to take a bus to the outskirts of Heaven.

Among these people is an artist who only wants to paint pictures of Heaven rather than wanting to stay and make Heaven her Home!

There is another busload coming of what Lewis calls the solid people. The two buses arrive at the outer gates of Heaven. The believers set about to mingle with the ghosts to help them make a choice for Heaven.

Though Lewis's book is fiction, and therefore not a totally orthodox picture of what will happen at the end of one's life, there are many great lessons to learn from it. Read it to find out what happened!

Books on Heaven

If you want a biblical picture of life after death, my non-fiction books *To Heaven and Back*[8] and *Heaven Tours – Astonishing Journeys*[9] give a close account of what it may be like. I invite you to visit my web site for details.[10]

Praying Always in the Spirit

Now let's put on the last and seventh piece of God's armor as we learn the language of prayer. It's the communication line that opens Heaven to us. It's communication with God Himself! "Praying always with all prayer and supplication in the Spirit ..." (Eph 6:18).

Thank You, Lord, for giving me some invisible armor that not even the enemy can see. This seventh piece of armor is not what I as a soldier wear, but rather what comes out of my mouth.

Thank You that when Your Son died, rose from the dead, and ascended to Heaven, He opened the way to Heaven potentially for all human beings. He said of Himself "I am the door: by me, if any man enter in, he shall be saved ..." (John 10:9 KJV).

Prayer is my connection with You Lord.

"I will pray with my spirit and I will pray with my understanding also."

"I will pray against temptation."

"I will pray everywhere, lifting holy hands" (1 Cor 14:15, Matthew 26:41, 1 Tim 2:8).

As You say through the Psalmist, "Let the saints be joyful in glory: let them sing aloud upon their beds. Let the high praises of God be in their mouth and a twoedged sword in their hand" (Psalm 149:5-6). Praising You is also armor.

As I stand here, I am fully clothed with the protective full armor of God. I have on the:

1. Truth – belt
2. Upright character – breastplate
3. Gospel – shoes
4. Faith/trust – shield
5. Salvation, eternal life – helmet
6. Bible – double edged sword
7. Prayer and praise – voice

I am equipped to walk with my brothers and sisters of all nations, denominations, and walks of life.

May we band together in love to make this world a better place. Help us to receive our marching orders from our one and only Lord, God Almighty. In Jesus name I pray. Amen.

Next time: God. Loves Children and Babies.

He Who Loved Children Defended them, and Babies

I was asked by a student in my university class to pray for her baby who was due to be born in six weeks. She was still counseling clients and sometimes they used profanity and were very angry. It concerned the new mother to be.

I was pleasantly surprised by the request. This was my second year and it was rare to see anyone pray aloud much less talk about prayer. Wondering how to pray for her, by faith, I lay my hand gently on her stomach and found myself praying a baby-sized *Armor of God Prayer*. It was given as I prayed. She seemed pleased.

Then I came home and wrote it down for my column in the Beacon Paper, so that you might pray for your baby, or grandbaby, and for all little children.

I think St. Paul would be pleased with this rendition of his teaching to the Ephesians.

A Baby's Armor of God Prayer

Dear Little Child, I put on you the whole armor of God so that you will be able to stand against all fiery darts from hurtful people and places.

I put around your waist, the solid belt of truth. It will keep you balanced, and make you strong. I pray that you will be able to know the difference between good and bad, light and darkness.

Around your chest, little child, I place the breastplate of righteousness which wraps its protection around you, front and back. The breastplate covers your heart to keep it safe and blessed. I put the all-wise one, Jesus' right thinking and acting power upon you.

I put on your little feet boots – spiritual booties of peace, booties of shalom. May the chaos of any angry words melt away in your presence. A great man, Isaiah, said, "A little child shall lead them." Let that be you, dear child.

I place in your left hand the Shield of Faith. It is able to resist all fiery arrows of harmful words or deeds aimed in your direction.

In your beautiful heart, a measure of faith was placed there to enable you to believe. Faith is pleasing to your Creator. Faith is like trusting your mom and dad. It is believing they want the very best for you. That's also true of your Creator.

Upon your head, I place the soft inside but firm outside helmet of salvation. Salvation means forever preserved from danger.

I pray for spiritual earmuffs that will keep out all words that un-well people might say around you. May your mind grow and be filled with wisdom and truth. This gift of salvation shows you how eternally loved you are.

In your right hand, I place the sword of the Spirit which is the Word of God. May you be fed by the milk of His Word even now in this prayer. And with joy, be fed by your mother's milk. You are awesome and wonderfully made.

Later on, as you learn to spell, you'll see that sword has word in it. That Word means ancient wisdom, called scripture, which is very old. It is older than your grandpa's and grandma's. It will give you much wisdom as you grow up to help you resist evil.

In your mouth is an invisible weapon. Your Creator has placed it there. It is praise and prayer. When the little children saw Jesus heal people's emotions and bodies, they cried out praises to Him in the Temple! Jesus said to them, "Have you never read, Out of the mouths of babes and sucklings God has perfected praise?"

He loved little children and always defended them. He said it was not His will that one little child should perish and that you, dear child, have a guardian angel watching over you!

Always remember that you are loved. I pray this In the Name of Thy Holy Child Jesus.[11]

Amen.

Next time: Armor of Prayer for Everyone.

Armor of Prayer Is for Everyone, Especially Teens

An impressive e-mail from a new friend said:

"Rita, I was reading your articles on your website about putting on the spiritual armor. I have been praying this on myself and my husband Eric and my children David and Gabriel for about a year. I try to do it at least a couple of times a week ... Does it count when I pray for the armor to be upon my husband and children, even if they do not pray to put it on themselves?

"I have been praying that just as I used to dress my children, I pray it on them now.

"Just like a wife helps to dress her husband, I pray it on him."

My Response

I am delighted with the way, you my friend, are being guided to apply these biblical truths. Yes, we can have faith for our families even when they cannot have faith for themselves. It is a very wise wife and mother who takes the time to pray for protection over her family.

We all grow at different rates. The eyes of spiritual understanding open for each person individually, even as the petals of a flower open one by one. What I am sure about is our young people need more awareness of praying for protection. The media are consistently telling about how some unaware teen has a drug slipped into her cold drink, or a young boy is picked up at gunpoint when he gets off a school bus.

How many more preteens and teens are we going to lose to these satanic activists? I get mad and sad, alternately, at what the destroyer of our souls gets away with! We need to arm our kids spiritually!

Let's Put on the Armor of God Dear Teen

Are you ready? Stand and proclaim:

I put the belt of truth around my loins to protect the center of my being and my sexuality. I will not allow anyone to tempt me to give a part of my body to another outside of marriage. I am not a subhuman animal but a human being made in the likeness of God. He's given me the power to say "No."

I put on the breastplate of right thinking, speaking and acting, the righteousness of God who came to earth through Jesus Christ. When I accepted Him, I exchanged my sins for His holy and wholesome life.

I put on the teen-boots of peace as I join God's army to pray and act on behalf of babies, and children.

I take the shield of faith in my left hand to resist the fiery darts of the enemy. I will help my faith grow by praying and studying the Bible with my friends and family. It's one of my life's goals – all sixty-six books.

I put on the helmet of salvation that is my greatest gift. It gives me a fantastic life now and for all eternity. "The Lord is my light and my salvation; whom shall I fear? ..." (Psalm 27:1).

I take the sword of the Spirit in my right hand. It is the Word of God that is a double-edged sword. Help me to memorize verses that work as spiritual swords to defeat temptation.

"Praying always with all prayer ... in the Spirit ..." (Eph 6:18). This is my invisible armor of the gift of talking to God and listening to His response with my spiritual ears and writing it down. I will pray with my spirit and with my understanding also. (1 Cor 14:15). How awesome it is to know that I, as a teen have an eternal connection with God Himself!

In the name of the Mighty Warrior, Jesus Christ, I pray. And they all said, "Amen!"

Since these verses in Ephesians 6:10-18 are so powerful as we apply them, what about: *The Lord's Prayer* that's coming up soon, then The Beatitudes, The Ten Commandments, and much more.

Next time, Breaking News: Terrible Events Put Real Values in Focus.

Terrible Events Put Real Values in Focus
Breaking News

After some years, many in our country are still feeling the effects of the April 17th, 2007 massacre of 32 and wounding of 15 more students, and teachers at Virginia Tech.

The murderer, Cho Seung-Hui, at his conclusion also killed himself, making thirty-three dead. This is the worst massacre on American soil in our history up to this time.

Mr. Seung-Hui, 23, was from South Korea, and at the age of eight immigrated to America with his family. There were warning signs that he was mentally ill but no one seemed to know how to get him the psychological and spiritual help he needed.

He hardly ever talked, and walked with his face and eyes looking down as if he had a poor self-identity. He really was not integrated into his new society. Cho was a lost soul, an empty vessel.

What We Can Do

What can we do now that this horrific, inhuman act has been done? We can seek better plans for protection on campuses. We can teach laypeople the signs to look for in mentally unbalanced people. We can investigate who made the mistakes and feel better to be doing something. We can stop making atheism the religion of choice at universities, which can lead to a cavalier way of looking at life!

Last, but not least, we can pray! A lot of people need prayer with all the 33 families and their friends in shock and pain. We can prayerfully put on the armor of God that I've been teaching about in this column for about twelve weeks. We can also pray *The Lord's Prayer* verbatim each day and when we have extended time to do so, we can pray it as an intercessory prayer outline. We can pray both of these prayers not only by ourselves but with our loved ones.

As Columbine High School, Virginia Tech, and 9-11 have proven, it is dangerous out there in the world!

Our Father

Let's look at the opening words of the prayer God gave us. It begins, "Our Father."

It is first of all a corporate prayer in that we can join together as one person in our place of worship. We are a family. God can be Our Father together. We can also pray it alone personalizing it, My Father.

How could I be so fortunate to obtain a perfect, unconditional, loving, Father? One who is omnipresent, omniscient, and omnipotent. One day in the future, I will walk up and say, "Hi Dad," or in Aramaic "*Salam Abba*," or in Hebrew "*Shalom Avee*," meaning Father.

The answer is that after the Son of God, the Lord Jesus, gave His life for this broken, human race, giving us eternal hope, He let us know that His Father is willing to become our Father.

How? It is by simply asking Him to be our Father, as we pray to Him, through His Son.

That's one reason Jesus gave us *The Lord's Prayer* as He told us to pray it to His Father and to do it in His name. The first and most important step in *The Lord's Prayer*, then, is to get us connected with Father God.

The Prodigal Son

The clearest picture the Bible shows of our Father is the famous story of the prodigal son. In it, a trusting father allows his younger son to leave home with his full inheritance.

This is a challenge all parents experience. Though we would like to protect our children and keep them from making major mistakes, holding on to them can have even more damaging results than letting them go.

You'll remember the story of the prodigal son who left home and also left his father to worry about him! Yet, the father never gave up on his son, but would walk down the desert roads, or daily look at the post box hoping, praying for a word from his son. Then one day he saw his ragged and dusty son, walking toward home.

The father ran out to meet him, and threw his arms around him and kissed him. The generous father gave his son water for a bath, new clothes, sandals, a ring, and a big dinner party (Luke 15:11-32).

This vignette Jesus gave of a loving father shows us the kind of Person we talk to when we pray, "Our Father." Let's make our world a better place by praying *The Lord's Prayer* soon. See Matthew 6:9-15.

Next Time: Preserve Environment, As Our Gift From Above.

Preserve Environment, As Our Gift from Above

Saving the environment is a subject that often comes up for politicians, movie producers, and concerned citizens. In addition to praying the awesome words of *Our Lord's Prayer* verbatim, one can also pray it reflectively on different subjects such as care of our planet.

One of these creative times of prayer was when I was in Hawaii in 1989 snorkeling in the warm, blue ocean. As I fed the beautiful, colorful fish with green frozen peas, I began to pray *The Lord's Prayer.*

I thought of how we humans can be thoughtless when it comes to taking care of God's planet. Here's the prayer

"Our Father," Abba, Daddy, I love You. Father of the depths as well as the heights. Father who, through Your Son, divided the great land mass from the waters, and fashioned the world beneath the sea and all that live in it – such as these beautiful tropical fish swimming here with their blues and greens, their yellow and red rainbow hues.

"Who is in Heaven," and also on earth, You are omnipresent. You came down to earth through Your Son in a special way, to rescue us from drowning in our own sin.

"Holy is Your name." By Your name all things, all creatures above and below the sea exist. I reverence Your name. I will keep it holy.

"Your Kingdom come." May human beings revere Your creation, and stop poisoning and polluting the waters, contaminating them and killing the whales, the fish, the ducks, the seagulls, and others of Your creatures.

"Your will be done." May we help clean up Your oceans, rivers, lakes, and the air we breathe (that I'm breathing now through this snorkel).

"On earth as it is in Heaven." May we stop making money our god – messing up and destroying this earth. May our air and water be purified as they are in Heaven. Show me what I can do to help, even in choices in my own home and city.

"Give us today our daily bread." Thank You for nourishment from the sea. Your own Son was a fisherman, and chose most of His twelve disciples from those who made their living from the fish of the sea. Now we have to kill fish to live. How great it will be one day in your fulfilled Kingdom where we won't need to kill any creature in order to live.

"Forgive us our sins." If we humans take more than our quota of fish or crabs or other sea creatures and so deplete the necessary supply, or cause an imbalance in nature, please forgive us. If we've helped to cause the sea mammals to give up hope – washing up on the seashore to die – please forgive us. Forgive us for polluting the oceans of the world with oil spills; give us creative ideas on how to stop this as well as delivering the oil to those who need it.

"As we forgive those who have sinned against us." I do forgive all others who have done these things. Please help me and those in authority find ways to stop the offenses against nature, until the offenders become wise enough to stop themselves.

"And lead us, not into temptation." Show us the way to live simply in harmony with nature, the water, air, ozone layer, land, flowers, trees, and animals on land and in the sea. Help us not be so self-centered that we forget those generations yet to be born.

"But deliver us from evil and the evil one." Help us not get our directions from the destroyer but from our Creator. Show us how to make a firm but kind stand against those who maim and kill for the love of money. Deliver us from destructive experimenters with nature.

"For Yours is the Kingdom, and the Power, and the glory, forever – Amen."[12]

Next time: An Old Story … But It's Often Told Wrong

An Old Story – But It's Often Told Wrong

The Bible helps us discover that Jesus is eager to share His Father with you and me.

How do I know this? It's because of what He has said. After Jesus' death and resurrection, the Apostle John records that Mary Magdalene was the first person to see Him.

I believe Jesus was smiling and perhaps lifting His hands with joy when He commissioned her, "… go to My brethren, and say to them, 'I ascend to My Father and your Father, and to My God and your God'" (John 20:17 NASB).

These were His first recorded words after His resurrection and they were unfathomably important. His great work was accomplished! The way had been opened for human beings to be adopted into the heavenly Father's family. Jesus could have innumerable brothers and sisters now, as well as the Father having innumerable (perhaps trillions of) children through His only begotten Son.[13]

Let's look at the idea of Jesus' death for us because it is crucial to have understanding of our Father's love. Some people look at Jesus' agony in the Garden of Gethsemane this way: He was trying to get out of giving His life, but His Father was determined to put Him on the cross where He would pay for the sins of the whole world!

That is not true! The truth is Father, Son, and Holy Spirit decided ahead of time, together, how to save this world from the power of Satan (Gen 1:26-27). This was before our first parents would give over their dominion of this planet Earth to the fallen angel, through their willful disobedience to God.

The effect of this – separation from God – has come down upon us all.

At this point God could have said, "Let's forget this whole race of people. They are a mess. They started killing right away, and doing all manner of evil because of their fallen condition, and they are only going to get worse and worse."

God could have then said, "Let's wipe them out and start over again." The wondrous thing is that our triune God had fallen in love with us, His own creation.

The great thing for us is that Jesus did not only die; He rose from the dead. The Bible clearly gives a picture of what the Father and Son's relationship is really like as we saw previously in the story of the Prodigal son.

The Father's Pain

Several years ago I heard about a young man who was an actor in *The Passion Play,* which tells the awesome story of Christ's life. He played the role of the Father in Heaven, and as he watched Jesus being beaten and crucified, the young actor had such physical pain he thought his physical heart would break.

I think our Father allowed the actor a little glimpse of His own pain so he would realize how the Father suffered, too. If you've ever lost a child through death, you will especially be able to identify with our Father God's pain.

The point is that Jesus did not seek a way of escape, though His Father would have immediately provided it at His Son's request. Jesus' heart's desire and purpose for coming to earth was to complete the rescue of mankind, to restore us to the Father, by giving up His own life and fulfilling God's plan as revealed in Scripture (Matt 26:53-54; John 14:6).

Jesus Gave it All

At Calvary, Jesus prayed that the cup of suffering might pass from Him, not because He didn't want to die for us, but because on the cross He had all the sins of mankind, beginning with Adam to the very last person to be created, laid upon Himself. That is a lot of sins!

All those sins were piled on Jesus Christ, and during His separation from His holy Father, He experienced hell for the whole human race.

Hell is separation from God, the One who loves you most. Jesus experienced hell so that you and I do not have to. God's Son prepared the way of escape for us.

Why do I tell this old and glorious story again? Because many people have heard it, but heard it wrong, and they unknowingly promote an unloving picture of our Father God. Sadly, this keeps a lot of people away from Father's house.

Let us now with gratitude pray, **"Our Father Who is in Heaven ..."** (Matt 6:9-13).

So Soon the Memory Fades – or does it?

In my graduate school class June 2007, Professor Tim was talking about how brief life is and how fast the memory of a person who dies fades away. He said something like,

"After one family generation goes by, the children will probably remember Uncle Joe's name and something about him. Add another generation and it will probably be, 'Didn't grandpa have an older brother? What was his name again?'"

Our leader and class discussed how fleeting life is, and how soon it is all over. Perhaps "that's all there is" was the tone. A dark cloud of unknowing was descending on our class of twenty-two soon-to-be-graduating counselors.

I was sitting there feeling like I had to speak.

"Professor Tim, I have something to say about the end of life," I interjected. "I've done research on near-death experiences and wrote a book about it, *To Heaven and Back.*

"I found that the NDE experiences and the 151 Scriptures on Heaven agree remarkably." I continued. "Science and faith can meet together here.

"I consequently believe there is more to come beyond this life. This realization and hope for my future, takes away the worry of not being remembered a long time after my death."

Did anyone have ears to hear? One student did, and thanked me after class.

Heaven?

The first construct we looked at in *The Lord's Prayer* was: "Our Father."

Now the second one is, "Who is in Heaven."

So where is this place called Heaven? Every time you see the word heaven in the Bible it is not necessarily referring to the abode of God, the faithful angels, and the saints who have died.

There are three heavens in the Bible. Two of them are related to earth: the atmosphere around the earth where clouds are and birds fly, and the second one is outer space where the sun, moon, planets, and stars exist.

The Apostle Paul indicated that the third Heaven is an actual location beyond earth's atmosphere and outer space. He said, I was caught up to the third Heaven (2 Cor 12:2).

His experience fits the description given today for those having a near-death experience. Consequently, when I speak of the third Heaven, I capitalize it.

Since God's Son came down from Heaven by the power of the Holy Spirit and was incarnated in the Jewish Virgin, Miriam, (Mary, in English). I am always reminded that Hebrew is a heavenly language.

It was fun when I was given *The NIV Hebrew-English Interlinear Old Testament* [14]from Betty Bell for my birthday back in 1996. The first Hebrew word I chose to look up was Heaven and I found that it is *Shamayim.*

It refers to both a physical heaven and a spiritual realm of Heaven. It is neither singular nor plural, but dual, meaning that it confirms a real place. That was an important discovery to me.[15]

And Heaven would not be Heaven unless our Triune God – *Elohim* is there. It is the habitation of God.

Of this location Jesus said, "In my Father's house are many mansions: if it were not so, I would have told you. I go to prepare a place for you" (John 14:2 KJV). Jesus has been on this project for over two thousand years now – speaking from our earth time perspective.

Heaven is twofold. It is first of all within all believers, and then it's in the universe.

As wonderful as it is to know we have a heavenly home awaiting us, for now it is even more important to know that Heaven has come to dwell in us when we accept God's Son.

Are you enjoying Heaven within you right now? Are you drinking from the pure fountain, the refreshing rivers of living water that Jesus gave you when you were reborn? Are you feasting on delicious fruit of the Spirit from the inner Tree of Life – love, joy, peace (John 7:38, Galatians 5:22-23)? Rejoice, as we pray together, "Our Father who is in Heaven ..."

Next time: Living a Life that is Whole, Holy, and Healthy.

Living a Life That is Whole, Holy, Healthy

How many counseling agencies begin their weekly group leadership meetings by spending an hour in devotions, scripture, and prayer? I don't know the answer, but Cedar Park Counseling Network in Kenmore, Washington has this qualification.

I had personal experience there because it is the location where I spent nine months in 2007 working as an intern for a master's degree in marriage and family therapy. For several months we had been trying a prayer approach with therapists and our supervisor rotating leadership.

After this hour of prayer/study, we then took an hour to have a professional case discussion.

Today was a devotional leadership day for me. The form of prayer I shared was on my recent *Beacon* news topic: *The Lord's Prayer.*

I asked when each person had first learned, *The Lord's Prayer.* To my recollection, one said she began at age 4; another was 5; I was 9; others were 7, 10 or 11, and 25.

I wonder about you, my reader. Do you have a story about your beginning prayer or are you just beginning to learn *The Lord's Prayer* with me?

Praying in Different Languages

We began our hour by all praying this most famous prayer verbatim. I heard several different languages since we are a multi-cultural group.

I then asked a colleague to pray Jesus' Prayer in Mandarin singly so we could enjoy the music of her native language. Then I asked another to pray *The Lord's Prayer* for us in Japanese. I then prayed our Lord's Prayer in Jesus' (*Yeshua's*) native language, Hebrew.

So to begin our workday, the six of us prayed *The Lord's Prayer* in four different languages, including English. Two other counselors joined us later.

We also prayed *The Lord's Prayer* as intercession for one another, which means we inserted our prayer partner's name into the prayer to personalize it. We also prayed it in seven categories of need where we stop a while to do intensive prayer for: father relationships, physical healing, or wounds from your sins, to name a few.

Holy is Your Name

Our study continues in this issue with the construct: "Holy is Your Name." What do the words holy, whole, and health all have in common?

Holy simply stated is set apart to the service of God. Whole is free of wound or injury, or recovered from a wound or injury. Health is the condition of being sound in body, mind, and spirit.

If you are dedicated to God and relating to Him closely, it is more likely that you will become whole, holy, and healthy. These three attributes go together.

How do you learn to live this way? How do you learn to talk this way? God's name is holy and is to be honored. We are not to use it carelessly or drag it down with profanity.

119

One answer for wholesome living is to use the prayer Jesus gave us: frequently, preferable daily, and live it. Practice doing what Jesus tells you to do. Read through the Gospel records and the first chapters of Acts to see that His early followers considered it vitally important to put what He commanded into practice. Ask the Holy Spirit to show you how to do this.

Live in that first love relationship with God (Rev 2:1-7). Don't let yourself get stale. Keep learning and growing. Keep sharing the good news with others.

I believe that true holiness – wholeness – should make you free to love, laugh, give, receive, stand for the right, be who you really are, get up wiser and stronger if you fall. Affirm others, mend the broken, heal the world. This is what I hope for you as you pray the holy and healing prayer that our Lord gave us.

As you're sitting down and relaxing, take a few deep breaths of God's healing love, and pray together with us: "Our Father, Who is in Heaven, Holy is Your Name ..."

Next time: Thy Kingdom Come – Your Kingdom Come!

Thy Kingdom Come – Your Kingdom Come!

In April 2007, the *Seattle Times* carried a story of Billy Graham's monumental loss of his wife, Ruth, at her death – age 87, and of his grief. Associated Press reporter Mike Baker says, "Ruth Graham retained her beauty even in death and surely 'had a great reception in heaven,' an ailing Billy Graham told mourners who gathered Saturday to remember his wife . . . She was remembered as a spiritual stalwart and modest mentor." [16]

It is at times such as these that a staunch believer, such as the world renowned Evangelist Dr. Graham, is counting on God's Kingdom to go on beyond this life. I'm sure that he believes he will see Ruth Graham again, as will his five children, and 19 grandchildren. That is a Christian's hope.

The Bible is full of Scripture passages about the Kingdom of God. Jesus said, "But seek first his Kingdom and his righteousness, and all these things will be given to you as well" (Matt 6:33 CJB). "Have no fear, little flock, for your Father has resolved to give you the Kingdom" (Luke 12:32 CJB).

"The wolf also shall dwell with the lamb, The leopard shall lie down with the young goat, The calf and the young lion and the fatling together; And a little child shall lead them" (Isa 11:6 NKJV).

To give God's Kingdom the broadest perspective, we must see that it is three-dimensional. That means:

The Kingdom has come.

The Kingdom is coming.

The Kingdom will come.

It is past, present, and future.

Past: The Kingdom came when Jesus was born, lived, died, resurrected, and ascended, to bring the Kingdom of unconditional love and redemption to the whole world.

Present: By your faith, His headquarters has been set up in your spirit's inner temple (*pneuma*), and in your soul's (psyche) composed of your intellect, will, and emotions. "… behold the kingdom of God is within you" (Luke 17:21). You do this by inviting Jesus, the King of kings, to live His life through you.

Future: His Kingdom is coming in its fullness when He will reign forever. The famous *Nicene Creed,* written in the 4th Century A.D., proclaims this in historic fellowships each week, "He will come again in glory to judge the living and the dead, and His Kingdom will have no end."[17]

In the King James Bible it reads, "Thy kingdom come." This phrase is not only a prayer but a declaration.

It is not, "Well maybe it will come," or "We hope it will come." It is "Thy kingdom come!"

Christ wants us to make a statement of faith, and that is far stronger than mere speculation.

Pass it On

I'm always amazed at how God works. When I was a teenager, I recommitted my life to Christ at a Billy Graham Crusade in Tampa, Florida. Now decades later in the northwest, providentially, I was contacted by Dr. Graham's youngest son, Ned, and his wife Tina. Together with prayer and counsel, we saw God bring healing from life's hurts.[18]

A more compete testimony, was told by Ned to *Charisma Magazine* writer, Sandra Chambers, in the May 2007 edition.[19]

This is the way God's Kingdom works on earth. We are healed and then we pass the blessings on. What a joy it was to send on the blessings I had received, from Billy Graham's ministry to his son.

And now pray with me: "Our Father, who is in Heaven, Holy is your Name, Your Kingdom come ..."

Next Time: Not My Will, But God's Will Be Done!

Not My Will, But God's Will Be Done!

One of the most important matters for you and me to pray for is God's will. In Jesus' prayer for us, He teaches us to pray a submissive and powerful prayer, "**Your** will be done!"

Knowing God's will is sometimes difficult. People may want God to tell them what to do: who to marry, where to live, where to work, etc. These considerations are important for us to pray about but we eventually have to move ahead believing that God is guiding us.

Romans 12:2 tells us, "Do not conform any longer to the pattern of this world, but be transformed by the renewing of your mind. Then you will be able to test and approve what God's will is – His good, pleasing and perfect will" (NIV).

Romance & Proposal

When my husband, Dennis, proposed to me I responded, "Yes I love you, but before I give you my answer there's one stipulation – that I take three days to fast and pray for confirmation from God."

During that time I received two scriptures from the book of Esther.

One is, "So Esther was taken into King Ahasuerus into his house royal in the tenth month, which is the month Tebeth, in the seventh year of his reign" (Esth 2:16). There were spiritual connections to this verse. Dennis had become Rector of St. Luke's Episcopal Church that year. Rector comes from the Latin *Rex* which means King, and it was in his seventh year as leader at St. Luke's Church. Also we were married in the tenth month, October 15, 1966.

So he was Rex (king), reigned for seven years and proposed, and we were married in the 10th month.

Another verse from the same book of the Bible also seemed to speak to me then. It says, "And who knows whether you are come to the

Kingdom for such a time as this?" (Esth 4:14b KJV-MOD). Dennis and I became a writing and traveling team to many nations during our marriage of twenty-five years.

Dennis had a confirmation himself. It was an unexpected phone call from a former parishioner during those three days of prayer and she said, "I feel strongly that you and Rita are going to be married." Dennis called me right away to let me know of this message through his former parishioner.

Two or Three Yes's

There are at least two confirmations of God's will for any given situation.

1. Make sure what you are asking for or considering doing is not something the Bible forbids. "Thy word is a lamp unto my feet, and a light unto my path" (Psalm 119:105 KJV).
2. Make sure what you are asking for will glorify God and will be good for your spirit, soul, and body.

When God created you He gave you the priceless gift of free will; it is part of the image of God in you. He could not take it away from you without totally changing your created nature. Without free will you would be a robot, not a human being. Your will is free, but as you bring it into line with what God wants, He can guide you and bring you His best will. I sometimes picture my will as a swinging door between my soul and spirit. The question is which way is it going to swing? Christ's will for us brings us inner rest.

I, by my choice, can determine whether my decision will come from God, who dwells in my recreated spirit, or from my soul which is still in the process of being healed.

St. Augustine said it this way, "Thou hast made us for Thyself, O Lord, and our heart is restless until it finds its rest in Thee."[20]

We may pray *The Lord's Prayer* all our lives, and in the various seasons of life. We are being transformed by the mysteries of this prayer. We are being changed.

Let us pray together: "Our Father who is in Heaven, Holy is Your Name, Your Kingdom come, Your will be done ..."

Next time: Pathway to Heaven is Paved by Believers.

Pathway to Heaven is Paved by Believers

"Thy will be done on earth, as it is in Heaven" (Matt 6:10 KJV-MOD).

Author George MacDonald said, "There are only two kinds of people in the end: those who say to God, 'Thy will be done,' and those to whom God says, in the end, 'Thy will be done.'" (So George MacDonald is imagined saying in The Great Divorce.[21])

That hurts to consider making such a mistake! The last thing most people would loath to hear is God saying, "Your will be done."

However, there are some belief systems today that teach we humans are gods ourselves! Not long ago I heard a university student proclaim her deity to a group, "I have just realized that I am God! I have no sins to confess or to worry about now!"

For a person to think he or she is God used to be considered a mental illness. The professor did not challenge her at all. An individual with this belief would of course not be at all concerned with C.S. Lewis's statement quoted above. Heaven would be of little concern.

Heaven Exists

So I am speaking to you today who might just have a glimmer of hope that such a place exists. We have two biblical witnesses of men of God who died, had a trip to Heaven (we call near-death experiences today) and then came back to earth to live a little longer.

These two witnesses are Lazarus, who was dead four days, and the Apostle Paul, who was killed by stoning for his faith.

Both were raised from the dead, after having heavenly experiences, and lived for a time before dying again. Now they await bodily resurrection (John 11:43-44; 2 Cor 12:2-4).

I only know of one person who has died, was raised from the dead, briefly went to Heaven, came back and witnessed to his disciples for 40 days, then left with a promise that He'd be back. That is Jesus Christ.

Plan Ahead

Five hundred thirteen people saw Jesus during those forty days (1 Cor 15:4-8). If you believe Jesus' words in the Scripture, and His historical witness on earth, then the concept of Heaven will not be difficult for you.

When do we humans get serious about whether there is an afterlife, and perhaps a place called Heaven? Most often it is when one is getting ready for major surgery. At that time, one begins to review or write his will.

It's also time to write up a living will after deciding for or against life- support equipment. One decides whether or not to have resuscitation.

That individual may talk to a clergy person to encourage his faith. Maybe he decides to open his Bible and look up verses telling about the place called Heaven – in some of the 151 places in Scripture. It's a trip each of us will make. Fortunately, we can check the travel brochure long before it is our time to go. You can take a Tour by reading *Heaven Tours: Astonishing Journeys.*[22]

On Earth As It Is in Heaven.

There are some places on earth that I think are like Heaven. Today as I drove home from counseling internship and looked at the sunset-kissed cumulus clouds tinted with mauve and blue-gray, I felt that it was breathtaking heavenly.

When a baby I've never seen before smiles at me, at those times I've felt a touch of Heaven.

When the Lord speaks to me through a sermon, a song, a poem, or a special verse from the Bible, I sense a heavenly touch.

How about you? Let's expect to be touched by Heaven.

Now let's pray together: "Our Father who is in Heaven, Holy is Your Name, Your Kingdom come, Your will be done on earth as it is in Heaven …"

Next Time: Our Daily Bread a Metaphor for Life.

Our Daily Bread is a Metaphor for Life

In *The Lord's Prayer* we are advised to pray, "Give us this day, our daily bread."

There are at least three kinds of bread spoken of in the Scripture: physical, spiritual, and everlasting.

Don't you love fresh ground wheat flour, mixed with warm milk, whole grains, active yeast and your favorite seasonings, then baked to perfection? Then there's that first bite, warm and layered with butter or for me olive oil blended with butter! Yum – Jesus knew what it was like to eat fresh bread.

Near the end of His life, Jesus was tempted by this very enjoyable bread which mankind has needed for survival. It came at the most crucial time and that was at the end of His 40-day fast.

This fast was for the purpose of gaining victory over the Great Temptation He would suffer from His archenemy, Satan. The battle took place at the Mount of Temptation in the dessert of Israel.

Story That Began in Genesis

Let me tell you about this battle that was won for you! Ever since the original temptation of humankind on Planet Earth and our weakness to resist the Tempter, an invasion of evil penetrated our world.

A time would come when these two forces of good and evil would face one another in a duel over what weak human beings gave away to this dark satanic spirit. This was the moment. Satan sneered as he spoke to Jesus Christ, "And the Devil said unto Him, 'If You are the Son of God, command this stone to be made bread'" (Luke 4:3 KJV-MOD).

The enemy of our soul knows our weakness, which his suggestion here reveals as he said, "Command this stone to be made bread." Satan knows of Jesus' miracle-working power when He turned the water into wine at the wedding in Cana in Galilee (John 2:1-11).

Yes, this cunning enemy knows Scripture. He has been tempting humankind since our fall in the Garden of Eden six millennia ago. You and I are in no easy winning position unless we are students of the Bible. Needless to say, it is most important to know the Savior of the World personally; He has won our battles for us.

Jesus, of course, had the right Scripture sword and answered the Tempter. "It is written, that man shall not live by bread alone, but by every Word of God" (Luke 4:4b). This is just one of the Scripture swordfights between the Light and the darkness. Jesus is letting us know that we do not live by physical bread alone.

Need Living Bread

To have the best life now and everlasting life, we humans need the Living Bread, the Bread of Life, who is Jesus Christ, Son of the Living God (John 6:48-51, Deut. 8:3b).

126

Jesus spoke to His disciples and said to them, "I am the bread of life: he that comes to Me shall never hunger, and he that believes on Me shall never thirst" (John 6:35 KJV-MOD).

He continues, "This is that bread that came down from heaven: not as your fathers did eat manna and are dead: he that eats of this bread shall live forever" (John 6:58).

Here we see Jesus proclaiming Himself as our Spiritual Bread who gives us everlasting life. Millions of believers around the world, every week, proclaim these truths through *The Lord's Supper*. Within one service, all these teachings on *The Lord's Prayer* can be proclaimed and participated in today.

The good news is that Jesus has won the eternal spiritual battle for His followers. The warning is that in each individual's life there will be temptations, both physical and spiritual, throughout our earthly journey.

Yet you and I have the ultimate victory that, through prayer, The Lord's Supper, the living and the written Word of God, and sometimes fasting, we will be able to successfully fight our own battles.

To review the entire three-point battle in the Great Temptation Jesus had with the Satan, take time to review in chapter two, *Nuclear Threat or Not, Sword Will Prevail.*

Now take a deep breath of God's victorious love, and let us pray: "Our Father, who is in Heaven, holy is your Name. Your Kingdom come. Your will be done, on earth as it is in Heaven. Give us this day our daily bread …"

Next Time: Even Science Agrees: to Forgive Is Divine.

Even Science Agrees: to Forgive Is Divine

The secular world as well as the religious world believes that people are healthier if they attempt to forgive one another. It's nice when both sides can overcome differences enough to see a truth together.

The scientific world is also in agreement with forgiveness. We're told that even our body's vital signs may show a shooting peak in blood pressure or in elevated heartbeats when we are angry and raging at one another.

This is an ideal time for a stroke or heart attack to happen. Our bodies must be treated kindly and respected in order to give us the best service.

Jesus, in *The Lord's Prayer* teaches us to pray to our Father, "Forgive us our sins." Why does He say this?

For one thing, the very first brothers born on earth had such anger that the older brother, Cain killed the younger brother, Abel. The effect of sin has escalated from that time on.

The recent worst one, to me, is the killing of little children.

How do we know what sin is? Moses went up to Mount Sinai to receive the Ten Commandments from God. Number six is, "Thou shalt not kill" (Exodus 20:13).

Jesus clarifies it, "Thou shalt do no murder ..." (Matt 19:18).

That is premeditated killing. If you want to know the nine other categories of what God calls sin, read further in these references.

The prophet Isaiah explained sin this way, "All we like sheep have gone astray; we have turned every one to his own way; and the Lord has laid on him [Jesus] the iniquity of us all" (Isa 53:6).

Saint John quotes Jesus on sin, "And when He [the Holy Spirit] is come, He will reprove the world of sin, and of righteousness, and of judgment: Of sin, because they believe not on Me; Of righteousness because I go to My Father, and you see me no more; Of judgment, because the [evil] prince of this world is judged" (John 16:8-11 KJV-MOD).

Loving God and Others

In Jesus' Two Great Commandments, He summed up the ten given to Moses, "You shall love the Lord your God with all your heart, soul, and mind. This is the first and great commandment. And the second is like it, you shall love your neighbors as yourself" (Matt 22:37-39 KJV-MOD). The big ten fall into these two categories: loving God and loving others.

In review: Sin is going your own way, not God's way.

Sin is not believing in the One who gave His life for you.

Sin is breaking and continuing to break the Ten Commandments, "You Shall Not," and the Two Great Commandments: "You Shall."

Lest we think we have escaped from the effects of the fall of man, Saint Paul reminds us, "For all have sinned, and come short of the glory of God" (Rom 3:23). That covers us all.

The only one who led a sinless life on earth was Jesus Christ; therefore, He was the only One who could die to take away our sins.

In church you may have prayed or sung the penitential *Agnus Dei,* (Latin for O Lamb of God). A great thing about believing these truths is that the moment you pray to be forgiven, you are forgiven. You can tell because you have inner peace.

Jesus gave this message, "I say unto you, that likewise joy shall be in Heaven over one sinner that repents ..." (Luke 15:7 KJV-MOD). One pastor friend looked at this verse and said that every time a Christian repents the angels rejoice. In other words if you repented seven times this week, the angels had seven parties.

Perhaps, but it sounds more like what Jesus was alluding to is when a sinner comes to Jesus for salvation for the first time, then the angels really have a great celebration of dancing, blowing trumpets, and praising God.

Let's keep those parties in Heaven coming with winning souls and repenting by praying, "Our Father who is in Heaven, Holy is Your Name, Your Kingdom come, Your will be done on earth as it is in Heaven, give us this day our daily bread, and forgive us our sins ..."

Next Time: Acts of Forgiveness Enhance Our Lives.

Acts of Forgiveness Enhance Our Lives

What is hard to do but yet you have to do it all your life, and perhaps even to your final microseconds on earth? You guessed it, forgive!

When we ask God to forgive us, He does. The other side of the coin is this truth, you and I then need to forgive others. *The Lord's Prayer* says we're to forgive, **as we forgive those who sin against us.**

Herein lies our gamble with life: either we have the good life where we live in reconciliation and inner serenity, or the good life gone bad with constant complaining and getting even with those who've done us wrong.

Forgiveness a Process

In the late afternoon one spring day, I was sitting in the car while my friend, Joan Longstaff, did needed grocery shopping. I usually read a book when I have free time, but I didn't bring one with me this time.

That day my schedule had been particularly busy. I hadn't even put the armor of God on my soul, though I'm quite certain I had prayed *The Lord's Prayer.* The parking lot was not busy so I had solitude.

I prayed for about fifteen minutes, when all of a sudden I was prompted to pray for a few people who had done what the ninth commandment warns against, "Do not bear false witness against another."

This caused me to realize that I was still hurting and needed to release some emotions. I fumbled around in my purse for some Kleenex to help the process. I was soon ready to speak forgiveness to them in prayer.

I felt light and happy when my friend Joan returned. I had not realized that I still needed to forgive more from this past memory.

Pelosi Prays

Looking back to 2007 I remember how prayer hit the spotlight on the media that week. The main reason for this is that Nancy Pelosi, then Speaker of the House, announced on October 7th that she was praying for President Bush.

The interviewer, Chris Wallace on Fox News, asked her, "Do you pray for Bush to change his policies?" Her answer was, "Yes. All the time."[23]

Most of us have tried the tactic of praying for God to overrule an individual's will. Yet the scriptures indicate that one thing God chooses not to do is change a person's will.

Each of us must come to Him by our own free will. In fact, the reason Jesus came to save us is because the first humans chose to disobey the first commandment, which plunged the world into darkness (Gen 3:11-24). "You shall not have another God before Me" (Exodus 20:3 KJV-MOD). Our first parents chose and obeyed another god and died spiritually. Four thousand years later, Jesus came to rescue the human race from this fallen condition.

One of the treasures we've discussed in our Beacon Newspaper study of *The Lord's Prayer* is that it is a perfectly crafted closing prayer for anyone, including our President, "Thy will be done."

Mrs. Pelosi was right about the importance of praying for our president back then (Heb 13:17). Her witness about prayer also reminded me to ask myself, "When is the last time you sincerely took time to pray for the president and his family?" I think there is an urgent need for prayer for our leaders.

I will close with an acrostic based on the word forgive. Check out these seven steps, plus the scriptures given. These came to me fresh, with you in mind:

Forgive yourself (Mark 12:33b)
Others, also forgive (Matt 6:12)
Reconciliation, a ministry of unity (2 Cor 5:18)
Grace to you, God's unmerited favor (Eph 2:8,9)
I am not on the throne (Exodus 20:3)
Victory that overcomes the world (1 John 5:4)
Everlasting life, the forever Gift (1 John 5:13).

Meditate on these seven constructs. When ready, sit back, relax, and pray *The Lord's Prayer* with new and fresh meaning.

Next Time: Be Sure to Select a Leader with Care.

Be Sure to Select a Leader with Care

The next part of *The Lord's Prayer* in our series is, "And lead us, not into temptation." I choose to add a comma after us, so I will concentrate on this first thought. Or I may personalize it with, "And lead me."

We are all so aware of the temptations we have in life, that we can skip over the positive words, "And Lead Us."

Why do we focus on the, temptation part? Perhaps it is because we are all aware of this constant battle in our lives. In order to live in victory we need to think about the first part of the sentence, before the second part.

The 23rd Psalm begins, "The Lord is my Shepherd, I shall not want, He makes me to lie down in green pastures, *He leads me* beside the still waters, He restores my soul ..." (KJV-MOD).

Let's stop here and unpack these first points.

Jesus is called the Good Shepherd. In fact, the Apostle John in the 10th chapter of his Gospel writings describes Jesus as the Good Shepherd three times. In other words, He is the "good, good, good" Shepherd (John 10:11, 14).

So if anything in your life is bad, it is not from your good and loving Lord and Savior. It's always wise to check out who or what is leading you.

Are you led by constant food cravings, your addiction to be admired or by your desire for someone to take care of you? Are you led by your craving to make money?

Dealing with food cravings: When you are personally led by the Lord of the universe, He will guide you to good food spiritually as well as physically. It's best in that order.

As you balance your needs holistically – spirit, soul, and body – your eating habits will begin to come into order. Wash your mind with health food books. Read a new one each year.

Constant need to be admired: Take time to write down any special compliments you receive, and read them when you need a lift. Also write what the Scripture says about you: a King's kid, a new creation, a child of God, an heir of eternal life, God's temple, never condemned, loved by God unconditionally, filled with God's gifts, saved by grace through faith, on the way to Heaven.

Get a *Strong's Concordance*[24] and a *Spirit –Filled Life Bible* and search for more of God's affirmations. Review them often. Affirm your mate or children with them.

Your frequent worry about getting money: Have you read a good book on finances lately? We can go along in business for years and not read one book about finances. There are many good books out there.

You might try, *Business by the Book*[25] by Larry Burkett. Also a good visual example of not being lazy is the proverb by King Solomon about the ant's behavior, "Go to the ant, thou sluggard; consider her ways, and be wise" (Prov 6:6 see vs. 7-11).

A fixation on someone to take care of you. This sounds co-dependent. Choosing a partner should be for a healthier reason than a mother-child or father-child relationship. For this person, I would recommend soul-healing prayer, and/or see a qualified counselor to help in your area of need.

Please get your wounded, neglected inner-child healed before you get married. As the Psalmist says so well, "He leads me beside the still (healing) waters and restores my soul" (Psalm 23:2b,3 KJV-MOD).

Have you ever taken Jesus the Good Shepherd by the hand? If you'd like to, you can pray *The Lord's Prayer* from the beginning (Matt 6:9-13).

When you get to the place where it says, "And lead me," pause and ask the Lord to become your Good Shepherd. Reach out your hand, and ask Him to lead you. Take time to meditate on this picture of you and God.

When ready, complete *The Lord's Prayer*. Matthew 6:9-13.

Next Time: Everyone is Tempted, but Strength is Nearby.

Everyone is Tempted, but Strength is Nearby

Temptation is a challenge you and I will battle all the time we are on Planet Earth. It comes in different guises at different ages.

In *The Lord's Prayer,* the twelve disciples are taught to pray, "Lead us, not into temptation." Or we could paraphrase it, "Lead us away from temptation," since Jesus would not purposefully lead His own into temptation.

The warning to pray against temptation is built into *Jesus' prayer*, which then became the *Disciples' Prayer* as a daily reminder.

One of the best extra-biblical examples of temptation is from C.S. Lewis's science-fiction book, *Perelandra*. It shows us a creative reframe of the original temptation reenacted on a different planet, this time Venus. Ransom, Cambridge philologist, is the hero, and Weston, a physics professor, is the tempter.

The lady is tempted to stay overnight on the fixed, unmoving island where God (Maleldil) has commanded her not to go. She is also tempted with vanity – looking into Weston's looking glass for the first time.

She is tempted to allow harming of animals when Weston makes her a beautiful coat of colorful feathers of animals he killed. She is tempted with information about fallen women on earth and their supposed wisdom.

Read Perelandra

Her temptation by Weston goes on 24/7 day after day … until it looks almost hopeless. Then Ransom catches a tame dolphin and gives chase after the demonized professor Weston on his dolphin.

After the mad ocean chase, the enemy's power is finally broken. The king of the island and the lady are married, and life begins as was originally intended. (I hope you read it.)[26]

Near the time of Christ's arrest, while in prayer He kept warning His disciples: "Pray that you may not enter into temptation" … "Rise and pray, lest you enter into temptation" (Luke 22:40; 46 NKJV).

Scripture says Jesus was "in all points tempted as we are, yet without sin." "For in that He Himself has suffered, being tempted, He is able to aid those who are tempted" (Heb 4:15b, 2:18 NKJV). The Great Temptation when Jesus went toe to toe with Satan is referred to here. Jesus was tempted in body, soul, and spirit, and won.

On Temptation

What is your present calling? Mine in 2007 was to continue working on my master's degree so that I'd be able to be more effective as God's child in the fields of counseling and writing. My threat would be to want to give up. Or to worry that some people will think furthering my education is to be one-up. Fortunately I won that battle when I graduated in 2008.

What is it that only you can do in this world to make a difference? What is keeping you from it? What is your intentional first step?

Now let's pray *The Lord's Prayer* and when you get to "Lead us (me) not into temptation," stop and meditate on what the divine Creator wants to show you. Finish the prayer. Amen.

Next time: We Love Our Animals – But They Are Not Us.

We Love Our Animals – But They Are Not Us

In my mid-20s, I had become an enthusiastic believer. One day at my job as a Social Worker, I was asked to attend a meeting to hear an agency invited guest speaker and Ph.D. For an hour his basic topic was, "Human beings are animals." To him we are no different than our four-footed furry brothers and sisters.

As a university student I had wavered between different ways of thinking about our origin, but now I had a check somewhere inside. I knew that since I had become spiritually alive, in what the scripture calls one's spirit (*pneuma*), I was living with a healthier moral stance and purpose in life. That night, still concerned about the speaker's message as I lay down to sleep. I prayed a simple prayer: "Dear God, please let me know if I am just an animal."

Early the next morning I was awakened with these words: "Since you are made in My image, how can you be an animal?"

Surprised by such a quick and clear answer, I lay in bed amazed. This is the first time I had ever heard from God directly. The words were so wise, and yet so simple. In other words, if I am just an animal and made in God's image, then He too is an animal (Gen 1:26, 27). So there would be no God.

But He had now clearly spoken to my heart that since I am made in His image, I am not an animal.

Of course animals are wonderful gifts to us humans and some animals are more loving than some humans. But animals are not restricted by sexual morality. They do not have to get a marriage license in order to have offspring! The problem is when we humans do not know who we are and who we were meant to be, we often live on the morality level of the animal world. Some live much lower than animals. In fact, animals might be ashamed to claim any connection with such humans!

Spiritually Dead Behavior

When the serpentine being in the garden successfully tempted the first humans to turn away from God, they died. That is, their spirits died – and they fell to a soul-body-animal level. Unless life from Heaven comes to resurrect one's spirit, it lies dormant, inactive, and less able to resist evil.[27] The Bible calls this the carnal nature.

It is the carnal nature that says: "Let's go to the casino, and skip church. Let's cheat on our mate. Let's have group sex – since there is no God anyway. Let's use alcohol and drugs until our teeth fall out, our eyes glaze over, and our brain is fried."

Examples of individuals who epitomize evil follow:

Adolph Hitler, who was anti-God took advice from mediums (channelers), murdered three million Jewish adults and children, blaming or scapegoating them to appease his own evil heart.

Saddam Hussein, in our day, had large groups of people shot and shoved into open graves. He tortured, beheaded, and shredded people.

Osama bin Laden on September 11, 2001 directed 19 Islamic terrorists from his al-Queda group into four suicide planes. They crashed two planes into the World Trade Center in New York, one plane crashed into the Pentagon in Washington DC, and another headed for the U.S. Capital Building was side tracked by brave Americans to crash the plane in a field in Shanksville, Pennsylvania. Total dead was nearly 3,000.[28]

The evening news constantly gives us more examples of evil.

But Love Wins

This is the reason Jesus told His disciples and us, to pray: "Deliver us from evil." He saw plenty of evil in His own day, and it nailed Him to a cross.

But love won. Christ rose from death and was seen by many witnesses before He returned to His Father in Heaven. He took the sins of the world to the cross with Him so that anyone can have their sins pardoned just for the asking. Jesus said, "Ask and it will be given you …" (Matt 7:7 KJV-MOD).

The Apostle Paul said, "For to be carnally minded is death, but to be spiritually minded is life and peace" (Rom 8:6). Jesus showed us a pathway of life that brings abundance. As you pray *The Lord's Prayer,* ask Him to deliver you from evil and to resurrect your spirit that has been dead to Him. You are then made in God's image, and can know and experience that truth, eternally.

"Father in Heaven … deliver us from evil and from the Evil One". In great thanksgiving we say, "Amen."

Next time: Lord's Prayer Doxology Inspires to This Day.

Lord's Prayer Doxology Inspires to This Day

This Advent and Christmas season I want to share with you inspiration from the closing words of *The Lord's Prayer.*

The earliest manuscripts of the New Testament do not have the familiar ending to the Lord's Prayer, "For Thine is the Kingdom and the power and the glory forever. Amen" (Matt 6:13 KJV-MOD).

These words are often called a doxology, meaning a liturgical expression of praise to God.[29] Most scholars do not believe Jesus Himself put these words of praise at the end of the prayer, but that they were added later.

If so, whoever added them was certainly led by the Spirit of God, obviously feeling that the Lord's Prayer should culminate in praise. I'm glad, too, that the Holy Spirit saw to it that it was left in the manuscripts chosen by the 47 scholars who translated the King James Version (KJV) in 1611.

Many other translators have followed suit including the New King James Version (NKJV) of the Bible.

About thirty years ago I climbed down the stairs into the crypt of Westminster Abbey, London where this intellectual and spiritual translation of the KJV Bible was accomplished. How in awe I felt to stand on this holy ground contemplating all the discussions, debates, and prayers that must have occurred during this project.

Most churches in the Protestant tradition use *The Lord's Prayer Doxology* because the closing words are so revered and such a tool of praise. I have included it, too. I love its victorious words, which bring Jesus' prayer to a triumphant conclusion, as well as to remind us of the importance of praise to God.

For Yours is the Kingdom

To have a kingdom there has to be a king. In our society, the idea of a king ruling over us is foreign. Caution is understandable due to the long list of good and bad kings recorded in the Bible and in human history since.

But Jesus is a different kind of King. "The King of love my Shepherd is whose goodness faileth never," proclaims hymn writer John Bacchus Dykes, in 1868.[30] His title describes Jesus' kind of rule, "The King of Love My Shepherd is."

On earth Jesus had a cross rather than a throne. He had thorns in His brow rather than a crown. He had abuse rather than respect. Christ the King was crucified between two thieves, further degrading Him by association. Yet one criminal grimacing in pain called out, "Lord, remember me when You come into Your Kingdom!" That makes me teary eyed just thinking about this scene.

Jesus' answer, given through unbelievable pain, including the weight of all humanity's sins, must have echoed throughout the universe, "Today – you will be with Me in Paradise" (Luke 23:43 KJV-MOD). How electric was this loving exchange from God the Son to man!

He Came to Save

The very reason Jesus went through all His pain and degradation on earth was for this alone – to save souls and pull them out of their hell on earth, and the one later.

His plan is for us also to have a very close friendship where we can look forward to taking walks together with Jesus in His heavenly gardens in Paradise.[31] Such an event is exactly what a king would choose to do with His friends.

If you like to walk, you can take prayer walks in which you enjoy conversing with the Lord right now, in earthly gardens. If you can't physically walk, you can picture yourself walking with God in the heavenly city, one day.

Let us close by praying in its entirety *The Lord's Prayer* together:

"Our Father who is in Heaven [fill in here from memory]. For Yours is the Kingdom ... and the Power ... and the Glory ... forever and ever. Amen."

Next time: Lord's Prayer: A Gift for a Lifetime.

Lord's Prayer – Gift for a Lifetime

In my last column we looked at each phrase of *The Lord's Prayer Doxology*, which contains the final words of praise to this greatest prayer ever written. There I mentioned the *Doxology* was most likely added by early Christians for the joy of what Jesus' prayer did for them.

Why is *The Lord's Prayer* called the greatest? Because it was written by God Himself for all people to benefit. It is a prayer to use in any situation, every day of your life. It is an outline and a checklist to see how you're doing in your walk with Christ.

"For Thine is the Kingdom and the power and the glory forever." "Yours is ... the power." What does our Lord say about power? Just before Jesus went to take His place at His Father's right hand, He told His friends the good news, "All power has been given to me in Heaven and on earth!" (Matt 28:18, literal Greek[32]).

We don't know the actual Hebrew (or Aramaic) Jesus used, but the Greek here is *exousia,* which means authority.

When the originator of this doxology said, "Thine is the power," he used another Greek word for power, *dunamis* – the one from which we get the word dynamite. Jesus demonstrated this kind of power when He turned water into wine, healed the sick, and cast out evil spirits.

Imagine a policeman directing traffic. He has *exousia* (authority) to make you stop, but he does not have *dunamis* (dynamite power) to stop your car forcibly, superman style by pushing on the front bumper!

While the war between God's light and Satan's darkness is still going on in the world, the Lord Jesus limits His own *dunamis* – His power – because although it could wipe out the destructive behavior in the world, it would also destroy multitudes who might yet come to know God.

Age of Grace

This is what the age of grace means – God limiting His power instead of exercising it directly, thus by His love giving the world a chance to change. At this time we're still in the time of Grace.

Meanwhile our Lord works wonders through His spiritual family today. His power and love are available in His people who are infused with the Holy Spirit. His *dunamis* begins to be released through you when you follow in Jesus' footsteps.

God can then work through you to heal the sick, set captives free, help the brokenhearted, feed the hungry, and in every way possible draw people to Him. Jesus exercised great power when He was on earth, but His *dunamis* in Heaven and earth will not be fully released until the end of this age.

To confirm this in the book of Revelation both *exousia* and *dunamis* are used together to describe God's Kingdom coming in its fullness: "Now have come the salvation and the power [*dunamis*] and the kingdom of our God, and the authority [*exousia*] of His Christ." (Rev 12:10 NIV). That is a dynamite scripture verse!

Because you are in Christ, through *exousia* you can say stop to the enemy, and he must obey you. By God's *dunamis* Jesus can work through you to implode the works of the age-old enemy by which he harasses and tries to destroy the people of God.

You may function in both God's power and His authority; in fact He is counting on you to do so! The power and authority of God are available to His people now because we are already in His Kingdom.

Flash of Glory

His is also the glory. I believe that when Jesus, by the power of the Holy Spirit, was raised from the dead there was such a flash of resurrection glory that it created the imprint of His body and wounds on the white linen cloth that covered Him. It's now called the Shroud of Turin. I saw it at St. John the Baptist Basilica in Torino, Italy!

This last year in 2012, October 26th and 27th I was asked to teach the course *The Lord's Prayer Heals* at St. Paul's Episcopal Church in Chattanooga, Tennessee. It has a 200-page syllabus. One student said to me, "I never knew that there would be enough one could say about *The Lord's Prayer* to fill 200 pages." She said further, "If I had known that, I would have joined the class sooner!"

I do not at this time have musical notes to give you, but if you know Malotte's music or some other melody, let us sing together:

"Our Father, who is in Heaven,
hallowed be Thy Name.
Thy Kingdom come,
Thy will be done,
On earth as it is in Heaven.
Give us this day our daily bread,
and forgive us our debts as we forgive our debtors.
And lead us,
not into temptation, but deliver us from evil.
For Thine is the Kingdom,
and the power,
and the glory forever.
Amen."

Chapter 4

Eternal Romance, The Beatitudes Series and the Ten Commandments Series with Hebrew Lessons

Redeemer, High Priest, King (illustration above) – This picture of Jesus Christ is a symbolic one, but through it we discover many of His ministries on earth and in Heaven. His hands are outstretched to us. When we accepted Jesus, our Eternal Friendship and Romance began.

Tracing the Steps – Seeing the Imprint

Let us look at the very last phrase of *The Lord's Prayer Doxology*, "and the glory forever. Amen."

What do these words mean? What is the glory? In Hebrew, "*kavod*" or glory means literally weight. The weight of God's manifest presence or His glory can at times cause people to be overwhelmed and not to be able to stand up.

For example, when the soldiers came to the Mount of Olives to arrest Jesus, they asked which one was Jesus of Nazareth, and He answered, "I AM." As He said these words, "I AM" the soldiers all "went backwards, and fell to the ground" (John 18:6 KJV). With these words, Jesus, God's Son, was proclaiming Himself God.

The glory or shining forth of a halo of light is another way the glory of God is seen. When Jesus came to earth from His home in Heaven, He was willing to lay His glory down so that He could communicate with us humans on a natural plane. (Theologically this is called *kenosis*.[1]) Every once in a while, this divine light or presence was seen upon Jesus.

Mount of Transfiguration

One of these occasions took place on the Mount of Transfiguration when, "… His face shone like the sun, and His clothes became as white as the light" (Matt 17:2 NIV). This divine meeting with Jesus, Moses, and Elijah arranged by Father God was to prepare Jesus for His exodus from earth, literally His death. Peter, James, and John were chosen by Jesus to go with Him to this divine meeting.

Some believe that Mount Tabor, six miles east of Nazareth and 1,350 feet tall, was the location. On my second trip to Israel, my tour group and I drove up this mountain to pray in the church on the very top. To climb this mountain must have been an all day trip for Jesus and His disciples.

Yet another contender for the transfiguration location is Mount Hermon which is the tallest in Israel, 9,101 feet.[2] We'll have to wait until Christ returns to know the real location. My vote is for Mount Tabor.

Another glory scene was the resurrection. The night before Jesus' crucifixion He prayed, "And now, O Father, glorify Me together with yourself, with the glory which I had with You before the world was" (John 17:5 KJV-MOD).

This greatest manifestation of Jesus' glory was seen when He rose from the dead in His resurrection body. The radiation from His body at that moment was so powerful many believe it imprinted a three-dimensional picture on His burial clothes.

Perhaps this was what caused the imprint of a crucified man on the Jewish burial cloth presently kept at St. John the Baptist Basilica, in Turin, Italy. If this is truly the burial cloth of our Lord, then that is as close as anyone can get to Jesus in this life. It's just like Him to leave us evidence via the negative of His own photograph!

Forever!

Forever is what Dr. Gerard Landry, NDE survivor calls Eternal Now. Landry describes his own death and return, "It's like finally getting to the nanosecond, where time stops for us. Like a watch, our body stops at that time. Yet our spirit and consciousness continue to live on a dimension beyond sequential time. We go beyond nanoseconds into a space-time measurement we cannot know here on earth. I call it the eternal now, because that's how it felt to me. The past, present, and future are all merged into what Scripture calls eternity. Eternity is the present, the now that never ends."[3]

The Lord's Prayer ends with, Amen.

Amen means, it is true, so be it. The Hebrew root means truth and faithfulness.[4]

A good way to experience His glory is to pray *The Lord's Prayer* in some way daily (Matt 6:9-13). Another great way would be to make a pilgrimage to Israel, the Holy Land.

In May 1997, the night I returned from taking a group of 25 to Jerusalem, I had a dream about Jesus. It was like a visit when he spoke to me as a bridegroom mentioning how He was looking forward to seeing His bride and the long awaited wedding in Heaven. Of course all of us children of God, female and male, are spoken of as the Bride of Christ. Yet, I think He was especially pleased that I had taken a group of Christians to see where He was born, lived, died, rose again and ascended to Heaven. This was my reward!

At Last! A Promise of Eternal "Romance"

Each year on February 14th when we think of Valentine's Day, we think romance. "Romance means a loving relationship, marked by courage, and adventure," so says Daniel Webster.[5] Isn't that appealing?

In the beginning of a romance, we have visions of prince charming coming to rescue us from the mundane and whisking us away to a glorious castle where we are fully loved and cared for, or a princess most beautiful, without one mean bone in her body, paying attention to our every word, and giving up everything else to meet our needs. There is a great market for romance novels and women are the biggest market for such. In fact, it's hard for the male to ever measure up to these heroic novels.

After a time, unless we work at it, our loved one can become plain old Joe or just plain Jane. He may develop a distended stomach and she may get sloppy by not grooming herself as she once did.

All relationships, in time, will wear down and have problems. Through the second law of thermodynamics we find that in our world, things wear down or break down when given enough time. This is also true of relationships.

The hero in the Song of Songs describes true romance for us:
"The voice of my beloved!
Behold, he comes
Leaping upon the mountains,
Skipping upon the hills.
My beloved is like a gazelle or a young stag.
Behold, he stands behind our wall;
He is looking through the windows,
Gazing through the lattice"
(Song 2:8-9 NKJV).

The beloved is full of energy and life. He is very interested in his intended and admires her but waits for an invitation to be with her.

First, he woos her with words as he stands gazing through the lattice:
"Rise up, my love, my fair one,
And come away.
For lo, the winter is past,
The rain is over and gone.

144

The flowers appear on the earth;
The time of singing has come,
And the voice of the turtledove
Is heard in our land.
The fig tree puts forth her green figs,
And the vines with the tender grapes
Give a good smell.
Rise up, my love, my fair one,
And come away!"
(Song 2:10b-13 NKJV).

The words we speak in a relationship are vitally important. They can make or break a romance or a marriage. These poetic words of the lover in the Song of Songs are caressing words that heal the soul.

Oh, how inviting are the words, "Come away with me" with the one who loves you most in the whole world. Who wouldn't want to go? But she must respond as he is ready to make a decision. He has found in her all he desires. Will she say yes?

God's Love Song

This ancient poetry of Solomon to the Shulamite woman has also been called God's Love Song. The Lord wants to have a love relationship with you that will not only be for this life, but for eternity.

It starts now and enriches all your relationships on earth because you can rest in His constant love which helps you be more loving.

His tender words will heal the wounds you've received in this earthly vale of tears. And with the Lord there is no natural law that is going to break down your relationship with Him but it will only get better and better as the centuries roll by.

Who wouldn't want to go with Him when He calls for us, male and female, to come away with Him? Come away to the eternal vineyards and mountains of spices, and soul-caressing words from God's own love poetry – sung especially to you. Will you say yes?

Spark your eternal romance by reading the Song of Songs also called Song of Solomon, the 22nd book of the Bible. Read it with your loved one for a Valentine's Day or Weekend gift.

The Beatitude Series
Beatitudes Beckon as Gateway to Happiness

The beatitudes are the beginning of a five-part sermon Jesus gave to His disciples as He prepared them for leadership. I think the beatitudes are even more valuable for His followers today than they were 2,000 years ago because we now have a clearer picture of the value and progression of His message.

For instance, no believer can fully obey God without the power of the Holy Spirit indwelling and filling him or her. Before Jesus' ministry was over on earth, He kept hinting at the fact that, "It is expedient for you that I go away: for if I go not away, the Comforter will not come to you; but if I depart, I will send Him to you" (John 16:7 KJV-MOD).

"And being assembled together with them, He commanded them not to depart from Jerusalem, but to wait for the Promise of the Father, 'which,' He said, 'you have heard from Me … you shall be baptized with the Holy Spirit not many days from now'" (Acts 1:4-5 NKJV).

Eight Point Beatitudes

The eight-point beatitudes sermon has rich teaching for the Christian believer who has experienced the power of the Holy Spirit dwelling within and as an artesian well overflowing to others.

So Jesus teaches all He can and as much as He can to those who come to Him. He knows full well that before the time of Pentecost, unconverted and un-empowered humans will find it hard to live an obedient, Spirit-led, dedicated life.

Saint Peter is a good example of this in that he denied knowing Jesus after his Lord's arrest, but after his experience of receiving Holy Spirit power on the Day of Pentecost (*Shavuot*) he boldly preached a sermon that brought 3,000 souls into the Kingdom in one day!

There are seemingly two beatitude sermons: one called the Sermon on the Mount as given in Matthew Chapters 5,6, and 7, the other, the Sermon on the Plain as recorded in Luke 6:20-49.

In 1997 on a tour to Israel, I had the opportunity to visit the lovely Church of the Beatitudes, which is built on the Mount of Beatitudes near the Galilee (*Kinneret*) shore. Behind the church is a natural amphitheater where archeologists believe Jesus preached His Sermon on the Mount.

the

The ice blue sea is very calm in the morning hours but is quite choppy in the afternoon. The town of Galilee on the sea was one of my favorite places, and where I learned Jesus spent a lot of His time teaching and praying for people.

Secrets of a Happy Life

These eight beatitudes have been called The Secrets of a Happy Life.

Beatitude Number One

The first beatitude is, "Blessed are the poor in spirit, for theirs is the kingdom of heaven" (Matt 5:3).

In studying *The Jewish New Testament Commentary* I discovered: "Greek *makarios* corresponds to Hebrew *asher* and means blessed, happy, and fortunate all at once, so that no one English word is adequate."[6]

Poor in spirit here describes the character of those who realize their great need, and thus are humble. Jesus tells us that unless we become as little children we cannot enter the Kingdom of Heaven (Matt 18:3). That's a very serious point for us to consider.

Even religious leader Nicodemus had to recognize his poverty, to the extent of needing to be born again of the Spirit before he could see or experience the Kingdom of God here or in the world to come (John 3:5).

As one realizes his spiritual need by humbly coming to Christ, he or she can at last know the awesome joy of being included in the eternal Kingdom of God.

Beatitude number one will get you started on a happy, fulfilling, and eternal life.

Prayerfully ask Jesus to help you become humble in spirit.

This week meditate on Nicodemus's full story in John 3:1-17 and ask Jesus to bless you in this way.

Life-changing Event Awaits Those in Need

Jesus' Sermon on the Mount can only be fulfilled in your life because the Messiah's life is being manifested now through the power of the Holy Spirit. This power to live a blessed, happy, fortunate life has been available on earth since Christ's resurrection, ascension and the sending of the Holy Spirit 2,000 years ago.

After Jesus' baptism in the Jordan, then the three-fold temptation by Satan, and Jesus' victory – His public miracle ministry and teachings began. One of His announcements was, "Repent: for the kingdom of heaven is at hand" (Matt 4:17b).

The good news is that the Kingdom of God is still at hand even though Jesus the Christ is no longer physically on earth. At hand means Christ's presence is always available to you. All you need to do is call upon Him.

Jeremiah 33:3 is like God's telephone number, "Call to Me, and I will answer you, and show you great and mighty things, which you do not know" (NKJV).

In our last column we looked at the first beatitude: "Blessed are the poor in spirit for theirs is the Kingdom of Heaven" (KJV-MOD). How could one know that the Kingdom had come? There weren't buildings with words painted on the front: "The Kingdom Church or Synagogue."

The New Bible Dictionary says, "The Kingdom has come in Him and with Him; He is the 'auto-basileia' ... [It] is concentrated in Him in its present and future aspects alike."[7]

Scripture shows us how Jesus manifested God's Kingdom of Heaven through casting out demons, miraculous healings, and other supernatural gifts of the Spirit (Luke 11:20, 1 Cor 12:7-11).

Beatitude Number Two

"Blessed are those who mourn for they shall be comforted" (Matt 5:4 KJV-MOD). How can mourning be a blessing from God when mourning is an outward expression of sadness and sorrow?

The Bible speaks of individuals who have over the years hardened their hearts to God. Apparently people can go too far as Hebrews 3:13 says, "But exhort one another daily, while it is called 'Today,' lest any of you be hardened through the deceitfulness of sin. For we have become partakers of Christ if we hold the beginning of our confidence steadfast to the end" (NKJV).

Our past is not as important as our life is now and our life at our end. How you began your spiritual race is not as important as how you end it.

Have you ever seen an individual mourn for their sins? Have you ever mourned for yours? I have.

148

I was a Sunday go-to-church believer most of the time, but I was not being fed spiritually. During my college years I was slowly falling away from my childhood faith. After graduation, I was invited to a home where people gathered together to have Bible study and to pray. A close friend of mine had just died.

The leader asked if I would like to pray. Several people gathered round me to join in. All of a sudden, I began to weep many tears of sadness about how I had often ignored my first love – Jesus.

I could have been embarrassed but the tears felt so good and cleansing. All I can say is that my life has never been the same since that day.

Mourning Is a Gift

I mourned and repented for my sins, and I also mourned the death of my friend, Gail. She was one of the best Christians I had ever known. I believe mourning is a gift and a blessing. Truly I was comforted and Jesus has remained my forever-best Friend. (For more see: My Personal Story Series in Chapter 6 – Part 2.)

Jesus is near, He is at hand for you too. Try calling His phone number Jer 33:3 – "Call to Me, and I will answer you …"

While there, ask to speak to my best Friend, Jesus. Share your heart. Tell Him your needs. You'll be glad you did.

Meekness, Understanding is a Lifelong Journey

We are continuing to look into the very famous Sermon on the Mount Jesus taught in Galilee sometime during His last several years of ministry on earth (Matt 5:5-12). He may have proclaimed these concepts a number of times in different locations.

Each of the eight beatitudes begins with blessed which can be modernized as happy.

Finis Dake reports, "Happy is used nine times here of people who have godly characteristics"[8] *The Amplified Bible* explains blessed as: "happy, to be envied, and spiritually prosperous" (Matt 5:3 AMP).

Beatitude Number Three

The third beatitude is, "Blessed are the meek: for they shall inherit the earth" (Matt 5:5). Meek is a primitive word to us today but it is used in many places in Scripture so it's important to understand it. Meek or meekness may sound weak to us, but not so.

In the earliest example of the word, Moses, the most powerful man of the Old Testament, led over a million children of Israel out of captivity through the wilderness and is described as, "... very meek above all men which were upon the face of the earth" (Num 12:3).

Praus or *praos* (meek, Gr. adj.) denotes gentle, humble, lowly. "Christ uses it of His own disposition (Matt 11:29); He gives it in the third of His beatitudes (5:5); it is said of Him as the King Messiah (21:5); it is an adornment of the Christian profession (1 Peter 3:4)."[9]

I'd like to delve into one of these verses. Here Jesus quotes and fulfills words from the prophet Zechariah, "Rejoice greatly, O Daughter of Zion! Shout, Daughter of Jerusalem! See, your king comes to you, righteous and having salvation, gentle and riding on a donkey, on a colt, the foal of a donkey (Zech 9:9 NIV).

Messiah Proclaimed

During the last week of Jesus' ministry, He deliberately fulfilled messianic prophecies such as Zechariah 9:9. The week before Easter (Resurrection Sunday) is Palm Sunday. This is the time we celebrate His triumphal entry into Jerusalem, which took place shortly before the crucifixion.

Perhaps your church handed out palm fronds on Palm Sunday and your congregation walked around your building enacting the worshippers of 2,000 years ago.

Or perhaps you, as I did in 1996, went to the actual Mount of Olives in Jerusalem and walked down the long pathway – which is now of necessity, concrete steps. This marks the location where Jesus rode the donkey that awesome day.

The second part of the beatitude is, "... The meek shall inherit the earth," Matthew 5:5 JNTC[10]) which has three applications.

First, as it is applied to the present. Spiritually meek individuals have already entered into this promise. How, you may ask? Because they are assured that God loves them and continually has their welfare

150

in mind. He who is meek has given His Spirit to those who ask. We are told in Galatians 5:22-23 that the fruit of the Spirit is meekness.

Second, there is a future reference. The Apostle Paul says, "The Spirit Himself bears witness with our spirit that we are children of God, and if children, then heirs – heirs of God and joint heirs with Christ, if indeed we suffer with Him, that we may also be glorified together" (Rom 8:16-17 NKJV). The spiritually meek have joy now in the midst of trials and look forward to the joy of our future inheritance on this earth.

Third, a second future reference is specifically for the Jews. The natural, literal promise for this beatitude refers initially to the meek of Israel who will inherit the land of Israel.[11]

Christ did not come as a conquering, warrior King but as a humble, unconditionally loving King to all who dare to proclaim, "Blessed is He who comes in the name of the Lord!' Hosanna in the highest!" (Psalm 118:26, Matthew 21:9, Zechariah 14:3–11).

With a meek spirit, take time to practice reading aloud or spontaneously singing the words written above, in unity with the billions of worshippers throughout history.

Quest for Righteousness is a Lifelong Journey

Beatitude Number Four

The fourth beatitude in our series is, "Blessed are those who hunger and thirst after righteousness, for they shall be filled" (Matt 5:6 KJV-MOD). How many people today do you know who would say their greatest desire is to hunger and thirst after righteousness? Fortunately we may think of some.

Yet it seems like many more people on Planet Earth are hungering and thirsting after unrighteousness. How do we know? Look at the commandments. Number 6 says, "You shall do no murder."

A friend of mine, Cherie Calbom, was house-sitting during her college years and a seventeen-year-old drug addict broke into that home. He beat her head with a led pipe and strangled her.

She felt herself leave her body and start her homeward journey. Somehow it was not her time as she found herself back in her body, outside the house – screaming for help.

The neighbors were instrumental in saving her life. The would-be murderer did succeed as a thief of four hundred dollars for his habit, so also commandment number eight was broken. (More is told about this true story in my book called, *Heaven Tours, Chapter 8*.)[12]

Then there's Commandment Number Seven, "You shall not commit adultery." The news is replete with those who spend large quantities of money in brothels looking for something or someone to meet their deep needs – perhaps from wounds left from parents who neglected or physically abused them. Or with some it's from plain addictive, indulged lust cravings.

It's easy to think of other examples.

Rightwiseness

In contrast, what is righteousness? The Hebrew word *tsdaqah* means: do justice, have moral virtue, make right, cleanse self.[13] *Tsadee* is the 18th letter of the Hebrew alphabet, which means holy. For example, "he is *tsadeek*."

In Greek the word righteousness is *dikaiosune* meaning, "the character or quality of being right or just"; it was formerly spelled "rightwiseness", which clearly expresses the meaning. It is used to denote an attribute of God e.g. Romans 3:5.[14]

How in this world-system can a person appropriate beatitude number four? It is very other worldly for human beings to consider thirsting for righteousness. Here David's Psalm describes it: "As the deer pants for the water brooks, So pants my soul for You, O God. My soul thirsts for God, for the living God" (Psalm 42:1, 2a NKJV).

In our hearts we are like the thirsty deer. We desire something pure and satisfying to quench our thirst. We want a connection with the living God.

Be Spirit Filled

How can we be filled? Here's the answer from Jesus: "On the last day, that great day of the feast, Jesus stood and cried out, saying, 'If anyone thirsts, let him come to Me and drink. He who believes in Me, as the Scripture has said, out of his heart will flow rivers of living water" (John 7:39 NKJV).

Jesus invites you to come to Him and drink in His beauty, His holiness, His wise counsel and sheer joy, and His heart of love for you.

In this beatitude, we can seek rightwiseness, moral virtue, justice and we shall be filled. Righteousness is also right thinking, speaking, and acting; it is right standing with God through Christ.

Ways you can be filled are: attend inspiring Bible studies, sing in a choir, experience Holy Communion, hear Spirit-filled pastor's sermons, attend healing seminars, journal your inspiring dreams and insights, pray *The Lord's Prayer*, study The Ten Commandments, read the Psalms of David, read *The Holy Spirit and You*.[15]

Now I invite you to pray or sing a chorus with me.

Fill my cup Lord,
I lift it up Lord,
come and quench
this thirsting of my soul.
Bread of Heaven, feed me
till I want no more,
fill my cup, fill it up and overflow.[16]

Lift your cupped hands up to God for Him to fill you. Breathe. Rest.

An Act of Kindness is Easy to Recognize

Beatitude Number Five

The fifth beatitude in our series is, "Blessed are the merciful, for they shall obtain mercy."

After I graduated from college, I chose to share a year of my life working in a multi-racial agency in New Jersey for emotionally broken children ages five to sixteen.

On one of my free weekends, I went into Manhattan on a double date. We four walked down the street together through the Bowery headed to Greenwich Village. I was shocked to see a man lying on the sidewalk near the curb; his balding head was injured and bleeding. I said to my date, "Can we stop and help him?

He said in measured tones, "Keep walking and do not look at him. He's just a drunk." I was saddened by the situation but no one seemed to care.

This is obviously not a good example of being merciful.

In contrast to the incident in New York is the Bible story of The Good Samaritan.

The Good Samaritan

It goes like this. Jesus had just finished speaking to the crowd on the two-part Great Commandment that concludes with the admonition to love your neighbor as yourself.

A man wanting to justify himself asked, "And who is my neighbor?" Jesus responded with an example:

One sunny afternoon a man walked from Jerusalem to Jericho and was cruelly attacked by a group of thieves. He was wounded, stripped of clothing, and left to die. Two people, a priest and then a Levite, passed by on the other side of the road.

The third man, a Samaritan, acted like a neighbor to this stranger. With concern he knelt down and used his oil and wine from his saddlebag to clean and bandage the wounds.

The good neighbor then put the wounded man on his own animal and brought him to the nearest inn. The Samaritan stayed overnight and paid the innkeeper the next day. As he was leaving, he told the innkeeper he would be back again to pay for further expenses.

Jesus asks, "Who of these three do you think was neighbor to him?" (Luke 10:36 KJV-MOD).

The questioner was caught, "He who showed mercy on him."

"Then Jesus said to him, 'Go and do likewise'" (Luke 10:37 KJV-MOD).

Practice Mercy

Perhaps Jesus was thinking about the Good Samaritan experience when He gave what we now call the fifth beatitude. "Blessed are the merciful …" Mercy (*chesed,* Hebrew) is also translated as loving-kindness," "unfailing love" or "steadfast covenant love," and is similar to the New Testament word "grace".[17]

God gets blamed for many of the bad things that go on in the world. As a consequence some may erroneously think God is not a merciful God. This attitude keeps many people away from God and His house.

A good antidote is to get a Bible concordance, look up the word mercy, and read the many verses. Mark the ones that speak to you. My favorite concordance is *Strong's Bible Concordance* and that lists 228 verses about mercy.[18]

I was impressed to see that Psalm 136 has 26 verses in it and with each one there is this constant refrain: "For His mercy endures forever" (NKJV). Wonderful words.

After you read this refrain 26 times, you might get the point God is trying to make! He is a God of mercy and He loves you.

The second part of the beatitude is, "They will receive mercy." Mercy is a gift but you have to receive it.

A Prayer of Mercy

I reach out my hands to You Lord God and say, "I joyfully receive Your gift of mercy. Thank You for being merciful to me! Now help me be merciful to others. I want to be a good Samaritan on this road of life. Amen."

Soul, Heart: Two Words for the Same Thing

As Jesus looked down from the Mount of Beatitudes where He was teaching his disciples, He saw a multitude of faces at the bottom looking up at Him in rapt attention.

Beatitude Number Six

Many of them could be called the pure in heart. These were among the citizens gathered in Galilee who were downtrodden by self-righteous religious and governmental leaders. One day He was speaking to them on what we today call the sixth beatitude: "The pure in heart shall see God."

I can imagine some of the discussions on this beatitude. "What does He mean by that? Do I have to be totally pure at all times in order to go to Heaven? What is the heart? Is He speaking about the organ that beats in my chest?

First let's see what Jesus means by heart. Dr. W.E. Vine says, "*Kardia,* the heart, the chief organ of physical life, occupies the most important place in the human system. By an easy transition the word came to stand for man's entire mental and moral activity, both the rational and the emotional elements ... The heart, in its moral significance in the Old Testament, includes the emotions, the reason and the will ..."[19] The heart is the seat or center of the soul, and part of the soul's intellect, will, and emotions.

Scripture teaches us that we are also composed of spirit *(pneuma)*, soul *(psyche)* and body *(soma)*. The heart and soul are a mixture of purity and impurity. They're in the process of being healed and cleaned up. To have a clean heart requires cooperation from the individual. Some of the ways to do this officially are during Lenten season fasting, *Yom Kippur* repentance, pilgrimages, revivals, healing seminars, Bible studies, Spirit-filled prayer meetings, attending scripturally based church.

Our hearts are also changed as we help the sick, bring or send aid to countries suffering from disaster, visit the elderly who are homebound – to name a few.

Your spirit has been purified

One part of us has been purified; that part is the renewed spirit that has been cleansed through spiritual new birth. This new creation core part can see God spiritually in prayer, dreams, visions and biblical meditations.

The Apostle Paul said, "But he that is joined to the Lord is one spirit *(pneuma)*" (1 Cor 6:17 KJV-MOD). "... Christ in you, the hope of glory" (Col 1:27). The pure in heart shall see God. It is imperative that our hearts be changed to be more like Christ; otherwise we will not be good witnesses for Him or be happy and fulfilled. Unless our vulnerable hearts are healed, our spiritual eyes may be swollen and shut so that we cannot see God as we grope in darkness for something to satisfy.

We see that the sixth beatitude has both a present and a future fulfillment. In the future, one day we will see God face to face. The Apostle John says, "... we know that, when He shall appear, we shall be like Him; for we shall see Him as He is" (1 John 3:2).

Saint John was speaking from experience when he said these words. We know this, because in a vision he was caught up to Heaven and given a tour of the city of God. He wrote a book about it, the book of Revelation. "And when I saw Him [Jesus], I fell at His feet as dead. And He laid His right hand upon me, saying to me, Fear not; I am the first and the last; I am He that lives, and was dead; and, behold, I am alive for evermore, Amen" (Rev 1:17,18a KJV-MOD).

In review, we see God spiritually in this life, until we see Him face to face in the next life.

Role of Peacemaker a Ubiquitous Blessing

The angels sang at Jesus' birth, "Glory to God in the highest and on earth peace among men of goodwill" (Luke 2:14, *Nestle Greek New Testament*).

This verse is read and sung at the Christmas holiday season. The literal Greek here indicates that peace is most likely to come to men and women who extend goodwill to others.

Beatitude Number Seven

In this section of the series, we're looking at the seventh beatitude: "Blessed are the Peacemakers, for they shall be called the sons of God" *(Ibid. Gr.),*

Peacemaking is a supernatural work. Peace not only means reconciliation between conflicting parties but further it is actively working at making peace. It is bringing about wholeness and well-being among the alienated.

Galatians 3:26 says, "For in Christ we are all sons of God through faith."

An acrostic for faith that I like is, "**F**orsaking **All I T**ake **H**im" Sounds like a wedding vow, and I guess it is, in that it speaks of an eternal spiritual union with God.

This is the greatest inner peace event in one's life. Before Jesus' death and resurrection, He said to His followers, "Peace I leave with you, My peace I give to you, not as the world gives do I give to you. Let not your heart be troubled, neither let it be afraid" (John 14:27).

A Personal Example

I'll give you a personal example of needing peace. In school I was in a confrontation class where students were encouraged to let their feelings about one another be known. One man began to make a negative connection with me. Having spoken only a few words with me previously, Tom *(pseudonym)* said, "I don't like you!"

157

This comment me took me by surprise, especially because no one had ever made a comment to me like that. Maybe they had thought it, but never said it.

My response came effortlessly, "Well, just because you do not like me doesn't mean that I do not like you." I actually felt peaceful as I said this. He said, "If you had spoken that way to me, I would not have respond like you did!"

I had several other word hits from him that year but each time I responded and engaged him in group to work through the conflict. By the end of the year, we had both practiced our skills and were on a friendship basis.

As I look at this seventh beatitude, and my class, I feel like a peacemaker. I have to admit I was often uncomfortable thinking and planning how to interact with him in class. It was not fun, but I also grew from the experience.

Peace Keeping

One of my favorite verses describes God's help to me, "And the peace of God, which passes all understanding, shall keep your hearts and minds through Christ Jesus" (Phil 4:7 KJV-MOD).

There are nine fruit of the Spirit and one of them is peace. There are seven pieces of the Armor of God, one being the shoes of the Gospel of peace.

In the King James Version of the Bible the word peace is mentioned 400 times. If a person wants to absorb some peace, they can check a concordance and read these peace verses. The entire Bible can be downloaded on computer, *gratis*.

Shalom is peace in Hebrew. In a secular sense it means, hello and goodbye. In a spiritual sense it means wholeness, health, the absence of agitation and discord, and peace. Jesus is called the Prince of Peace or in Hebrew *Sar Shalom* (Isa 9:6).

I love to hear the Aaronic peace blessing sung or prayed in English and in Hebrew. I'll share it in English:

"The Lord bless you and keep you; The Lord make His face shine upon you, And be gracious unto you; The Lord lift up His countenance upon you, and give you peace" (Num 6:24-26 NKJV). Amen. Please bless your children with this scripture.

Truest Lessons are Delivered From the Heart

We've been studying the beatitudes in my previous columns. As we conclude, I'll give my concise list of how I see the eight beatitudes: 1. spiritually-reborn, 2. repentant, 3. fruitful, 4. Spirit-filled, 5. merciful, 6. pure-hearted, 7. peacemaker, and 8. witness.

I'll be talking about **Beatitude Number Eight** comprised of seven articles in *My Personal Witnessing Story* in Chapter Six- Part 1 of this book *A New Look at the News.*

The key Scripture in the beatitudes is, "... the kingdom of heaven is at hand" (Matt 3:2). God is available. "Blessed are you, when men revile you, and persecute you, and say all manner of evil against you falsely, for my sake. Rejoice and be exceedingly glad ..." (Matt 5:11-12 KJV-MOD, Eighth Beatitude).

We can have all these beatitudes in our lives because the Kingdom came to earth when Christ was born.

Be-Attitudes

Now let's segue from the beatitudes to a dimension of counseling not often practiced. A friend of mine with a PhD in clinical psychology tells about this dimension in his book, *A Far Better Life.*[20]

Dr. James Friesen, after years of counseling from what he says was more from his head than from his heart, realized that his clients were not making enough progress. He decided to add on to his field of psychological training a spiritual dimension. Jim asked some of his colleagues who used prayer in counseling to meet with him two hours once a week to pray for individual clients. This prayer experiment lasted two years.

To his delight he found that people got better faster when he added healing prayer to his counseling practice. Great breakthroughs began to happen for people with wounded hearts and souls.

Dr. Friesen says, "Now that I am a few years down the road since my initial spiritual training, I have met people of all sorts who are involved in the psychological-spiritual counseling field ... I have come to value the leaders in this field who never lose their quest for learning from both psychological and the spiritual realms. What I have found is that most of my work seems to center around Jesus' concerns, namely, that hearts need to receive healing for the wounds that produce hopelessness, contempt, lust, dishonesty, retaliation and false righteousness."[21]

My Response

I have found that the beatitudes in Matthew chapter five are only the beginning of Jesus' Sermon on the Mount. Another main theme is when Jesus elaborates on the Ten Commandments and warns us not to break them nor teach others to do so. The next primary section of Matthew is chapter six on *The Lord's Prayer*. In Matthew chapter seven, Jesus speaks against judging others, to ask God for what we need, and bear good fruit.

He ends His Sermon on the Mount with: "Therefore whosoever hears these sayings of mine, and does them, I will liken him to a wise man, who built his house upon a rock" (Matt 7:24 KJV-MOD).

Dr. Friesen's book gives inspiring teachings on Jesus' entire Sermon on the Mount, beginning to end. He also incorporates these teachings in his counseling and in his life-style. I hope you will follow his example.

This has also been my goal in what I call prayer counseling since my Inner Healing work got started back in 1976. My major book on this subject is called, *You Can Be Emotionally Free*.[22]

I like the term be-attitudes since it has the major word attitudes in it. We need to have healthy and healing attitudes not negative ones. The word comes from "Old French beatitude or Latin *beatitudo*, from *beatus* blessed."[23]

We will be a Blessing to others as we cultivate God's beatitudes.

The Ten Commandment Series
Ten Ways to be Happy – and Stay That Way

The only way we can be full of happiness and comfort is to hear God's voice.

Happiness is wonderful but fleeting. It's here today or for a moment, and then flies away. It can be as elusive as a butterfly lighting on a flower. But once you have a permanent connection and relationship with the God of the universe and know He loves you, it is easier to keep that inner happiness, or joy as the Bible terms it.

When you love someone, you want to hear his or her voice. You want your loved one near you.

One night shortly before my late husband Dennis died, he was leaving the house to drive to our nearby post office to mail some bills he had paid.

I called to him, "Dennis, do you want me to go with you?" He answered, "I always want you with me." How comforting those words were. From time to time I think about them, even now years later. They were unconditional love expressed.

The only way we can be full of happiness and comfort is to hear God's voice speaking to us in prayer and in His Word. Imagine God saying to you, "(fill in your name here), I always want you with Me!" Awesome isn't it?

Yet Jesus, the great connection between God and man, does say something similar to us recorded in the Gospel of Matthew prior to His ascension, "And, I am with you always, even to the end of the world (or age)" (Matt 28:20b KJV-MOD). He is here with you. You need to believe and hear, with your inner ears, what He says.

There are eight places in the Gospel records where from Heaven Father God publicly acclaimed His Son Jesus, "This is My beloved Son, in whom I am well pleased; hear Him!" (Matt 17:5b KJV-MOD). See also Matthew 3:17, 12:18; Mark 1:11, 9:7; Luke 3:22, 9:35, 20:13).

Mary, Jesus' mother, said to the servants at the wedding feast, "Whatever He says to you, do it" (John 2:5 KJV-MOD). Almighty Father God, and Blessed Virgin Mary are both calling us to listen to and obey our Savior Jesus Christ who, as Moses did, teaches us the Ten Commandments.

In the Beginning

The first and foundationally important time that God spoke to man was at Mt. Sinai in Arabia the third month after the children of Israel had come out of Egypt (Gal 4:25). They were beginning a long, glorious, but arduous journey. Through their leader Moses, God gave Israel Ten Commandments because He loved her and was betrothed to her.

The commandments gave the people boundaries, and yet they were also wedding vows. If they kept them, it would be a happy marriage; otherwise things would not go well (Exodus 20:1-18). I want to show you the commandments as given to Moses nearly 3,500 years before Jesus was born.

Jesus, of course read the *Torah* and these original commandments. I've heard various people say that the commandments are not needed today in the 21st century. They have also said that Jesus did not teach the Ten Commandments and I want to set that record straight.

Jesus Teaches the Ten

In the New Testament, Jesus gives us the moral law of the Ten Commandments as recorded in the Gospel of Matthew. In one powerful verse of Scripture, Jesus teaches six of the Ten Commandments of Exodus that I'll list and number for you.

"For out of the heart proceed evil thoughts (10), murders (6), adulteries, fornications (7), thefts (8), false witness (9) blasphemies (3). These are things which defile a man ..." (Matt 15:19-20 NKJV). Earlier in Matthew 15, He teaches another of the commandments, "Why do you also transgress the commandment of God because of your tradition? For God commanded, saying, 'Honor your father and mother (5) ...'" (Matt 15:3b, 4a NKJV).

In Matthew 22:37 He teaches another one, in fact the first of the ten, "... You shall love the Lord your God with all your heart, with all your soul, and with all your mind (1)" (NKJV). Then "You shall worship the Lord thy God, and Him only shall you serve (2)" (Matt 4:10b).

And "... Keep the Sabbath rest (4)" "Come unto Me, all that labour and are heavy laden, and I will give you rest ..." (10) (Matt 6:19-21) "Where your treasure is ..."

Here we see that if an individual had only one book of the Bible, the Gospel of Matthew he could find all ten of the commandments taught by Jesus Himself. I love hearing how Jesus teaches the commandments. In Matthew 5:19 Jesus strongly says that we are to teach the commandments.

1. Love God is number One (Matt 22:37).
2. Have no other gods – (idols) (Matt 4:10b).
3. No blasphemies (Matt 15:19, 20).
4. Keep the Sabbath rest (Matt 11:28-29).
5. Honor parents (Matt 15:3b, 4a).
6. No murders (Matt 15:19,20).
7. No adulteries or fornications (Matthew15:19-20).
8. No thefts (Matt 15:19-20).
9. No false witness (Matt 15:19-20).
10. We are not to covet; treasure is in Heaven (Matt 6:19-21).

Following our Lover's ten vows to Israel, and now also to us, will help us stay happy all our lives and the blessings will last through eternity! How great that is.

The commandments, or *mitsvot* (Hebrew), were the only words written by God's own hand. The Ten Commandments are honored by being put in the most Holy Ark of the Covenant. With all of this in mind, don't you think we should pay more attention to The Ten Commandments and study them more deeply?

Next time: Road to Happiness Begins with First Step.

Road to Happiness Begins with First Step

This is my second column in a series on the famous Ten Commandments.

Let's walk through these important words written to us, His followers, not looking at them as though God wants to take our fun away. Rather, let us see them as they were intended – to show how our Mighty God loves us and wants to give us a happy life, now and forever. In any activity, whether it be a church or synagogue service, a woman's retreat, or a sports activity, there must be rules and boundaries or no one will be happy. I don't know about you but I definitely do not want to live in chaos. Here is the first commandment as given to Moses:

"I am the Lord your God who brought you out of the land of Egypt, out of the house of bondage" (Exodus 20:2 NKJV).

The specific commandment is, "You shall have no other gods before Me" (Exodus 20:2 NKJV).

God begins by reminding Israel about its bondage in slavery and literally how, through His servant Moses, they were delivered. When chased by the Egyptians in horse driven chariots, miraculously Israel walked through the Red Sea as upon dry land. They received The commandments at Mt. Sinai and headed for the Promised Land.

Christians look at these words spiritually and know we too were in slavery and bondage to sin. Our leader, Jesus Christ, delivered us from slavery. He also gave The Ten Commandments and the indwelling Holy Spirit to enable us to keep them.

God is No. 1. As His betrothed bride we are told not to have any other gods before Him.

The first temptation in the Garden was to worship and obey the imposter Satan who was and is fixated on being worshipped. Speaking of being narcissistic, he expresses this malady here big time.

A few of the basic characteristics of narcissism are: excessive self-admiration, thinks he or she is always right, lacks empathy to others feelings, and has a grandiose sense of importance.[24]

What does it mean to have other gods before the Lord? Is there any entity, person, habit, or activity we are worshipping or putting in place of God?

The First Commandment is challenging us to love the Lord (*Adonai*) our God who has delivered us from spiritual death and eternal bondage. We must not have other lovers before Him but make Him first and foremost.

Of course He wants us to love our mate, children, parents, and friends. But He is talking here about an exclusive relationship with God our Creator.

Mnemonics to Help You

To help you remember the order of the commandments I want to teach you the first ten letters of the Hebrew Alphabet. These letters also are numbers and have spiritual meanings. When we finish this study together, and someone asks you what commandment number seven or four is, you will be able to answer him. Here we go.

Aleph is the first Hebrew letter "a" and numerically it means No. 1. Spiritually, *aleph* is defined as being strong and mighty. That describes God well.

It was not possible to write Hebrew letters in a news column, so I used another method. I suggested you look up the Hebrew letters in Psalm 119 in the KJV, NKJV, NIV Bibles, and of course in the Hebrew *Tehillim* (Psalms).

Why do I tell you this? Because Psalm 119 is actually an octagonal Hebrew acrostic prose poem. This means in every eight verses a new Hebrew letter begins that next series of lines. It totals 22 which equals the 22 letters of the basic Hebrew alphabet. The message of the Psalm is to help Jew and Christian – all believers – live a faith-filled live.[25]

Hebrew Lesson: To draw the letter "*aleph*" begin making a capital N. Now draw the diagonal line a little higher and a little lower than a capital N. The letters I will give you are how the original Phoenician letters changed when the children of Israel were in Babylonian captivity.

To me Babylonian derived Hebrew letters are easier to write and remember than Phoenician letters.

Jesus learned these Hebrew letters when He was a little boy. Have fun learning what He was taught in childhood.

Make God No. 1. "You shall have no other God's before Me."

False Idols Beckon but True Path Is Clear

The Ten Commandments are not out of date but more relevant and important all the time. There are numerous promises of blessings in the Bible for those who keep God's moral law.

Our last time together we reviewed God's First Commandment: "You shall have no other gods before Me" (Exodus 20:3 NIV). That is short and easy to remember. The second is longer and therefore a bit harder to recall.

"You shall not make for yourself an idol in the form of anything in heaven above or on the earth beneath or in the waters below. You shall not bow down to them or worship them; for I, the Lord your God, am a jealous God ..." (Exodus 20:4 NIV).

Why does God say He's jealous? Because His chosen people got into idolatry big time while Moses was seeking God on Mount Sinai.

The sin of idolatry or seeking another god, a false god, is best represented in the orgy of the golden calf. God had just brought the children of Israel out of slavery in Egypt, and now while Moses is with God on Mt. Sinai, they are committing spiritual adultery against God! How soon we forget. (Exodus 32:1-25).

Dr. Laura says, "The Israelites, after waiting 40 days for Moses to come down from Mount Sinai, thought he was dead or had deserted them. They fell back into old patterns by building themselves a god representation – a golden calf. Idolatry, with its physical representation of gods, was so enticing to the Israelites that the prophets had to chastise the people about it repeatedly."[26]

Pornography

What is the particular relevance of idols to our day? One idol is pornography, especially of the female body – often smuggled into our homes by the internet. This is a big temptation for emotionally needy men or women. It can become an addiction, waste a lot of time and money, set a bad example for the children, eventually harm one's marriage, make one vulnerable to spiritual attacks and cause separation from God's presence.

Astrology

Another example of an idol is astrology. Webster says it is "a method or theory based on the assumption that the positions of the moon, sun, and stars affect human affairs and can be used to tell the future."[27]

In other words, instead of seeking their Creator and His Word, they may choose to let a pseudoscience astrologer guide them to make important decisions about his or her future. This is not the way to know who to marry, where to live, where to work, what to believe!

One of the serious effects of allowing astrological teachings to direct one's life is they can bring about negative repercussions for a life time (Deut 18:10-12).

No, the American Idol TV program is not necessarily an idol, nor is a decorated Christmas tree, unless of course you bow down to worship a person or a tree! Personally I'd prefer American Ideal rather than use the term idol.

You can think of other true idols to avoid. The Bible has at least 50 Scriptures on this topic.

Hebrew Lesson: In our study of the First Commandment we learned how to write No. 1 or *Aleph*. This time we'll learn the letter *Bet,* the second letter in the Hebrew alphabet.

Numerically, *Bet* means No. 2 and, spiritually, it's a symbol of blessing and creation. The two-syllable word *Beit (Be-it)* literally means home.

To draw the *Bet,* it looks like a backwards capital "B" with the middle of the front open and a large dot called a doggish in the top. Check Psalm 119 in the NKJV Bible to see the Hebrew letters. Without the doggish the letter becomes a V.

A good question to ask is this, Are there any idols in my home (*Be-it*)? If so, let's clean house physically and spiritually and then call for the dump truck.

Abusing God Verbally Is Not Acceptable

The Third Commandment is broken by a lot of people, and if you work in a job in the marketplace you'll know what I mean. The commandment is:

"Do not take the Name of the Lord your God in vain. For the Lord will not hold guiltless one who takes His Name in vain" (Exodus 20:7 KJV-MOD).

First of all, we need to know who God is when trying to obey His commandments. God encountered Moses at a burning bush that did not burn up. Once God had Moses' attention, He told him that he wanted him to go to Egypt to bring the children of Israel out of Egyptian bondage.

Moses asked this God of the burning bush, "Who shall I say sent me?" God told Moses to tell them, "I am who I am" sent you (Exodus 3:14).

When you're talking to the Creator of the universe and all that is in it, including yourself, you can expect an answer that is beyond your understanding.

Well, Moses decided to go on this extended rescue mission camping trip which would include over a million people. Moses accepted the challenge because God promised to go with him; he trusted Him and believed he would succeed. And he did, eventually.

Theologically we find, "The two essential and personal names of God in the Heb. Scriptures are *Elohim* and Jehovah (more correctly *Yahweh*); the former calling attention to the fullness of divine power, the latter meaning 'He who is' and thus declaring the divine self-existence."[28] God is a Spirit and reveals Himself in the Old Testament through His mighty acts.

In the New Testament, God the Father often reveals Himself through His Son, Jesus Christ. Now for the first time we can physically see God because Scripture teaches that Jesus is made in the likeness of His Father and is "... the brightness of His glory and the express image of His person ..." (Heb 1:3 (NKJV).

Before Jesus returned to His Father in Heaven we are introduced to the Holy Spirit who will reveal Jesus to those who are open (John 16:5-15). Here we see the Triune God.

167

Taking God's Name in Vain

When a person takes God's name in vain, he is speaking against God: Father, Son, and Holy Spirit! Often Jesus Christ, Son of God, gets the brunt of the offences of cursing or damning His name.

Have you ever been around a person, perhaps in your place of business, whose language is filled with expletives that are cursing or damning Father God or Jesus? Actually this person may have learned his form of speech from father, mother, or siblings. He may or may not realize what he is doing.

Not only is this individual breaking the Third Commandment and abusing God's name, he is abusing the people who are hearing him speak this way. When these words are spoken over and over they may go down into the subconscious of the speaker and the hearer. It's like bad seeds being planted in the garden of the soul.

Perhaps you've found it necessary to walk out of profane movies or turn off profane TV programs. Don't let your mind get hardened into accepting profane speech.

Hebrew Lesson: This time we'll learn the letter *Gimel* (the third letter in the Hebrew alphabet – G). Numerically *Gimel* means No. 3 and spiritually it means to humble yourself before God.

To make the letter you will draw a camel starting with a flat line for its head. Bring the line down for a long neck, then branch out for the right leg. Now make the left leg.

Gamal is the Hebrew word for camel, an animal that must kneel to lap up water. This third letter, *Gimel,* reminds us to humble our tongues.

This letter has helped me, and I believe it will help you remember the important Third Commandment.

Sabbath Is There for Those Who Reach Out

Why is it a good idea to go to a place of worship and fellowship at least one day a week?

Pick out your answer: (1) It's good for my business. (2) Who knows, I just might learn something. (3) It's a good place to find a date. (4) I like their coffee bar. (5) God commanded me to have one special day a week devoted to Him, family, and friends.

Did you have one or several answers? I hope you'll eventually choose the concluding answer.

Let's see what the Bible says about the Fourth Commandment: "Remember the Sabbath day to keep it holy" (Exodus 20:8).

"Six days you shall labor and do all your work, but the seventh day is the Sabbath of the LORD your God ..." (Exodus 20:9 NKJV). See also Exodus 10:10-11.

The Jews celebrate their Sabbath on the seventh day of the week according to Exodus 20:9. Deuteronomy 5:12-15 adds that it is in commemoration of coming out of Egyptian bondage, and Moses receiving the commandments on Mount Sinai. The Jewish holy day begins at sunset on Friday and concludes at sunset on Saturday.

The Christian celebrates the Lord's Day, their Sabbath, on the first day of the week, commemorating the Resurrection of Jesus Christ that brought them out of bondage to sin and death (Luke 24:1, John 20:1).

While there are some differences in the way these two faiths celebrate their chosen Sabbaths, it is a day revered by both as a holy, peace-filled day. It is healthy to have one day a week for a Sabbath rest.

United Nations Prayer

In October, 2008, I was invited to a meeting at the United Nations building in New York City. The World Prayer Congress (WPC) group led by Roberta Hromas came to the UN to pray for protection for New York City, for those injured during the 9-11 attack in 2001, and for the survivors' emotional healing.

This experience reminded me of how many people came to church or synagogue in large numbers in the months following 9-11-2001. All of a sudden, people realized the importance of being in closer touch with God. All of a sudden, life as usual could not be counted on. All of a sudden, we wondered how we could learn to hear God's voice.

Then – life returned to normal with a huge hole left at ground zero and in many hearts.

Yes, we at World Prayer Congress prayerfully drove by ground zero on 9-11 and saw the work that was at a standstill with scaffolding and machinery stopped. It's expensive to finish this memorial to the 3,000 dead.

Progress is finally being made on this location now.

Pray for our president and all governmental officials, and our candidates and their families. Pray and, if you can, fast, for America!

Let us fill the churches and synagogues, including every religion that would like to pray with us, and see what God can do to show us the way out of fiscal cliffs.

Let us take time to get into prayer.

Hebrew Lesson: Let's learn the fourth Hebrew letter. *Dalet* numerically is No. 4, and means door. It reminds you to be present at the door of God's House. Remember the Sabbath Day, to keep it holy is the Fourth Commandment (Exodus 20:8).

Draw a straight horizontal line for the top of the doorway. Now draw the right side of the doorway down to the bottom of the door. See that the lintel of the door goes a little past the vertical line. Now stop.

You have to visualize the left side of the door, as it isn't there. Can you picture it? Good. See the door by faith. Now practice your "a, b, g"s and now "d"s in Hebrew.

Trouble at Home? Honor Your Parents

How hard it is to hear about a child who, after reaching nineteen years of age, turns against her mother and will have nothing to do with her. She won't even speak to her unless her words are full of profanity.

Think of how many meals that mother has prepared, clothes she has bought, shoes she has tied, baths that have been given, time spent cooking and feeding the child, help given with the child's homework. All these gifts are just for starters.

What about the Fifth Commandment? It seems that many children and adults have not learned about this commandment or its value:

"Honor your father and your mother, that your days may be long upon the land which the Lord your God is giving you" (Exodus 20:12 NKJV).

When I realized Dennis was going to propose to me, I phoned my father and got his approval. He said, "If he proposes, do not hesitate to say yes."

My Father over many years had verbally disapproved of most young men I had dated, but this time he gave me the okay. I'm sure Dennis was the next one to call my dad. I was honored to have Dad walk me down the aisle to give me away.

Family's Support

My mother had late onset diabetes so I needed to shop for her. I was able to buy an aqua blue two-piece dress for her to wear to my wedding.

My brother, Bob, and his wife put on the reception at their country club and my parents were the last ones there, laughing and having fun until Dennis and I left to board our plane to the Bahamas.

My parents lived in their own home to the end of their days and never needed a retirement home. After my parents' death, my siblings and I got together to purchase headstones for their graves.

If in your young adult years you were so wrapped up in yourself you didn't have or take time to remember your parents, what we did could give you some ideas. It's not too late for you. You could also purchase flowers for your church in memory of your parents.

Maybe you and your siblings, and grandchildren, could help write their memoirs. Or, if they are still alive, you can record the messages they want to leave behind.

Psychologist Dr. Laura says, "The command to honor parents cannot be absolute. If a parent tells his or her child to violate a civil or moral law, the child has no obligation to honor the request … Our relationship to God always has precedence over our relationship to our parents"[29]

In other words, not every parent can be fully honored, but do work on healing your past memories to forgive him or her. If you do, you may eventually want to dust off an old picture of that parent and restore it to the gallery of family photos. My book on emotional healing can help you.[30]

Dishonoring One's Parent Is Not Healthy

The Fifth Commandment is the only one with a promise – that of a long life. This can also mean that living a life of love and respect will make you healthier in the years you do have to live.

It is important to teach your children The Ten Commandments, "And you shall teach them thoroughly to your children" (Deut 6:7 KJV-MOD). It does not say for the pastor or rabbi to teach them, but you, dear parent.

Hebrew Lesson: Let's learn the fifth Hebrew letter: *Heh* numerically is No. 5, and means breath of God and long life. The sound of the h is made by an exhalation of breath. To draw a picture, make a capital H. Now erase the bar across the middle of H and put it on top. Then on the top left side, erase one-fourth of it. This leaves a chimney space where you can imagine the breath going out. Ready everybody? Say, "Heh."

This should remind you of the longer and better life you can have by honoring your parents.

Murder of Innocents Is the Epitome of Evil

Moses recorded the sixth commandment received from God on Mount Sinai about 3,500 years ago: "Do not murder" (Exodus 20:13 CJB).

A simple meaning is the premeditated taking of another person's life. The Hebrew word for murder is *tirtzach*, which reflects wrongful killing.

The deaths of 3,000 souls at the Twin Towers in New York City on Sept. 11, 2001 by foreign hijackers of jet airliners, planned and premeditated for years, was outright murder. The terrorists on each plane also murdered themselves by committing suicide, a crime against self and their Creator.

Self-defense, individually or in war or capital punishment, is allowed in the Bible. Self-defense is very different from murder. Also, an accidental death is not considered murder. One can think of many examples.

My late husband, Dennis, in his early years was a pacifist – that is, opposed to war. It seemed to him the right way to go, until he was married in his early twenties to Elberta and began to have children. Then he knew he would certainly have to defend his family if their lives were threatened.

Dr. Laura Schlessinger says, "As for the notion that 'only God can take a life,' note that capital punishment for murder of an innocent is mandated in each of the (*Torah*) Five Books of Moses ... In fact it is the only law in the *Torah* repeated in each and every one of the Five Books! Obviously, this was an important divine consideration! I find it morally abhorrent that some equate capital punishment with murder. The murder of an innocent is clearly different from the societal determination to eliminate an evildoer."[31]

Jesus' Example

Jesus warns against abusing an innocent child. "Whoever causes one of these little ones who believe in Me to sin, it would be better for him if a millstone were hung around his neck, and he were drowned in the depth of the sea" (Matt 18:6 NKJV). Here, Jesus is saying that this sin is deserving of most serious consequences.

When Jesus died on an old rugged tree formed into a cross, it was a case of premeditated murder by the Romans and religious leaders of that day. Jesus told the people about another Kingdom to come and demonstrated it by feeding the multitudes, healing the deaf, the lame and the blind, restoring the brokenhearted, setting captives free, and saving human souls.

His spiritual Kingdom talk and action perhaps made these leaders fear they would lose their jobs, their following, and their popularity. They did not understand that this loving man was the Son of God and that He and His Father, *Yahweh,* actually created The Ten Commandments that were given on Mount Sinai.

His Kingdom was not of this world system and He had come to rescue them from the dark kingdom of greed, betrayal, and lostness.

Though the Son of God was murdered and martyred, He rose from death and after 40 days ascended into Heaven. Before Jesus left He said He'd be back for us. "... I will come again and receive you to Myself; that where I am, there you may be also" (John 14:3 NKJV).

In this day of banking instability, we need money market values we can count on. One unfailing currency value you and I can always bank on is the written and living Word of God.

Hebrew Lesson: Let's learn the sixth Hebrew letter: *Vav* numerically is No. 6, also the number of man, and it means hook or nail. The letter reminds us that when Jesus, the sinless Son of God, was nailed to the cross, redemption for mankind's sin became possible.

To draw this letter, draw one straight vertical line a quarter of an inch long. Now draw a flat head on the nail, extended slightly to the left. It looks something like a nail. By backsliding from our faith, we crucify Christ afresh (Heb 6:6). *Vav,* when added to the front of a word with vowels, means and. Its sound can change: *Veh, Vah, Voo.*

Vav has many meanings, but remember it is Commandment No.6.

Roadmap Shows Way to Non-adulterous Life

A specific rule is set up with the Seventh Commandment to honor the institution of marriage. "You shall not commit adultery" (Exodus 20:14 NKJV). Adultery is voluntary sexual intercourse between a married person and someone other than the lawful spouse. Adultery comes from the term adulterate, which means to make impure or contaminate.

Biblical, marital sex is a sacred act within a relationship – between two people of the opposite sex who are committed to one another for life. From the beginning this was God's prototype.

Since men are God's sparkplugs to keep the human race in existence, they may be more easily tempted. It is important for married men to have moral boundaries to protect themselves from being vulnerable.

Recently a friend told me that Billy Graham, throughout his marriage, kept the rule that he would not go out to lunch with a woman other than his wife. Ruth Graham died June 14, 2007, after a long and happy life with Billy. Dr. Graham had his 90th birthday in November of 2008. He's 95 in November 2013.

Stephen Arterburn's book *Every Man's Battle* is a great help to win the war on sexual temptation. "From the television to the Internet, print media to videos, men are constantly faced with the assault of sensual images. It is impossible to avoid such temptations … but, thankfully, not impossible to rise above them." [32]

When tempted sexually by one's unregenerate nature and hormonal rush – good advice is, "Run like mad, and do not look back!" Although a Hebrew slave in Egypt, Joseph, Jacob's youngest son, knew the Seventh Commandment. One day Joseph was pursued by his master Pontiphar's wife to commit adultery. He followed this commandment by running from her as fast as he could go (Gen 39:10-12)!

Women Tempted Too

Women have their sexual needs and temptations, too. There are seductive women, with flattering lips, who steal financially stable husbands from their mates at the prime of their life. The book of Proverbs warns of such women in chapters 6 and 7. "Whoever commits adultery with a woman lacks understanding; He who does so destroys his own soul" (Prov 6:32 NKJV).

As the marriage years go by, couples must keep strengthening their relationship. Physical changes through age, disease, or surgery can challenge a marriage. Children and their multitude of problems can weigh heavily on a couple. Sex is a gift and an important part of a healthy marital relationship. Of course love is more than sex. True love is for eternity. (See *Sexual Happiness in Marriage* by Herbert J. Miles, Ph.D.)[33]

Adultery vs. Fornication: One thing that concerned me about Commandment No. 7 is that it spoke against adultery but didn't mention fornication. Fornication is voluntary sexual intercourse between two unmarried adults. It is a huge problem in our culture, with growing numbers of young people tossing marriage out the window.

English editions of the Old Testament use the word fornication only six times. The New Testament gives 35 references (Strong's Concordance). I found also that in most new translations or paraphrases of the Bible, the term sexual immorality is used to cover both adultery and fornication. I gained more clarity as I studied.

Fornication in Greek comes from *porneia*. See the comparison with the words pornography and pornographic. Pornography is considered a form of either adultery or fornication.

The good news is we have a road map, the Bible, that shows us how to live an abundant life. It shows that God is merciful, and when asked He will forgive our sins and set us on the right and happiest pathway. The Ten Commandments are part of those guidelines for life. You're on your way!

Hebrew Lesson: The seventh Hebrew letter *Zahyin* (z) numerically is No 7. It means weapon and looks like an axe, reminding us that adultery cuts between a man and woman. To draw this Hebrew letter, make one straight vertical line a quarter of an inch long. Now draw a horizontal line on top of the axe handle, facing left. Make a short vertical line for the cutting edge. This symbol reminds you to honor, not destroy, your marriage.

Steal Now, Pay Later With a Shriveled Soul

The Ten Commandments are a large part of my value system. They are boundaries assisting my conscience.

The conscience develops from our environment – what we see, and also what we are taught by the adults in our lives. If those parents have healthy biblical values, the healthier their children have the opportunity to become.

It's just the opposite with parents whose values are, "Do your own thing. Anything goes."

The Eighth Commandment God gives us is clear and concise: "You shall not steal" (Exodus 20:15 NKJV). See also Mark 10:19.

We are not born with a value-coded conscience so we must be taught and born again into God's family, and changed from the inside out. God then puts his law in our spiritual hearts but we have free wills and can still resist. We believers still need to learn the moral laws of God's Ten Commandments in order to live righteous lives. We also need to teach them to our children.

A friend told how she had repeated the commandments to her pastor from her childhood days as she went to confession monthly. Now as a senior citizen, she realized through further study that she had never been taught the meanings. It was all by rote. This was a revelation to her!

Knowing right from wrong does not come automatically. We must continue to be students of the Bible all our lives. Our born again spirits are new creations joined to the Lord, but our Christian souls – intellects, wills, and emotions may need to be cleansed daily. If that's not true, then why did Jesus teach us to pray: "Forgive me my sins as I forgive those who sin against me, and lead me, not into temptation but deliver me from evil" (Matt 6:12-13 KJV-MOD and personalized).

The more we live the right way according to God's Word, the healthier our souls become and better witnesses we will be.

Harassing Phone Calls

Some of the dishonest people who bother me today are those who call on my phone with an anxiety-producing electronic message: "I'm calling to warn you that your credit card is overdrawn. Contact company X immediately or you will be in serious trouble!"

Since I pay my bills on time, I can with assurance hang up the phone immediately. Calling on the phone in this fashion is not what a legitimate business would do. You would first be notified in the mail, not by a recorded phone call or an email.

Lying usually accompanies stealing. These people are out to make you fearful, so you will tell them about your finances. Then you may have further trouble financially.

Honest Abe

Have you ever gone to the grocery store and found that you weren't charged for an item? Have you gone to a restaurant and found that you were under-charged? Have you ever found lost money in a store? What did you do? Was it the right thing? Did you feel good about it? Or did you take what wasn't yours and harden your heart?

It is said of Abraham Lincoln that he was very honest from his youth. As a young clerk in a store, he accidentally overcharged a customer by a few cents. Abe walked several miles to the person's house to return it.

Becoming known then as Honest Abe, he is an example to us, and became a great 16th President.

There are so many things that can be stolen, such as your reputation, identity, job, mate, family, place in politics, credit card, exam information, computer information, mail, your innocence.

Today, with the falling economy, we seem to be paying the price for having had an over-abundance of prosperity. We've gotten greedy in wanting more and more money for more and more possessions.

When will God say, "It is enough!" Maybe He will give us time to repent from greed, pride, and immorality, and give our country – and us individually – a chance to make a new start.

We cannot, however, spend our time blaming others. We have to start with No. 1. This change for our country starts with me and with you.

Hebrew Lesson: Let's learn the eighth Hebrew letter. *Chet* numerically is No. 8. This letter has no English equivalent. It looks like the top of a fence. A fence keeps people from stealing and for trespassing on another's property.

To draw this Hebrew letter *Chet*, draw a lower case "n" in English. Enlarge the "n" and place other "ns" beside it and another to make what looks like a fence. Remember the meaning of this important letter is: do not steal.

Hurtful Lies Define Those Who Tell Them

I think one of the reasons an adult gossips, or gives false evidence against another, is that she or he is modeling after a parent who spent a lot of time on the phone or with friends criticizing others. Too often we pass on our sins.

In this column we'll look at the Ninth Commandment given to Moses on Mt. Sinai 3,500 years ago. "You shall not bear false witness against your neighbor" (Exodus 20:16 NKJV). A short way to say this is, "You shall not lie."

Webster's Dictionary defines a lie as: "To make an untrue statement with intent to deceive." [34]

Daniel Webster knew that in politics it is common practice to make numerous promises that one cannot keep. Yet we, the public, hang on to every word and sincerely hope that what we hear is the truth.

When the media shares all the rumors about the candidates, it turns out to be one of the greatest legitimate gossip sessions imaginable. It's also great for ratings as the public is glued to the media hoping to learn something beneficial.

Some, of course, are listening for any gossip they can glean to use against the opposition.

Honest George

History shows that George Washington, our first president, was reluctant to tell a lie. Yet a hoax was begun about George – that he as a child cut down his father's cherry tree. Supposedly, he had to admit, "Yes, father I cut down the cherry tree."

So this false story has followed a great president's memory to the present. I know I've heard it in a joke form. It goes around just like many unfortunate hoax/lies on internet.

A friend of mine was sued by her neighbor. She fought the false accusation for seven years in order to clear her name. What fortitude and faith she had! During what became the final court session the judge said to her, "You are a fine woman of integrity. This case is closed." In anger, the accusing neighbor pushed over the table where he and his lawyer were sitting. The anger was a shock in the courtroom, but it was great that truth won!

Says Dr. Laura, "The Ninth Commandment specifically prohibits lying under oath in a court of law. We call it perjury when a person knowingly gives false testimony under oath ... More than one witness is required for convictions, especially of capital crimes."[35]

"A single witness shall not rise up against a man on account of any iniquity or any sin which he has committed; on the evidence of two or three witnesses a matter shall be confirmed" (Deuteronomy19:15 NASB).

How does God feel about lying, one may ask? Proverbs tells us. "There are six things the Lord hates ... a lying tongue ... " (Prov 6:16-17 NKJV). "Lying lips are an abomination to the Lord ..." (Prov 12:22 NKJV).

Truth is a divine characteristic. Let us allow His divine life to shine through us to our world.

Hebrew Lesson: Let's learn the ninth Hebrew letter. *Tet* (English t) numerically is No. 9 in the alphabet (*Alef-Bet*), and in ancient Hebrew means to surround or to twist.

To draw this Hebrew letter, make a lower case u, several times larger than mine. Leave the left top side as it is – straight up, but make the right top beginning to twist like a snake around the letter's shoulder.

This letter represents a person who through false speech is lying about a known or unknown neighbor. He or she is therefore hob-knobbing with the dark lying spirit – and is spiritually in a dangerous position.

Let this letter "*tet*" remind us of the danger of being a false witness.

Acquisition of Things Is Not the Right Answer

Many wars in our world have begun through the sin of coveting. Consider the tiny land of Israel (about the size of New Jersey). When the famous writer Mark Twain was alive, he visited Israel and reported that he was not impressed with its barren land.

But when Israel became a nation in 1948, its people made great sacrifices to develop their new homeland. One plan was to develop Kibbutzim where many of the population lived in different communities. Their success took three decades of hard labor, and children being cared for by the community while parents went out to work in the farmlands. A Hebrew tutor told me what that was like in his childhood.

Now, 60 years later, the land has blossomed and as the Scripture says, it is a land of milk and honey. Israel's produce shipped abroad is some of the best.

When I was there in Israel in 2004, most everyone in my tour group planted a tree in the forest. This constant planting helps the land and environment greatly. Yet, constant bombing through covetous hearts is destroying parts of Israel.

Every successful nation has to protect what is theirs, because someone will want what they have and may try to take it by force. This is true for America and for all successful countries. It would be so nice not to need the great sacrifice and the expense of our military forces for protection, but it won't easily happen on a fallen planet.

Until our hearts are changed, we will continue to covet what another has. Some wise people have allowed God to touch their hearts to heal them from greed, but the percentage is not enough for a safe world. In this column, I'm sharing on Commandment No 10: "You shall not covet your neighbor's house; You shall not covet your neighbor's wife, male servant or his female servant ... or anything that belongs to your neighbor" (Exodus 20:17 NASB). This gets right down to our own personal property. Our neighborhoods. Our family.

A Covetous Heart or a Healed Heart

A covetous person is never happy or satisfied for long. He or she always wants what others have, their home, their car, their boat. They are constantly over-spending, then have to borrow money in order to have what the Jones's have. This attitude and lifestyle are part of the explanation for our recent economic failures in America. You and I may not be able to change the whole world but we can change ourselves, with help from our higher power – who is God.

"How?" you may ask. Try praying and ask your heavenly Father to change your craving for things. Have fellowship with believing people who are givers and not takers. Hang out with non-covetous people. Look up the words covet, covetousness in the concordance of your Bible, or Google the words online.

Look up Jesus' words in Luke 12:15-21, which begins: "And He said to them, 'Take heed and beware of covetousness, for one's life does not consist in the abundance of the things he possesses'" (NKJV).

180

Immerse yourself with healthy thinking. You will then have a much happier time during the holidays and birthdays. Be free! Covet only God's spiritual beatitudes, fruits, and gifts.

Hebrew Lesson: Let's learn the tenth Hebrew letter: *Yod*. It is the smallest of the Hebrew letters! Draw an English comma, only increase it about five times its size. This letter has no English equivalent.

The *Yod* is close to the word for hand in Hebrew, or *yad*. Your memory prompter is to remind you of the connection of the hand *yad*, and the Hebrew letter *Yod*. "You shall not covet" is Commandment No. 10.

You now have collected the ten Hebrew letters and lessons during these last ten columns. Do practice saying them aloud. Dave, one of my early column readers, recited his letters to me at the Driftwood Players Theater where *Fiddler on the Roof* was playing. You will soon be able to remember The Ten Commandments in order.

Chapter 5

Jesus' Commands Series
Seven Festivals Fulfilled Series, Psalm 91 Series
Breaking News and Healing Prayers - Poetry
Psalm 23 Series, Christmas and New Years

Front Door of Heaven (illustration above) – The glorious main entrance makes an awesome boulevard leading us to the throne of God which is encircled with an emerald rainbow of light. Jesus the good Shepherd led you safely Home. One day we'll be dancing down the streets of gold to our Triune God's throne. Abba is waiting.

Jesus' Commandments (Six Articles)
Resolve to Learn [and Obey] The Commandments

We have been doing some pretty deep and creative studying of the Ten Commandments in chapter four and going on to build on them in this and further Chapters.

I have enjoyed doing the research for this important topic. Just seeing the Ten Commandments concisely printed somewhere is not as clear or interesting as it is when delving into the text more deeply.

It could be compared to swimming on the surface of the ocean, or donning a snorkel mask or scuba diving equipment and going deeper for a better look at the sea creatures around you.

Learning to recite the Ten Commandments is taught in many churches and synagogues. Yet I've noticed that over the years remembering the commandments in order is often forgotten or perhaps never learned.

Ever since I learned the commandments, together with the ten letters of the Hebrew Alphabet as mnemonics (letters, pictures, ideas for remembering), I have not forgotten them or the order. That's why I taught you the Hebrew letters to go along with the commandments. For review see below the commandment, Hebrew letter, and mnemonic.

1. "You shall have no other gods before Me." "*Aleph.*" One Strong, mighty God.
2. "Do not engrave idols nor worship them." "*Bet.*" What's in your home (*beit*)?
3. "Do not take the Name of the Lord God in vain." "*Gimel.*" Humble camel (*gamal*) kneels to drink. We need to humble our speech.
4. "Remember the Sabbath day to keep it holy." "*Delet.*" Door to God's house.
5. "Honor your father and mother – for a long life." "*Heh.*" Human breath – expel.
6. "You shall do no murder." "*Vav.*" Hook or nail. He was nailed.
7. "You shall not commit adultery." "*Zayin.*" Weapon or axe cuts between a couple.
8. "You shall not steal." "*Chet.*" Looks like a fence. A fence keeps out intruders.

9. "You shall not bear false witness against your neighbor." "*Tet.*" Like a snake wraps around shoulder.
10. "You shall not covet a neighbor's wife, servant, property." "*Yod.*" A hand or "*Yad*" that covets, then takes.

Why learn the Ten Commandments? Because God said to. Because you'll be happier if you do. Because it will keep you out of a lot of trouble. Because you'll be able to teach them to your children, siblings, and others. Because these were the only words written by God's own hand on tablets of stone. Because when you see God at the end of your life you'll be glad that you lived as His disciple.

In fact, for your New Year's resolution, or Lent, or Day of Atonement or *Yom Kippur*, learning and practicing the commandments would be a great decision and would have life-lasting effects.

Psalm 119 has all 22 letters of the Hebrew alphabet in increments of every eight verses. It is quite an amazing chapter. You already know the letters and spiritual meaning for the first ten. Try applying the spiritual meaning to the octave stanza of the same letter. *Aleph* (1) for the first eight verses.

If you could read it in Hebrew, you would see that each octave begins the sentence with that exact Hebrew letter. Psalm 119 is the longest and most unique Psalm in the Bible. Read it.

Here are some good commandment verses. "And I will delight myself in Your commandments, which I love. My hands also will I lift up to Your commandments … And I will meditate on Your statutes" (Psalm 119:47-48 NKJV).

If you make obeying the First Commandment your priority, it will help you keep all the others. Make God number One in your life, your one and only triune God.

Deuteronomy says, "And You shall love the Lord Your God with all your heart, and with all Your soul, and with all your might" (Deut 6:5 KJV-MOD). He will love you back.

Guidelines: For the best listing of the Ten Commandments go to Exodus 20:1-17 and Deuteronomy 5:1-22.

After The Ten Commandments, What's Next?

One Sunday at St. Albans during the coffee hour, quite a few parishioners were reading *The Edmonds Beacon.* Betty Bell had been faithfully bringing the paper to church, and consequently this column had been read by quite a few members.

In conversation I said to Pastor John, "I've now completed teaching The Ten Commandments so I'll have to think of another topic."

He said grinning, "Is there an eleventh?"

I responded with a smile. "Well, I have been thinking a good follow-up to the Ten Commandments, through Moses in the Old Testament, would be to give some of Jesus' commandments in the New Testament."

Now I'll continue my thoughts with you, the reader. I know Bible commentators do not normally describe what Jesus says as His commandments. For instance, The Twelve Commandments of Jesus are, and then a list.

We know all His words are important. Yet what I consider commandments by Jesus are concise statements He made that are very emphatic. This will be the basis of my new series.

A good quote from Jesus says it well. "If you keep My commandments, you will abide in My love, just as I have kept My Father's commandments and abide in His love" (John 15:10 NKJV).

Jesus goes on to say, "This is My commandment, that you love one another as I have loved you" (John 15:12 NKJV). Here is that most wonderful word, love.

Life giving,

Other centered,

Victorious living,

Everlasting love.

I think God sets standards too high for us to reach so that we'll keep on our toes reaching for the heights.

To love as He loved us is to be willing to lay down our lives for one another. That's going all the way with love. Some have done this in a heroic moment on the battlefield, or a mother has when giving birth to a baby, or a father when searching for his lost child in a hurricane or snow bank.

Even humanistic psychologists such as Carl Rogers taught students to treat clients with "unconditional positive regard."[1] That is well said and a positive goal that can help the client begin to accept him or herself.

But beyond that is Jesus' concept that we should treat one another with unconditional *agape* love.

185

There are three levels of love in Greek, *eros, phileo* and *agape*. The first is physical love, the second is friendship, and the third is self-giving unconditional love. The Amplified Bible in John 21: 8-17 greatly amplifies the Greek meanings in English. As I tell the fishing story of Jesus and His disciples, I use the more concise Greek meanings for these three levels of love. [2]

Greatest Kind of Love

In the gospel of John, chapter 21, there is the story of reconciliation of Peter and the newly resurrected Lord Jesus.

Peter saw a man on the beach who called out, "Cast your net on the other side of the boat!" As soon as they followed His instructions, the disciples miraculously had an overflowing catch of 153 fish!

Realizing it was the Lord, Peter jumped in the water to go to Him.

Jesus had been cooking fish and bread so was able to feed the disciples right away. When they were full and relaxed, Jesus asked Peter, "Do you love [*agape*] Me (love Me unconditionally) more than these [monetary value of the fish]?"

Peter answered, "Lord, you know I [*phileo*] like you as a friend." Jesus says, "Feed My lambs."

Jesus asks again, "Peter do you [*agape*] Me?"

Peter answers, "Jesus You know that I [*phileo*] like you." Jesus says, "Feed My sheep."

A third time Jesus asks the question differently, "Peter do you [*phileo*] like Me?" Peter with grief answered, "Lord, you know that I [*phileo*] like You." Jesus says, "Feed My sheep." (John 21:15-17, Author's paraphrase from the Greek.)

By the third time, Jesus had revealed to Peter that his love for Him had been diminishing. We too need to check our love for God and see if it has been diminished or if we're really on fire for Him.

Peter had also three times denied knowing Jesus before His crucifixion. It shows Jesus' unconditional love for him in that He asked three times if he loved Him. He also took time to make sure that Peter knew he was forgiven. The Lord was also calling Peter to carry on the Christian faith after Jesus' return to His Father in Heaven. Peter was asked, metaphorically, to feed the adult human sheep and the young human lambs.

Fortunately, a short time later the Day of Pentecost arrived and Peter's love for God the Son would be ignited forever, with the greatest love, *agape*. The power of the Holy Spirit was just what Peter needed for his call to ministry.

A New, Different Life is Just a Prayer Way

Together we have intensely studied the great Ten Commandments God gave to the world through Moses. Jesus also taught the Ten Commandments in the New Testament. If you only had the Gospel of Matthew, you could find these same Ten Commandments given to Moses on Mount Sinai as I demonstrated in the previous chapter.

Now I want to show you some of the emphatic words of Jesus that are believed by many to be God's further commandments to us.

To His followers Jesus said, "Go therefore and make disciples of all the nations … teaching them to observe all things that **I have commanded you**; and lo, I am with you always, even to the end of the age" (Matt 28:19-20 NKJV).

What are the all things He has commanded us to do?

You must be born again is one of these commandments (John 3:7b). What we might call the eleventh commandment.

Let me give you an example of what this means. I'm a member of a book club that read the *New York Times* bestseller, *Amazing Grace* by Eric Metaxas.[3]

It is about an Englishman, William Wilberforce, who lived several centuries ago and made a great impact on the world. He headed the heroic campaign to end slavery in England.

Three days before his death, July 29, 1833, the House of Commons passed the bill abolishing slavery in the British Empire. He heard the news before his death.

Amazing Grace describes how untold thousands of African men from their coasts were picked up in boats, shackled together in twos and packed like sardines on ships. Many died before they were ever sold into slavery. Some were thrown overboard so the ship captain could receive insurance money for their lives!

Many of the British populace were not aware of these horrific activities of slave trade as it was kept quiet.

Born Again

Why am I telling you this? Because chapter five of Metaxas's book is called, *Ye Must Be Born Again.*

As a wealthy young man in England, Wilberforce spent much of his time eating, drinking, and partying. He had become close to the prime minister's son, named Pitt, and through their friendship had become a popular member of Parliament.

Young William at age 26 was led to Christ through some spontaneous Greek New Testament studies with a Methodist scholar and friend, Isaac Milner. Milner was eventually able to answer all of Wilberforce's questions.

At this time, evangelist John Wesley was still alive and the fledgling Methodist denomination was Wilberforce's choice.

The book describes the young political orator's spiritual experience.

"He had lived so long for his own ambition that to live for God, as he now longed to do, was a foreign and strange proposition and would take time to sort out. Two changes manifested themselves right away: the first was a new attitude toward money, the second toward time."

The Great Change

"Before 'the great change,' Wilberforce had reckoned his money and time his own, to do with as he pleased, and had lived accordingly. But suddenly he knew that this could no longer be the case."[4]

Jesus said, "… Most assuredly, I say to you, unless one is born again, he cannot see the kingdom of God" (John 3:3 NKJV).

When Wilberforce's eyes were opened spiritually, he realized he had been wasting his life and time in meaningless pursuits. If he had not been born again, which he also called the great change, he would not have been given the commission, desire and strength from God to be the point man bringing about the abolition of slavery.

This changed life is a good example of what it is like to be born again.

A year and two days after William Wilberforce's death, Sir Reginald Coupland describes it in his 1923 biography:

"At midnight on July 31, 1834, eight hundred thousand slaves became free."[5] This was the beginning of a great movement that not only changed African and British history, but changed the world!

One does not have to be a member of a particular group to have a life changing experience. The new birth is just a prayer away.

It's Never Too Late for a New Beginning

In this new series, we are looking at the emphatic words, the commandments of Jesus. The first one I chose to list in my last column was John 3:6-7, which I'll repeat here more fully:

"That which is born of the flesh is flesh, and that which is born of the Spirit is spirit. Do not marvel that I said to you, 'You must be born again'" (NKJV).

Jesus was explaining a brand new experience for humankind.

Everyone, since Adam, was born into a fallen race when the first couple had obeyed the Tempter rather than their Creator. At that moment, they were tricked into turning their own dominion of Planet Earth over to God's archenemy Lucifer (AKA Satan), the fallen cherub, whose goal was to be God and usurp His throne.

Yet, instead of our Lord deciding to wipe out the initial disobedient human beings He had created and start over, He had fallen in love with us. The great romance had begun. He decided to save us.

Our Triune God had a war room meeting. Jesus, God's sinless only Son, offered to go to earth, be born as a baby, grow up, and become the perfect sacrifice for all humankind's sins. He would then offer us a new birth.

Then anyone who believed in and received Jesus, the Lamb of God, would have his or her original sins removed, be forgiven from actual sins and be born into the family of God. Further sins committed in life would be removed through prayer to our Father in Jesus name.

Forgiven people of God would become His **Beachhead Kingdom** on the fallen planet Earth.

At the very end of the Bible, we find that in the seventh millennia of mankind's biblical history, in Heaven the dark seals of bondage on earth's title deed – from earth's fall – are broken by Jesus. He is the only One who can open the seals (Rev 5).

John Gets a Glimpse

The Apostle John, who was given a peek into Heaven, saw this scenario:

"Then I saw a strong angel proclaiming with a loud voice, 'Who is worthy to open the scroll and loose its seals?' And no one in Heaven or on the earth or under the earth was able to open the scroll, or to look at it … "Then He [Jesus] came and took the scroll out of the hand of Him [the Father] who sat on the throne … And they [angels and elders] sang a new song, saying:

"You are worthy to take the scroll,

"And to open its seals;

"For You were slain,

"And have redeemed us to God by Your blood …" (Rev 5: 2-9 NKJV).

The action that seals our covenant with God is simply our invitation inviting the Savior into our life. This invitation can be given any time and any place, by you, or with others.

William Wilberforce in the book, *Amazing Grace*, became like a different man and described it as the great change.

John Wesley, the founder of Methodism, said he had a heartwarming experience.

The Apostle Paul describes his experience, "… if anyone is in Christ, he is a new creation; old things have passed away; behold, all things have become new" (2 Cor 5:17 NKJV).

One day while driving along the Bay Shore in Tampa, Florida after making a deeper commitment to Christ, I found, "The blue jays were a deeper color blue that day, the grass was greener, and the sunlight on the bay sparkled like thousands of diamonds."

Yes, I changed too. I became a great lover of Christ and the Bible, and care much more about other people now. Not perfect, but forgiven, and I have hope for life after this one.

There's a divine romance waiting for you – with God: Father, Son and Holy Spirit. Take a moment to relax, breathe deeply, and think about how much God loves you. If you haven't done it yet, then invite Jesus to be your Savior and Lord today. He will lead you to His Father and the comforting Holy Spirit.

Passing on the Torch of Light and Power

Do you want to know what Jesus' personal commandments are? For the last two columns we studied Commandment No. 1.

Now here is Commandment No. 2. "And being assembled together with them [Jesus' Apostles] He **commanded** them not to depart from Jerusalem, but to **wait** for the Promise of the Father, which," He said, "You have heard from Me; For John truly baptized with water, but you shall be baptized with the Holy Spirit, not many days from now" (Acts 1:4-5 NKJV – emphasis mine).

Jesus had been raised from the dead and was seen by over 500 people (1 Cor 15:6). For 40 days He completed His final work before He returned to His Father in Heaven.

During this time, He appeared in the upper room where the Apostles were gathered and in His eternal, timeless body was able to enter the room without a key. This day He commissioned the Apostles.

"Then Jesus said to them again, Peace to you! (which is '*Shalom*' in Hebrew) [Just] as the Father has sent Me forth, so I am sending you.' And having said this, He breathed on [them] and said to them, 'Receive (admit) the Holy Spirit'" (John 20:21-22 AMP).

Here they were indwelt with the Holy Spirit, born again.

Thomas Has an Encounter

After this is that famous time when the Apostle Thomas told the other Apostles he would not believe that Jesus was alive unless He personally showed him the wounds in the palms of His hands and His side. You see Thomas, the twin, missed the commissioning experience the previous day.

Some of Jesus' unfinished business was to help Thomas believe. After eight more days the Apostles were again in the upper room, this time Thomas was there.

"Jesus came, the doors being shut, and stood in the midst, and said, 'Peace to you!' Then He said to Thomas, 'Reach your finger here, and look at My hands, and reach your hand here, and put it into My side. Do not be unbelieving, but believing.'

"And Thomas answered and said to Him, 'My Lord and my God!'" (John 20:26b-28 KJV-MOD). This was one of the greatest biblical

191

declarations of who Jesus is. At that moment Thomas experienced spiritual rebirth.

Two Steps

The first step of a believer's life is to be indwelt with Jesus' life by the Holy Spirit – a new birth (John 3:3).

The second step is what Jesus said to His disciples in Acts 1:8, "But you shall receive power when the Holy Spirit has come upon you ..." You will receive power that is in Greek *dunamus* or literally dynamite!

When Jesus, God's only Son, was ready to leave Planet Earth for His home above, He did not leave His chief Apostles without the power to carry on His work. They needed to be ready every day to defeat the kingdom of darkness, and passing the torch of God on to others who would be running the race eventually worldwide, down through the millennia.

The power is passed on not only to apostles and to pastors in our day, but to laymen and women, to teens, to children. We too are commissioned to be indwelt, and empowered to pass on the good news of Jesus' redeeming love. We need it now more than ever.

Next time I'll tell you more about the dynamite power of God which is a major part of this second commandment.

My friend, you have not been left alone. God's omnipresence is here the moment you call upon Him. He brings a refreshing presence. He brings powerful gifts to sustain you. He gives you wisdom beyond your own.

Breathe deep, relax, and talk your needs over with Him.

Ask, Seek, Knock – And the Door Will be Opened

I do not know what would have happened to me spiritually if I had not learned there is personal empowerment available for God's children. When I found out, all I had to do was ask, seek, and knock on God's door.

At age 9, I had opened my heart to Jesus, was indwelt with the Holy Spirit, and given eternal life. I was then baptized in water. I had actually been baptized as an infant earlier, so God had had His eye on me from infancy.

So why wasn't this enough for me to live a strong, committed life? The world around me seemed a lot more exciting than going to church, reading a few ancient scriptures, and mumbling a quick prayer when in trouble. In fact, I can identify with the waffling disciple Peter.

In my last column, I began with Jesus' second commandment, "You shall receive power after that the Holy Spirit has come upon you: and you shall be witnesses to Me ..." (Acts 1:8 KJV-MOD).

These were Jesus' last recorded words from earth, for you and me. The word for power in Greek is *dunamis* or, specifically, "Inherent power; power to reproduce itself, like a dynamo."[6]

"When did this spiritual power show up?" one may ask.

The answer is, "On the Day of Pentecost."

That happened exactly ten days after Jesus' ascension into Heaven, two millennia ago in Jerusalem.

The twelve Apostles, Mary the Mother of Jesus, and His siblings were there. A total of about 120 disciples were present in the upper room.

"When the Day of Pentecost was fully come, they were all with one accord in one place.

"And suddenly there came a sound from Heaven, as of a rushing mighty wind, and it filled all the house where they were sitting.

"And there appeared to them cloven tongues like as of fire, and it sat upon each of them.

"And they were all filled with the Holy Spirit, and began to speak with other tongues, as the Spirit gave them utterance" (Acts 2:1-4 KJV-MOD).

A great change took place in the 120 disciples as they were filled with God's power.

Peter a Primary Example

Scene No. 1. On the evening before Jesus' crucifixion, Peter was challenged three times to know if he had a connection with the One who was soon to be nailed to a tree. Peter three times, with profane expletives, denied ever knowing Jesus (Matt 26:69-75).

Scene No. 2. Jesus appears to Peter and the other Apostles and breathes resurrection life into them. They have new birth (John 20:22). Yet Jesus instructs them to wait for the power in Jerusalem (Luke 24:49).

Scene No. 3. After the crucifixion, Peter goes back to fishing. The disciples were coming to shore without catching any fish until a Man on the shore tells them to throw the net on the other side. They catch 153 fish. On the shore the resurrected Jesus asks Peter three times if he loves Him and if so to feed His sheep (John 21).

Scene No. 4. Peter receives his personal Pentecost. The fire of God lights upon his head and he is anointed with the Holy Spirit praising and praying in the Spirit. Immediately he is no longer afraid of being known as one of Jesus' disciples. He cannot wait to be a witness!

A crowd having gathered, Peter stands up to preach from the prophet Joel's book about signs and wonders; Peter tells of Jesus' miraculous healing power, then about His crucifixion and resurrection (Acts 2:14-39).

Three thousand souls come into the Kingdom that day (Acts 2:41).

These examples of Peter's journey were eye-openers for me. They convinced me that God not only wants me to have a great spiritual new birth, but that the empowering experience of Pentecost is also available for me today. It's true for you also.

Seven Festivals Fulfilled
Steps to Empowerment Begin with Three Feasts

Why do you think tongues of spiritual fire landed on the heads of 120 seekers in Jerusalem on the day of Pentecost?

I wonder if it was a picture to teach us a lesson. For instance, what is the main obstacle that prevents human beings from believing in God's Word with simple, uncomplicated faith?

Could it be the brain? The brain is described as being soft as butter. But the connections that can be made in the brain through hurts in life can create unbelief that is as hard as a rock.

Sometimes God chooses to give spiritual signs to get a point across to us: "God is not dead. He is alive and well!" For the brave early believers 2,000 years ago, they needed all the power they could get. These Jewish believers of The Way, were for those ten days praying while sequestered behind closed doors as they waited for Pentecost – or as they would say it in Hebrew, *Shavuot.*

Forty-one years later the early believers we're first called Christians in Antioch (Acts 11:21-26). Historically, on Mount Sinai in B.C. 1706, God (*Yahweh*) instructed Moses about the importance of the children of

Israel celebrating seven annual feasts (Lev 23). God would meet with them in special ways during these feasts or festivals. Pentecost is the fourth of those feasts.

So Pentecost had been celebrated for 1706 years until the actual Day of Pentecost had its fulfillment in the upper room in Jerusalem after Jesus' crucifixion, resurrection and ascension. Scripture says it this way: "When the Day of Pentecost had fully come, they were all with one accord in one place" (Acts 2:1).

Festivals (Feasts) Fulfillment

Each of these seven feasts either has or will have its fulfillment or time of fully coming. For instance, Passover or *Pesach* has been celebrated every year since the children of Israel escaped from Egyptian slavery in B.C. 1706. For the early believers of The Way, that feast was fulfilled by Jesus when He met with His Apostles for the Passover Feast that Jesus had celebrated every year of His life. Only this Passover was different in that Jesus would become the Passover Lamb, the One who once and for all would make it possible for the sins of the world to be removed (John 1:29).

This fulfillment of Passover was the reason for all the annual Passovers that had taken place from B.C. 1706 to A.D. 32[7], total of 1,738 years. The first four feasts – Passover, Unleavened Bread, First Fruits, and Pentecost – were all fulfilled through Jesus the Christ. They represent Him as:

- Lamb of God who takes away the sin of the world
- The pure sacrifice, without blemish or sin
- Our resurrected Lord – the first fruits of God's family, who are also promised resurrection from the dead
- The fourth feast, Pentecost, was the fulfillment of Jesus' promise to send the Holy Spirit with power ten days after His ascension. (John 16:7).

Consider us in the 21st Century

We are presently living between the fourth and fifth festivals, Pentecost and the Day of Trumpets. One festival was fulfilled (Pentecost) and the next festival is yet to be fulfilled (Trumpets). Trumpets always remind me of the trumpet sounding when Messiah Jesus comes for his body of believers (1 Thess 4:16-17).

Now for us today, we can look back 3700 years and see these first two major feasts, Passover and Pentecost, as eternally important and foundational in the formation of the Christian faith – as well as for the Jewish faith.

For the Christian's faith to have your Pentecost experience, you must first take step No. 1 – your Passover experience. Said another way, to have your *Shavuot* you must first have your *Pesach*.

For the Christian Track

- The Lamb's blood over your heart's door (Good Friday);
- Your Unleavened Bread or sin removed (Holy Saturday);
- Your First Fruits of spiritual resurrection (Easter Sunday).
- Walk with Christ, and renounce cults and occult (Pentecost Sunday).

Remember the value of *The Lord's Supper* or *Holy Communion*. That is the major way Christians remember the Passover and Christ's death until He returns. Jesus said about this holy celebration, "**Do this** in remembrance of Me" (Luke 22:19 NKJV). This is the **third** of our Lord's commandments to us.

Take some time to ask Jesus to fulfill these feasts in you. Try opening your hands in a receptive position. Relax, close your eyes, and speak praises to the Lord who loves you.

Tell Us More about the Seven Festivals

I find that I need to tell you the rest of the story before I get back to our subject of empowerment to sustain us while on earth. Immediately after the last column came out April 2, 2009, I received an online request from a minister and friend saying, "Tell us more about the seven festivals!"

Was he perhaps voicing a request other readers may have today? I will try to give you a column-sized answer to a book-sized subject.

In my last column, I explained my view that steps of empowerment begin with three feasts (AKA festivals).

For The Jew It Is:

- Passover: the blood of the lamb on each door saving Israel from judgment.
- Unleavened Bread: clean out all yeast from cupboards, and sin from hearts.
- First Fruits: Bring the first fruits of the harvest to God (*Yahweh*) in the Temple.
- The fourth Feast: *Shavuot* means seven weeks, Feast of Weeks and the morrow after the Sabbath makes 50 days (Lev 23:15).

For The Christian It Is:

- Good Friday: Jesus' blood shed on the tree, placed over hearts for salvation.
- Holy Saturday: Our Lord dying as the sacrifice for all humankind, forgiveness.
- Easter Sunday: Jesus glorified as First Fruits bringing us, His family eternal life.
- Pentecost, *pentecoste* Gr. means the fiftieth day (Acts 2:1). This feast came exactly 50 days after First Fruits or Jesus' resurrection. He was the first fruit that prepares the way for His believers to be resurrected also.

This was the time of the empowering of the Church for more harvest of souls. Jesus said, "You shall be witnesses to Me in Jerusalem, and in all Judea and Samaria, and to the ends of the earth" (Acts 1:8b NKJV). The world has been filled with believing witnesses for over 2,000 years.

The fifth Feast: Feast of Trumpets or *Yom Teruah:*

- Jews today put most emphasis on their second New Year, *Rosh HaShanah; Yom Teruah* is part of their festival with blowing the *shofar* many times.
- Christians do not usually celebrate the Feast of Trumpets. Some who have studied the Jewish feasts see a connection between it and the rapture of believers and are watching for the New Moon.

The Feast of Trumpets, also called, The Day of the Awakening Blast, or the fifth feast, is obviously next on God's calendar.

It is a fall feast and comes in the seventh month at the very beginning of the New Moon as seen from Jerusalem. In the first century, there had to be two witnesses who saw the new moon and would then rush to tell the rabbi in the temple. The second witness made it valid. This is the reason why no man knew the day or the hour of this feast until it occurred and why two days are set aside on the Jewish and the Christian calendars. (See my story: *My Birthday Gift from Heaven* on our website EmotionallyFree.org[8]).

The sound of a trumpet or a *shofar* indicates something important is happening.

The *shofar* is made from a ram's horn. The first biblical example represented Isaac on Mount Moriah who was spared when a ram became the sacrifice in his place. God's voice was like a trumpet on Mt. Sinai as He gave the Ten Commandments – rules for good living – to Moses for the people.

Zola Levitt, Jewish Bible Scholar, said: "The trumpet unquestionably represents the Rapture of the Church."[9]

"For the Lord himself shall descend from Heaven with a shout, with the voice of the archangel, and with the trump of God: and the dead in Christ shall rise first: Then we which are alive and remain shall be caught up together with them in the clouds, to meet the Lord in the air: and so shall we ever be with the Lord" (1 Thess 4:16-17). (See Rev 3:11, John 14:1-3, Matt 24:40-44).

Zola says, "We remain partly under orders of Pentecost, continuing the summer crop cultivation. We remain 'workers in a field' until that day of the great harvest marked by the next feast."[10]

In the next two columns, we'll conclude the seven festivals. Keep tuned in.

Mystery of Festivals Explained and Resolved

In looking at our Jewish and Christian heritage as believers, we have been studying the seven festivals (AKA feasts) as listed in Leviticus, chapter 23.

This is one of the most important chapters in the Bible, as it concisely tells the whole story of the spiritual redemption of humankind from Genesis to Revelation.

Isaiah prophesies with these words:

"Remember the former things of old; for I am God, and there is no other; I am God, and there is none like me, declaring the end from the beginning and from ancient times things not yet done, saying, 'My counsel shall stand, and I will accomplish all my purpose'" (Isa 46:9-10 RSV).

Here we find God declares or tells the end of the story from the very beginning. Only God can predict the future 6,500 years ahead of time!

He gave the whole picture in Leviticus, Chapter 23. Of course we're still counting the years, as the last days are not over yet.

In past columns, we have reviewed Passover, Unleavened Bread, and First Fruits, the three spring festivals.

We have reviewed the Festival of Weeks or Pentecost which comes 50 days after these festivals.

Three Fall Festivals

In my last column, we began the series of the three fall festivals starting with the Day of Trumpets. I mentioned that the first four festivals have been fulfilled in Jesus, but the last three have not as yet.

All the festivals were, or will be fulfilled, through Jesus personally.

We look forward to the upcoming fulfillment of *Yom Teruah* or The Day of Trumpets the fifth festival, or the first fall festival. The best way for you and for me to know where we are on God's time clock is to study these festivals, the Jewish calendar, and understand what they mean. It is also most important for all believers to have a personal experience of the four that have already been fulfilled in Christ. We need to keep our lamps full of oil of the Holy Spirit for Jesus says at the midnight hour He, the Bridegroom, will come (Matt 25:6).

Yom Kippur: *Yom Kippur* or the **Day of Atonement** is the fall festival, number six. It is the holiest festival of the Jews.

In Leviticus 23:27 *Yahweh* says, "Also on the tenth day of this seventh month there shall be a Day of Atonement: it shall be an holy convocation unto you; and you shall afflict your souls, and offer an offering made by fire unto the Lord."

Since there is no temple in Jerusalem at present, the Jews cannot make an offering by fire on the bronze altar to the Lord, but they do have a special holy service of a twenty-four hour fast and repentance on this day. It is their Day of Atonement for the year.

While *Pesach* is for humankind's personal atonement, *Yom Kippur* is a picture of the national redemption or atonement of Israel, which is yet to be fulfilled through Messiah (Rom 11:25, 26).

The Jew's "best defense [to persecution] will be to stand back-to-back with their brethren in the Holy Land. This is how the Lord will find them regathered when He returns."[11]

At a *Yom Kippur* celebration, people often wear white for purity. Near the end of the service you will hear a door slam shut. This reminds Jewish believers that the door to Heaven will close someday as the day of *Hesed* (grace) is over, even as the door to Noah's Ark was closed by God. Christians may prayerfully attend this service as I had a chance to do several years ago.

The *Shofar HaGadol* is the trumpet sound given at this Festival. *HaGadol* means the great. This trumpet blast will herald the return of Messiah to rule on the earth during the coming *Sabbath Millennium.*

We will look some more at the seventh and concluding festival in my next column. Keep listening for the joyful sound!

Peace Must Begin in Each Human Heart

Will Messiah come to rule and reign bringing peace on earth in some future day? If you pose this question to Christians and Jews alike, some will say yes and some no.

Laying aside the politically correct answers, let us examine some biblical answers.

In this column we are concluding with this seventh festival or feast in our series.

The Jewish festival of *Sukkot* or Tabernacles is the seventh and final one God gave to Moses and ultimately to us all.

"Speak unto the children of Israel, saying, The fifteenth day of this seventh month shall be the feast of tabernacles for seven days unto the Lord. That your generations may know that I made the children of Israel to dwell in booths, when I brought them out of the land of Egypt: I am the Lord your God" (Lev 23:34, 43 KJV).

It seems that God (*Yahweh*) wanted to celebrate that He provided the tabernacle in the wilderness for the Jews.

Even today devout Jews build small shelters outside their homes to worship in them part of the time each day for seven days during that season. Another name for this occasion is Festival of Booths. In Jerusalem near Jaffa Gate, there is a municipal shelter built for this yearly festival observance.

Today Christians and Jews both may celebrate the Festival of Tabernacles for seven days in Jerusalem. I've celebrated the Festival of Pentecost and the Festival of Trumpets in Jerusalem, but have not yet celebrated the Festival of Tabernacles there. I've heard it is a wonderful celebration.

Zechariah prophesies the future Kingdom, "And it shall come to pass that every one that is left of all the nations which come against Jerusalem shall even go up from year to year to worship the King, the Lord of hosts, and to keep the feast of tabernacles ..." (Zech 14:16-19).

Ezekiel says prophetically that the Lord will establish His tabernacle in Jerusalem (Ezek 37:26-27).

Though Tabernacles is not officially one of the Christian celebrations today, a main purpose of this festival is to celebrate Messiah's rule on the earth during the Sabbath Millennium. Christians in the historic churches repeat these words in the *Nicene Creed* each week.

> ... For our sake He was crucified under Pontius Pilate;
> He suffered death and was buried.
> On the third day He rose again
> In accordance with the Scriptures;
> He ascended into Heaven
> And is seated at the right hand of the Father.
> He will come again in glory to judge the living and the dead,
> And His kingdom will have no end ...[12]

Christians also each Sunday repeat *The Lord's Prayer* which says in part, "Thy Kingdom come, Thy will be done, On earth as it is in Heaven."

Yes, His Kingdom came when we individually accepted Jesus Christ. But in these two examples we are still praying for His Kingdom to bring total peace to the earth as it is in Heaven.

Jesus, the Christ, (*Messiah*) annually celebrated this seventh feast of Tabernacles (*Sukkot*) which is commemorated by His words spoken in the Gospel of John, chapter seven:

"If anyone thirsts, let him come to Me and drink. On the last day, that great day of the Feast [of Tabernacles], Jesus stood and cried out saying, 'He who believes in Me … as the Scripture has said, out of his heart will flow rivers of living water'" (John 7:37-38 KJV-MOD). See Isaiah chapter 12.

"They have seduced My people, saying, Peace; and there was no peace" (Ezek 13:10). Though the world cannot bring lasting peace, it is vitally important to work and pray for peace.

Yet peace must first begin in each human heart. Ask the Prince of Peace to indwell, to tabernacle with you in your heart today.

Take a breath of sweet, everlasting peace. Sit quietly and let peace fill your soul. Let that peace flow through you to the world.

Psalm 91 Series (Seven Articles)
A Spiritual Antidote Exists for Swine Flu

Does the world seem filled with more chaos and fear than usual? swine flu was one of our concerns in 2009.

Science says there is a war between microbes, animals, and humans. In fact, that has been true for millennia.

When a mutation of a new configuration of an unholy three combine i.e. – human flu, bird flu and swine flu – these new microbe combinations have to find hosts to survive.

We humans have not yet built immunity against them, so one can be infected more easily. These mutations keep finding new hosts and either make them sick or destroy them. They continue this process until they can find no more hosts, or until mankind stops them with a new vaccine.

Meanwhile during this new microbe attack we have to frequently keep washing our hands, stay off planes or wear a surgical mask, and stay away from the person who is sneezing or has a cold. Too much refined sugar also feeds viruses. I keep my vitamin C up to 1,000 mg. daily and more when I think it's necessary.

Spiritually, know that God will lead us in all circumstances. Scripture says, "A merry heart does good like a medicine" (Prov 17:22a KJV-MOD). Let us be happy and rejoice in God. Find time to read and reflect on Scripture daily. Use reading aids such as *Daily Bread* or *Forward Day by Day.* Pray *The Lord's Prayer* (Matt 6:9-13) and put on the armor of God daily (Eph 6:10-18). You might read this, my latest book, *A New Look at the News* for daily devotions. Get out in the sun when time permits.

Psalm 91 for Health

To me, Psalm 91 is the perfect Scripture antidote to a pandemic.

It begins: "He who dwells in the secret place of the Most High (*Elyon*) shall abide under the shadow of the Almighty (*Shaddai*). I will say of the LORD (The Name, *Yod Heh Vav Heh*), 'He is my refuge and my fortress; My God (*Yahveh*), in Him I will trust'" (KJV-MOD). Everything else in Psalm 91 depends on these first two verses. Here God's name is given in four Hebrew dimensions which one only realizes if you know Hebrew, or when reading an interlinear Hebrew and English Bible or book of Psalms (*Tehillim*). I discovered these four names of God listed while reading Psalm 91 in the interlinear *Tehillim*. It was therefore emphatically clear to me that God's presence is our place of protection.

Historically the most holy place was considered to be the temple in Jerusalem. It was burned by the Romans in A.D. 70. The altar of a synagogue or church is considered holy today. The reserved sacrament of Holy Communion is left in the tabernacle near the altar with a light burning. Receiving the Eucharist at the altar is considered being in a holy place. Praying to God in your home and studying your Bible in a special place is considered holy.

God Confirms My Trip

Back in 1963 I lived in Van Nuys, California and one day went to Christ the King Church in Studio City to pray. I was surprised to be met by a friend there as I was seeking God for an answer about moving. As we knelt, I was looking at the huge carving of Christ the King on the cross with His arms outstretched.

As the afternoon sun began to set in the west behind me, all of a sudden I was surprised to see the shadow of wings, one over each of Christ's arms!

I quietly said, "Norm, look at the shadow of angel's wings!"

He looked and began to quote, "He who dwells in the secret place of the Most High shall abide under the shadow of the Almighty."

I was amazed and encouraged. I felt that God was letting me know He was going with me when I traveled from California to the Northwest. I will never forget those shadows of wings.

The next verse gets to more of the antidote. "Surely He shall deliver you from the snare of the hunter ("snare that entraps," *Tehillim*) and from the perilous pestilence" (Psalm 91:3 KJV-MOD). Now this is getting specific.

Read on, and next time we'll look at more of Psalm 91. Take time to seek God's presence for safety and guidance. You can choose to be, under the shadow of the Almighty.

Revealed: The True Author of Psalm 91

Psalm 91 is one of the most beautiful psalms ever written. There is a debate about who wrote this psalm, as some versions do not name an author.

After researching Psalm 91, I am convinced that Moses wrote it. Psalm 90 precedes it wherein Moses prays to God for mercy upon the people that they will live their allotted days wisely and not sin against their Creator.

Psalm 91 seems to be God answering Moses' prayer.

I'm a fledgling but I like to practice reading in Hebrew. I realized even before I read my commentaries that God's Hebrew name is given four times and each time differently. I mentioned in my previous column on this Psalm that I saw it as a spiritual antidote for the plagues of this world.

Here is a review of the verses and the Names of God in Psalm 91:1-2:

"He that dwells in the secret place of the Most High shall abide under the shadow of The Almighty.

"I will say of the LORD, He is my refuge and my fortress: my God; in Him will I trust" (KJV mod).

1. *El Elyon* – God Most High, no one is above Him.
2. *El Shaddai* – God Almighty, tender, lean upon His chest.
3. *Yod-Heh-Vav-Heh* – four Hebrew sacred letters, in English YHVH, LORD. Hebrews say *Adonai*.
4. *Yahveh* – Jehovah, Yah, my God.

"In Him I will trust" reminds me of our U.S. money, which says, "In God we trust." Perhaps that, or a similar verse, was where our founding fathers chose the words to mark our money for God.

I wonder how often we think of whether God approves of the way we personally spend our money or how our country spends it?

Yet the most important point to consider is whether we have made God our refuge and fortress – the One above all we can sincerely trust. Stock markets rise and fall but the One who does not have negative change is God.

Moses the Author

Some reasons I see Moses as the author of Psalm 91 are the use of these four Hebrew names of God.

When God called Moses to free the children of Israel from slavery, he was a wise Jewish man at the age of 80. It was through him we have the *Torah* or the first five foundational books of the Bible. (Christian theologians use *Pentateuch* from the Greek.)

Also, in the book of Exodus, we learn how God taught Moses to make the furniture to be used in the tabernacle in the wilderness. He was given the details about how the Holy of Holies was to be created in a perfect cube shape, and how the Holy Ark of the Covenant and Mercy Seat were to be made and covered with precious gold.

So when I read that God wants me to dwell in the "secret place of the Most High under the shadow of the Almighty," I believe it is referring to the Holy of Holies.

"Under the shadow of the Almighty" again confirms this location because a huge cloud of God's presence covered this part of the tabernacle as Moses led Israel away from bondage through the wilderness. The cloud also protected the people from the hot desert sun as they traveled to the Promised Land.

Application

How does this Scripture apply to us today? When you and I put our trust in God, by inviting Him and His Son into our lives, God is joined to our born again spirits (1 Cor 6:17).

You are triune, spirit, soul and body (*pneuma*, *psyche*, and *soma*, Greek). Now your spirit has become a spiritual Holy of Holies where God dwells. Your greatest safety comes as you are led by the Holy Spirit who indwells your spirit.

We'll continue here next time. Try memorizing the first two verses of the famous Psalm 91. Meditate on it. Take it as spiritual medicine. Be healthy!

When God Speaks to You – Write it Down

Meditating on Psalm 91 can be a lifelong journey. One day you read it for the first time and then peruse it once in awhile. That's the way it was with me. Then on May 18, 2002, I was driving along in my blue Honda and a person on the radio quoted Psalm 91:3, in a translation new to me:

"He Himself will deliver you from the hunter's net, from the destructive plague." (Psalm 91:3, HCSB)[13]

It was just what I needed. Strange, I thought, "I just happened to turn on the radio and seconds later I heard the words that spoke to a very personal need."

Instead of the King James Version using the word fowler, here's the word hunter. When I heard the words, the hunter's net, I realized that God was speaking to encourage me in a spiritual battle.

In that moment, I knew He would deliver me, and He did.

Apply This to You

Perhaps your good name has been attacked by someone who is jealous of your opportunities. He does not like your success in business, or he or she seriously and publicly disagrees with your politics.

If a Scripture speaks to you, put the date in your Bible next to the verse. If your Bible is too fancy to write in, get a paperback Bible that you can use as your journal. You do not want to miss those moments when God speaks specifically to you through His Word.

This way your personal Bible will get more valuable as the years go by.

God Loves You

Continuing with our Psalm 91, verse 4 says of God, "He shall cover you with His feathers, and under His wings you shall trust: His truth shall be your shield and buckler" (KJV-MOD).

The wings of God are a picture speaking of His comfort and His desire to take care of you. To be under this tender care and comfort of God, you must be willing.

Jesus the Messiah spoke about this. He said to the leaders of the holy city, "O Jerusalem, Jerusalem, who kills the prophets, and stones those sent to her. How often would I have gathered your children together, even as a hen gathers her chicks under her wings and you would not" (Matt 23:37 KJV-MOD).

How can we desire to be elsewhere other than close to, abiding in and learning from Him? We are His chicks and He wants to nurture us, protect us, feed us, warm us, and hold us close to His heart.

God shows His mothering nature here, which is also found in His Hebrew name *El Shaddai*.

Your Armor

"His truth shall be your shield and buckler" (Psalm 91:4b KJV-MOD).

The buckler is armor carried on the arm to intercept blows (synonym: shield). The buckler-shield was small and for quick action in battle. [14]

The Hebrew word for truth is "*emet*," spelled: *aleph, mem,* and *tav,* the first, middle and last letters of the Hebrew alphabet for the word truth.

Aleph stands for God's strength and for having no other God but Him. Do not let idols replace God.

Mem stands for water that refreshes. Psalm 23:2 says, "He leads me beside the still waters" (KJV-MOD). The Holy Spirit's presence refreshes.

Tav stands for truth itself. God and His written Word are truth. Jesus is the truth (John 14:6).

Your shield and buckler of truth are even found in the Hebrew word Jesus would have spoken and known, *emet*.

Jesus said, "If you continue in My word, then you are my disciples indeed; and you shall know the truth [*emet*] and the truth shall make you free" (John 8:31-32 KJV-MOD).

Sit back now, breathe deeply, close your eyes, and meditate on thoughts and pictures that come to you from Psalm 91, especially verses three and four.

Fear May Be Real – But Victory Is Near

I don't know about you, but the three columns we've studied together have helped me to understand and memorize the first four verses of the healing Psalm 91. How about you? Do want to go for two more?

My memory code words are:

Verse 1 – We may dwell in the secret place of the Most High, the inner Holy of Holies.

Verse 2 – The Lord is our refuge and fortress, Him will I trust.

Verse 3 – He will deliver us from the trap of the hunter.

Verse 4 – He will cover us as chicks under feathers, and truth of His Word is an arm-shield.

Delivered from Fear

Our next verses help with unreasonable fear.

"You shall not be afraid for the terror by night; nor for the arrow that flies by day; nor for the pestilence that walks in darkness; nor for the destruction that wastes at noonday" (Psalm 91:5-6 KJV-MOD).

I remember when my late husband, Dennis, and I went to North Pole, Alaska a few decades ago. You might feel that since the small town wanted it to be Christmas-all-the-time that there was no fear there. But that was not how it was.

Dennis and I were speaking at a small country church in North Pole (near Fairbanks). Dennis shared his message in a homey style that was more like talking to a friend. In this way, he often taught the truths of the Scriptures and the power of the Holy Spirit.

My part was to explain *Inner Healing Prayer* and how we can practice the loving presence of Jesus to heal the hurts in our lives. Through prayer and God's omnipresence, we can go back to the hurtful scene and practice Jesus healing presence, hearing what He would say to us. As I explained this, I was aware of only one young boy in the congregation of adults.

The next day as the pastor asked for testimonies of how people had been helped, the lad stood up and said, "I have been afraid of the dark since I was a child of two. I remember how I ran to my parents' room and said something dark and scary was in my room. Would they come and help me?

"Many times they said, `Go back to bed. There is nothing to be afraid of.'

"This one night, I got in bed and pulled the covers over my head, and fell asleep in tears. I have slept with covers over my head for 10 years. When the Bennetts had us pray about a fearful memory, I went back to that scene, this time with Jesus, and He took the fear away. Last night I no longer needed to sleep with my head under the covers!"

I was full of joy over the emotional healing of this 12-year-old. His childlike faith was contagious. He was "not afraid for the terror by night; nor for the arrows (of doubt) that fly by day" (Psalm 91:5 KJV-MOD).

When you and I are made aware of God's omnipresent love with us and realize we can appropriate His timeless presence in our past – as well as in our present – great things can happen.

To learn more read, *You Can be Emotionally Free.*[15]

No Pestilence

Verse six says not to be afraid of the dark, "Nor for the pestilence that walks in darkness; nor for the destruction that wastes at noon time" (Psalm 91:6 KJV-MOD).

Pestilence is an archaic noun meaning "a fatal epidemic disease, esp. bubonic plague."[16]

Previously in verse three, we talked about this word pestilence and saw Psalm 91 as a good spiritual antidote against undue fear of swine flu.

An additional connection we can make with this beloved Psalm is that if you add another number one to its title, you have 911 – the number to call in emergencies. Call up, or re-call, Psalm 91 when you need it.

I'll close with this saying:
Fear knocked at the door.
Faith answered it.
There was no one there.

If fear is knocking at your door, try sending faith to answer it.

Vacation Bible School Increases Awareness

Many children's vacation Bible schools (VBS) have been meeting all over America and right here at St. Albans Church in Edmonds by the sea.

One summer day, Joyce Carver, the Sunday school director, and I met on her sunny porch to discuss the theme of the event, July 13-17, 2009. It was called the *Jerusalem Market Place and Synagogue.*

As I understand it, the children draw, color, and paint their lessons and put their wares in the market for parents and children to admire.

Retired lawyer, Chuck Becker, took the role of rabbi to teach the children from the *Torah* in the outdoors under the blue canopy tent, Sunday school synagogue.

On the altar was a little wooden Ark with a curtain contributed by Gaylord Sisk, a church vestryman. Next to the Ark is a child-size *Torah* scroll with scripture written artistically within and attached to wooden handles. A mother was the scribe.

To the Christian, the *Torah* is understood to be the first five books of the Old Testament and the foundation for the rest of the Bible.

In the Jewish synagogue, the altar is called the *bema*. Set upon it is the usually ornate container or Ark in which an ancient *Torah* scroll is placed.

So much important history and inspiration are taught to these fortunate children who attended St. Alban's. I experienced VBS in Florida as a child, but I don't remember it including our Jewish roots.

My first trip to Israel in 1996 was when I began to dig deeper into Judeo-Christian understanding.

Back to Our Theme

Now to segue to our continuing study of Psalm 91 beginning at verse seven. "A thousand shall fall at your side, and ten thousand at your right hand; but it shall not come near you. Only with your eyes shall you behold and see the reward [the retribution] of the wicked" (Psalm 91:7-8 KJV-MOD).

What fantastic promises have been made to the believer! There is no room to sit around worrying about the missiles of North Korea, or the potential nukes of Iran.

Rita Bennett

Like fighters in a boxing ring, oppressive rulers beat on their chests to make everyone afraid because they themselves are afraid. But fear can cause such leaders to become wicked and do wicked things. The reward of the wicked, will be seen in this life, but more so in the life to come.

Why are these protections offered us in this Psalm?

"Because you have made the Lord, who is my refuge, even the most High, your habitation; There shall no evil befall you, neither shall any plague come near your dwelling" (Psalm 91:9-10 KJV-MOD).

We found in verse one that the secret place of the Most High refers to the Holy of Holies. The Holy of Holies was first in the tabernacle in the wilderness, then later in the temple in Jerusalem.

Through practicing the Lord's presence, by accepting Him, we can today go to our own spiritual Holy of Holies – our refuge.

In prior articles, we studied the Hebrew names for God found in the psalms earliest verses, two and three.

Now later in the Hebrew translation it says: "You *Hashem* are my refuge in the Most High ..." (Psalm 91:7a TEHILLIM).

Ha Shem means The Name, a reverent substitute the Jews use for the holiest Name of the Lord, the four sacred Hebrew letters. They are being careful not to take the Lord's Name in vain.

Next is my refuge which many believe refers to the Holy of Holies.

And third is the Most High, *Elyon* – no one, god or man, is above Him. These three holy Names reveal in whom we are putting our trust.

You now have four more verses on which to meditate. When the news scares you, go to your refuge of prayer. Slowly, prayerfully repeat these verses (Psalm 98:1-10). And please teach them to your children, before bed at night, before they go to school, or perhaps at VBS next summer. The word pictures would also make good art projects.

Join me next time for the concluding five verses.

The Importance of Who You Know

We are now near completion of our gleanings from Psalm 91. It was written 3,500 years ago by *Moshe* (Moses) as inspired by the Holy Spirit.

"All scripture is given by inspiration of God, and is profitable for doctrine, for reproof, for correction, for instruction in righteousness" (2 Tim 3:16 KJV).

The hundred and fifty "Psalms as we have it today is just like it was when Christ used the book [scroll]." [17] It was "written in Palestine [now Israel] and Babylon [Iraq] from about 1,500 – 450 B.C.

Protection of Angels

"For He shall give His angels charge over you, to keep you in all your ways. They shall bear you up in their hands [palms], lest you dash your foot against a stone" (Psalm 91:11-12 KJV-MOD).

To my knowledge I have never seen an angel, though Scripture says you and I may have "… entertained angels without knowing it" (Heb 13:2 NIV).

My dear daughter-in-law, Diane Bennett, did see an angel. Diane had terminal cancer. The Christmas before she died she told me that a large, beautiful angel had flown over her bed. She explained that he seemed to be doing a fly by, observing, checking on her.

I thought to myself, perhaps he would come back later to carry her to her heavenly Home. I think he did.

The Great Temptation

It's interesting that at the time of Jesus' Great Temptation by the fallen traitor cherub, Lucifer, he used this very scripture to tempt Jesus. It is partially quoted by Satan in Matthew 4:6 and Luke 4:10. [18]

"The phrase, 'in all Your ways' is omitted but, the phrase, 'at any time' is added by Satan, showing how he misquotes and misapplies Scripture. Also vs. 13 is omitted by Satan, because it predicts his own crushing defeat (Gen 3:16, Luke 10:19). This promises power over wild beasts and creeping things, as well as power over all satanic powers symbolized by them." [19]

Psalm 91:13 reads, "You shall tread upon the lion and adder: the young lion and the dragon shall you trample under feet" (KJV-MOD). This verse has a double reference of humankind's dominion over animals, as well as well as a Spirit–led believer's power over all satanic power symbolized by them.

How awesome to think that Moses prophesied scriptures of Jesus' temptation, battling for the human race, 1,500 years before it happened. This is also effective for believers now 3,500 years later!

Who You Know

There is an old saying, "It is not what you know but who you know."

Let's apply this to Psalm 91:14, "Because he has set his love upon Me, therefore will I deliver him: I will set him on high because he has known My Name" (KJV-MOD).

This speaks of a devoted person who spends time with God in prayer and study of the words He left to help us know Him personally. In this very chapter, we have gone deeper into the name God:

El Shaddai – God Almighty,

El Elyon – God most high,

Yod-heh-vav-heh (four most sacred letters) LORD spoken as *Adonai* by Jewish leaders today.

In the New Testament we read, "Wherefore God also has given Him a name which is above every [earthly] name; that at the name of Jesus every knee should bow, of things in Heaven, and things in earth, and things under the earth; And that every tongue should confess that Jesus Christ is Lord, to the glory of God the Father" (Phil 2:9-11 KJV-MOD).

The most important person we can know is God: Father, Son, and Holy Spirit. In fact, the reason we were born was to meet Him personally, and become part of His eternal family. This is our greatest decision in our one and only life.

We have two more verses and a review next time. Now close your eyes, relax, and see how far you can go in quoting Psalm 91.

He Will Rejoice Over You With Joy

The famous Psalm 91 has taught, healed, and inspired people for over three millennia. This is our sixth and concluding column on it.

I'm sure untold thousands upon thousands have memorized it. Good at memorization are those not allowed the privilege of owning a Bible, the blind, the musically talented who creatively put scripture to music, and those who began memory work in childhood.

During our study together, I discovered a website *Bible in Song*. There you can listen to Psalm 91 sung by Janelle Ing. The music was composed in 1982. It was fun to hear it sung via my computer.[20]

Decades ago, my friend, Cordie Barber, of Deer Park, Washington put the comforting verses about the angels guarding God's people to music. I can sing it to this day.

The Scottish and Welch, and charismatic Christians of all brands are good at putting scripture to music. In Jerusalem standing at the remaining holy temple wall, one will find males and females with their books of Psalms (*Tehillim*) often bowing in rhythm as they read.

The cantor in the synagogue will chant from the *Torah*. Notations for this musical activity have been written with the words – for thousands of years in the opening five books of the Bible.

One of the 28 unfulfilled predictions about our Lord is: "He will rejoice over you with joy, He will rejoice over you with singing" (Zeph 3:17b KJV-MOD). We can look forward to Cantor, Jesus Christ, singing to us!

Who Wrote the 150 Psalms?

"Authors of 100 of the Psalms have names prefixed to them. They are Moses, David, Solomon, Asaph, Heman, Ethan, and sons of Korah … Ezra is perhaps the collector and compiler of Psalms in its present form."[21]

"The *Talmud* writers consider that when the author's name is not mentioned we may assign the Psalm to the last named writer; and, if so, this is another Psalm of Moses, the man of God.

Many expressions used here are similar to those of Moses in Deuteronomy, and the internal evidence, from the peculiar idioms, would point towards him as the composer."[22]

Eight Blessings for You

We are completing verses 15 and 16, but 14 goes with it so I will begin there.

There are eight promised blessings in these three verses.

"From here to the end of the psalm, God speaks in praise of and with assurances to the person who has faith in Him."[23]

"Because he has set his love upon Me, therefore I will deliver him:

I will set him on high, because he has known My Name.
He shall call upon Me, and I will answer him:
I will be with him in trouble;

214

I will deliver him,
And honor him.
With long life will I satisfy him,
And show him my salvation,"
(Psalm 91:14-16 KJV-MOD).

The *Tehillim* commentary indicates this final verse, "And I will show him my salvation," is prophetic.[24]

"He will witness the salvation. I will bring about at the advent of *Messiah*, at the time of the revival of the dead, and at the salvation of the World to Come." [25]

Jews and Christians are looking for *Messiah*. Jews for the first time and Christians for the second time. Fortunately we are both looking.

I do not have enough space to write down the entire Psalm 91 for you to have a master copy for practicing your memory work. Therefore I recommend you copy the King James version and modernize it from the old fashioned wording of thee's and thou's.[26]

Add any wording that helps you remember some of the unique lessons from the psalm study we've experienced. Put these helps in parenthesis, add Psalm 91 to the armor of God, and you have two powerful weapons!

In learning this psalm, you will be walking in the footsteps of millions of believers through thousands of years.

You are not alone.

And you are walking in the footsteps of Moses, David, and Jesus. Yes, walking in the very footsteps of God.

Amen.

Healthcare and Prayer Must Go Together
Breaking News & Healing Prayer —Poetry

Today as I was driving home from meeting with Andrea, my exercise trainer, I was feeling good. Yes, I got to my club to take care of my body today! I felt even better as I slowly drove down the steep hill on Main Street and my eyes scanned the evening sky.

The moon was crescent-shaped and bright in the south sky. Directly in front of me facing west were gray-blue rays like sun streaks across the sky. It seemed that they were rays from Heaven reaching out to bless all the Edmonds community.

To the far north side were white fluffy banks of clouds. I chose to drive slowly and take time to look up and see the beauty around me. I was overwhelmed. I thought of the scripture, "I will lift up my eyes to the hills, from where comes my help. My help comes from the Lord Who made Heaven and earth" (Psalm 121:1-2 KJV-MOD).

God wants us healthy. He wants us whole. The words holy, whole, and healthy surprisingly have meaning in common.

If one goes back to Middle and Old English language roots one will see that holy (*halig*), whole (*hal*), and health (*haelth*) have all descended from a common prototype.

- Holy simply stated is "set apart to the service of God."
- Whole is "free of wound or injury."
- Health is "the condition of being sound in body, mind, and spirit."[27]

If you and I are dedicated to God and relating closely to Him, we are more likely to become holy, whole, and healthy.

Take Care of You!

There are some things a healthcare bill cannot do for the population. The government cannot take care of our bodies as only, we the people, can do that for ourselves.

It cannot call you up and see if you exercised today, if you made healthy choices in your diet, or chide you if you have begun to look pregnant from drinking too much beer. The government is not your sweet Uncle Sam but laws, guidelines, and wisdom which have been passed on for centuries to help our country function to the best of its ability.

The main concern in our nation at present has to do with the health and care of our bodies.

Though the inner part of our being is as important as the exterior, yet without a healthy body the life of our whole person is shortened.

Healthcare Concerns

I'm glad the healthcare bill slowed down so more people can read and discuss it. Though some resist the idea, it is healthy for citizens to express themselves in town hall meetings across our land.

On August 30th 2009 we had our own Edmonds town hall meeting hosted by U.S. Representative Jay Inslee.

In my grad school, a major part of our training as therapists was to learn to confront one another in class. At the same time, we were required to use fair rules of engagement.

Recently, online I was impressed to receive a physician's abbreviated outline of the present healthcare bill. We are told through the media that such bills are impossible to read and understand; yet some people have taken the time and effort to do that.

A Holy Calling

My brother, Bill Reed, MD and Surgeon, in his *Progress Notes* newsletter wrote, "To take care of fellow human beings and other needs was, and has continued to be a 'Holy Calling' and a most rewarding life of God directed experiences.

"This has been an era of magnificent progress in medicine and surgery in phenomenal areas of therapeutic development in this last century. During my life as a physician, I have had the privilege of being involved in medicine and surgery across the world.

"Let us look to our Great Healing Physician, Christ the Lord, to guide us in the many important decisions facing our country. Get together with friends to pray that we and our government will make right decisions; for only God knows the right answers – (Matt 18:20)."[28]

Alfred Tennyson said, "More things are wrought through prayer than this world dreams of."[29] As I've written much on prayer in this book, you'll understand why, "I know he's right."

Dear God, Please Turn the Water On!

In 2009 I had been concerned about the economic crisis of California, especially in these last few years. It seemed so prosperous when I lived in the Los Angeles area in the early 1960's.

That October, I was especially concerned about the horrendous fires burning homes of the wealthy community. Some fires have been set by humans, others resulted from lightening strikes in dry areas.

Now while this beautiful state was trying to recover its losses, the new crisis was the effect of the government Endangered Species Act. It has seemed necessary to turn down the water supply to one of the great

217

fruit and almond production centers of America, the San Joaquin Valley. The reason given is to save the rare three-inch delta smelt.

Here we see quite a balancing act between human beings and the animal species. Nature verses farmland.

On television, I saw how dry the San Joaquin Valley farms were becoming. It looked like a huge dust bowl. One farmer opined that with only 10 percent of the previous water supply allowed, his almond farm would no longer be there next year.

Many farmers were out of work. This situation affected thirty million people.

There are a few things we can do as citizens, we can pray for wisdom for our leaders, we can pray for rain, and we can pray for more new inventions to help quench the destructive fires.

Books to Help Us!

C.S. Lewis's science fiction space trilogy is a must read! Out of the three books, the significant one that deals with trying to save our planet amid things going awry is told in the novel, *That Hideous Strength.*[30]

I had to read the book twice to get the full impact and then realized just how powerful it is. Clive Staples Lewis in *That Hideous Strength* warns us about what might happen to the world in a battle between environmental concerns and those who control society.

I read it during the time of George H.W. Bush's presidency and felt it would be a valuable gift so mailed the trilogy book Series to him. On Feb. 28, 1990, I received a letter from President Bush from The White House thanking me for remembering him and his wife Barbara "in such a thoughtful way…" His letter is one of my keepsakes.

Our Fallen Race

What concerns me in our fallen race is when a nation gets a perfectly good idea to help improve its world, but then it in time changes to something less than having the welfare of others at heart. Over a lifetime one notices this scenario being replayed.

You can see it in the Barnes & Nobles book synopsis, which follows: "*That Hideous Strength* concludes the adventures of the matchless Dr. Ransom … A sinister technocratic organization is gaining power throughout Europe with a plan to 'recondition' society, and it is up to Ransom and his friends to squelch this threat by applying age-old wisdom to a new universe dominated by science. The two groups struggle to a climactic resolution that brings the Space Trilogy to a magnificent, crashing close."[31]

Let's work to make sure that America and our world will have victorious closing scenes.

What else can we do? We can prayerfully let our age-old wisdom gained from application of God's Best Book make an impact on our world. We could begin by making a goal to keep the 3,500-year-old wisdom of the Ten Commandments (Exodus 20:1-17).

Instead of being reconditioned, the Apostle Paul exhorts us: "Do not be conformed to this world, but be transformed by the renewing of your mind, that you may prove what is

> that good
> and acceptable
> and perfect will of God"
> (Rom 12:2 NKJV).

Healing Your Past May Heal Your World

Over several decades I have learned that it's very important to get my childhood memories healed. It has been curative for me ever since I realized that God's omnipresence has been with me from my very beginning and that this fact is true for my entire life.

Whenever a hurt from my past comes to mind, I try to access the truth given in Psalm 139 proclaiming that my healing Lord is outside of time, and is eternal. And I as a believer, indwelt with the Holy Spirit, can appropriate His healing presence in that situation.

As I meditate on His love for me, God can speak to me in the Holy of Holies in my spirit (*pneuma* Gr.). The words are always full of love and insight, even if they may also be corrective.

Then I have the further benefit of Scripture study to feed and nurture my new creature spirit.

Omnipresence

For others to get started, I recommend studying Psalm 139 as it is another one of the great Psalms to teach about God's omnipresence.

Once I realized the importance of God's omnipresent Being, I found more and more Scripture to study and feed on spiritually.

For instance, "How precious also are Your thoughts to me, Oh God; how great is the sum of them! If I should count them, they are more in number than the sand; when I awake, I am still with You!" (Psalm 139:17-18 KJV-MOD).

When you see the Hebrew word *selah* in the Bible, it means stop and meditate on these words or "measure carefully and reflect upon the preceding statements."[32]

The Bible is filled with God's omnipresence – His always-present nature – always available to help when called upon. I realize that bad things can happen in anyone's life since this world has plenty of evil in it, but that fact can never keep me from accessing God's healing love as I go back with Him to meditate on what Jesus' would want to say to me about those old wounds in life.

When I claim His lordship, and seek to know His message to me in that situation, His wise, gentle, cleansing words restore my soul (*psyche* – intellect, will, emotions).

I like to journal what I hear Him saying to my inner being and date the entry. Looking back in my journals and reviewing His guidance keeps me affirmed and looking straight ahead on the pathway He has cut out for me.

More Examples

Some other Scriptures that reflect the truth of God's omnipresence are:

"… He is not far from each one of us; for in Him we live and move and have our being, as also some of your own poets have said …" (Acts 17:27-28 KJV-MOD).

"Therefore know this day, and consider it in your heart, that the LORD Himself is God in Heaven above and on the earth beneath; there is no other" (Deut 4:39 KJV-MOD).

Another wonderful healing part of the Bible is Psalm 91 that we've dealt with in seven columns. You may find this archived on http://www.emotionallyfree.org/articles.html. You can also use this part of Chapter Five for your Bible study with friends.

I wish I had known these healing truths earlier in my life, but it took me until my early 30s to begin to grasp it fully. Then as I prayed with people and saw emotional healings occur, my journals flowed into a book on the subject called, *You Can be Emotionally Free*.[33] I had no idea I was writing a book that would reach several nations.

The truth of this inner healing concept became part of my life's journey. It changed my history, my present, and my future. God's omnipresent transforming presence can do the same for you. *Selah*

You Too Can Touch the Hem of His Garment

Have you heard about the exciting day when Jesus Christ healed a dying 12-year-old girl, and a woman slowly bleeding to death for 12 years? Both happened on the same day 2,000 years ago and many of His followers still talk about it today.

These true stories recorded in three of the four Gospel accounts give great confirmation and validity to the miracles. Nearly everyone must have known about it in these two communities.

The girl was the only child of Jairus, the synagogue leader. He fell at Jesus' feet and implored Him saying, "My daughter has just died ... but come and lay your hand upon her and she will live" (Matt 9:18, NKJV).

Jesus and His disciples arose and followed Jairus to his home. As they hurried to the child, a crowd followed. Can you imagine how thrilling it was to be in the throng that followed this teaching, healing rabbi?

Woman with Faith

Surprisingly, a woman having a constant flow of blood for 12 years inserted herself into Jesus' schedule. She was considered ceremonially unclean, and touching a rabbi would have had severe consequences.

But suddenly she saw her moment of deliverance from this plague and regardless of the cost made a leap through the crowd for the hem of Jesus' garment.

"She said to herself, 'If only, I can touch the hem of His garment, I shall be made well'" (Matt 9:21 NKJV). She did not just hope, or wish, but her faith was strong enough that she from within proclaimed, "I Shall Be Made Well!"

During this healing, Jesus stopped and said, "Who touched Me?"

"When all denied it, Peter and those with him said, 'Master, the multitudes throng and press You, and You say 'Who touched Me?' "

But Jesus said, "Somebody touched Me, for I perceived power going out from Me" (Luke 8:45-46 NKJV).

As the power of healing flowed out of Him, He physically felt it. He was truly a conduit from Heaven to earth!

Here Jesus was in a hurry to pray for the little girl, but the bleeding woman's faith reached out – causing Him to heal her first. "And He said to her, Daughter be of good comfort: your faith has made you whole; go in peace" (Luke 8:48 KJV-MOD).

"The woman touched the hem of Jesus' garment, the tassels hanging from the edge of a Jewish cloak, that reminded the Jews of the *Torah* (Num 15:38-39)."[34]

This Jewish woman actually touched one of the four sacred Hebrew letters of God's proper Name, (*YHVH* or *yod heh vav heh*). And, Jesus, who wore them was and is the healing Son of God!

Healing the Child

In Luke's account of resurrecting the girl, Jesus had said to the crowd, "Do not weep; she is not dead but sleeping" (Luke 8:52 NKJV).

Some on-lookers thought this was humorous. It must have been obvious that she was dead (Luke 8:40-56).

After Jesus instructed all who laughed and ridiculed to leave, only then did He speak the command, "'Talita, kumi!' (which means, 'Little girl, I say to you, get up!') At once the girl got up and began walking around ... everyone was utterly amazed" (Mark 5:41-43 CJB).

Then Jesus in a fatherly way said, "Give her some food."

What about Today?

Maybe you have felt the healing touch of God in this 21st century, at Holy Communion, while enjoying a sermon, or during a special prayer. At times, His power is tangible today.

Believers who pray – can represent the hem of Christ's garment to others.

As Jesus' power is in us and with us, His anointed Word leads us. The commandments, and His mighty Name are our tassels. Take a moment to meditate on His love for you. Then reach out and touch Him to meet your own needs.

Rita Bennett

Hem of His Garment, Now[35]
One day a woman in great distress
didn't know where to turn for help,
Doctors tried every cure to make whole
to quench her bleeding, body and soul.

Rumors were flying about a Healer.
Blind can see, dead raised, lepers cleansed.
What about her? Could He quench the flow?
Where could she find Him in City aglow?

On Via Della Rosa Street, or soon to be,
A holy Man would come to carry a cross
Now, throngs of humans, hands imploring,
Outstretched to One with love, adoring.

Could it be the Healer, Jesus Messiah?
My divine appointment in this hour?
Joining the needy, she edged in
"I can be clean, can be whole again!"

With one big leap, hand touched His hem,
Woven tassel, a letter in God's Name.
Anointing power through her body flowed
She knew right then, new life was bestowed.

Jesus stopped, "Who touched Me?" He called.
"Daughter, your faith has made you whole."
"How did He know? I am over-awed.
Reached out my hand, and I-touched-God!"

You can be touched by the King of Kings
You can have life with a heart that sings.
Reach out your hand as an act of faith
Reach out your soul to amazing grace.

© 2009 by Rita Bennett

223

Psalm 23 Series (Five Articles) Holidays & Poetry
Psalm 23 For You and Me

Psalm 23, a psalm of David, is full of healing words millions of people have memorized and meditated upon over the centuries. They have comforted people in times of challenge, temptation, sickness, and loss.

I memorized the twenty-third Psalm when I was a child, perhaps you did, too. It continues to have fresh meaning for me.

Do you ever, in the morning, evening or some other time during the day, take a passage of scripture and think about it awhile? The Word of God renews your mind and sometimes a certain part of it will be healing to you and speak to you in a personal way.

As I was reading the twenty-third Psalm recently, I could see in it major keys for healing the soul and confirmation of several other insights received through praying for others and myself. Let's look at it together.

"The LORD is my **Shepherd**"

When you think about this first phrase, you may put emphasis on different words in it. For instance, "The Lord is my Shepherd" does not speak of another human being the shepherd, but about God Himself.

There is a tendency in human beings to want to control others and even in Christian circles it may come out, though in "Christianish" wrappings. If others try to lord it over us, we must obey God as did Peter, and the other Apostles.

When religious leaders tried to dominate and persecute them they responded that they should obey God rather than men (Acts 5:28-29).

God does give under-shepherds in the Church to guide us. He knows that we need them. But those truly sent by God will have the characteristics of our Lord and not try to replace Him in our lives.

"The **LORD** is my Shepherd"

A shepherd is someone who loves his flock, tends his flock, cares for them when they are tired or sick, and would lay down his life for them.

224

That is the kind of good Shepherd Jesus was and is. He laid down His life for us. If He had not given His life for us, there would be no spiritual healing for spirit, soul, or body. Without Him there is no complete wholeness now or ever.

There is no other Shepherd. Jesus Himself said, "I am the good Shepherd: the good Shepherd gives His life for the sheep," (John 10:11 KJV-MOD). He is the only One who knows all about us and therefore, knows exactly what we need.

"The LORD is **My** Shepherd"

This emphasizes the personal. The Psalm is referring to our first and most important healing experience, salvation. Jesus could be someone else's Shepherd, that's great, but it will not help you.

Is He your Shepherd? If you've asked Him to be, then you have access to the range of a thousand hills, the everlasting spring fed streams, and tender care when you're hurting, wounded, or sick.

Jesus said, "My sheep hear my voice, and I know them, and they follow Me: and I give them eternal life, and they shall never perish: neither shall anyone snatch them out of My hand" (John 10:27-28 KJV-MOD).

There are six promises Jesus gives His sheep in this verse:
- You will hear His voice.
- He knows you personally.
- You follow Him.
- You have eternal life.
- You will never perish.
- No one can take you from His loving hands.

Pray with me. "I claim these promises in Psalm 23 to be mine. Please be my personal Good Shepherd, Jesus. Forgive me from straying from the fold and away from the safety of Your presence. Help me to always hear and know Your voice, so I will come when You call me. Thank You for the awesome gift of eternal life, and for the safety of being in Your care, supported by Your loving hands. Amen."

Join me next for more thoughts of Psalm 23 for you and me.

Give God the Primary Place in Your Life

LORD (*YHVH*), is the proper name of God and *Roi* is one of His titles as the good, the great, the Chief Shepherd. *HaYahveh Roi* means the Lord is Shepherd of me (transliteration).

Shepherd comes from one Hebrew letter *resh,* and the word head begins with it pronounced *rosh.* To help you visualize this Hebrew letter *resh,* it looks like a shepherd's crook or curved staff. In the historical church, bishops and archbishops during special services process into a church with staff in hand showing they are shepherds under God.

The LORD is the head person in charge of the flock. There must be one central person in charge; otherwise it can cause chaos for the sheep. They may become confused in the direction they must go for safety, water, food, and rest.

People of The Book

This is also why there is one central Book that both the Christian Church and the Jewish Congregations see as primary, and that is the Bible. For the Jew, the Bible includes 39 Books, (Genesis to Malachi) and for the Christian, sixty-six Books (Genesis to Revelation).

The Jew has One God. The *Sh'ma* says: "[Hear, Isra'el! *Adonai* our God, Adonai is one]" (Deut 6:4 CJB).

The Christian has One God. Apostles' Creed: "I believe in One God [*Yahweh*], Creator of heaven and earth. I believe in Jesus Christ [*Yeshua haMashiach*] His only Son our Lord. He was conceived by the power of the Holy Spirit [*Ruach haKodesh*] ..."[36]

I Shall Not Want

The Lord is my Shepherd; I shall not want. "Just as sheep feel no anxiety, because their shepherd sees to their every need, so do we express our complete contentment in the knowledge that God will not deny us any legitimate need"[37]

That's quite an encouraging biblical promise for the world today. America has had its ups and downs, but in the past we have always been there to help other countries during environmental challenges or financial needs.

My dad was born in 1893, and at the age of sixteen during the financial depression he had to leave his home in Port Huron, Michigan, and catch a train to the big city of Detroit. As an assertive, young Scotsman, he walked into the office of the president of the Postal Service, and landed a job. In those days, the postal delivery was done with horse and buggy.

There have been other times of financial depression in our country, including market crashes. But during my lifespan, I have never before seen the challenging conditions we are presently experiencing. Over 100 banks failed in 2009. America is in debt, even needing to borrow survival money from other nations. If there are lessons we need to learn, let's find out what they are, and soon.

The LORD Loves Us

I like Rabbi Meiri's quote, "God will not deny us any legitimate need." [38] We Americans may have to tighten our belts. Many have overspent by misusing credit cards, and a lot of those material things we have bought were not legitimate needs.

Psalm 34 says to us, "Oh, taste and see that the LORD is good; Blessed is the man who trusts in Him! Oh, fear the LORD, you His saints! There is no want to those who fear Him. The young lions lack and suffer hunger; but those who seek the LORD shall not lack any good thing" (Psalm 34:8-10 NKJV).

What we can do to be blessed:
• Partake of the Lord and His Word
• Trust in Him
• Fear the Lord – that is, hold Him in awe
• Seek the Lord

God has the answers for your life. He will guide you as you give Him the primary place in your life.

Join me as we continue the Psalm 23 Series next time.

Take Time to Relax and Hear God's Voice

"The Lord is my Shepherd; I shall not want," (Psalm 23:1).

In Psalm 23 there are two metaphors: 1.) Jesus is the Shepherd and 2.) you and I are the sheep. We are carefree and totally provided for.

"He makes me to lie down in green pastures" (Psalm 23:2a KJV-MOD).

Meditating on this beloved Psalm can help to take stress away. When I think of my childhood in Florida, what this verse reminds me of is rolling down a beautiful green hillside in my neighborhood. At age six or seven, I was totally relaxed as I rolled round and round until I came to the bottom of the hill. The fresh cut grass also had a sweet smell and, as usual, the sun was shining. Then I wanted to go to the top of the hill and do it again.

I can picture Jesus, my Good Shepherd, sitting there on the grass watching me and enjoying my childlike activity. Maybe He would begin to quote Psalm 23, which He had learned from the scrolls in the synagogue. Closing my eyes and thinking about this makes me want to take a deep relaxing breath.

"He leads me beside the still waters" (Ps. 23:2b).

If a sheep wanted to take a drink of water from a spring fed river, the water would be running, but not rushing water. Rushing water and a sheep's heavy coat of wool would be a dangerous combination.

One of my favorite memories at the University of Florida in Gainesville was going tubing. Each of us had an inner tube. Clad in our bathing suits, we sat in the tube and let the river gently carry us for several miles downstream.

Sometimes the inner tubes would go 'round and 'round. Never wanting the adventure to stop, we met up with friends who had driven to a special location to meet us. They took care of us by providing nice warm towels and delicious food and cold drinks.

They were like good shepherds. I'd like to be there right now but those pleasures are only for me to meditate on. Good memories are wonderful gifts.

I think Jesus would have liked to be in an inner tube beside me.

Even more wonderful, maybe He'll meet me at the 750-mile long River of Life for the swim of my life upon entering Heaven. Those trees with twelve kinds of fruit on each one will be a delicious treat after our swim.

"And He showed me a pure river of water of life, clear as crystal, proceeding out of the throne of God and of the Lamb. In the midst of the street of it, and on either side of the river, was the tree of life, which

bore twelve manner of fruits, and yielded her fruit every month ..."
(Rev 22:1-2 KJV-MOD).

To learn more about this river, read my commentary in chapter six
of *Heaven Tours*, "Front Door View of Heaven."[39]

The Gospel of John

One of the great New Testament chapters that elaborates on the
theme of Psalm 23 is the 10th chapter of the Gospel of John. Here Jesus
is speaking.

"... He who enters by the door is the shepherd of the sheep. To him
the doorkeeper opens, and the sheep hear his voice; and he calls his own
sheep by name and leads them out" (John 10:2-3 NKJV).

The voice of Jesus is rich and powerful. He called to the twelve
disciples one by one, "Come follow Me." And they did. Somehow He
called to you or is calling you. He is drawing you to follow Him, to
study His life and messages. He's calling your name. Will you follow?

Join me again for the Psalm 23 Series next time.

Overcoming Our Failures by Confession and Soul Restoration

"The Lord is my Shepherd I shall not want. He makes me to lie
down in green pastures. He leads me beside the still waters" (Psalm
23:1-2 KJV-MOD).

**"He restores my soul. He leads me in the paths of righteousness
for His Name sake"** (Psalm 23:3 KJV-MOD). This phrase is the one we
will look at today.

What does David mean in his 23rd Psalm when he says God
restores his soul?

Soul is *nehfesh* in Hebrew. It refers to the psychological part of a
human being: the intellect, will, emotions, and subconscious. This is in
contrast to the holiest part of man that is his spirit or *ruach* (Hebrew)
when connected to God at salvation (1 Cor 6:17).

Why did David need restoration? Rabbi's Radak and Hirsch point
us to David's words in Psalm 26, "Examine me, Lord, and test me;
scrutinize my intellect and my heart" (Psalm 26:3-4).[40] God tested King
David's unlawful desire for Bath-Sheba. David failed the exam.

David then regretted his presumptuous request and said: "You tested me – You found [me] not [perfect]; my scheming will not again pass my lips." [41]

We Are Not Immune

Why do God's people in this 21st century continue to need restoration? The Apostle Paul answers this, "For all have sinned, and come short of the glory of God" (Rom 3:23). The Apostle John gives the remedy, "If we confess our sins, He is faithful and just to forgive us our sins, and to cleanse us from all unrighteousness" (1 John 1:9).

One may ask, "What is sin?"

In our example, King David's three sins were:

• Adultery – with Bath-Sheba,

• Murder – of her husband by putting him in the front lines on the battlefield, and

• Coveting – his neighbor's wife.

These were breaking the Seventh, Sixth, and Tenth Commandments (Exodus 20:1-17).

The Prophet Isaiah describes sin this way: "All we like sheep have gone astray; we have turned everyone to his own way; and the Lord has laid on Him [Jesus Christ] the iniquity of us all" (Isa 53:6 KJV-MOD).

Jesus was willing to die for our sins and in our place to rescue us. When we confess, repent, and receive Him, the sting has been taken out of our death. We will then never die – spiritually.

Restoration

If we should back-slide as King David did, we will need soul restoration.

Restoration Defined:

1. to bring back into existence, use, or the like; reestablish: to restore order.

2. to bring to an unimpaired or improved condition.

3. to give back; make return or make restitution of (anything taken away or lost).[42]

How Are Our Souls Restored?
- By studying and applying the Ten Commandments (Exodus 20:1-17).
- By studying the Bible – all sixty-six books (Psalm19:7).
- By daily devotions from faith building books, Bible studies, or online studies, etc.
- By repenting when you know you've sinned (1 John 1:9).
- By practicing the Omnipresence of God (Psalm 139).
- By receiving Soul Inner Healing Prayer & Counsel.[43]
- By receiving Holy Communion as Jesus commanded (Luke 22:19-20).
- By studying and praying *The Lord's Prayer* and forgiving (Matt 6:6-13).
- By meeting with a biblically based, qualified counselor.
- By helping those less fortunate than you are (Matt 25:40).

How could God say of David, "The LORD has sought Him a man after His own heart, and the LORD has commanded him to be captain over His people" (1 Sam 13:14b KJV-MOD)?

The reason is that King David had lived a righteous life until his great temptation as described. When Nathan the prophet challenged David's behavior, he truly repented from his sins and thereafter walked in God's ways (2 Sam 12:1-23, Psalm 25:1-13).

I first visited Jerusalem in 1996 and saw King David's casket in a separate location in the building where the Day of Pentecost is remembered – located on Mount Zion. King David is honored to this day! When God forgives, it is permanent.

How we live our life at its ending is even more important than at its beginning. King David therefore had a good ending. When our name is honored, God's Name is honored too. *Selah*

Join me for the continuation of the Psalm 23 Series next time.

Knowing Our Weaknesses – God Made Provision for Our Failings

"The Lord is my Shepherd I shall not want. He makes me to lie down in green pastures. He leads me beside the still waters. He restores my soul" (Psalm 23:1-3a KJV-MOD).

231

"He leads me in paths of righteousness for His name's sake"
(Psalm 23:3b KJV-MOD). This phrase is the one we will look at today.

What did the shepherd boy David, who later became King David, mean by these words in Psalm 23? We discussed in my last column that David had a great fall after he was elevated to power as king. He thought he could have what he wanted including another man's wife. The more earthly power humankind has the more temptations there are.

The historian and moralist, the first Baron Lord Acton (1834–1902) speaks of this condition, "Power tends to corrupt and absolute power corrupts absolutely."[44]

Does this mean that we should not try to become great men and women such as presidents, vice-presidents, governors, members of Congress or the Senate, sports men and women, movie actors, TV personalities, leaders of large corporations, bankers, pilots, famous authors, priests, or pastors? Of course not.

But as we have opportunity to become well known, we need to be aware of the pitfalls as well as the opportunities given us. I think a good plan is to spend more time in prayer and study of the life-lessons given in the Bible.

It might be beneficial to meet consistently with an accountability group of peers who are also seeking wholeness. Balance out your life by not having a steady diet of secular TV. Get some good CDs and DVD teachings to watch during your evening hours.

Does righteousness mean having a holier than thou attitude? No! To me it means right thinking, right speaking, right acting, and to have right standing with God through Christ.[45] Jesus showed us by His life how we could be like Him. He is our greatest role model.

God Made Provision for Our Failings

Knowing our weaknesses, God made provision for our failings by the way of repentance.

He also made provision for believers to be empowered with the Holy Spirit (Acts 1 and 2). We cannot live a righteous life without divine help.

One day, as I was meditating on Psalm 23, I noticed that the phrase, "He restores my soul" comes just before, "He leads me in paths of righteousness." That is experientially true.

The healing of the soul needs to take place before we are able to live righteously. In my last column, I got into this subject more thoroughly.

"He leads me in the paths of righteousness for His name's sake." Our earthly family has a reputation, and if it is good, it would be unfortunate to dishonor it by living unrighteously. This is true also with God's spiritual family to which every believer belongs.

For God's name's sake, and due to our love for Him, we want to be good representatives of His family. How we live now has eternal value. Jesus, our great Intercessor, is praying that we'll have strength to do the right thing.

Are We Tzaddikim?

Tzaddik in Hebrew means a righteous person. At Acts 7:52 and elsewhere 'The *Tzaddik*' with the definite article, means the Messiah (Matt 10:41)[46] (The Just One, the righteous man's reward.)

Tzaddik is the 18th letter of the Hebrew alphabet. It is interesting to see that the letter looks like an individual kneeling and lifting his or her arms in praise. It is written in Hebrew like a capital "Y" that is bent at the bottom. Kneeling with arms lifted in praise is a good way to become more *tzaddik.* King David became *tzaddik.* So can you and I.

Jesus said in His Sermon on the Mount, "Blessed are they who hunger and thirst after righteousness, for they shall be filled" (Matt 5:6 KJV-MOD). See also Psalms 119:137-144.

If we ask God to fill us with more of His righteousness, I am sure He will answer our prayer.

Join me for an interlude of two Holiday Messages

Wise Men Will Seek Him and Find Him

For about 35 years I have created my own Christmas cards. A friend encouraged me back then so I took her up on it. Daring huh?

Last year, my graphics designer friend, Pat, suggested that we go down to Wight's Home and Garden Store in Lynnwood to take a picture for the card. There we found a life size display of the three wise men with their gifts for the Holy Child.

I had already written my annual Christmas poem. It emphasized the two-year-old Jesus and the Wise Men from the East so that was the scene I posed by.

In years past, I wasn't aware that the wise men did not come to visit baby Jesus, but rather came to see Him when He was about age two. We know this because when the wise men were looking for the location of

233

Jesus' (*Yeshua's*) house, they visited King Herod the Great in Jerusalem.

"And he [Herod] sent them to Bethlehem, and said, Go and search diligently for the young child; and when you have found him, bring me word again, that I may come and worship him also" (Matt 2:8 KJV-MOD).

Unbeknown to the wise men, Herod had also been looking for this child, but not for good cause.

When the wise men found the Child Jesus, they worshipped and gave Him gifts of gold, frankincense, and myrrh. These were not birthday gifts, but gifts for a King.

The gifts had a double purpose of helping the Holy Family to escape and be cared for in a foreign land.

Divine Dreams Save Lives

The wise men did not go back to see Herod in Jerusalem, as he requested, but went home another way as they had been warned by God in a dream (Matt 2:12).

Foster father Joseph was also warned in a dream that the family must escape to Egypt, or their child would be killed. They obediently packed immediately and left in the middle of the night (Matt 2:13).

Herod, in a rage, realized that the wise men had ignored his request, and immediately sent out an edict that all males in Bethlehem and all the coasts, age two and under were to be slain (Matt 2:16). This horrific event is known today as the Slaughter of the Innocents.

Sometime later, a second dream and message came to Joseph. "But when Herod was dead, an angel of the Lord appeared in a dream to Joseph in Egypt, saying, 'Arise, and take the young child and his mother and go into the land of Israel: for they are dead who sought the young child's life'" (Matt 2:29-20 KJV-MOD).

Herod's son was now king, and so the Holy Family did not settle in Jerusalem. Joseph being warned by God in yet another dream, settled them about 90 miles north, in the city of Nazareth in Galilee (Matt 2:22-23).

The Righteous Infant Jesus

Jesus never had a birthday gift
That was not the Jewish way.

Sweetness, anointing, and purity
Frankincense, myrrh, and gold
Were the only gifts Jesus received
When He was but two years old.

Chosen Wise Men from the East
Followed a bright star to His home
The ultimate purpose of such treasure
Save Holy Family from tyrants of Rome.

Joseph took Mary and the righteous Infant
He was warned in prophetic dream
Fled to Egypt, 'til Herod's demise
As he had planned to kill the young King.

This Christmas let us be ever faithful
To the righteous Child who came to earth
Who made it possible for you and me
To have an everlasting second birth.

© 2009 by Rita Bennett

Your Days Are Like Pearls – Treasure Them Daily

A particular scripture has intrigued me for years. It is, "Teach us to number our days, that we may apply our hearts to wisdom" (Psalm 90:12 KJV-MOD).

My question is, "How do I number my days?"

I think it is fair to deduce by biblical reasoning that only God knows the beginning and ending of each of our lives. I do not mean that He controls our every step and action, and like floundering marionettes we have no freedom to choose.

But rather God who is omniscient or all knowing, is outside the confines of time (past, present and future) and can therefore see the decisions we will make down to the very last day, hour, and microsecond of our lifespan.

Don't be Lured with Trifles.

Some people attempt to find out their life span by going to a fortuneteller. Just think if the information received is wrong then one will plan his or her life according to deceptive information! Deuteronomy 18 gives a strong warning against this activity (Deut 18:9-14).

Shakespeare describes such deception with Banquo speaking: "But 'tis strange. And oftentimes, to win us to our harm, The instruments of darkness tell us truths, Win us with honest trifles, to betray's In deepest consequence ..."[47]

If God's Holy Spirit has something to say to you, He can tell you in a dream, in Scripture, or in prayer. He has given me guidance in these safe and biblically sound ways throughout my adult life.

Take a Lesson from Solomon.

When King David died, Solomon his son became the King of Israel. Though he did not become a faultless ruler, at this beginning stage, Solomon sought the Lord for guidance for his life as a king.

"That night God appeared to Solomon and said to him, Ask what I shall give you" (2 Chron 1:7 KJV-MOD).

Solomon responded with, "Give me now wisdom and knowledge, that I may go out and come in before this people; for who can judge this Your people, that is so great?"

"God replied to Solomon, Because this was in your heart, and you have not asked riches, possessions, honor and glory, or the life of your foes, or even long life ... Wisdom and knowledge are granted you, and I will give you riches, possessions, honor and glory ..." (2 Chron 1:11-12 AMP)[48]

Because of Solomon's thoughtful response, God gave what he asked for – and much more!

One of the ways you can gain the wisdom and knowledge of Solomon is to read and study his writings found in the 31 chapters of the book of Proverbs. If you are looking for a New Year's resolution, this is a good one for you and perhaps your family.

Numbering Our Days

In 1969 my Dad, William Harvey Reed, wrote a tender poem called, "My Days Are Numbered." He was a widower in his older years as my mother died fourteen years before him. Married and living in the northwest I knew he had many family members around him in Florida, and that he was a strong Christian. He made friends easily. However, I never knew how much he loved each and every day of his life, until I read this poem after his death.

My Days are Numbered

My days are numbered,
Like leaves on a tree,
Each day that passes
Is gone from me.

When the sharp winds blow,
More than one leaf drops to earth,
In the setting sun,
No one notices its worth.

The barren tree greets dimming eyes,
And a few leaves cry –
For they are like our days
Before we too wither and die.

For our days are numbered.
This I know
And each day that passes,
Draws closer and to me does show.

There are very few days left
They are like pearls to me,
Are like the last fallen leaf
From a beautiful barren tree.

Numbering Your Days

1. Value your life and treasure it
2. Do not waste your valuable gift of days
3. Learn all you can on your trip
4. Practice God's loving presence
5. Help others along your pathway
6. Spend time with God each day
7. Read books of wisdom, especially His Book
8. Pass on the pearls you have discovered
9. Rejoice, this life is not all there is.

Happy New Year and Happy Hanukkah!
We'll continue with Psalm 23 in Chapter 6 Part 1.

Chapter 6
Part 1

Psalm 23 continues
Breaking News – Earthquakes, Lenten Series
and Global News, My Personal Story Series

Rita Bennett and Dove (photo above) – Rita visited the Holy Land Experience in Orlando, Florida. She is standing in front of the replica of the Garden Tomb in Israel. Holding a tame dove, Rita is comforted as she thinks about why the gentle dove represents the Holy Spirit. She loved the dove and was inspired to write a poem, *The Dove*, in 2003.

Psalm 23 Series Continues (Six Articles)
The Valley of Death and It's Several Meanings

"The Lord is my Shepherd I shall not want. He makes me to lie down in green pastures. He leads me beside the still waters. He restores my soul. He leads me in paths of righteousness for His name's sake" (Psalm 23:1-3 KJV-MOD).

"Yes, though I walk through valley of the shadow of death, I will fear no evil; for You are with me" (Psalm 23:4a KJV-MOD). This verse is the one we will look at today.

What is the valley of the shadow of death?

Often people would guess that this Scripture refers to the end of one's life or physical death. Death is not a favorite topic for most people.

The comic Woody Allen says, "I don't mind dying as long as I am not there when it happens."[1]

Yet the Jewish interpretation of this verse is different, "The morbid valley characterizes exile … It is a place so dangerous that it is as dark and forbidding as the grave."[2] The Jews know what it is like to be in exile for hundreds of years in Babylon, Persia, Egypt, Greece, Rome, Poland, and Germany until it became worse than exile. Experiencing holocaust is beyond death itself.

Persecution of any individual or group of people is truly, a valley of the shadow of death.

The 1994 Rwandan genocide with one million people killed is a most recent holocaust. Immaculee Llibagaza prays through her many close calls with death, "God, I am really walking through the valley of death – please stay with me. Shield me with the power of your love. You created this ground that we're walking on, so please don't let these killers spill your daughter's blood on it."[3] This is a very moving book to read. I highly recommend it.

The Valley of Death

Another way to look at this verse in the 23rd Psalm is to see each person's death as walking through the valley of the shadow of death. When we know the Lord, our Good Shepherd, we can see death as only a fleeting shadow. We walk out of the shadow lands into the true reality of the fullness of God's Kingdom. "... There shall be no more death, nor sorrow, nor crying. There shall be no more pain, for the former things have passed away" (Rev 21:4 NKJV).

When my friend Dianne's husband Dave Herivel died in the mid 1990's, I had the sad and joyful experience of praying with him while he was near the very end of his life.

I bowed my head, and suddenly it seemed right to pray Psalm 23 over him. I began, "The Lord is Dave's Shepherd he shall not want. You Lord are leading him beside the refreshing still waters. You are restoring His soul. Lord Jesus You have led him in the paths of righteousness for Your name's sake.

Yes, though Dave is walking through the valley of the shadow of death, he will fear no evil. For You Lord are with him."

"Your rod and Shepherd's staff they comfort Dave. You've prepared a table before your child in the presence of his enemies. You have anointed Dave's head with oil; his cup runs over.

"Surely goodness and mercy have followed Dave all the days of his life. And he will dwell in the House of the Lord, Forever! Amen."

Though Dave could not speak, his eyes looked over to his wife, Dianne, on the other side of his bed. She whispered to me softly, "He said, 'Thank you.'"

How grateful I was to know that and to be there.[4]

God's Omnipresence

"I will fear no evil; for You are with me" (Psalm 23:4b KJV-MOD). Dave was a faithful husband and father to his three daughters and a strong Christian.

You and I can be free from fear also when in the valley of death. These words are a promise to us too.

As long as God is with you, you can handle anything. Dianne, Dave's lovely wife, was supernaturally strong that day. It was amazing to see her as a strong soldier of Christ, even leading their musical family in song, by his hospital bed, in his last moments on earth.

God is with you; you can acknowledge His presence now.

Tell Him: "Abba, Jesus, and Holy Spirit, I want You with me always. Come to me dear Lord." Now sit back and relax, and wait to sense God's loving presence with you – Amen.

See you next time at the 7th Psalm 23 series.

Only One Person Can Separate You from the Love of God – You

"The Lord is my Shepherd I shall not want. He makes me to lie down in green pastures. He leads me beside the still waters. He restores my soul. He leads me in paths of righteousness for His name's sake. Yes, though I walk through the valley of the shadow of death, I will fear no evil; for You are with me" (Psalm 23:1-4a KJV-MOD).

"Your rod and your staff they comfort me" (Psalm 23:4b KJV-MOD). We will look at this verse today.

What do the words rod and staff really mean?

Jewish thinking sees the rod as God's punishment for sin, while His staff is support for the believer in time of affliction. "Both are equally comforting for a Jew's greatest consolation is that he is not an insignificant straw blown about in chance winds. Rather, God is cognizant of his behavior, and rewards or punishes accordingly."[5]

Generally speaking, Christians are quite grace-centered. Their first choice would probably be that the main purpose for the shepherd's rod is to beat off the sheep's enemies.

I discovered in the first column on Psalm 23 that the Hebrew spelling for shepherd is *Roi.* Coincidentally, or by God's design, the first letter "R" in Hebrew looks like a shepherd's crook or curved staff. It was fun to discover that while writing my first column in this series.

The staff is very handy for the shepherd while walking in the hills and dales to let the sheep graze. If a sheep falls into dangerous craggy rocks, the crook at the top of the staff can help the shepherd reach down and rescue his sheep. Also, the sheep pass under the staff when they are counted each night.

So the rod and the staff both comfort the believer. Jesus Christ, our Shepherd and King, has power and authority over all the forces of darkness, and we, His sheep, have His protection.

A Place for Discipline

But how about discipline? We know that is important, too. Discipline has the word disciple in it. The two are closely related. You cannot have one without the other.

A good parent must use some form of effective discipline. When we do wrong, I believe the greatest discipline for God's children is that we feel separated from the One who loves us most. God doesn't leave us, but it is as though we create an airtight capsule around ourselves that thoroughly blocks our fellowship with Him. He's there all right, but we are blocking His presence.

There's only one person who can separate you from the love of God and that is yourself! And there's only one person who can restore the fellowship and that, again, is yourself, when you humble yourself before God and repent from your sins.

The Good Shepherd

In the Gospel of John, chapter 10, Jesus describes Himself as the good Shepherd. In fact, He states He is the good Shepherd three times in this chapter.

When Jesus gave His life for His sheep, He was showing the greatest love that could ever be expressed for us personally and for the entire human race. The Good Shepherd made *agape,* God's unconditional love, available to us not only at the time of our first accepting Him, but every day of our lives!

God is good and He is love; He's concerned about you personally and longs to bring you into His fold to heal you, feed you, and restore you. When you accept the Shepherd, all this and much more is possible.

One day I wanted to be Jesus' disciple, so I said, "Yes Lord." We've been traveling together ever since. I've been grazing on awesome eternal food, and drinking pure living water. His rod protects me. His staff leads me. He is *Roi Tov,* my good, Shepherd. Make that triple good.

His invitation is open. Whosoever will may come.

See you next time at the 8th Psalm 23 series.

You've Prepared a Banquet for Me – In front of My Enemies

"The Lord is my Shepherd I shall not want. He makes me to lie down in green pastures. He leads me beside the still waters. He restores my soul. He leads me in paths of righteousness for His name's sake. Yes, though I walk through the valley of the shadow of death, I will fear no evil; for You are with me. Your rod and your staff they comfort me" (Psalm 23:1-4 KJV-MOD).

"You prepare a table before me in the presence of my enemies" (Psalm 23:5a KJV-MOD). This verse we will look at today.

The shepherd David, who wrote this psalm, was set apart by God to be King of Israel. Since he was the youngest of his brothers and was simply a shepherd boy, it did not seem logical for him to have this great honor. But God looked at his heart, not his size or age.

As it is with many leaders who rise to the top, they are not happy when qualified younger persons threaten to take their place. That's exactly what happened here.

King Saul was on the hunt to destroy his contender to the throne. Even though David had a group of followers – a rag-tag army of 400 to 600, he had to be on the move so as not to be taken out by Saul. Interestingly, Jonathan, the king's son, was secretly on David's side.

Dealing with an Enemy

David could sing to God these positive words in the midst of the threat of death: "You prepare a table before me in the presence of my enemies." Many times the Scripture says, "And David behaved wisely in all his ways, and the LORD was with him" (1 Sam 18:14 NKJV).

For example, two times David could have killed King Saul and taken his throne, but he would not do it. Why was that? Because David feared displeasing his Lord more than he feared letting the anointed but sinful king continue to live.

During a battle, David cut off part of the hem of Saul's garment, and he showed it to him (at a healthy distance). He told Saul "I will not stretch out my hand against my lord, for he is the LORD'S anointed" (1 Sam 24:10b NKJV).

David's humble, godly behavior had won the king over, and Saul said, "And now I know indeed that you shall surely be king …" (1 Sam 24:20 NKJV). They even made a covenant together to protect Saul's offspring.

Singing Your Way through Battle

David was a psalmist who filled his life with music. I can picture David taking time during days of hiding in the hills to sing and write down a song or two. The psalms he left are a spiritual banquet for us today.

Perhaps you can write a song about your emotional pain. Songs often tell of pain in a relationship. Singing songs of praise in worship services are very comforting to congregants. In fact, it is healthy to fill your lungs up with fresh air and sing out with praise.

I've written a few personal songs. One related to a challenge I was facing. Words and music came as I was playing my ukulele.

"I am heavy hearted. I hear my Savior whisper: 'This too shall pass away. This too shall pass, this too shall pass, this too shall pass away'" (Chorus).

"I carried all your burdens, I said, 'My yoke is easy.' Yes, I will help you in this hour. Yes, I will help every second, every minute; Help you with My pow'r." Pretty simple, I admit, but meaningful to me. I published it in a song book, *Singing to be Emotionally Free*, in 1996 and titled it "You're Coming Though."

The many psalms that David the shepherd wrote are quoted and sung all over the world. Psalms can even be downloaded to your iPod.

David was victorious in battle because he put God first. He kept a Spirit-inspired song of praise in his heart consistently.

You, too, can sing your own psalms of victory. Write a poem and then try to sing it. Try it.

See you next time at the 9th Psalm 23 series.

Samuel Took the Horn of Oil and Anointed Him

"The Lord is my Shepherd I shall not want. He makes me to lie down in green pastures. He leads me beside the still waters. He restores my soul. He leads me in paths of righteousness for His name's sake. Yes, though I walk through the valley of the shadow of death, I will fear no evil; for You are with me. Your rod and your staff they comfort me. You prepare a table before me in the presence of my enemies." (Psalm 23:1-5a KJV-MOD).

"You anoint my head with oil; my cup runs over" (Psalm 23:5b). We will look at this verse today.

David, who had written a large portion of the book of Psalms, is here referring to one, or all three, of the anointings he had received during his life.

The first one occurred when Samuel the prophet was told by God to go to Jesse's house and anoint one of his sons to be King of Israel. Saul who had been anointed king over Israel years before was often not walking in God's ways so it was time for a change of leadership.

All seven of the sons passed before Samuel as possibilities, but Samuel prophetically said, "The Lord has not chosen these" (1 Sam 16:10b NKJV). The Prophet wanted to know if Jesse had another son. He said he had one younger son who was tending the sheep.

So the father sent for his son. "… Now he was ruddy, with bright eyes, and good-looking. And the LORD said, 'Arise, anoint him; for this is the one!' Then Samuel took the horn of oil and anointed him in the midst of his brothers; and the Spirit of the LORD came upon David from that day forward …" (1 Sam 16:12-13 NKJV).

David was about 15 years old at this time. He would later be anointed king over Judah at Hebron for seven years and over all Israel at Jerusalem for 33 years (2 Sam chapters 2 and 5). He reined a total of 40 years.

So now we know why David explains his anointing with oil in Psalm 23, which caused his inner cup to run over with joy!

Aaron Anointed High Priest

David wrote another Psalm about anointing. It was about Moses' brother Aaron when he was anointed High Priest. It is also one of my favorites.

"Behold, how good and how pleasant it is For brethren to dwell together in unity! It is like the precious oil upon the head, Running down on the beard, The beard of Aaron, Running down on the edge of his garments. It is like the dew of Hermon, Descending upon the mountains of Zion; For there the Lord commanded the blessing — Life forevermore" (Psalm 133 NKJV).

The Church is Anointed Today

There are many anointings with oil in the church. The oil used is olive oil, sometimes with frankincense or another perfume added. There is anointing with oil after baptism, with prayer for healing, and for those near or at death. Anointings for ministry positions held in the church are deacon, minister or priest, bishop, and archbishop.

On the Day of Pentecost about 2,000 years ago, 120 disciples and Apostles in the upper room were anointed with the Holy Spirit. This was not an external anointing with oil, but an internal one. Tongues of fire were seen over the people's heads and they spoke with languages of praise beyond their own understanding. Their speech centers were anointed and as a result they became capable speakers and witnesses for their resurrected Lord.

Peter, who had vacillated from time to time, was so empowered that he preached to a crowd in Jerusalem, and 3,000 souls were born again in one day! Now that was a catch of fish for the fisherman Peter (Acts 1:8, 2:4).

Some churches believe that the anointing of the Holy Spirit is still available for believers today.

Take a moment to relax and pray, "Dear Lord, I need your power. Please anoint me. I want to be your witness. In Jesus' name. Amen."

See you next time at the 10th Psalm 23 series.

Get Acquainted With the Good Shepherd

"The Lord is my Shepherd I shall not want. He makes me to lie down in green pastures. He leads me beside the still waters. He restores my soul. He leads me in paths of righteousness for His name's sake. Yes, though I walk through the valley of the shadow of death, I will fear no evil; for You are with me. Your rod and your staff they comfort me. You prepare a table before me in the presence of my enemies. You anoint my head with oil; my cup runs over.

"Surely goodness and mercy shall follow me all the days of my life: and I will dwell in the house of the LORD for ever" (Psalm 23:1-6 KJV-MOD). We will look at verse six today.

The story is told that a young man heard this verse read aloud, and thought it was speaking to him personally. He was dating a woman named Shirley. He heard, "Shirley, with goodness and mercy (like two little puppies), will follow you all your days." So he decided to propose!

This is of course not the best way to use Scripture! Nor should we close our eyes, open the Bible, point, then open our eyes and read expecting the best answer for our need!

I also like the Hebrew rendition of this verse: "May only goodness and kindness pursue me all the days of my life."[6]

The word kindness comes from the word *chasadh* (Heb). "In a little wrath I hid my face from thee for a moment; but with everlasting kindness will I have mercy on thee, saith the LORD thy Redeemer." (Isa 54:8)[7]

Looking at two of the words used in verse six – goodness is God's Spirit working within us, and kindness is us reaching out to others. "The combination of the two terms expresses a desire that one will experience personal growth while not neglecting to help others."[8]

God's Grace is Eternal

Chasadh is also close to the Christian word, grace, which means receiving "God's unmerited favor."

The prophet Isaiah puts it this way, "For the mountains may leave and the hills be removed, but My grace will never leave you, and My covenant of peace will not be removed," says *Adonai*, who has compassion on you" (Isa 54:10 CJB).

Another Dimension

"I will dwell in the house of the Lord for ever" (Psalm 23:6b). How is that going to happen for us? Where is this house, this place, located?

In 1996 I was getting into the subject of Heaven. I believed in it personally, although I hadn't heard a *bona fide* sermon or read a book specifically on the subject. Since I was preparing to write a book that included that topic, my publisher back then, required me to read all published books on Heaven. I think there were only five non-fiction books I could find in print at that time.

That year I was able to obtain the first edition of *The New NIV Interlinear Hebrew –English Old Testament*,[9] and also used my scholarly late husband's commentaries and my own many editions of the Bible. I found that the word Heaven when it referred to the spiritual abode of God, saints and angels, and not the sky and space (heavens), had to be referenced in context. As I studied, I found fifty-four references in the Old Testament and ninety-seven in the New Testament – or a total of 151 references. Of those accounts thirty-nine are Jesus' own words.

My two books on Heaven total 483 pages, not counting this present book, but as we know there is an awesome amount of knowledge to be revealed to us all, one day. God Himself is of course the final word on Heaven (*Shamayim*). In my studies I've found,

"Heaven is a real eternal place, and not only an earthly spiritual experience. There, we will find unconditional love, tangible peace, beauty, total acceptance, history, heavenly music, praise, worship, dancing, friendship, family reunions, fulfillment, amazing light, mountains, rivers, and rainbows. We will experience shining gemstones, wisdom, knowledge, learning, thirst-quenching drinks, delicious fruit in variety, heavenly manna, trust, joy, kindness, health, timelessness, and eternal life. These are for starters"[10]

After Jesus completed His "operation rescue" for the human race with His death and resurrection, He said, "I go to prepare a place for you. And if I go to prepare a place for you, I will come again and receive you to Myself; that where I am you may be also" (John 14:2b-3 KJV-MOD).

This is what the Good Shepherd of Psalm 23 meant that forgiven believers can look forward to; the reward of eternity with God in His home with His family forever.

Tell the good Shepherd that you want to belong to Him. Then take some time to repeat Psalm 23 quoting it in first person.

"You Lord are my good, my very good, Shepherd and that means I shall not want. You make me to lie down in green pastures. You lead me beside the still waters." Use the scripture in the first paragraph to help you.

Take your time. Enjoy every moment. Say "Amen" meaning "so be it" at the end of your prayer.

See you next time at the 11th Psalm 23 series.

A Lasting Valentine Gift of Psalms 23

Pray aloud or write "The 23rd Psalm for My Valentine" adding his or her name as an *Intercessory Prayer*.

The Lord is Mary's Shepherd
She shall not want.
The Lord invites her to lie down in green pastures.
He leads her beside the still waters.
He restores Mary's soul.
He leads her in paths of righteousness for His name's sake.
Yes, though she walks through the valley of the shadow ...
She will fear no evil; for You Lord Christ are with her.
Your rod and your staff they comfort Mary.
You prepare a table before her in the presence of her enemies.

You anoint Mary's head with oil; her cup runs over.
Surely goodness and mercy shall follow Mary all the days of her life:
And she will dwell in the house of the LORD *forever"* (Psalm 23:1-6
KJV-MOD).

Listed below are eleven blessings given to His sheep, a metaphor for us. The list below is a brief review of my eleven previous Beacon Columns.

1. The Lord is my Shepherd (vs. 1). A shepherd is someone who loves his flock, cares for them when sick, and would lay down his life for them.
2. I shall not want (vs. 2). "Oh taste and see that the LORD is good; blessed is the man who trusts in Him! ... Those who seek the LORD shall not lack any good thing" (Psalm 34:8-10 KJV-MOD).
3. He makes me to lie down in green pastures (vs. 2a). I can picture Jesus, sitting there on the grass watching me (or you) and enjoying childhood activity of rolling down the beautiful, green hillside.
4. He leads me beside the still waters (vs. 2b). I think my good Shepherd would have liked to be in an inner tube beside me (or you) that summer in Florida, and joined us for a picnic at the beach.
5. He restores my soul (vs. 3a). The soul refers to the psychological part of a human being, intellect, will, and emotions. If we should backslide in our faith, we will need soul restoration.
6. He leads me in paths of righteousness for His name's sake (vs. 3b). Our Lord also made provision for believers to be empowered with the Holy Spirit. We cannot live a righteous life without divine help.
7. Yes, though I walk through the valley of the shadow of death, I will fear no evil; for You are with me (vs. 4a). During the 1994 Rwanda holocaust, Immaculee Ilibagaza prayed through her many close calls with death, "God, I am really walking through the valley of death – please stay with me. Shield me ..." [11] God heard her prayer!
8. Your rod and Your staff they comfort me (vs. 4b). There is only one person who can restore fellowship with God and that is you,

when you humble yourself before Him and repent. The rod and the staff of our Shepherd, comforts the believer.

9. You prepare a table before me in the presence of my enemies (vs. 5a). Though David was often pursued by King Saul's army, still he found time as a psalmist to fill his life with music. The psalms he left are a banquet for our table. Pray that your enemies will join in your songs, and be healed.

10. You anoint my head with oil; my cup runs over (vs. 5b). On the Day of Pentecost, the 120 disciples gathered in the upper room were anointed with the Holy Spirit. Their speech centers were so anointed that they praised God beyond themselves.

11. Surely goodness and mercy shall follow me all the days of my life; and I will dwell in the house of the LORD forever (vs. 6). "For the mountains may leave and the hills be removed, but My grace will never leave you, and My covenant of peace will not be removed, says Adonai ... (Isa 54:10 CJB).

Forgiven believers can look forward to the reward of eternity with God – in His home – with His family forever. Amen.

Have a wonderful Valentine's Day with romance (human or divine) and chocolates!

I'll see you next time as we explore more of God's bestseller.

Lenten Series (Seven Articles)
A Touch of God's Grace – Without End

As a writer and president of a non-profit organization in Edmonds, I often find my schedule going into the early hours of the morning. On Wednesday, February 28, 2010, I was working until 5:00 am on my newsletter. I had gotten a few paragraphs beyond the point where I mentioned earthquakes. What I had written was:

"While the problems with the Israelis and Palestinians continue to escalate, students of prophecy are studying their Bibles and checking to see where we possibly are on God's timetable ... Many prophetic books in the Bible foretell a final challenge for the Jews in their homeland before Christ (Messiah) comes. More earthquakes are shaking the world every few weeks ..."

I did not realize that just six hours later, we were in for a 6.8 earthquake in Edmonds and the greater Seattle-Tacoma area. The timing of my newsletter seemed almost prophetic.

When the quake came, I was in bed trying to make up for my late night's work and was awakened with the earth's shudder at 10:54 am. I saw my hanging lamp swinging and felt like I was on board ship. Realizing it was an earthquake; I jumped out of bed to the floor and laid down face to the ground. I stuck my head and as much of me as I could under the bed! I'm rather small, but my bed is low and has some items stored under it.

As soon as the floor stopped shaking, I got up and headed for the kitchen to locate my emergency radio. I listened to the news for half an hour, learned no aftershocks were expected and went back to sleep in total peace.

Though there were two small aftershocks, we know how fortunate it was that the quake was thirty miles deep so it did not do the horrendous damage it could have.

Ash Wednesday Service That Night

Later that night happened to be Ash Wednesday where ashes are placed on one's forehead to remind us of what Genesis 3:19 says. "… For dust you are, and to dust you shall return" (NKJV). Here God is correcting mankind for his woeful disobedience in what is known theologically as The Fall of Man.

The following selections of scripture are normally read as the church begins its forty days of penitence. The Old Testament scripture read, Joel 2:1-2; 12-17, was significant. "Blow the trumpet [shofar] in Zion, Consecrate a fast, Call a sacred assembly; Gather the people …" (Joel 2:15-16 NKJV).

Writing my column for February 25, 2010 Lent had begun again. Lent is a time of extended reflection of our lives, which helps to keep us grounded and aware of more important values. Some are:
- Prayer (justice towards God),
- Fasting (justice towards self), and
- Almsgiving (justice towards neighbor).[12]

Let's look at almsgiving. Our earthquake in the northwest has little comparison to the disastrous earthquake of Haiti on January 12, 2010.

Ours was 6.8 and theirs was 7.0 on the Richter scale. The most fortunate difference for us is that ours was 30 miles deep!

I'm sure anyone reading this column either has sent a contribution to help Haiti, or has prayed for the people affected. These are part of the good works we might do at any time, but especially at times of disaster.

January 16, 2010 Port-au-Prince – CNN. Anderson Cooper reports, "From a distance it looks like an ordinary land-fill. The true horror is clear only up close. The dead of Port-au-Prince are slowly disappearing. Now we know where many end up ... This entire mound is already filled with bodies. As you walk, you come across a hand sticking out from the dirt; you see a foot sticking out ... It's incredibly quiet, all you hear is the wind blowing, and buzzing of flies ... We saw at least 100 bodies clearly visible ... There's no system of identification ... People will simply disappear and no one will ever know what happened to them. Another truck approaches with another load of the dead. Who they are, who they were, the lives they led: none of that now will ever be known. Anderson Cooper, CNN, Port-au-Prince."[13]

God Helps the Living and the Dead

You and I cannot help the dead, but only the living. Our Creator is the only one who can help the dead, as everyone will experience resurrection some day (2 Tim 4:1). He is the just and righteous King.

"God is our refuge and strength, A very present help in trouble. Therefore we will not fear, Even though the earth be removed, And though the mountains be carried into the midst of the sea; Though its waters roar and be troubled, Though the mountains shake with its swelling. Selah. There is a river whose streams shall make glad the city of God, The holy place of the tabernacle of the Most High" (Psalm 46:1-4 NKJV).

Lots of Worldwide Shaking Going On
Breaking News

Wow, we had three more earthquakes since my earthquake report in *The Edmonds Beacon* last week. It was interesting to me that all three are reported occurring at different times but on the same day!

- 2-27-2010 Concepcion, Chile 8.8 magnitude, This is a megathrust type that occurred along the fault zone.

- 2-27-2010 Okinawa, Japan 6.9 magnitude, and
- 2-27-2010 Lincoln County, Oklahoma 4.4 magnitude.

Chile Earthquake: The Next Big One – The Washington Post

"So: Is this the Next Big One? Here's what we can say at the moment: There's a lot of devastation in the images on CNN. You see crumbled buildings, collapsed highways, major fires. This was certainly a huge quake. About three million people were subjected to extreme shaking, and another 12 million to very strong shaking, according to a USGS email circulating this morning. That said, Chile is not nearly as vulnerable to quakes, from an infrastructure standpoint, as most other South American countries. This wasn't nearly as powerful as the 1960 quake.

"Here's an email I got from Susan Hough, a USGS seismologist, this shrove morning:

"'3 million people exposed to MMI 8 is not good. The shaking level is largely an estimate and may be too high: there is some evidence that big subduction zone quakes produce relatively low levels of shaking for their magnitude. And construction in Chile is better than Port au Prince, although a big step down from Japan and California …'"[14]

Chile Quake Similar to 2004 Indian Ocean Tremor – The Seattle Times

"The Nazca tectonic plate, the section of the earth's crust that lies under much of the Eastern Pacific Ocean south of the equator, is sliding beneath another section, the South American plate. The two are converging at a rate of about 3 ½ inches a year."[15]

Tsuanmi Warning Downgraded – Stars and Stripes

"Japan suffered only minor flooding and no injuries Sunday despite predictions of massive tsunami waves spawned by Chile's earthquake that forced the evacuation of hundreds of thousands of people - including thousands of US military personnel - on mainland Japan and Okinawa."[16]

Oklahoma Reports 4.4 on the Rictor Scale – Allvoices

"Shortly after 4 pm on Saturday Oklahoma reported an earthquake with a 4.4 magnitude. There is no injuries to report and only minor damage.

"The 911 centers say the tremor could be felt from Lincoln County to Prague, Norman, Seminole, and even as far as Tulsa."[17]

Wendy Case is based in Luray, Virginia, United States of America, and is a Stringer for Allvoices.

Bible Confirms Tectonic Plates

Dakes Bible reports:

"Today there is mounting evidence that our continents were at one time joined together.

"It is said that the continents could be fitted together like a jigsaw puzzle. The east coast-line of South America matches the west coast of Africa with the rounded corner of Brazil fitting into the gulf of Guinea. Facing coasts of the United States and Europe can be fitted together etc.

"At last scientists are awaking to facts that the Bible recorded as truth 4,000 years ago (Gen10:25).

"It was in the days of Peleg that God divided the earth, after the confusion of tongues and scattering of the people abroad upon the face of the earth."[18]

Peleg (Hebrew) was a son of Eber (1 Chron 1:19). Interesting that *Peleg* prophetically means canal, channel, or division!

What We Can Do to Be Safe

I tried to update myself while watching the news, reading the paper, and checking online news this week.

First of all, I learned that during an earthquake, if possible, it is important to move fast to get out of the building you are in. It is normally the building that may kill you, not the earthquake. (Unless a fault line is at your front door!)

Earthquakes usually last from two to three minutes, so you do not have a lot of time.

Ladies it is good to have your keys or purse close at hand to grab and run out of your house.

Leave your house the quickest way.

Lying flat on the floor between two tables may be recommended, however, only do that if you cannot move out of the building.

If a tsunami is expected, you need to evacuate to the highest point of a building or a hillside.

Wrapping It Up

A text message or text may be typed to send a brief, electronic message to a loved one over a cell or smart phone network. In battle situations, as in Iran, on TV I saw how people connected with their loved ones who otherwise would have been lost in a crowd. You may also use your Twitter or Facebook account for this purpose.

By your bedside, you also need a small emergency radio, small Bible, and wallet. My purse has everything to go. The trunk of my car has a backpack with warm clothing, blanket, snacks, and bottled water.

Pray, give, learn safety rules, have updated fire extinguishers in your home and car, educate your children, have a rendezvous plan.

When you've done your best, rest in God's peace.

Lenten Series (Five Articles)
From Ashes of Repentance to Epiphany of Glory

I did not celebrate the spring Lenten season of the Christian Church in my childhood, but only in my adult life. Jesus did not give a commandment about keeping a season of Lent, but the Church under God, beginning in the fourth century, recommended keeping an extended time of reflection and repentance. Some believers do it this way.

In the Episcopal, Anglican, and Catholic churches, for example, the tradition is to prepare for Ash Wednesday services by meeting on Shrove Tuesday for a pancake supper. Delicious fresh pancakes are an easy way to use up butter, eggs, and yeast before the less fattening, frugal days of Lent begins.

I try to attend the pancake supper of my church, especially for fellowship during the meal. It is fun to see the guys working in the kitchen, flipping those hundreds of pancakes!

Pancakes Anyone?

Pancake supper is done in recognition of removing from our lives old leaven (yeast) that usually represents sins in the Bible. Saint Paul says, "Purge out therefore the old leaven, that you may be a new lump [of bread dough] …" (1 Cor 5:7a KJV-MOD).

I think of this lump as pita bread or matzah, that has no yeast in it. The Church followed Jesus' tradition when as from a child, He and his parents followed the feasts of God (Lev chapter 23).

The feasts of God in Scripture began in the spring with Passover (coming out of Egyptian bondage), next Unleavened Bread (confess sins – rid self of old leaven – now receive holy wine and matzah wafers), and then First Fruits (Jesus death and resurrection).

Paul tells the Church, "For even Christ our Passover is sacrificed for us: Therefore let us keep the Feast" (1 Cor 5:7b-8a KJV-MOD).

Lent officially begins a day later on Ash Wednesday.

Ash Wednesday

The name Ash Wednesday comes from the ancient practice of a minister placing ashes on a worshipper's forehead, sometimes in the form of a cross. It is a sign of humility that is expressed well in these words, "For dust you are, and to dust you shall return" (Gen 3:19b NKJV).

This was a decree from God as a result of the treasonous choice our first parents made to follow another god before Him. It was then necessary for Jesus to buy us back from the pharaoh-like usurper, Satan – and to redeem Adam and Eve from the results of turning over their lives and dominion of the world, to this king of darkness (Rev 5:3-14).

The good news is that by Jesus' death and resurrection, salvation and restored dominion comes to all who receive the Savior, Jesus Christ. You could be on a desert island or in a foxhole, and pray to God to receive Christ, just as easily as someone who walks down the aisle of a church. If you'd like to do this, pray, "Lord Jesus please forgive my sins, and come into my heart today. With Your help, I will follow You as Your disciple. Thank You Lord Jesus. Amen." (Put today's date in your Bible next to John 3:16.)

The Biblical Number Forty

"Since Sundays celebrate the resurrection of Jesus, the six Sundays that occur during Lent are not counted as part of the 40 days of Lent, and are referred to as the Sundays **in** lent. The number 40 is connected with many biblical events, but especially with the forty days Jesus spent in the wilderness preparing for His ministry by facing the temptations that could have lead Him to abandon His mission and calling."[19]

We need to pray for ourselves that we will not be tempted by the deceiver who would like us to abandon God's mission and calling for our lives. "If it feels good, do it," is not the pathway for a healthy, exemplary, influential life. Father God does not want to see us mindlessly fumble our way through life not knowing where we're going, who we are, or why we are here.

Repentance and Restoration

During these six weeks, we will remember that through our unrepentant sinful life-style, we in essence may have crucified Jesus afresh (Heb 6:1-6). The commandments of God are broken or possibly not even known (Exodus 20:1-17). If we, like Peter, do not admit to those asking us about our Friend Jesus or do not admit that we even know Him – we may all the while deny our Best Friend who loved us to His death.

Peter repented from his denial of the Lord and was empowered with the Holy Spirit. His life of victory is proclaimed in the Bible and his name is written as one of the twelve Apostles of the Lamb! At God's twelve gates to Heaven there are welcome mats in stone foundations there. Peter's name is listed as one of those twelve names (Rev 21:14)![20]

Every Sunday *The Book of Common Prayer* used in many churches proclaims the mystery of faith:
Christ has died.
Christ is risen.
Christ will come again.[21]

This Lenten season begins with ashes. We walk with Christ through His challenge to the world's darkness. It concludes with joyful fulfillment in the epiphany of His resurrection light.

I'll see you next time as we continue to explore the news through God's bestseller.

Fasting and God's Word for Your Battles

We are still in the Lenten season of the Church. Eating less and more frugally, it is hoped will bring our bodily appetites more under control. Not all, but a good number of church members, try to follow this Lenten discipline.

Annually I attend my church's soup and bread supper. We enjoy hearty soup and a variety of breads. Some golden delicious apple slices dipped into lemon juice and a sprinkled with a little sugar were the only dessert.

Later food for the soul may come in the form of Scripture study, discussion, and intercessory prayer. Clergy couple, John and Sarah, teamed up to lead us. We sat around a large double rectangular table in the parish hall. Sharing was encouraged. We broke out into laughter from time to time.

As I mentioned a few columns ago, Lent means a time of humbling our souls and bodies with fasting, repentance, and forgiving. The kickoff to this event begins at Ash Wednesday service. Count forty days and nights from February 17, minus Sundays, brings you to the triad of Good Friday, Holy Saturday, and Resurrection (Easter) Sunday.

What does the number forty make you think of? You will remember Moses on Mount Sinai near the Red Sea 3,500 years ago, and Jesus on the Mount of Temptation in the Judean wilderness 2,000 years ago. There is also forty days of Noah's great flood, and forty years of the children of Israel traveling to the Promised Land.

Therefore in Hebrew biblical numerology, forty means trials, tribulation, and testing.

Jesus in the Desert

Let's choose the event closest to our time, Jesus in the desert of Judea. After three days of fasting, one's stomach begins to shrink, so the faster loses his desire to eat. One's energy eventually is depleted, in fact, after a week the body begins to lose weight and slowly shut down.

Jesus did not go on a 40-day fast for fun!

Like the Olympic game stars, Jesus put His body under serious discipline in preparation to fight His greatest personal enemy and the greatest enemy of the human race. No fans were watching the battle, but

I think the banisters of Heaven were crowded with saints and angels looking on.

Who is this enemy? He is Lucifer the former angel, son of the morning, who after his treasonous rebellion against God Almighty, morphed into Satan.

Through Jesus' 40-day battle, and confrontation by Satan, the Lord won His victory with three sword-like Scriptures originating in Deuteronomy.

Round One

Prince of Darkness: "... If You are the Son of God, command this stone to become bread" (Luke 4:3 NKJV).

Jesus, King of Light: "... It is written, 'Man shall not live by bread alone, but by every word of God'" (Luke 4:4 NKJV).

Round Two

Prince of Darkness: "... All this authority I will give You, and their glory; for this has been delivered to me, and I give it to whomever I wish" (Luke 4:6 NKJV). This happened with Adam and Eve when they obeyed Satan and gave up their dominion and ours. Satan continued: "Therefore if You will worship me, all will be Yours" (Luke 4:7 NKJV).

Jesus, King of Light: "... Get behind Me, Satan! For it is written, You shall worship the LORD your God, and Him only you shall serve" (Luke 4:8).

Round Three

Prince of Darkness: "... If You are the Son of God, throw Yourself down from here. For it is written: 'He shall give His angels charge over you, To keep you, And In their hands they shall bear you up, Lest you dash your foot against a stone'" (Luke 4:9-11 NKJV).

Jesus, King of Light: "... It has been said, 'You shall not tempt the LORD your God'" (Luke 4:12 NKJV).

Jesus answered perfectly, powerfully. Satan is seeing stars in the knockout.

This battle is ended until the biggest battle of all. It happens on what the Church calls Good Friday. Get your Scripture swords ready. I'll tell you more next week.

Rita Bennett

At Times It Is Wiser to Fast Than to Feast

I was thinking about my last column and the three rounds in the spiritual boxing ring Jesus and Lucifer had starting at the Mount of Temptation in the Judean dessert. It really was a "one, two, three, and you're out" situation. Jesus won that battle hands down. He did it for you and me. In 1996 I took a tour group of 25 to Israel. I looked at the dry, lifeless, mountain where Jesus had his battle. It impacted me strongly when I saw from my bus the actual biblical location where the Great Temptation took place!

Of course the preparation Jesus had to participate in was very painful, almost to the point of starvation – as He fasted forty days and nights. That is totally opposite to any kind of training a boxer or fencing champion would take. It doesn't make sense to the natural mind.

Others Fasted

Many other people fasted in the Bible. Daniel chose a simpler fast when he was in Babylonian captivity around 605 B.C. His fast was not total as Jesus' was. Daniel fasted like a vegetarian. That is, he did not eat meat, drink wine, or eat dessert from King Nebuchadnezzar's table.

He asked the cook to prepare vegetables and light healthy meals for him and the other Jewish youth's who had been taken captive from Jerusalem. At the end of ten days they looked much healthier than those who had eaten sumptuously at the palace. Daniel, renamed Belshazzar, and his three friends were allowed to continue on the vegetable and water diet.

Daniel was in training for three years to prepare to serve the king. This was forced upon him and his Jewish friends, renamed Shadrach, Meshach, and Abednego. He said they did not want to be defiled with the king's food (Daniel, Chapter 1). He was a devout man who could interpret spiritual dreams and survived being thrown into a lion's den.

Fasting Today

My late husband, Dennis and I, went on a 3-day fast of fresh vegetable juices and water, along with prayer and scripture. We did this when we realized that we needed to pray against an attack on our seminars. In three days, we had evidence that the spiritual battle had been won.

While I was at the university and nearing graduation for my Master's degree, I had some uncomfortable challenges. I was concerned about whether I would be graduating. I new friend, Carol, a counselor with her PhD said, "Rita I'm going to fast and pray for you on the last days of your classes." I was amazed at this gift.

I said, "Though still in class, I will fast part of the time with you." We journaled as we prayed and sought clear guidance from Scripture. We checked in with one another several evenings and shared what we had learned.

It was a great support and needless to say nothing could come against my success in graduating from LIOS/Bastyr University at the Seattle Center Opera House, June 21, 2008.

Jesus' First Attack

The first test for Jesus was when Lucifer, Prince of Darkness said: "… If You are the Son of God, command this stone to become bread" (Luke 4:3 NKJV).

Jesus could create miracles and had with His Father made manna come down from Heaven to feed the children of Israel on their journey in the wilderness. The resurrected Christ had also provided a fish and bread dinner when Peter and the other disciples had been out fishing.

Reading about this round one battle, I thought, "That was a low blow to say to the fasting, starving, Lord that He should make bread!" Maybe the Tempter wanted to get Jesus' salivary glands and memory of favorite breads pumping up His desire for bread.

But Jesus would have none of it. With all His strength Jesus, King of Light declared: "… It – is – written that man shall not live by bread alone, but by every Word of God" (Luke 4:4 KJV-MOD).

During the Lenten season, you have been strengthening yourself for the battles you are in or may yet face. Through the ages believers have fasted and prayed for various needs.

Jesus said, "For the bread of God is He who comes down from Heaven and gives His life for the world" (John 6:33 NKJV).

Those who receive Him will never suffer from spiritual starvation.

When Palm Sunday Was Inaugurated and More

When I visited Israel for the first time, for five afternoons, pilgrims from many countries gathered on the beautiful Mount of Olives for our program. We sat on blue blankets provided by The World Prayer Congress and their leader Roberta Hromas. We faced the massive, glowing eastern gate. Prophecy declares that one day Christ/Messiah will walk down the mountain and through this gate.

In modern times they now have a large white cement walkway going down the southeast side of The Mount Olives. The Bible tells us that this is the location where Jesus was proclaimed Messiah on Palm Sunday when He was there two millennia ago.

Of course believers back then had not named it Palm Sunday as many do in our 21st Century. They did not have a New Testament to read about this holy day as we do!

What happened was that Jesus and His disciples were traveling in their healing ministry and came from Bethpage, also called Bethany, to The Mount of Olives. The distance was about a mile and a half. Jesus knew that the time of His crucifixion would soon occur. Regardless of all the miracles He had done for several years, He did not often admit that He was the Son of God. He knew that this fact could only be revealed to others supernaturally, by the Holy Spirit.

Prophecy Fulfilled

Now was the time that He would intentionally fulfill the prophecy given 400 years before by the prophet Zechariah:
"Rejoice with all your heart, daughter of Tziyon [Zion]!
Shout out loud, daughter of Yerushalayim [Jerusalem]!
Look! Your King is coming to you.
He is righteous, and he is victorious.
Yet he is humble—he's riding on a donkey
yes, on a lowly donkey's colt" (Zech 9:9-10 CJB).
Jesus asked His disciples to search for a donkey for Him. He told His men where to go, who to see, and what to say. The disciples eventually returned, put their own garments on the animal, and set their Master on it. The huge crowd of men, women, and children Jesus had ministered to over the months and years had gathered.

Where We Get Palm Sunday

"And a very great multitude spread their clothes in the ground; others cut down small branches from the trees, and spread them as a carpet. And the multitudes that went before, and followed, cried, saying, 'Hosanna to the son of David: Blessed is He that comes in the name of the Lord; Hosanna in the highest'" (Matt 21:8-9 KJV-MOD).

We Too Can Enter In

I didn't see any palm trees on the Mount of Olives. There were mainly beautiful olive trees that looked something like small weeping willows, only with round leaves. Some areas of Israel have date palms.

Liturgical Christian congregations are given slender palm fronds. Before the service begins, they may choose to march around the church building waving palm branches. Singing songs of praise, and hearing Scriptures read as they walk are often part of the service. When you experience this personally, it helps you **feel a part of the crowd that proclaimed Jesus as Messiah 2,000 years ago**.

I've participated in numerous Palm Sundays. Palm Sunday prepares us for the next most important Sunday. Resurrection or Easter Sunday tells us of the biggest battle and the biggest victory Jesus had, and because of Him – victory for you and me.

When you accept His love and relationship, you will not become just a pile of dust when you die. Your life on earth is then only the Preface to your Book of Life.

Your Chapter One will begin with fulfilled eternal life in the awesome Kingdom of Heaven with your Savior.

Proclaim It

Today you can begin proclaiming what Matthew taught: "Blessed is He that comes in the name of the Lord; Hosanna in the highest" (Matt 21:9b KJV-MOD). And Zechariah taught, "Look! Your King is coming to you. He is righteous, and He is victorious" (Zech 9:9a CJB).

"Hosanna" means "Save now." Save me now. Save my mate now. Save my children now.

Take some time to think about God's love for you this very moment. Take a deep breath. Relax. You are blessed and safe in His arms.

The greatest story ever told continues next week.

Choose Life on Easter or Any Day of the Week

Jesus' birth occurred about 2,000 years ago, although God planned it before the foundation of the world. Why did Father God send His Son, Jesus, to Planet Earth two millennia ago? Because the first couple He created horribly failed a spiritual test.

Lucifer, who was cast out of Heaven after his treasonous attempt to take over God's throne, then went after God's first created people. He's been in a war to get the most people on his side ever since.

Lucifer, known as Satan, made Adam (man) and Eve (life) doubt God's Word to them. First he tempted the woman to eat the forbidden fruit.

The woman responds, "But the fruit of the tree in the midst of the garden, God has said, you shall not eat of it, neither touch it, lest you die" (Gen 3:3 KJV-MOD).

The Tempter cunningly says to Eve, "You shall not surely die. For God knows in the day you eat thereof, then your eyes will be opened, and you shall be as gods, knowing good and evil" (Gen 3:4b-5 KJV-MOD). Here Lucifer, i.e. Satan, is attacking God's Word!

The food looked so good, also becoming a god no doubt lured her, and so Eve was the first to be convinced by this devilish, slithery salesman.

Sin, sickness, and death entered into our human race and the whole of creation. "For we know that the whole creation groans and travails in pain together until now" (Rom 8:22 KJV-MOD). The "now" is speaking of God's plan being fulfilled through the redemption of our bodies in years to come (Rom 8:23, 1 Thess 4:13-18, 1 Cor 15).

But in the beginning, Adam and Eve immediately died – not physically but spiritually. Physical death happened to them some years later.

Our LORD's plan had to be put into place to rescue mankind from the evil kingdom and from our own fallen selves.

God's Plan of Redemption

Easter or Resurrection Sunday is not just lovely folklore carried down through generations by numbers of believers. It is the greatest story ever told! It is the story of a choice of either eternal life, or eternal death for each person.

This is the reason Jesus, the Son of God, came to the Middle East to be born to Mary, a lovely Jewish virgin, who was betrothed to Joseph. **Jesus was on a self-sacrificial mission to save us**. The sinless Christ Jesus chose to come as a perfect sacrifice for our sins. That was His plan from the beginning to die in your place and in mine.

What could have happened if this rescue had not been carried out? It would have been **hell on earth** with no ending even at death. Think of the most hellish place on earth and multiply that by millions and you can see from what God rescued us.

How did Jesus accomplish this amazing rescue for us once He grew into manhood? He had twelve Apostles, though one betrayed Him. He gave numerous dynamic life-changing sermons, healed thousands of people, raised the dead, fed multitudes, cast out evil spirits, baptized new disciples, and loved us.

Before his death He was tortured, beard pulled out, slapped, spit upon, ridiculed, beaten 39 stripes with a whip, starved, a crown of thorns pressed into His head, paraded naked in the street, carried His own execution cross beam, and nailed to a tree.

From the cross Jesus gave His mother's care to the Apostle John. Then He saved the soul of one thief on the cross next to Him and told him, "Today you will be with me in Paradise" (Luke 23:43 KJV–MOD). With all the strength He could gather He shouted, "It – is – finished!" and died (John 19:30).

Death and Resurrection

His friends, Joseph of Arimathea and Nicodemus, prepared a Jewish burial with spices, myrrh and aloes, and a linen cloth that covered his body front to back, head to toe. Since Jesus was in the tomb three days and nights the fragrances counteracted the smell of death.

But Jesus did not stay in the grave. He, who paid the price of redemption for you and for me, was raised from the dead. He accomplished all this because He wants us to be rescued, safe, and with Him always (John 11:25-27).

When we accept Him and His sacrifice for us, He gives us a new spirit and a new heart. We are born from above. We are now in His Kingdom as His ambassadors on earth. And our new Spirit-filled life has just begun.

It Is Not Politics, Race, or Religion

The problem in this world is not political parties fighting one another, or people thinking critically of others because they were born into different races, and it is not different religious denominations challenging one another's validity.

It is actually a problem of two spiritual kingdoms at war! Jesus rose again, but the dark kingdom – though defeated – is for a time still seriously at war.

Each individual has an opportunity to choose either the Messiah's Kingdom of love, peace and life, or the imposter's kingdom of hate, cruelty, and death. To learn more, study the Bible, as the answers are all there.

I hope you will say, "I choose life." Even today – Even now.

Next column: St. Francis of Assisi.

Make Me an Instrument of Your Peace

I was invited by new friends, Katy and Nick, for lunch at Arnie's some months ago. Katy is a beautiful, young married woman who met Nick, an older Irish gentleman, at an Alcoholic Anonymous meeting. Nick became her sponsor. They meet often to work through the Alcoholics Anonymous Twelve Step Program and he also shares spiritual insights with her.

The way I met Katy was when both of us were called to jury duty at the courthouse in Everett. After all the preparation for hearing one of three trials, Katy and I and five others were not called but would simply be substitutes – if needed. We were told to go have lunch! This was a turn of events.

I looked at our small group and found one woman. I asked if she'd like to have lunch with me, and so I met Katy. We got acquainted over lunch. She lives in Lynnwood, which is near me, so we had more time to visit as she drove me home.

Katy and I were willing to be juror's, as citizens, to bring the peace of law to the land, and discovered we were called to another kind of peace – that of friendship.

When Katy shared with Nick our experience at the courthouse, Nick said it sounded like God's plan. I, in fact, felt the same way that morning in February 2010. I love God's divine appointments.

The Prayer of Peace

Now I segue to our recent lunch. In saying our goodbyes, I met Katy's friendly, big, yellow Labrador retriever, Filson. She and Nick were taking him to the dog park for a swim.

Later, I received an email from Katy, who said,

"One of Nick's main goals in life, besides helping people get sober, is to give the *St. Francis Prayer* to them.

"He believes that this prayer helped him find God and get sober, and feels it will also help other people too.

"Nick has had thousands of copies made at his own expense and hands them out at all the AA meetings he holds and goes to, and at all the conferences he attends. He hopes that in this way he may help and save someone, and is **very** passionate about it.

"I don't know if it is possible or not," said Katy "but I had the idea that maybe you could use the St. Francis Prayer as a subject for one of your Worship Columns. In this way, I feel I can help Nick spread the prayer for him. I would feel like I'm doing something special to pay Nick back for all the help he has given me."

I Love St. Francis of Assisi Too

When I took a small tour group to Italy in 1998, two of the pilgrims chose to catch a train to the monastery in Assisi where a Franciscan Order had been founded. There had been a recent earthquake and so the walkways had not been repaired. It was too rough for me, but these real hikers were able to go regardless.

"*St. Francis of Assisi,* the patron saint of animals and ecology, was a Roman Catholic saint who took the gospel literally by following all Jesus said and did. Christians everywhere celebrate the feast of St.

Francis of Assisi on October 4 by having their pets blessed in the spirit of this patron saint of animals and ecology."[22]

Here it is for Nick and Katy, and all who want a more peace-filled life.

Peace Prayer of St. Francis

> LORD...
> *Make me an instrument of your peace;*
> *Where there is hatred, let me sow love;*
> *Where there is injury, pardon.*
> *Where there is doubt, faith;*
> *Where there is despair, hope;*
> *Where there is darkness, light;*
> *Where there is sadness, joy.*
> *Grant that I may not so much seek*
> *To be consoled, as to console;*
> *To be understood, as to understand;*
> *To be loved, as to love;*
> *For it is in giving that we receive.*
> *It is in pardoning that we are pardoned.*
> *And it is in dying*
> *That we are born to eternal life.*

Empowered21 Global Congress On The Holy Spirit[23]
Global News

Two years ago I returned home from "Empowered 21st Century." It took place in Tulsa, Oklahoma April 7-10, 2010. Eight thousand people, half of whom were age 30 and under, came together to celebrate their faith. Oral Robert's University (ORU) hosted the event, and William Wilson from International Center for Spiritual Renewal was Chairman. All university classes were closed so students could attend. There were workshops as well as morning and evening large gatherings.

The theme was "Purity, Passion, and Purpose." Six speakers from mega churches came from Africa, Asia, Australia, Europe, South America and North America.

Empowered21 Global Congress on Holy Spirit Empowerment Conference chose the dates April 8-10, 2010 because it was the 50th anniversary for those historic, charismatic churches who proclaim empowerment of the Holy Spirit today, and the 109th year of the beginning of the Pentecostal outpouring in Topeka, Kansas.

My late husband, the Rev. Dennis J. Bennett, was honored with a "2010 Pioneer Award for Spiritual Trail–Blazing" trophy. It was for having been a primary leader in the Holy Spirit revival that had begun 50 years prior to this ORU event. I was asked to receive the honor for him in front of 8,000 or more cheering people!

Mrs. Bobi Hromas, was asked to receive the honor on behalf of her grandfather, Rev. Charles F. Parham, for his trail-blazing that had begun 109 years ago, at Topeka, Kansas.

Both trophies were presented to us by Dr. Mark Rutland, President of ORU.

PowerPoint Presentation

I presented a "Learning Conversation" along with a group of four other charismatic leaders in the Golden Update Panel. They were Gary Moore – Methodist, Larry Christensen – Lutheran, Oreste Pesare – Roman Catholic, Julia Duin – Washington Times author, and myself – Episcopalian.

I shared a message about Dennis' life and our international outreach ministry together for the 25 years of our marriage 1966 – 1991.

History

In the early church, 2000 years ago, it was common for Christians to believe in the supernatural gifts of the Spirit such as, healing, discernment, words of wisdom, and to expect them in their meetings. After Jesus' resurrection and ascension, this went on for quite a few centuries. Eventually it began to fade.

Dennis began to personally re-discover these nine gifts of the Holy Spirit in 1960. He found that there was no place in the Bible that said they had passed away.

"If they were no longer available," he taught, "it would be like christening a new ship with champagne and thinking after that, No more fizz water and excitement is needed or wanted."

In his metaphor, the Church is the ship, and the champagne is the power of the Holy Spirit and His imparted gifts. The Church today needs more power rather than less power!

The Nine Supernatural Gifts Are:
- **Revelation Gifts** (Knowing):
  1. A word of wisdom, 2. A word of knowledge, 3. Discerning of spirits.
- **Power Gifts** (Doing):
  4. Gift of Faith, 5. Healing gifts, 6. Gift of Miracles.
- **Vocal Gifts** (Speaking):
  7. Gift of Prophecy, 8. Gifts of Spiritual tongues, and 9. Interpretation.

We Need Empowerment

The gifts of the Spirit come from the Greek word *charismata* and are listed in 1 Corinthians 12:7–11. Dennis said, "What is happening to people today when they receive the freedom of the Spirit is just the same as the first, except that now we understand much more about it. The Church is not primarily a preaching or teaching institution. It must be charismatic.

"It must manifest the gifts and fruit of the Spirit, for they are the continuing signs that Jesus is alive and ready to bless people now."[24]

Now I invite you to take some time to pray, "Come Holy Spirit, reveal the supernatural gifts to me, as shown in the entire Bible. Empower me to do the work You've called me to. Amen, may it be so."

My Personal Story Series (Seven Articles)
A Personal Story of Divine Purpose in Life

Recently I wrote an article about a conference I attended in Tulsa, Oklahoma, called Empowered21 Global Congress on the Holy Spirit.

A friend emailed me to say, "The Empowered Celebration article is a good entrance to a discussion about the gifts of the Spirit. I'm sure people would be blessed," she said.

Dennis and I wrote a 241-page book on this subject, *The Holy Spirit and You*.[25] Writing on this topic in the newspaper would have to be greatly condensed; yet with that in mind, here I go.

My Spiritual Roots

When I was an infant, my parents took me to a Presbyterian church in Port Huron, Michigan to be baptized. The Holy Spirit came upon my life according to the minister's prayer and my parent's faith for me. I believe there was protection over my life from this act by my parents.

We moved to Tampa, Florida when I was age two. In my new Florida full gospel church at age nine, I responded to an invitation to accept Jesus personally as Savior and was immersed.

I went to church with my parents and to Sunday school. Then I grew into the challenging teenage years. My church was rather rigid regarding movies, dancing, and lipstick. I eventually was less involved in my church and tried others.

Seeking

I tried to read the Bible from time to time but did not have help from a qualified, caring person. When as a teen I got to the "begats" in Genesis and Matthew, I thought, the Bible was not for me. I had little guidance and so gave up. Besides, I was not aware that in Bible reading you do not usually start on page one, like in a regular book, but it's best to begin with a book of the Bible such as the Gospel of John or Matthew.

Fortunately today we have many more translations than the King James Version which was all I had then. Now I understand and appreciate the KJV but it was archaic to me in those days. Good commentaries are also great teacher helps to students of the Bible.

At that time, the world seemed more interesting to me than the religious life. I spent my time going to high school, then college, socializing, dating, and going to parties. I still tried to attend church on Sundays, but most of the time the sermons were not life changing and often uninteresting.

I do not remember hearing a sermon on morality, the Ten Commandments, or Heaven. These subjects would have been helpful to me. I usually went to church one hour a week and the world had my attention all the rest of the time. This was rather a losing battle for developing a life of faith.

Finding

I eventually became an Episcopalian. When I was leading the junior choir one Sunday, I ran into an old friend from my teen-age years, Gail Miller. I invited her to my new apartment near the school where I was a teacher.

She told me her husband had divorced her and yet I saw she was at peace. I asked her how she could be so calm in this kind of a storm.

Gail said she had a very close relationship with the Holy Spirit. I found out later that the Holy Spirit is called the Comforter and that His presence is what she was experiencing.

Before Jesus left Planet Earth for Heaven He said, "If you love Me, keep my commandments. And I will pray the Father, and He shall give you another Comforter, that He may abide with you forever" (John 14:15-16 KJV-MOD).

Though Jesus would no longer be on earth, I learned that He and the Father would be with me through the Holy Spirit.

If you are where I was at this time, please pray the following prayer:

"Dear Lord Jesus, I want to be a less worldly believer. I want to be empowered by the Holy Spirit so I can be an effective witness. Quicken your Scriptures to me. Fill this hunger in my soul and spirit. I want Your divine purpose for my life. In Your Name I pray. Amen."

Join me next time on my journey and direction in discovering God's gifts.

A Story of Divine Purpose – Continues

Last week I attempted to begin a transparent story of my early spiritual life or lack thereof. Writing about this was harder than I thought.

Now I'm back again to invite you to help me walk on my continuing journey. In my seeking, I mentioned becoming an Episcopalian. By saying this, please note that I'm not promoting a denomination but I am simply telling my story. Episcopal means having bishops. I guess any church that believes in a bishop's headship is in essence, episcopal.

When I joined the church May 14, 1959, my oldest brother, Bill Reed M.D., an Episcopal lay-reader was delighted. A lay-reader reads the Scriptures aloud at appointed times during a church service.

Bill told me that at my confirmation service, when the Bishop laid his hands on my head and prayed, I would receive the power of the Holy Spirit. That meant my spiritual life would be strengthened. This sounded important, as I did need deeper spirituality. I found out later that reading the book of Acts, chapters 1 and 2, would have helped me understand more.

Working in Newark

After graduation from my university, for a year I was a volunteer in New Jersey working at the Youth Consultation Service Center. This was when I made my step toward confirmation. My three friends, also college grads and apprentices in social work at YCS, joined me for the church service.

The minister led us in Scriptures, prayers, renouncing evil, renewing our commitment to Jesus Christ, and the Apostle's Creed.

As I came forward for this special part of the laying-on-of-hands, the prayer given for me was: "Strengthen, O Lord, your servant Rita Reed with Your Holy Spirit, empower her for Your service; and sustain her all the days of her life. Amen."[26]

I do not think I heard or absorbed the words spoken over me, as I was probably a bit self-conscious.

It really was a good prayer. Empower her for service was one of the main reasons for this whole event. It is possible that I, not fully understanding, thought the main purpose was joining the church.

Endued with Power

St. Luke quotes Jesus who uses similar words, "And, behold I send the promise of My Father upon you: but tarry [wait] in the city of Jerusalem, until you are endued with power from on high" (Luke 24:49 KJV-MOD).

I had been a Christian for sixteen years, but I did not show evidence of any kind of spiritual power. Seems there was something missing.

Another quote includes Jesus' instructions. "And, being assembled together with them [the apostles] He commanded them that they should not depart from Jerusalem, but wait for the promise of the Father, that you have heard from Me. For John [the Baptist] truly baptized with water; but you shall be baptized with the Holy Spirit not many days from now" (Acts 1:4-5).

Forty Days Training

Here we find Jesus in His glorified, resurrected body – giving forty days of final training to His Apostles before His ascension. What extremely important words they were. He does not just suggest but He commands them to receive the power of the Holy Spirit before they travel outside the city of Jerusalem.

After Jesus' ascension, 120 disciples obediently gathered in the upper room on Mount Zion to wait and to pray for the Holy Spirit's power. Maybe they fasted with their ten days of prayer. I wasn't taught fasting during my childhood or young adult life.

My prayer life was rather light. But now I was getting some new ideas through my church. A challenge in my life would soon occur to cause me to rethink my life. Take some time to read Acts, chapters 1 and 2, and I will tell you more next time.

A Story of Divine Purpose and Kingdom Light

This column continues with an interlude where situations in life reveal how one's present level of faith is not enough. I told you about Gail Miller and how we were reacquainted after living in different parts of the United States. She had returned to my hometown, at that time Tampa, Florida. We had a chance meeting at my church and over lunch she let me know that her husband had divorced her.

She could not make her husband continue to love her, so she put her life and future into God's hands. Gail showed a kind of peace that was rare and appealing.

I invited her to share my apartment while she got on her feet. I continued to teach at an elementary school near my apartment.

I had taught school one year in Tampa and then worked as a social worker apprentice in New Jersey one year. Now I was back teaching in Tampa, this time working with exceptional children. Three years before I had graduated from the University of Florida, in Gainesville with a BAE degree and life seemed to be going quite well for me.

Two Directions

Gail's way of life was different from mine. She surprised me by attending a prayer meeting in Palma Cia every Friday night. I could not understand the appeal of this kind of activity for a woman in her early twenties. I wondered what could be drawing her to spend a perfectly good Friday night sitting around in the living room of a lady Bible teacher, her husband, and other assorted people from various religious persuasions.

I did not want to waste my weekends and I happily enjoyed going out to dinner, a dance, or a party with a date. Florida was quite a party state. Gail and I were both enjoying ourselves but we seemed to be drawn in two different directions.

One day Gail said, "Hey Rita, I've been given a reservation for us to go to a Camp Farthest Out retreat at Fort Lauderdale beach. Do you want to go this weekend?"

Right away I responded, "That sounds like a lot of fun. I love to swim and relax on the beach."

A Deeper Way

Frank Laubach began that first day with an early morning meditation on the molecular structure of the water, the consistent rhythm of the waves, and he continued by giving a microscopic view into God's creation.

The Florida sun was beginning to shine on the frothy blue, white capped waves and his deep, kind voice was restful. I had never begun a day like this. I was looking forward to the next morning.

After lunch in the afternoons, we met in different small groups with a prayer leader. It would start with inspiring words and biblical quotes. Our second day the teacher began sharing on the subject: "Keys of the Kingdom."

Apparently there are two different kingdoms on earth. She taught something like, "One kingdom is full of light and the other kingdom is full of darkness. It is up to us to choose which one we will live in. We need to receive the keys to enter God's kingdom."

Break Through

We eventually stood to join hands in our prayer circle, as people prayed spontaneously. I listened as they prayed. At one point I began to cry and try as I may, I could not stop! Maybe my sobs continued three or four minutes. I might have been embarrassed but somehow I felt relieved. No one bothered me, as they seemed to understand.

This was our last meeting, so I thanked the ten or twelve people and we hugged one another good-bye. As Gail and I drove home, I knew something was happening to me but I did not understand what.

Jesus speaks of His Kingdom, "My kingship [kingdom] does not derive its authority from this world's order of things ... My kingship does not come from here" (John 18:36 CJB).

I learned later that Gail had secretly paid my way to the CFO retreat. She was more tuned into God than I expected. Next time I'll tell you more.

A Story of Divine Purpose and a Wake-Up Call

Last week my divine purpose story ended where I had gone to a Fort Lauderdale, Florida beach retreat center. During a prayer circle, I was overwhelmed by what I now realize was God's grace-full presence.

I had been too busy courting the world to spend much time courting my Creator. I now found that the world had been crowding Him out.

I drove Gail and myself home in my apple-red convertible, MG TF-1500. The wind was blowing through our hair and the faithful Florida sun was shining brightly. Gail started singing some church songs that I had known in years past. I did not think these songs were cool, to use today's youth vernacular, but I joined in.

Some songs were *What a Friend We have in Jesus*, *Pass Me Not Oh Gentle Savior*, and *I Love Him - Because He First Loved Me*. This went on for most of our drive home.

Touched by a New Dimension

I had felt touched by a new spiritual dimension, but then life took on its usual routine. On Friday nights my friend still attended her prayer meeting and I realized later she was probably praying and having others pray for me.

I continued going to dances and parties. My activities were not all that bad. None of my friends used drugs or were alcoholics. But most of them would have thought it was strange to be so spiritually minded.

I did not know how to become a whole person, spirit, soul, and body. I did not know how to feed my spiritual inner being. In fact, I did not know there was a difference between my spirit and soul!

I had not been told that my spirit (*pneuma*) and soul (*psyche*) needed to be fed, just as my body needed nourishment. I did not have a daily devotional to help me start my day with food from God, nor did I have a Bible concordance to help explain Scripture so I could grasp it. In my early twenties, I was biblically illiterate!

God Met Us at the Beach

Gail and I decided to go to the beach, and this time to do some actual sun bathing. We found a white sandy spot at one of the gulf beaches, not far from my home in Tampa.

Spreading out our towels we were ready to get a dose of vitamin D and a good tan.

After a while, we had a cold drink and began to talk. Gail told me more about herself. She said she had been a believer from early childhood, but that she had never gotten into a satisfying spiritual life until she learned that God had provided something more for believers.

I never pinned her down about when that occurred. But here on the beach she distinguished between her conversion or salvation experience, and her empowerment.

She said, "After receiving the power of the Spirit, I began to study the charismatic gifts. One of them, sort of like a starter gift, helped me know how to pray when I did not know how."

I said, "Gail, I hardly even know how to pray nor do I spend much time doing it."

She smiled, then continued, "From that day on, I always had the words to pray beyond my own intellectual self."

I wondered how one prayed beyond one's self. Then I said aloud, "Oh I wish I could do that!"

I did not know it then, but I had prayed my first Spirit-filled prayer. And God was listening.

This was an important message from Gail and very timely.

I did not know that my dear friend would be moving to North Carolina and would die suddenly while on her lunch break. Gail's death was a shocking wake-up call to me!

Moses said, "So teach us to number our days, that we may apply our hearts to wisdom" (Psalm 90:12 KJV-MOD).

Next time I'll tell you what happened.

A Story of Divine Purpose and a Stark Look at Life

Last week my story ended where the best Christian I had ever known, Gail Miller, finally witnessed to me after a year of living the Spirit-filled life before me. That day we ended up at a beautiful Florida beach where she dropped the other shoe or should I say, sandal.

She gave the Holy Spirit credit for the joy she had in her walk with God. It was the Holy Spirit, third person of the triune God, filling and strengthening her along the way. She was in love with God.

It's as if the Holy Spirit is the Matchmaker who was sent by Father God to find a bride for His Son, Jesus. The Spirit was scouting for Gail to see if she would become a worthy bride.

Yet we are all included here, for humanity has the potential of being part of that corporate, spiritual Bride of Christ.

The Bible opened up to her and fed her spiritually. Her prayer life was energized. She talked to God as her best Friend. Sometimes she meditated on the Scripture and wrote in her journal. At times she simply praised God in her spirit and with her understanding also (1 Cor 14:15).

A New Kind of Friend

Needless to say I was impressed, as I had never had a friend who cared enough to speak to me like this. I was a 25-year old college graduate and teacher, a former university band dancerette and Miss Tampa contestant. Gail was a different kind of friend.

One day shortly after our beach conversation, Gail told me she had sought guidance from her prayer group leader. After their prayer together, she felt directed to return to North Carolina, the place where she had felt closest to God.

As time had gone by, there were now four of us young women who had rented a house together. Three of us were going to have to say goodbye to Gail. This was an unhappy farewell for me as she was the only one in the group who had a clear relationship with God.

A Dreaded Phone Call

Five or six months after our goodbye's, I received a phone call from Gail's aunt, whom I had never met.

She said, "I hate to tell you this Rita, but Gail Miller is dead. She was on her lunch break and began to faint, then had presence of mind to give her name and address before a cerebral hemorrhage occurred. She never regained consciousness but died eight hours later."

I was shocked and replied, "But I – I just got a letter from her and she was saying how right it was for her to have made the move."

"I'm sorry Rita. The whole family is saddened by this. I want you to know that the funeral will be this Saturday at 2:00pm, at the Baptist Church on North Florida Avenue."

"Yes, I know where that is. Thank you so much for calling. Of course, I –will – be – there."

I hung up the phone and sat in a stunned silence. I thought of Gail's life and said to myself, "Of course I know for sure she was ready to meet her Maker. But, I'm not so sure that I am."

Why, God?

I mused, "She had so much to live for. Why did God let this happen?"

Then I remembered how in her teenage years she was in a serious accident. Her parents were both killed but Gail lived. Her jaw was damaged so that she lost her lower teeth and had to have them replaced.

I then reasoned, "The effects of her head injury may have caused this hemorrhage 10 years later."

"No, God did not do this, but how will this terrible event have any benefit? I questioned.

Romans 8:28 says, "And we know that all things work together for good to those who love God, to those who are called according to His purpose" (NKJV). Gail certainly loved God.

Next time I'll tell you more.

Rita Bennett

A Story of Divine Purpose and Facing Death

I've been telling my personal story of how at age 26 – a 99-pound spiritual weakling – Biblically illiterate college graduate, I began to get new direction for my life.

The impact came through my friend Gail Miller who by providence had reconnected with me for about two years. During this time, three experiences with Gail affected me, her personal faith testimony, her life-style, and her sudden death.

I went alone to the Baptist church where her funeral would take place. I was seated on the front row right in front of Gail's open casket. I had never seen an embalmed body before and the reality of death shocked me. I do not remember what the minister said, as I sat there and cried throughout the entire service.

Gail's body was like a living sermon: "No one can control the length of his or her life. When your life is over will you have introduced anyone to God's saving grace and love? How have you prepared yourself for eternity?"

As I was leaving the church, I was introduced to Bertha and John Madden. This couple had the weekly prayer meeting in their home where Gail attended. I did not realize the importance of this meeting.

Sleepless Nights

I began to have some nights of insomnia. I was afraid of dying. One night I went to my parent's home nearby and told them of my fear.

Dad let me sleep with mom that night. My sweet mother calmed me by quoting a poem: "Safe in the arms of Jesus. Safe on His gentle breast. Sweetly His arms enfold me. Sweetly my soul shall rest."[27] I went to sleep.

Two weeks following the funeral, I received a phone call from Bertha Madden. She said, "I've been praying for you ever since we met at Gail's funeral. I began to receive some words I felt were for you. I wrote them down so I wouldn't forget them. If you would like to read them, please feel free to drop by my house."

My response was, "I'll be right over!"

I had never met a Christian before who said, "I've been talking to God about you and He said to tell you ..." I learned later that this is one of the nine supernatural gifts of the Holy Spirit called a Word of Knowledge (1 Cor 12:7-11).

I found Bertha's house, a white frame building, having a nice porch, and well cared for lawn. My new acquaintance opened the door to welcome me into her comfortable home.

A Spiritual Gift

We visited for a little while and then she gave me the written words resulting from her prayer time.

I read: "Expedient is it that you shall be no more a part of those abandoned to this world. Stay out of their cars. To do under My hand is ordained for you.

"Ask Me for the longings of your heart. Did I not make man? To you is there one ordained.

"Pick up the things [gifts] you have dropped; they are still at your feet. Scatter not among thorns, sit here by Me for a while and learn. Achievements are for all born to man, and for each is the good place given. Watch for the high place is yours – but to qualify you must in time.

"Follow Me, is My Word to you. Seek My face for the joy you crave."

I was amazed. These words registered with me as truth. I told Bertha I would attend her prayer gathering that Friday night rather than driving to the beach with girl friends to audition with a band. In that prayer gathering, my life's goals would be set in a new direction.

Confirming Bertha's spiritual gifts to me, within six years, I would marry a clergyman and there was a narrow margin of time in doing so.

To see how this transpired, join me next time.

A Story of Divine Purpose and God's Intervention

I've been telling you about my wake-up call at the death of my best Christian friend I had ever known, Gail Miller.

At Gail's funeral I met Bertha Madden who had a few weeks later phoned me saying that God had a message for me. That Gift of Knowledge I read rang true to me.

I had turned down a group of several young women as we had planned to audition to sing with a music group. My purpose in doing this was to go to a prayer meeting instead. If God was speaking to me, then that was more exciting than the band trip. Making such a spiritual choice was unheard of in my group of university friends.

When I arrived at the Madden's home that night in 1960, it was hard to find a parking place. I walked through the unlatched front door and saw that the large screened-in porch had wall-to-wall people. The living room was also crowded, but there my host guided me to a seat. This did not look as though it was going to be a boring meeting!

There was an air of excitement as the meeting began. We sang choruses, shared how God answered prayer, read from the Bible, and took turns praying.

Yet, at this point, I was simply an interested observer.

Getting Involved

Eventually, the leader asked if I would like to have prayer. You may remember from past columns that I had intermittent insomnia after Gail's funeral. So I thought to myself, "Maybe it would do some good and it couldn't do any harm."

My verbal response was, "Yes." I was guided to a chair more centrally located in the room. The prayer leader requested that the Rev. Bill Sherwood pray for me along with a few others. I did not know Fr. Sherwood, but since he was an Episcopal priest, I figured all would be handled properly.

He gently laid hands on my head and immediately prayed in a language I did not understand. It was beautiful and powerful. The thought came to me that this could be the spiritual unknown language that Gail had talked about. The realty of God's love and His presence touched me. I began to sob. Tears ran down my face.

Between the sobs came sounds and almost unutterable groans when I tried to speak to God. I was releasing a lot of hurt and pain in my 26 years of life.

Eventually the leader whispered in my ear to quiet my heart. For a time, I had forgotten about others in the room.

A Path for You

Later I read in the Bible, "Likewise the Holy Spirit also helps our infirmities: for we know not what we should pray for as we ought: but the Spirit Himself makes intercession for us with groanings that are beyond our power to say" (Rom 8:26 KJV-MOD). I would also discover that sounds began to form into words, just as Gail said at times she prayed beyond her understanding. That was also in the Bible (1 Cor 14:15). I would soon find that what I had experienced was right there in the words of Scripture. The Bible became spiritual food and the living words of God to me.

Following the meeting, my new friends congratulated me that I had received the power of the Holy Spirit. I smiled as I received loving hugs, said goodnight, got in my car and headed for home. It was a beautiful evening as so many are in Tampa, Florida.

My roommates were already asleep. I quietly entered my home and would discover my sleep sweet and my insomnia cured.

The next morning I drove to work by way of the Bay Shore Boulevard. Everywhere I looked there was more depth of color in the hibiscus flowers, blue birds, and sparkling Tampa bay. The world was new and I felt like a new person. I would never be the same.

Of course I am telling my own story; yours may be different.

All I know is that God loves you just as He does me. He has answers for you.

This book *A New Look at the News* shows you a lot of what has happened since those early days. Without the Holy Spirit's power and leading, I would not have written the columns you have read or the books I have been honored to write.

Next time, join me for my new segment on Spiritual Gifts and the concluding chapters. Thank you for walking with me this far.

Chapter 6
Part 2

Breaking News, Supernatural Gifts Series
The Fall Festivals Series, Breaking News
And Isaiah Revisited Series

Dennis Bennett, the Visionary (photo above) – Dennis received his Doctorate of Divinity degree in 2012 (posthumously) from Oral Roberts University in Tulsa, Oklahoma – 21 years after his passing! During his years of ministry, God gave him a world–wide platform to teach that the Holy Spirit's supernatural gifts are for today.

Supernatural Gifts are for Yesterday and Today
Breaking News

On Saturday June 5, our sunny day this week, I drove down Admiral Way in Edmonds. Cars lined the street. The ferryboat had landed. As I drove, I looked at our beautiful Puget Sound and felt thankful that it is lovely and clean.

I'd never thought to thank God for our waterway before. Today I am feeling grateful that we in the northwest have not had an oil spill disaster, as has Louisiana. The spill was, and is bad enough, but there is still danger of further seepage into the waters and beaches of Florida's Gulf Coast.

With the new partial well cap, 10,000 barrels of oil daily were being saved on tankers.

Unfortunately, at the same time, 10,000 barrels of oil were still flowing daily into the Gulf of Mexico.

British Petroleum's (B.P.) main goal was a relief well to be installed back in August, 2010. Though they saw some improvements, it still seemed a long time until a full cure. How painful it was to watch the news to see the damage that was being done to the environment!

What about Prayer?

Why didn't our churches have round the clock prayer for that oil contamination in the Gulf?

We need to forgive everyone we can think of who is connected with the oil spill. Pray for the families of those who lost their lives. Pray for loss of jobs and businesses. Pray for the environment that has been contaminated. Especially ask for divine wisdom to be bestowed on those in leadership.

Gifts of Faith and Wisdom

When I drove past the Edmonds United Methodist Church, during those days, I was given hope. On their reader board that day, I saw these words in large print: "Pray for the Gulf Coast."

I thought, "Now we're getting somewhere!" Here we see two of God's gifts, wisdom to know what to do – pray, and faith, to be able to pray – effectively.

Jesus Calms a Storm

I think of Jesus in the boat on the Sea of Galilee. He had fallen asleep and a storm had come up – probably late in the day. The disciples were frightened and awakened Him, as they had not learned this particular lesson from their Rabbi.

Jesus said, "… why are you fearful, Oh you of little faith? Then he arose, and rebuked the winds and there was a great calm" (Matt 8:26 KJV-MOD). The disciples were astonished that the wind and the waves obeyed Him (verse 27).

It was exciting when our tour boat crossed the Sea of Galilee in the spring of 1996. We were on our way to see the Church of the Beatitudes at Capernaum. I observed that morning the water was smooth, but it had gotten quite choppy by that afternoon as we returned.

A Word of Faith

I will tell you a present day story of faith. When my late husband, Dennis, was still here on earth, we loved to vacation in Hawaii on rare occasions.

One day on the island of Maui we were both having a great time playing in the ocean. At one point, I looked up to see a small whirlwind whipping up on the far side of the cove.

This shocked us both. There was no time to get to shore, to save our blanket and personal property! What to do? I spoke a word of faith out loud while holding Dennis's hand, "In Jesus name, I command you whirlwind to stay away from our blanket and all our personal property." Within seconds, we watched as many people's blankets, umbrellas, and other items flew through the air but we found ours had remained untouched!

If I had time to think of it, I could have asked protection for other's property as well. But then, I am a disciple who is still learning.

In recent columns, I told how I lacked depth of commitment to God until I was 26.

This event occurred after the Holy Spirit had empowered me. Before this change happened in my life, I would never have prayed as I did during the challenging whirlwind. Some might say, "That was just a coincidence." I would respond, "Before I learned that we are to pray as

Jesus prayed, the miracles never happened." See you for more miracles – in the Supernatural Gifts Series.

Supernatural Gifts Are For Yesterday and Today (Twelve Articles) A Supernatural Answer from God

This week we'll begin our investigation of spiritual gifts. Last time we gave an example – in a combination of faith and wisdom, and the importance of prayer. One of the leading gifts of God's Spirit is the Gift of Wisdom. Let's look at this together.

Four Kinds of Wisdom

Natural human wisdom is naturally applied knowledge. Wisdom in the fields of computer science and medical science have exponentially increased in the last two decades. Eighteen years ago, while doing my grocery shopping, I saw my first person using a cell phone. He was checking the grocery list with his wife. I was impressed.

Fallen supernatural wisdom was the very thing used to tempt the first man and woman to disobey God's commandment. "And when the woman saw that the tree was good (suitable and pleasant) for food, and that it was delightful to look at and a tree to be desired to make one **wise**, she took of its fruit and ate" (Gen 3:6 AMP). Saint Paul says, "But [now] I am fearful lest that even as the serpent beguiled Eve by his cunning, so your minds may be corrupted and seduced from wholehearted and sincere and pure devotion to Christ" (2 Cor 11:3 AMP). They fell for it.

Fortune telling is an example of counterfeit wisdom today (Dan 2:27-28). Those who fall for it will allow into their lives an inroad from the kingdom of darkness – with a small "k".

True intellectual wisdom comes by studying books of wisdom, especially in the Bible, and meeting with wise biblical counselors. "A wise man will hear, and will increase learning; and a man of understanding shall attain unto wise counsels" (Prov 1:5 KJV).

In my university studies, only secular books were required for a master's degree. Since graduating it is gratifying to once again buy and read faith–based counseling books. The wisdom of the author as well as the wisdom of God's Word underlying it, gives more benefits.

The **Supernatural** gift of the Word of Wisdom was expressed often in the prophet Daniel's life. As a Jewish prisoner, he was taken from Israel to King Nebuchadnezzar's palace in Babylon (Iraq). One of Daniel's first opportunities was to reveal to the King the interpretation of a dream he had forgotten. The gift of wisdom was supernaturally revealed to Daniel in a dream or night vision. None of the magicians, astrologers, or sorcerers could give an effective answer. Daniel's gave the correct dream and interpretation to the King and he was saved from death along with his Jewish friends – including all the false soothsayers. Daniel was honored with leadership at the King's gate (Dan 2:20-49).

God Speaks Today

In 1961 in Tampa, Florida, I was at a social worker's meeting. A behavioral scientist PhD during his lecture said, "We are animals." He then gave several gross examples that showed just how animal–like we are. Then he said, "Your clients will have good, and bad cycles. There is not much you can do to help them. That's the way it will continue to be."

In other words, don't get your hopes up.

As a renewed Christian, I felt confronted and challenged by this encounter. That night, as I lay in bed, I asked God a question, "Am I just an animal?"

I thought, "This would obviously mean that at death my body will go into the earth, and my spirit and soul will simply disappear."

During the night I awoke with the answer from God, in question form: "How can you be an animal, when you are made in My image?"

I came fully awake and turned over in bed. I thought over the message. "It must be the Lord. God is obviously not an animal nor am I, as His believing child!"

This was a Gift of Wisdom imparted to me as I slept. I had fought my way out of the world–system into the arms of God, so He – who is love – was not going to let me fight this battle alone.

Made in God's Image

In the first chapter of Genesis we are told that we are made in God's image (Gen 1:26-27). But what does that mean? God is speaking on a level deeper than the physical. "From the primal elements you brought forth the human race, and blessed us with memory, reason, and skill. You made us rulers of creation."[1]

Memory of mankind is beyond that of animals.

Reason helps us human beings to learn from past discoveries. We've even built a station in outer space. We have travelled to the moon. In 2012 we have sent the spacecraft Rover to Mars.

Skill to use our hands is unique in building, construction, surgery, art, and music. Our thumbs are unique to all living beings.

To top it all off, because we are joined to God through our faith, our spirit is already eternal because it is joined to Him.

The first three letters of these human qualities from the prayer book, I found, gave me the mnemonic MRS, helping me remember these important attributes. It will help you when you need to give an answer to someone in just a pinch of time.

More on Spiritual Gifts next time.

Concerning Supernatural Gifts be Knowledgeable

This week we are continuing our investigation of supernatural spiritual gifts. I believe it is important to know the real biblical gifts so we can distinguish between the true and the false occult copies. If the church does not teach about the real gifts, the church could also be trapped into believing the false ones.

Of this the Apostle Paul says, "Now concerning the spiritual gifts, brethren, I would not have you ignorant" (1 Cor 12:1). See verses 2–11 as we look at these gifts.

Four Kinds of Knowledge

First: **Natural Human Knowledge** is on the increase. Daniel wrote his book of the Bible from his life span of 606 to 536 B.C. at his death. To the present day of human biblical timing that's about 2,000 plus 536 years, or 2,536 years ago.[2] God sealed the understanding of Daniel's book "… even to the time of the end: many shall run to and fro, and knowledge shall be increased" (Dan 12:4 KJV).

"Concerning travel, for 6,000 years of recorded history, man's only means of travel on land, was either by foot or by horseback or by horsedrawn carriage. … By horseback and horse drawn carriage, the fastest a man could travel was about 25 miles per hour. Travel under these conditions was limited to 1,000 miles per person per year. At the turn of this century, however, transportation aids such as the automobile, diesel powered locomotives, airplanes, and even rockets have increased the distance man can travel per year from 1,000 miles to 25,000 miles per person per year.

"In 1962, John Glenn, Jr., a U.S. astronaut, circled the earth in 1½ hours. That's 12,000 miles in 1½ hours." Since this flight ... we have built even faster spacecraft ... including the Shuttle." [3]

I rest my case that scientific [and biblical knowledge] is increasing.

Second: This **Fallen World's Supernatural Knowledge**. I have seen on television a professed psychic telling a new widow that her husband is right there in the room wanting to speak to her. He then begins relaying a message to the biblically unaware widow with the supposed words from the dead. She begins to cry and think this is real.

The man is an individual practicing spiritism or spiritualism. "This is the attempt to get into contact with the 'spirit world,' especially with departed relatives and friends, through the help of 'spirit guides' and mediums. This is the cruelest of all satanic deceptions, and the one that is particularly abominable to God." For correct biblical teaching see the book, *The Holy Spirit and You – a Guide to the Spirit-Filled life*.[4]

Third: **True Intellectual Knowledge** goes to the level and depth of ancient wisdom as revealed in Scripture. Ask God "that you may be filled with the knowledge of His will in all wisdom and understanding; that you may walk worthy of the Lord, pleasing, being fruitful in every good work, and increasing in the knowledge of God" (Col 1:9b-10 KJV-MOD).

We pray for knowledge, and we study God's Word.

One of the reasons I enjoyed writing this column is that it provided an extra opportunity to dig into the Bible weekly. I'm also helped by studying the Scripture in Hebrew and Greek. The Bible is our best guide for successful living, yet how many of the sixty-six books have you and I seriously studied? I've been trying to make up for it for some decades now, yet I believe it's a lifetime work and a joy.

Fourth: **The Supernatural Gift of the Word of Knowledge** was very often manifested in Jesus' life. For example, He had a divine appointment with a Samaritan woman one day. He asked her for water at a well, and eventually asked that she bring her husband to meet Him.

She said, "I have no husband."

Jesus gave her this Word of Knowledge: "You have had five husbands, and he whom you now have is not your husband" (John 4:18 KJV-MOD).

She then witnessed to her whole town about Jesus, "Come, see a man, who told me all things I ever did: is this not the Messiah?" (John 4:29 KJV-MOD).

Jesus was not a psychic who told her fortune! He was manifesting the supernatural gift of Knowledge. Jesus was an exciting person to be around. He set people free everywhere He went.

We've taken a quick look at the big subject of wisdom, and knowledge. But these are formerly worship columns, now turned into a book, so I can take some liberties and space to update them for you.

Next time tune in for the Gift of Faith.

Get on the Train of the Faithful

The next spiritual gift we'll study is the Gift of Faith.

This is a primary gift. We won't get anywhere without it. If a minister or layperson tries to teach the Bible without a personal faith and a trust in the Bible, the listeners will soon find a lack of interest in the class. "But without faith it is impossible to please Him ..." (Heb 11:6).

The Bible talks about faith from Genesis to Revelation. Hebrews chapter 11 is the greatest chapter on faith in the Bible. And it begins with the best definition of faith in verse one: "Now faith is the assurance of things hoped for, proof of things not seen" (Heb 11:1 KJV-MOD).

Verse two says, "for by it [faith] the elders obtained a good report." The elders here are listed in the book of Hebrews chapter 11. It begins with righteous Abel, Adam and Eve's youngest son, and the list ends with the faithful prophet Samuel. I counted 18 on the list.

Two women are listed as elders here, along with the men, Sara, father Abraham's wife, and the woman Rahab, who formerly had been a woman-of-the-night. By faith and works, Rahab believed and put her life on the line to save the Jewish warriors who were spying out the Promised Land (James 2:25).

This list of the faithful is to encourage us to see them as a great cloud of witnesses and in seeing them "... let us lay aside every weight and the sin that so easily besets us and let us run the race that is set before us" (Heb 12:1 KJV-MOD).

When you study the lives of these 18 people of faith, you will see what they went through to be on such a prominent list.

Of course Noah, Abraham, Isaac, Jacob, Joseph, Moses, Joshua, and others are on the list.

It is believed by many that the Apostle Paul wrote this list. He also wrote two-thirds of the New Testament.

Paul is listing those from the *Torah* or the Old Testament since there was no New Testament yet. We know now that the New Testament believers are added to this list in Heaven. You can think of some of them?

So how do we get this faith?

"Looking unto Jesus the author and finisher of our faith; who for the joy that was set before Him endured the cross, despising the shame, and is set down at the right hand of the throne of God" (Heb 12:2 KJV). The answer Scripture gives is Jesus, the Messiah. Looking unto Jesus. He authored our faith. He finished it with His death, resurrection, and ascension.

I like the Faith acrostic created by an Anglican minister and missionary to Africa. His FAITH took him home to Heaven decades ago.

Forsaking

All

I

Take

Him

"Look unto Jesus (v 2). He is the head of the long train of faith heroes. He is the Author and Perfecter of our faith. Consider Him (v.3). Observe and analyze every part of His life and conduct, His courage in sufferings."[5]

Jesus is the *Alpha* and the *Omega* [*haAleph beh haTav*, Heb.] the beginning and the end, the first and the last (Rev 22:13).

He gave everything for us to redeem us, to show us the way of life now, and in eternity. He is the way to the Father and the Holy Spirit. When you receive Jesus, you right then and there received FAITH.

Prayer: "Dear Lord, I want to get on the train of the brave, faithful ones. I choose faith in You. Bring faith into my spirit and soul through Your Son. I choose life forever. In Jesus' Name. Amen."

Relax and breathe deeply of God's love and freshness. Take time to be thankful in His presence.

Join me next time, as we investigate the four types of faith.

God's Best-Seller Tells of Various Kinds of Faith

Last time we reviewed those famous individuals in the Old Testament whom the book of Hebrews calls Heroes of the Faith.

The subject that we are continuing is faith. *Pistis* is the Greek word for faith, which also means persuasion, credence, conviction, (Gospel) truth itself, assurance, belief, faith, fidelity.[6]

In the Bible, God's best-seller, there is not just one kind of faith, there are many kinds of faith.

Natural Human Faith is first on our list. All of us have this faith.

When I flew on a small jet to San Francisco in June 2010, I had to have a lot of natural faith. I needed faith in the pilots whom I had never met. I needed to trust the air traffic controllers that they would give the pilots all the right information for a safe takeoff and flight from Sea/Tac Airport. I had to have faith that the plane was not too heavily loaded with luggage.

Near our destination we had to fly over and through a dense deck of popcorn clouds for a bumpy descent but a safe landing. I always pray before and during takeoff and landing so my spiritual faith also came into play. When I talked to Ben, the soldier who was my seatmate on furlough from Iraq and encouraged his spiritual life – that was beyond natural faith.

Saving Faith is second. The Bible warns us, "But without faith it is impossible to please God" (Heb 11:6a KJV-MOD). Then it encourages us with, "For by grace you are saved through faith; and that not of yourselves: it is the gift of God: not of works, lest any man should boast" (Eph 2:8-9 KJV-MOD).

He tells us we must have faith and then lets us know that He has provided a measure of faith so that if we choose, we can respond to Him (Rom 12:3). This saving faith is a gift and not something we create. We learn about saving faith by the proclamation of God's Word (Rom 10:17). "… Believe [have faith in] the Lord Jesus Christ and you will be saved …" (Acts 16:31 KJV-MOD).

Once we have received the Lord as Savior, that measure of faith is activated and begins to grow. We all start out with an equal measure, yet some continue to grow and some do not, but the choice is ours.

Faith as a Fruit of the Spirit is third. Faith is also one of the nine fruits. "But the fruit of the Spirit is love, joy, peace, longsuffering, gentleness, goodness, **faith**, meekness, temperance: against such there is no law" (Gal 5:22-23 KJV).

When Dennis and I moved into our house in Edmonds, we ordered some fruit trees from a catalogue. They eventually came in the mail, and when we opened them they looked like old, dead, sticks!

But, we planted, nourished, and watered them and within five to seven years we had yellow Transparent Apples, red Jonathan Apples, red and yellow cherries, and purple plumbs.

The point I want to make here is the fruit of our faith was not immediate. It took a number of years to produce.

This is true of the fruit of one's spiritual faith. Your fruit of faith will grow when it is fed, nurtured, watered, pruned, harvested, and shared with others. This takes time. May the buds on your spiritual trees continue to develop into beautiful, savory fruit.

This fruit of faith comes from our union with Christ who says, "I am the Vine, and you are the branches. He that abides in Me, and I in Him, the same brings forth much fruit ..." (John 15:5 KJV-MOD).

The Holy Spirit "supplies the faith as we go along in the Christian life. Our part is to respond to Him. Faith in Jesus, both initial faith and continuing faith is the basis of all other fruit and gifts of the Spirit."[7]

Think about Saving Faith and Fruit of Faith and see if you have activated your faith and grown in it.

Next time, The Supernatural Gift of Faith and The Weapon of Faith.

Teenager Receives a Supernatural Gift of Faith

This is our second session on the gifts of faith. Thus far we've looked at natural faith, saving faith, and the fruit of faith.

Next is the **Supernatural Gift of Faith**. Unlike the fruit of faith, it is given instantaneously. It is a sudden surge of faith, usually in a crisis, to confidently believe without a doubt that as we act or speak in Jesus' Name, it shall come to pass. I never entered into an experience of faith like this until I was baptized with the Holy Spirit.

For example, before I was married I had moved from Van Nuys, California to Spokane, Washington. I was going on a retreat at Living Springs Ranch in Deer Park, and then stayed in Spokane for some months.

I attended a church prayer meeting. While there that morning, I learned about a seventeen-year-old boy who was severely injured when a car hit him as he rode his bike. His leg was broken and could not be set because of his condition. He also suffered a fractured skull and was being kept alive with a tracheotomy and a feeding tube.

A woman in the group said, "Sibley Bloyd has gangrene in his broken leg, and has been in a coma for a month. Unless God intervenes, Sibley does not have long to live."

The group then prayed for him. I felt inspired to say, "If someone in this prayer group goes to this teen, lays hands on him and prays for him, his life may be saved."

No one responded. Then I said, "Maybe that was for me. How can I see him?"

His mother was phoned and I met Dorothy at the Nursing Home. As we went into his room, I found this tall gangly teen was skin and bones. His beautiful red hair had fallen out except for a few patches.

I asked Dorothy, "Has Sibley been able to speak at all?"

She said, "No, but I think he raises his eyebrows sometimes when I speak to him."

Supernatural Gift of Faith

All of a sudden, *I knew what to do.* I took his hand in mine and said to this comatose patient, "Sibley, if Jesus heals you, will you live for Him for the rest of your life? If your answer is yes, squeeze my hand three times."

To my delight, I felt one, two, three squeezes! We had made contact and he had confessed faith in his Savior. Now I could pray effectively for him.

"Father I thank You for what You have already done and that Sibley has confessed you as his Savior. In Jesus Name and for your glory and Sibley's joy, I ask You to restore Your child Sibley and make him whole again. In Jesus' mighty Name. Amen."

Soon it was time to leave, so I gave Dorothy a hug goodbye.

The next day I received a phone call that Sibley had pulled his feeding tube out and the nurse decided to give him Jell-O to eat! Wow, things were happening!

I went to see him the next day. He had begun to speak again. It was good to get acquainted with him! I remember his eyes lighting up as he asked for a hamburger, milkshake, and other foods. I had to smile and almost giggle. After all, he was a teenager who had not eaten solid food for a month!

Not being my place to feed him, I assured him, "You will have plenty of food." And he continued to have all he could eat.

The doctors soon saw his improvement and felt he was now strong enough for major surgery. They put him in the hospital for amputation from the knee down due to the heel with gangrene. Gangrene in the other foot had already been healed.

Power of the Holy Spirit

I again visited him in the hospital – donning a white robe and mask. I now was led to pray with for him to receive the power of the Holy Spirit. He did with great joy and prayed aloud in the Spirit.

Sibley lived and Dorothy and her family were grateful for God's grace to them. It is amazing to have been a part of this miracle. Doctors and nurses were a part of the miracle also. Here it was faith and science working together. Faith had to come first in this healing, and then the doctors could act.

About a year later, when I visited St. Luke's Church in Seattle, Sibley and Dorothy also happened to be there from Spokane visiting that Sunday. Dennis had a chance to meet this recovering young man who now walked well with his prosthesis. His red hair was growing again and he was full of smiles.[8]

Dennis and I were married a year later, in 1966, and I then moved from Spokane to Seattle.

See you next time for The Weapon of Faith.

Speaking the Word with Confidence in Spiritual Warfare

We're looking at the Sword of the Word in this, our fourth session on gifts of faith. In the whole armor of God, we have a weapon called the Sword of the Spirit which is the Word of God (Eph 6:10-18).

The Sword is double edged, metaphorically speaking, of both the Written Word (Bible) and Jesus who is the Living Word. "And the Word was made flesh, and dwelt among us ..." (John 1:14 KJV).

There are two major Greek words for Scripture in the Bible.

One is "*logos*" concerning doctrine meaning: "Divine expression (i.e. Christ). Word, matter, or concern. Preaching, biblically it is the spoken, or written Word.")[9]

The other Greek word is *rhema:* "The idea of pouring forth; to utter i.e. speak or command."[10]

In Ezekiel 37:4, 7a: "Again He [God] said to me [Ezekiel], Prophesy to these bones and **say** to them, oh you dry bones, hear the Word of the Lord ... So I prophesied as I was commanded: and there was a great noise and a shaking" (KJV-MOD).

In Mark 11:23: "Jesus said ... Whosoever shall **say** unto this mountain, Be thou cast into the sea; and shall not doubt in his heart, but shall believe that those things shall come to pass; he shall have whatsoever he says" (KJV-MOD).

You will have what you say! It is most important to be in agreement with God's Word. Faith without doubting is the condition to meet if one wants the benefit (Mark 11:23). Here we have both of the Testaments, Old and New, talking about the importance of what we **say** in warfare.

Prayer is one thing. Speaking by faith is another. We pray to get the word. Then we can speak it with power. We can say to dry bones or to the mountains that block us, be healed or move out of my way, and we will see positive results.

Swords of the Word

We can find an appropriate Faith–Word or Sword of the Spirit from Scripture and speak that into our situation.

When I was nearing completion of my master's degree at my university, a male student said to me, "You are not going to graduate!" He had challenged me many times in class prior to this.

I was surprised to hear these mean and unfounded words. I paused to take a deep breath. Faith rose up in me and I said kindly but with great confidence, "J. you are wrong. I **am** going to graduate!" It was important that I made a positive response.

That afternoon as I concluded presenting my public self-evaluation chart, the teacher announced, "The professors in their evaluation of you have all agreed that you are graduating!"

I purposely kept from looking at my adversary, and tried my best not to gloat too much, as I heard these longed for words.

Breaking a Yoke of Bondage

Over a decade ago I was asked to pray for a young woman who was being emotionally abused by her boyfriend. As a result she was having pain in her shoulders and could not sleep well. I was impressed with a *rhema* Scripture sword for her.

I said. "L. This Scripture is for you. The words seemed to pour out, 'And it shall come to pass that in that day, that his burden shall be taken away from off your shoulder, and his yoke from off your neck, and the yoke [of bondage] shall be destroyed because of God's anointing'" (Isa 10:27 KJV-MOD). I said, "Today that bondage is broken off your neck and shoulders through God's anointing."

She had been yoked together in an unhealthy relationship. She was a believer and anointed by the Holy Spirit. That day, the abusive relationship was broken and she was both physically and emotionally healed.

Another Scripture that has been a *rhema* to me over the years is Jesus' words, "Behold, I give you power … over all the power of the Enemy; and nothing shall by any means hurt you" (Luke 10:19 KJV-MOD). This helped me as a young adult when I had made a commitment of Jesus as Lord, not only as Savior.

A spiritual battle began, with gory dreams at night. I quoted this Scripture in Luke whenever I needed to, and slept with the Bible under my pillow. I was totally and completely victorious but was in a spiritual battle for one month.

Find Scriptures to help you with your battles of faith. They are there in God's armory waiting to strengthen you.

More spiritual gifts next time.

Healing Miracles Happen Through God's Gifts Today

In August of 2006, a team consisting of Shirley Wilson, Rupert Walworth, Liz Glover, and I headed to Spokane, Washington to co-lead the *Emotionally Free® Media Course* held at the Immaculate Heart Retreat Center. Wonderful healings occurred.

Since I was in the location where I had lived for several years before my marriage in 1966, some of my old friends organized a 40-year reunion for me. In those early years, I had begun writing and teaching on the supernatural gifts of the Holy Spirit.

Two Spokane friends, Cordie Barber and Lucy Durham, prepared a reunion dinner and meeting which took place after the retreat seminar. We all had changed over the years, but when we spoke or smiled at one another we immediately reconnected in the spirit.

I recognized one of the guests, Fran Wray, who had received a miraculous healing from the Lord from deafness in one ear when we prayed for her in 1965. When the group gathered after our meal, I asked Fran, "How is the healing of your right ear?" She jubilantly replied, "It is still healed after all these forty years!"

That was an exciting witness to us all. Sometimes those who doubt God's healing for today will say, "The healed person only had a psychological reaction and it won't last." It is not so with Fran.

Fran Tells Her Story

I asked Fran to tell her story to the group who had gathered for the reunion. Some of the earliest participants were in our meeting.

"I was deaf in my right ear for about twenty years," said Fran. "I had become concerned about my teenage children and foster children, as I needed to be able to hear to take care of them.

"Rita Reed [now Bennett] had been teaching on the Gifts of the Spirit for a number of us meeting at Betty Moore's home. That night she was speaking on the gift of miracles.

"During prayer time Rita asked, 'Does anyone have anything wrong with their right ear?'" I was surprised in that I had told no one about the problem with my ear. I raised my hand and said, 'Yes, I do.'

"Rita said, 'Come and sit in this chair so we can all gather around you.'

"When she laid her hands on my ears and commanded my right ear to 'be opened,' I felt a warmth that went from my left ear to my right ear.

"Then Rita whispered in my right ear, 'Can you hear me?' And I said, 'Yes!'

"The next day I went to the office of my internist, Dr. Gene Beiver, to have him test my ear. He said to me, 'Fran, you've been healed. There is no doubt about it!'"

300

Fran quipped to me with a smile, "If people say they do not believe that God heals through prayer today, I would say, baloney."

When I taught on the supernatural gift of miracles in Spokane, it built faith in me and others to expect a miracle of healing. I believe that an instant healing is in the double category of miracles and healing.

When Jesus healed the deaf man, Scripture says, "Then looking up to Heaven, He signed and said to him, *Ephphatha,* that is, 'Be opened.' And immediately his ears were opened ..." (Mark 7:35-35).

Those were the same words I had spoken, only in English.

The Word of God and Faith

Since Jesus was Jewish, I will quote a Hebraic version of this Scripture. "Taking him off alone, away from the crowd, *Yeshua* [Jesus] put His fingers into the man's ears ... then, looking up to Heaven, He gave a deep groan and said to him, *Hippatach* [that is, 'Be opened!']. His ears were opened, and his tongue freed, and he began speaking clearly" (Mark 7:35-35 CJB).

No matter what language you speak in prayer, God the Holy Spirit understands and works on your behalf.

God, the Healer

I am not a healer. God is the Healer but He works through believers today when we obey His Word in faith.

In this instance, I was simply God's delivery girl. Fran was the one who received His gift of healing. Though I had the joy of following in Jesus' footsteps, all glory goes to Him.

Join me next week for more true stories of God's gifts today.

He Anoints You, Your Cup Runs Over

In July 19-24, 2010 was a special *Emotionally Free® Seminar* that I've had a part in presenting for over twenty years. Very diverse groups of people come from a variety of cultures, denominations, states, and countries.

We use Scripture, personal testimonies, and PowerPoint illustrations with inspired words, small group discussion, and most importantly, a large portion of time for individual healing prayers. As you can imagine, this takes quite a bit of preparation.

Shirley Wilson, National Lead Facilitator, works meticulously placing individuals in the most appropriate small groups. As CEO, planner, and co-teacher, my sleep often is shortened during these six days.

What I'd call the anointing of the Holy Spirit carries me through. Amazingly at the end of the event, I am still full of energy.

I am quick to get back to my proper sleep right after the event concludes. I believe in taking care of my temple of the Holy Spirit (1 Cor 6:19) even though I do have to push myself at times.

Gift of Energy

Don, one of the students who was a pastor from California was in recovery from a 10-year medical challenge. Before he arrived he said, "I don't think I'll be able to stay at the seminar all day but will have to take time off in the afternoons and evenings."

Yet he never did return to his apartment during the day or early evening, but was one of the last attendees to leave each night! He was quite surprised. He even met a beautiful woman, Sherry, at the Seminar and they are happily married today.

One of the special reasons why some facilitators have worked with me annually for fifteen or more years is that these leaders also receive emotional and sometimes physical and spiritual healing. Professional counselor, Judy Glenn has said, "I like to send my new counselees to *Emotionally Free*® *Seminars* – if possible both basic and advanced – as it takes off about a year of their counseling time."

Receive Anointing

As an example, David who wrote the 23rd Psalm was anointed with oil as King of Israel by the Prophet Samuel.

Jesus says of Himself and His own anointing: "The Spirit of the Lord is upon Me, because He has anointed Me to preach the gospel to the poor; He has sent Me to heal the brokenhearted, to preach deliverance to the captives, and recovering of sight to the blind, to set at liberty them that are bruised" (Luke 4:18 KJV-MOD).

What I like about my own calling is that Jesus' anointing comes to our meetings. Recently at the seminars in July, I saw it again. Many of the brokenhearted from divorce and sexual and emotional abuse were healed.

A couple who were only acquaintances last year, following the seminar and their inner healings – fell in love. They were married just before our July 2010 seminars that year. Daniel and Nancy told me that they wanted to take the advanced course again, and spend part of their honeymoon with us at the Embassy Suites Hotel!

In another of our sessions, we have biblical teaching and prayer for deliverance to the captives. Many were freed from cult and occult practices that had them bound (Deut 18:9-14). We may also pray for the anointing of the Holy Spirit, as it's important for staying free.

Many who had been bruised in life were set at liberty. Harsh, critical words spoken to a child, or young adult, can set them up for failure. It, however, is never too late for healing as we go back to the scene – this time with our omnipresent, healing Lord. We tell Him of our pain and in listening prayer – hear what He is saying to us with His unconditional love. Of course, then speaking forgiveness in prayer is a major part of the healing also.

The book of Acts says, "God anointed Jesus of Nazareth with the Holy Spirit and with power; Who went about doing good and healing all who were oppressed ..." (Acts 10:38 KJV-MOD).

Your Prayer: You too can be anointed. Just take a few minutes to pray now and ask Jesus, "Come into my life; please give me Your peace and Spirit-filled anointing. I want to be like You, Lord, and do good everywhere I go. Amen."

Now take a deep breath and close your eyes and wait in His presence. When ready, slowly repeat the 23rd Psalm.

More on healing and miracles to come.

God's Supernatural Healthcare Program in Action

These days, the subject of healthcare is often in the news. Yet, God's own health-care program has been in the good news of the Bible for over five millennia. Perhaps it is time to take God up on what He has freely offered us.

He tells His followers: "... These signs shall follow them that believe ... they shall lay hands on the sick, and they shall recover ..." (Mark 16:17a –18b KJV).

When Jesus was here, He healed everyone who came to Him. Today, those who ask followers of Christ to pray for them will have varying degrees of healing. Why? Because we do not live on the 100 percent level of faith, as did the healing Son of God. But it still happens.

At St. Alban's Church, I am part of the "Hem of His Garment" prayer team. Four of us pray at the two sides of the altar during Communion for those who want healing for themselves or others. Healing can be for any level of body, soul, or spirit.

We also pray for wisdom for doctors. My own brother, Bill Reed, M.D. was a Christian surgeon who has prayed for thousands of patients prior to surgery, and sometimes during surgery.

A Heavenly Tea Party

I have another healing experience to share with you from my Spokane days. I had been invited to Ann's home for a Women's Tea. While I was there, her neighbor, Juanita, phoned. Ann asked if I would speak to her.

When I picked up the phone I said, "Hello Juanita, how are you?" Her answer to my question brought up her need for healing. Then she asked, "Rita, I hear you are a woman of prayer, would you be willing to come to my home to pray for me?"

I said, "Yes, I'll be happy to do that." I wrote down her address and a short time later drove to her home.

When I knocked on her door, her husband Charles answered it and I explained why I was there. Charles graciously took me to Juanita's room where she lay in bed.

I was age 30 and I imagine she was in her late 50's. She was a gracious woman. Juanita told me that she had fluid around her heart that had to be removed as needed.

Getting Ready to Pray

I sat down and opened my Bible and began to read Scriptures to build her faith. The prophet Isaiah said, "Surely He [Jesus] has borne our grief's, and carried our sorrows: yet we did esteem Him stricken of God, and afflicted. But He was wounded for our transgressions, He was bruised for our iniquities: ... the chastisement of our peace was upon Him; and with His stripes we are healed" (Isa 53:4-5 KJV-MOD.).

304

I said, "Juanita – Jesus was crucified not only for our sins, but for our sicknesses." I also shared some personal healing examples, and then I asked if I could pray for her.

"Yes, please do," she said.

I anointed her with oil, and gently laid my hands on her head. I simply asked God to heal her physical heart and to remove the excess water around it. At that point, I felt a warm anointing in the center of my stomach. I told her, "I believe God has touched you." I said my goodbyes and returned to my home.

The next day, she went to the doctor's office in her wheel chair, as usual, but feeling much improved she decided to walk into his office.

He looked up from his desk and said, "Juanita what has happened to you?"

She cheerfully responded, "God answers prayer, doctor!" As he looked at her heart under the fluoroscope there was no need for his intervention, the fluid was normal.

I did not know until later that Juanita Beeman's diagnosis was heart failure and she had been given two weeks to live!

I'm happy to report that she lived a normal life for 14 more years. Her husband and children, and their mates all put their faith in the Lord and were spirit filled.

Once again I saw God's supernatural healthcare in action!

This is the tenth column in the Supernatural Gifts series. Join me next time for more gifts.

Every Good and Perfect Gift Comes Down from God

There is balance needed in manifesting God's supernatural gifts. The balance is between being ignorant brethren about the gifts, and being decent and in order, when expressing them (James 1:17).

In New Testament days, gifts of the Spirit were most often allowed publically in church gatherings. Today every church is not comfortable or aware of gifts, so God may use other ways.

I believe gifts such as wisdom, knowledge, or discernment can happen as a matter of course in conversation or prayer, where two or three believers are gathered.

I taught on Healing Prayer and Counseling in Southern California recently. When it came time for lunch, there were seven people who had personal needs. I decided to fast from lunch and give my time to them.

Some were out of jobs and were worried about taking care of themselves. One was in a fearful divorce and lives with an aging parent. Another had a pervading feeling of guilt that would come back when anyone spoke to another critically in her hearing.

Counseling would have taken too much time with each individual since there was only an hour for lunch. Instead, I seemed to have just the right word to speak for each person. I was told later that depression lifted, new ideas came for a better job, and fear was replaced by joy.

This reminds me of Jethro, who had a word for his son-in-law, Moses. He observed that Moses needed help in counseling large numbers of people otherwise he would wear himself out. Jethro advised him to select men to work in groups of 1,000s, 100s, 50s, and 10s who respected God, were truth lovers, and haters of covetousness. These men were to handle the light cases. Only the hard cases were they to send Moses (Exodus 18:13-27).

Something similar happened to me that day in California. The good thing is that trained laymen and women met as leaders over the small groups. I, with God's divine assistance, handled some hard cases. This is good information for all leaders.

Knowledge in Writing

I find that especially in writing, the gift of knowledge has come to me. During the time I wrote *To Heaven and Back*,[11] the first Christian near-death experience (NDE) book, I discovered something amazing. That is the twelve tribes of Israel written over the twelve doors of Heaven were encoded in Hebrew that's why I call it a "Welcome Home Message."

During my research, I decided to look up the Hebrew meaning of each name of the twelve tribes of Israel as listed in Revelation 7:5-8, 21:12. I just happened to follow the exact order as listed and the translation came out with this meaning:

Confessors and praisers of God,
Looking upon the Son,
A band of,
Blessed ones.
Wrestling is over,
Forgetting the pain.
Hearing and obeying His Word,

Cleaving to our Lord.
He is our reward.
We are Home.
We are added to the family of Jesus,
Son of the Father's right hand.[12]

A Second Happening

Another supernatural happening occurred when thirteen years later I wrote, *Heaven Tours.* I was researching the width of the beautiful jasper, transparent wall around the holy city. The Apostle John wrote,

"Then he [the angel] measured its wall: one hundred and forty-four cubits, according to the measure of man ..." (Rev 21:17 KJV-MOD).

There is only one measurement given for the wall and the reader has to decide either height or width. After much biblical research I chose width, which meant the wall was 72 yards wide or deep; that was almost the length of a football field. The measurement seemed odd until I sent it to my artist, Sally Moser. When she sent back her black and white sketch for my approval, I was amazed that it actually showed a tunnel into Heaven! With twelve entrances, that means twelve tunnels of light!

One reason this excited me is that some Bible teachers adamantly claimed that the tunnels that NDEs said they had experienced were wrong, since there was no Bible verse to confirm it.

But now, God had gifted Sally and me with the first known biblical confirmation of these tunnels! Unless a person chose the right dimension of the wall, and drew a picture of it, it would not have been discovered. We have this miracle also confirmed in *Heaven Tours – Astonishing Journeys*, published January 2009.

Join me next week to learn more about gifts.

A Menorah Miracle with a Message

"Christian reasoning says: 'The so-called laws of nature codified by human science are God's usual way of doing things.' God, however, for His people, will change His accustomed ways of doing things to meet their needs, and thus, too, show them that He is sovereign and has all power"[13]

"The record of Elijah and his disciple, Elisha, speaks to us today. Elisha asked that he might have a 'double portion' of the Holy Spirit that rested upon Elijah (2 Kings 2:9-14). Sure enough, the Scripture records that Elisha did twice as many miracles as Elijah. That equals 32 miracles!

"This is symbolic of what happened to believers after Jesus' ascension, although He did not bequeath only a 'double portion' of His Spirit – He set no limit. He simply said, 'Greater works than these shall you do, because I go to My Father' (John 14:12).

"The power to do greater works comes from the fact that Jesus ascended into Heaven, and the full power of the Holy Spirit was sent at Pentecost, and has been available to Christians ever since" [14]

When Jesus performed miracles, He did not do them for show, but to meet a human need. When He walked on water, it was done to comfort His fearful disciples. When He miraculously fed the multitudes, it was because food would not be available otherwise. When He turned water into wine, it was because it was needed at a wedding reception.

The disciple of Christ who wants to be used in any of the supernatural gifts, needs to practice the fruit of humility and be careful not to take personal credit.

Miracle of Scripture

I began studying Hebrew in 1995 and found how miraculous our Hebrew foundation is. Some Hebraic Christians are continuously discovering miracles in Scripture. One of those students is author, J.R. Church. He has written a book on the subject of the Jewish Menorah, the seven branch golden lampstand Moses was instructed to make.[15] The middle of the lampstand (called candelabra today) is called the Servant Candle and is used to light the other six candles. Christians automatically sense that the Servant Candle represents Jesus. Once you look for groups of sevens in Scripture, you may find your own sets of menorahs which aren't necessarily or literally candles.

For example, Isaiah 11:1-2 (KJV-MOD) is one of those biblical menorahs. "And there shall come forth a rod out of the stem of Jesse, and a Branch shall grow out of His roots.

"And *the Spirit of the Lord shall rest upon Him, the Spirit of wisdom and understanding, the Spirit of counsel and might, the Spirit of knowledge and fear of the Lord …*"

When you look at this Scripture in Hebrew, you would read it right to left, not as in English left to right. This provides the following order.

The Spirit of the Lord (Servant Candle, in the middle) (#7), Spirit of Fear of the Lord and of knowledge (#5 and 6), Spirit of Counsel, and Might (#3 and 4), Spirit of Understanding and Wisdom (#1 and 2)."[16]

My Menorah Miracle

I have traveled to Israel three times and each time God gave me affirmation when I returned home.

One Saturday while I was at a Judeo-Christian Bible Study, the Menorah candles had been extinguished before lunchtime. As we were all gathered at tables eating, my friend Erin said, "Look. A candle has relit itself."

"I wonder which one that is" I said, and looked up Isaiah 11:1-2. Counting right to left, I reported, "The third candle is counsel."

When I said counsel, the candle extinguished itself! It was almost as if the candle said, "You're right."

Erin and I looked at one another in surprise.

I can't prove to you it was a message, but later as I drove home I, as a counselor, began to feel like it was some kind of a personal message to me. I was touched by this idea as I drove home. This was three days after my third trip to Israel and every time God had spoken to me just before or when I returned home. Six months later, in 2005, I enrolled in graduate school and in 2008, I received my M.A. in counseling. It was also like an affirmation for going to our Lord's holy places and taking others with me.

I would soon understand the purpose of my menorah miracle.

Spiritual gifts will be continued next time.

Discover Healing and a Bible Code in Scripture

Two of the most intriguing healing stories in the Bible are written in three of the Gospel books: Matthew, Mark, and Luke (called the synoptic Gospels).

Jesus had a lot to accomplish during His three-year ministry. This day was a typical day for our Lord. It started by the president of the synagogue coming to Jesus (*Yeshua*) to ask for his child's healing;

eventually it was for resurrection of his 12-year-old daughter. Jesus tells Jairus, "Be not afraid, only believe" (Mark 5:36b).

The walk to Jairus' house begins, but on the way, a woman who has had a serious blood condition for twelve years pursues her own healing. She reasons, "If only, I can touch the hem of His garment, I shall be made whole" (Matt 9:21). This woman was an outcast because of her consistent flow of blood. If she touched a rabbi, he would have become unclean for a number of hours.

The woman did not touch Jesus physically. She touched the hem of His garment, and perhaps one of the four tassels sewn there.

With the crush of the crowd following Him, Jesus did not see her but He said, "Somebody touched Me for I perceived [healing] virtue is gone out of Me" (Luke 8:46 KJV-MOD).

She fell down before Jesus and explained she was the one who touched Him and was healed. Jesus said, "Daughter, be of good comfort; your faith has made you whole" (Matt 9:22b).

Why Touch His Hem?

She easily could have been a Jewish woman, and therefore she would have known that the four tassels on Christ's garment represented the original four Hebrew consonants of God's Name *yod, heh, vav, heh* (In English YHVH or *Yahveh).* They also represented the *Torah* and Ten Commandments.

Some Jewish men wear the tassels today to remind them to keep the commandments and live a holy life. In fact, God commanded Jewish men to make and wear these tassels (Num 15:38-40).

Death and Return Experience

Jesus was not worried about the situation or time of day; He pressed on – taking matters in His stride. Each person was precious to Him.

When Jesus finally arrived at Jairus' house, the mourners were weeping and wailing at the death of the 12-year-old daughter. Jesus assured them that she was only asleep.

Scripture says, "They laughed Him to scorn, knowing she was dead" (Luke 8:53, Mark 5:40a).

Jesus had enough of their unbelief and asked them to wait outside. Only His three Apostles, Peter, James, and John, and the mother and father were allowed to be with Him and the girl.

With all the unbelief gone, "He [Jesus] took her by the hand, and called, saying, 'Maid, arise.' And her spirit came again and she arose immediately: and He commanded them to give her food. Her parents were astonished" (Luke 8:54b-56a KJV-MOD).

Why the Number Twelve?

I was pondering why the Holy Spirit coupled these two healings together in the same scripture story, the woman with the issue of blood for twelve years, and the seriously ill little 12-year-old girl.

Then a plethora of biblical twelves filled my mind:

- 12-year-old daughter of Jairus, restored,
- 12-year-old importance of coming of age, for teens: Bar & Bat Mitsva,
- 12-year-old importance of coming of age, for Christians: confirmation,
- 12 year battle for a woman's life in the Scripture,
- 12 disciples of Jesus,
- 12 Apostles of the Lamb, on
- 12 thrones in Heaven
- 12 tribes of Israel, and message
- 12 Pearls, at
- 12 Gates in Heaven,
- 12 Angels at the gates,
- 12 Tunnels of light,
- 12 Rivers of life, (Rev 21:6, Ezek. 47:1-9),
- 12 kinds of fruit on trees of life,
- 12 precious and semi-precious jeweled foundations of the city,
- 12 months in a year of life to serve God,
- 12 biblical octaves in Psalm 119:1-176,
- 12th Hebrew letter *Lamed,* which we would call "L" in English, means to study and learn.

Is this a coded message encouraging us to **learn** all we can from these biblical twelves listed above?

The more we study the supernatural Word of God, the easier it is for our Good Shepherd to lead us.

Interestingly *Lamed* is the tallest Hebrew letter and looks like a shepherd's staff.

There may be others twelves God will draw our attention to.

Reach out and touch the hem of Jesus' garment today. Miracles await.

See you next time in the New Series of Fall Festivals.

The Fall Festivals Series (Three Articles)
A Day of Trumpets Is a Joyful Sound

Since Jesus is Jewish, I'm interested in the way He practiced His religious traditions when on earth. The Fall Festivals, as the Jews call them, come to mind. (Others may say Feasts.) The yearly dates show on the Jewish calendar as the month of *Tishri*, and on our Gregorian calendar as the month of September.

As a Christian, following the Day of Pentecost, I do not have any religious celebrations until Christmas.

That being so I like to follow along with my Jewish brothers and sisters as they celebrate their high holy days.

The Theme of these days is Repentance or *Tehshuvah.* The Festival listed in Leviticus 23 is *Yom Teruah* or Day of *Shofar* Sounding.

When I was in Jerusalem, Israel in 2002, I attended this fall festival in a large synagogue. The men were on the main floor and the women and children were in the balcony. It was exciting to hear the *Shofars* blowing that day.

The Day of Trumpets is preceded by a time of repentance for thirty days. Jewish purification continues on the first day of *Tishri* until the tenth day, making a total of forty days.

Christians and Lent

Christians have a 40-day purification also. It is a time of prayer, fasting, almsgiving, and reflection. We fast from things we want to change, like a habit we want to quit, giving up unhealthy foods, or frugal eating to help save money for alms. Keeping our 40-day commitment requires prayer. The season of Lent, begins with humbling ourselves on Ash Wednesday and concludes in an epiphany of light on Easter or First Fruits.

The Jewish *Shofar*

The first trumpet was actually the voice of God on Mt. Sinai giving the commandments. The *shofar* concept comes from the ram's horn and dates back to Abraham and his son Isaac on Mount Moriah. There, a ram's horn was caught in the thicket and the ram became the sacrifice in place of Isaac.

Blowing the *shofar* has three basic meanings:
- Sound of alarm
- Sound of joy
- Sound of a trumpet

I noticed when blowing the *shofar* it makes the sound of its Hebrew name, *Teruah*. Using two syllables, try singing the word as I did, from middle c to high c, ending with a crescendo, *T'ru*-ah – It will sound something like a *shofar* blowing. There are three kinds of *shofar* sounds; you musicians might want to research this further.

An increasing number of Christians are interested in The Day of Trumpets and connect it with the return of Messiah (1 Thess 4:16), even as some Orthodox Jews look for the first coming of Messiah. Either the date of September 16th or 17th was the date of Trumpets in the year 2012. If you are interested in the most official date for The Day of Trumpets each year, go on the internet and see when the New Moon is seen from Jerusalem.[17] For the "Watchers" they will be especially interested in knowing the date as one only knows it from the sighting of the New Moon in Jerusalem.

The Second Part

A second part to this season is the Jewish Day of Remembrance or *Yom Ha Zekaron.* This means to remember our failings, and behavior, with a desire to do better. It's to remember the commandments and have a desire to make this world a better place.

Rabbi Mark Golub on *Shalom* TV says sin means "Not going in the right direction. *Chate* is the Hebrew word for sin and is an archery term. It literally means, to miss the mark."

The Third Part

The third part to this season is *Rosh HaShana* or Head of the Year created by the Rabbis. It is called, The Birthday of the Creation of the World.

Rabbi Golub says, "This is the way Jews express a greeting of love on the Holiday of *Rosh HaShanah*. They say *LaShana Tova*. This means: 'May you have a wonderful, sweet, healthy, joyous, good New Year.'" He encourages everyone to use this greeting.

Yom Kippur and *Sukkot* are the two concluding festivals we will look at next.

By the way, *La-Shan-na To-va.*

The Holiest Festival for the Jews – Yom Kippur

God instructs Moses, "Also on the tenth day of this seventh month there shall be a Day of Atonement. It shall be an holy convocation for you; you shall afflict your souls, and offer an offering …" (Lev 23:27 KJV-MOD).

Yom Kippur, or Day of Atonement, in 2012 began in the evening of September 17 to the evening of the 18th.

For the Jewish people, the High Priest once a year brought sins of the entire nation before the golden altar in the Holy of Holies as the blood of the lamb was sprinkled on the Mercy Seat.

This was and still is the holiest day for Israel. But since the glorious temple in Jerusalem was destroyed in A.D. 70 there is no longer a temple and High Priest available. Now the Jews, guided by their Rabbis, have a day of prayer and repentance in their synagogues.

Atonement means a sacrifice has been made for a person's sins. The fast is a sacrifice Jews are making for themselves and their nation. They fast 24 hours, or if strong enough 25 hours. The worshippers dress in white, which represents striving for spiritual purity. Service in the synagogue begins with the leader singing a prayer called *Kol Nidrei*. They read prayers from the *Yom Kippur* prayer book and pray. In the afternoon, the Bible story of the prophet Jonah is read.

Jonah's Lesson

Briefly told, Jonah hears the voice of God telling him to go to the wicked city of Nineveh to convert them. That could be like God telling a spiritual leader to go to the border of Mexico and California and convert the drug cartel gangsters.

Even though Jonah knew he was called (that's always step number one) he was still fearful. He ran to the seaport and got on a ship going the opposite direction from God's call. Soon a great storm forms and the ship begins rolling and rocking. Jonah realizes he is the cause and asks the sailors to throw him overboard. They do and the sea immediately calms down.

Meanwhile a great fish swallows Jonah, and he begins a three-day prayer, fasting, and repentance meeting. The fish had a hard time digesting Jonah and throws him up (you guessed it) on the shore of Nineveh!

Jonah stops resisting and preaches the gospel there. The gentile nation gets its spiritual eyes opened and believes in the God of Israel. But Jonah finds he has a prejudice problem, as he is not happy about the results of the revival. God uses this opportunity to deal with Jonah about his attitude toward another culture. The book of Jonah reminds the Jews that if they repent, God will write them down for a good year in the Book of Life.

As the sun sets in this Jewish festival each year, the symbolic gates of Heaven begin to close and the congregation says the *Neilah* prayer, the holiest prayer of the Jews, a call for greater devotion to God. There is a long blast of the great *Shofar*.

The people go home to eat their first meal after the fast, and will soon prepare for the concluding festival of *Sukkot*.

Christian View

The Festival of Atonement is one that individuals in the Church have already entered into and celebrated at Good Friday, our Passover remembrance. So this can be a time of praying for our Jewish brethren who as a nation seek *Adonai* diligently on this festival day. King David said, "Pray for the peace of Jerusalem ..." (Psalm 122:6).

At the *Yom Kippur* service you would hear a door slam shut. For the Christian we are reminded that the door to Heaven will close someday when the day of grace is over. God is generous to have given our world many millennia to receive His son, *Yeshuah* (meaning Salvation).[18]

Remember Jonah's lesson, "He who wins souls is wise."

Next time join me for the festival of *Sukkot*.

Sukkot – The Joyful Harvest Time – Festival of Booths

When I realized that the Jewish people built *sukkot* (booths) when they camped forty years in the desert, that relieved me. At night they needed protection from the elements and certainly from animals.

The Bible says,

"Also in the fifteenth day of the seventh month, when you have gathered the fruit of the Land, you shall keep a feast unto the LORD seven days; on the first day shall be a Sabbath, and on the eighth day shall be a sabbath.

"You shall dwell in booths seven days; all that are Israelites born shall dwell in booths: That your generations may know that I made the children of Israel to dwell in booths, when I brought them out of the land of Egypt: I am the LORD your God" (Lev 23:39, 42-43 KJV-MOD).[19]

Sukkot Today

I originally wrote this for Sukkot. On the Christian Gregorian calendar that was October 1, 2012. And on the Jewish calendar it was Cheshvan 1-7, 5773. The Jewish date shows a closer timeline revealing how long human-beings have lived on the earth - nearing 6,000 years.

For one week Jews, and some Gentiles and Messianic believers build booths in their yards and gardens. Each day they may read from the Bible, sing, and eat a meal together with family and friends in a booth (*sukkah*).

The *sukkah* creates a humble position representing the nullification of material power and acquisitions. No matter how wealthy a person is, he is obliged to leave the realm of wealth, his home, and its symbols of status and power, and dwell in a temporary dwelling at least a part of each day for a week.

In this destabilized condition, he may feel how much he needs God's protection. Instability and vulnerability are hallmarks of exile.

For example, citizens of Haiti have lived in houses that look something like booths, with palm branches for a roof. On Daystar TV 2010, I remember seeing an evangelist who said he was building hundreds of small, well-equipped homes for the Haitians. That was faith in action!

God Uses Nature

"You shall take for yourselves on the first day the fruit of a citron, the branches of date palms, twigs of a plaited tree, and brook willows; and you shall rejoice before *HASHEM*, your God, for a seven-day period." (Lev 23:40)[20]

"In the four species, "The esrog (citron) resembles the heart; the lulav (palm branch) the spine; the hadasim (myrtle leaves) the eyes; and the (aravos) willow branches the lips. By holding all four [species] together, we symbolize the need for a person to utilize all his faculties in the service of God.[21]

The book of the Bible that is the recommended reading for *Sukkot* is Ecclesiastes, written by Solomon.

A Christian View Point

The feast of *Sukkot* or Tabernacles says to me that this world is a temporary dwelling place.

Jesus, of course, celebrated this festival while on earth as well as the six others. He also came down from Heaven, was born among us. "And the Word was made flesh, and dwelt [tabernacled] among us, and we beheld his glory, the glory of the only begotten of the Father, full of grace and truth" (John 1:14 KJV-MOD).

It also speaks to us that by the Holy Spirit God wants to come and live within us, in our earthly tabernacles. His life and presence is multiplied on the earth through all the people indwelt with His Spirit. This is His plan to change the world through God's obedient, loving, healing people.

This seventh festival will be fulfilled at harvest time and the millennial reign of Christ. *The Nicene Creed* says, "He [Jesus] will come again in glory to judge the living and the dead, and His kingdom will have no end."[22]

We work for peace now, but at harvest time there will be a millennium of peace on earth and good will to men.

"May the peace of the Lord be with you." Do pass the peace of God along to all people.

Join me again next time for *Breaking News,* and The Isaiah Series.

Breaking News
Who Was The 34th Man in The Depths of The Earth?

For three days, October 11–13, 2010, I was glued to my television screen, watching the miraculous news from Chile. Thirty-three miners were still alive even though they had very little to eat or drink after being trapped in a mine for 17 days, 2,000 feet below the earth's surface.

August 5th was the date that part of the mine collapsed leaving the miners cut off from escape. When two men drilling for 48 hours broke through the mine's rock formation to the miners location, a note was placed on the bottom of the drill which was then retrieved by the heroic drillers. All 33 men were alive!

I learned that never in the history of the world have people survived underground for 69 nights and days. A billion people watched the rescue of these men by television, computer, and radio.

Saving the miners lives is how, in the face of near tragedy, the whole world came together. For some days we forgot our differences, and were just one human family caring about one another. We cheered, we cried, we yelled! And we thanked God as each miner, and then the team of rescuers, returned to the top of the earth.

How did they do that? Westinghouse created the first rescue capsule 37 years ago and it was first used to help the nine Quecreek Miners in Pittsburgh, Pennsylvania escape from their collapsed mine in 2002. It became the prototype for the new capsule created for Chile, lovingly named Phoenix (meaning out of the ashes). It became the elevator for dozens of people between the dungeon below and the earth's surface above.

The plans called for boring a 28-inch diameter escape hole into the fragile earth; with the help of the new rescue capsule and a pulley – the men ascended one by one to the top arriving like men raised from the dead. The warm and kind President Sebastian Pinera and others said something like, "We and our country have had a rebirth."

Testimonies

"Jose Henriquez, a 55-year-old father of two, was the 24th man pulled out. A religious man, he had led prayer groups in the mine and had friends send 33 bibles down the rescue shaft."

"Mario Gomez, the ninth man to step into the sun after months in the dark, fell to his knees to pray after he stepped out of the capsule."

Gifts to each of the men were T-shirts with the inscription: "The depths of the earth are yours." This refers to Psalms 95:4b "The depths of the earth are in His [God's] hand ..." (HCSB). (See Psalms 71:20 KJV).

Reporter Trevor Persaud for *Christianity Today* Gleanings Blog quoted, "Jimmy Sanchez said, 'There are actually 34 of us, the nineteen-year-old miner wrote in a letter sent up from the mine on Tuesday, because God has never left us ...'"[23] That's like the fiery furnace example in the Book of Daniel.

Daniel and the Fourth Man

Daniel, a prince in Judah, in his youth was taken captive by Babylonian's Nebuchadnezzar, King of Babylon. The army took as prisoners many of the handsome, wise, and talented young Jewish youths from Jerusalem.

Daniel's name was then changed to Belteshazzar. The name change is done to show subjection. His three friends became Shadrach, Meshach, and Abednego (Dan 1:7b KJV).

King Nebuchadnezzar made an image in the likeness of what he saw in a dream and demanded that everyone bow down and worship it when they heard music from his palace. Not to obey meant death in a fiery furnace.

Daniel's three friends let it be known that they would not bow down and worship an image. These Jewish captives had learned the second commandment from childhood. "You shall not make any graven image ... You shall not bow down yourself to it, nor serve it ..." (Exodus 20:4-5 KJV-MOD).

Even when brought before the King, they did not back down (Dan 3:18).

The three Jewish youths were bound and thrown into the furnace. The king came to see how the destruction of Shadrach, Meshach, and Abednego was going. In surprise he said to the executioner, "Didn't we cast three men into the fire? ... I see four men loosed, walking in the midst of the fire, and they have no hurt: and the form of the fourth is like the Son of God" (Dan 3:24b-25 KJV-MOD).

Out of the Depths

Whether down in the depths of the 2,000 foot, hot dungeon in the San Jose Mine in Chile, year 2010, or in a red-hot furnace in Babylon, 586 B.C., the Son of God, Jesus Christ, is with us.

Whether there are 33 miners, or 3 Jewish teens, or you alone, just add one Man, Christ Jesus. Know that God incarnate is walking with you. You are not alone.

Join me next time for the Isaiah Series.

The Isaiah Series (Ten Articles)
The Book of Isaiah the Prophet Revisited

Isaiah is a very popular book of the Bible. Believers dip into different old favorite chapters or verses of it. I have certain portions that have been meaningful to me over the years and perhaps you do too.

The Judean prophet Isaiah was born in Jerusalem about 770 B.C. during the reign of King Uzziah 769 – 733 B.C.[24] Isaiah was called to be a prophet, that is a person who speaks by Holy Spirit anointing about future events. You will know a true prophet if his words come to pass in addition to being a person of integrity.

One of the exciting facts of the book of Isaiah is that God preserved the entire parchment scroll of this 2,000-year-old Hebrew manuscript. It is dated about 100 B.C. The discovery took place in 1947, as it was found in Cave I of the northern Qumran site in the Judean Desert. The Hebrew scrolls are now named by scholars as Isaiah A and Isaiah B.[25] These Isaiah scrolls were originally wrapped with linen, covered with black wax, and sealed in an earthenware jar.

In 1996 I visited the Shrine of the Book, Jerusalem's Israel museum. I saw a copy of the first chapter of Isaiah under glass. It was exciting as I was actually able to read some of the Hebrew words.

Study Isaiah

Isaiah has normally been used for inspiration but has not always been easily understood. Since it is composed of sixty-six chapters it is the longest book of the Bible other than Psalms; that can detour many working people from studying it.

I see Isaiah as a microcosm of the Christian Bible, that is, it has similarities to the whole of Scripture.

- For instance, the entire Bible has sixty-six books and Isaiah has sixty-six chapters.
- There are 39 books in the Old Testament and 27 books in the New.
- Isaiah also in its content easily breaks into 39 and 27 chapters.

Comparing: Isaiah Chapter 1, Genesis 1-3

Genesis chapters 1–3 show the creation, and the fall of mankind. "And the Lord God formed man from the dust of the ground and breathed into his nostrils the breath of life; and man became a living soul" (Gen 2:7).

The temptation by the serpentine spirit was, "For God does know that in the day you eat thereof, then your eyes shall be opened, and you shall be as gods, knowing good and evil" (Gen 3:5 KJV-MOD).

In comparison, Isaiah, chapter one, shows restoration after the fall. The prophet Isaiah is called to bring God's chosen people back to a consecrated lifestyle. God says, "Wash you, make you clean, put away the evil of your doings from before My eyes; cease to do evil; Learn to do well; seek judgment, relieve the oppressed, judge the fatherless, plead for the widow.

"Come now, and let us reason together, says the Lord;
though your sins be as scarlet, they shall be white as snow;
though they be red like crimson, they shall be as wool"
(Isa 1:16-18 KJV-MOD).

Here God is pleading with the southern kingdom of Judah in this instance, and pleading with all humanity in our present time. He wants to sit down and reason with us about why we are throwing our lives away on frivolous things, breaking down the safety boundaries of the commandments, and wasting time on activities with no eternal value. These are some of the similarities in content we can see.

Comparing: Isaiah 40 and Matthew 1-3

Isaiah, chapter 40 in the Old Testament begins similarly to Matthew chapters 1-3 in the New Testament.

"Comfort ye, comfort ye my people, says your God. Speak ye comfortably to Jerusalem, and cry unto her that her warfare is accomplished, that her iniquity is pardoned ..." (Isa 40:1-2 KJV).

"The voice of him that cries in the wilderness, Prepare the way of the Lord, make straight in the desert a highway for our God" (Isa 40:3 KJV-MOD).

God corrects Judah in Isaiah chapters 1 through 39, and now He comforts them in chapters 40 through 66.

Then there is the prophecy where Isaiah proclaims, hundreds of years before the birth of John the Baptist that he, John, will come to prepare humanity for the birth and ministry of the Messiah, Jesus.

Matthew one and two give the genealogy of Jesus and His supernatural birth in Bethlehem, and chapter three tells us again about the life work of John the Baptist.

"In those days came John the Baptist, preaching in the wilderness of Judea, and saying, Repent: for the Kingdom of Heaven is at hand. For this is he that was spoken of by the prophet Isaiah, saying, Prepare the way of the Lord, Make His paths straight" (John 3:1-3 KJV-MOD).

Take time to prayerfully sit and reason together with the Lord God in prayer. Are there any scarlet or crimson colors that need to be changed to white? Give them to Him.

See you next time.

Isaiah the Prophet Says, "Here Am I Send Me"

Last week I began a series on the book of Isaiah. Obviously with a book of sixty-six chapters, I will be touching on selective parts. Several years ago when the Dead Sea Scrolls were displayed in Seattle, I attended with my neighbor and friend, Esther Walker. It was inspiring to both of us.

I purchased my own replica of a cylinder shaped clay pot where a copy of the Hebrew scroll of Isaiah resides.

A special note about Isaiah (*Yeshayahu,* Hebrew) is that it is the only book of the Bible that was preserved totally intact when discovered 2,000 years ago! Perhaps Isaiah is being given special honor by God for his faithfulness. Or perhaps God is especially honoring this prophet whose words of truth cost him martyrdom. Isaiah was born in 770 B.C. His mission was to warn Judah of impending judgment. The reason for this was that they were rejecting the law of God's Word (*Torah*) which would help them be a light to the world.

They were apparently trying to keep in good with everyone by using double speak. Scripture says further that they drank and partied to excess. They bribed people in court, and the righteous were denied a fair trial. Occult beliefs replaced the Bible, and women's clothes became their idols.

Does some of this behavior sound familiar to us today? If so, we should do an about face, before we, like Judah, are sold into slavery (Isa 5:8-23).

In chapter 6, we see Isaiah being commissioned by God. Moses had his burning bush experience, and Isaiah also had a powerful encounter with God. This happened in 740 B.C., the year King Uzziah died.

At this time, Isaiah had a vision of God sitting on His glorious throne in Heaven. The train of the Lord's garment filled the temple. The six winged seraphs were gathered around the throne "calling to one another: 'Holy, holy, holy is the Lord Almighty; the whole earth is full of His glory.'

"At the sound of their voices the doorposts and thresholds shook and the temple was filled with smoke.

"'Woe to me!' I [Isaiah] cried. 'I am ruined! For I am a man of unclean lips, and I live among a people of unclean lips, and my eyes have seen the King, the Lord Almighty'" (Isa 6:3-5 NIV).

God's Call

Then a seraph flew to Isaiah, with a live coal in his hand which he had taken from the altar. Isaiah says, "With it he touched my mouth and said, 'See, this has touched your lips; your guilt has been taken away and your sin atoned for.'

"Then I heard the voice of the Lord saying. 'Whom shall I sent? And who will go for us?'

"And I said, Here am I, Send me!" (Isa 6:7-8).

Isaiah followed God's direction for his life; he was faithful to his calling.

You Are Called

I believe all of God's people have a calling. Once we find it we can feel fulfilled. Maybe it's being a minister like Isaiah, or a mother or dad with children to raise, perhaps a teacher, or a mechanic, a counselor or grandparent, or an author or librarian, an artist or a gardener.

We're all called to be lights in a world that is sometimes very dark.

If you have not found your place in the sun, pray, "Dear Lord, cleanse my mouth and mind with a coal from Your altar. If I've taken Your Name in vain. I truly repent. Thank you for Your forgiveness. Prepare me as I study the Great Book you've given me for salvation, spiritual growth, and direction for life.

"By your grace I say, 'Here I am Lord, send me. Amen.'"

The Prophet Isaiah and You, and How You Are Alike

Last week we looked at a life-changing vision Isaiah experienced when he was called by God to be His personal friend. After that day, Isaiah's life changed drastically. It was wonderful to at last be in God's wholesome presence and have His unconditional love. Now, Isaiah knew why he was born and that he was to walk with his Lord all his days. Interesting also that his name meaning, "God is Salvation" was being fulfilled.

But not long after this great visionary encounter, Isaiah noticed something else. Coming into the presence of the holy, living God caused his sins to be revealed.

Isaiah then said, "... I am undone; because I am a man of unclean lips, and I dwell in the midst of a people with unclean lips ..." (Isa 6:5 KJV). The result is that God's presence caused him to realize that he had been tarnished by the world in which he lived (James 1:27).

My Wakeup Call

I can identify with Isaiah in that I was a pretty good person and went to church on Sunday, but I was not a student of God's Word so I was not being changed. Compare one hour in a church service once a week to six days with little spiritual input. Guess what wins?

I needed to take a spiritual bath to wash away the mud that splashed on me as I walk through the world. I didn't even know that I was unclean until I found someone with whom to compare myself. Gail Miller showed me the pathway but within a year and a half she died of a cerebral hemorrhage from a childhood injury.

She was my wakeup call decades ago, at age 26.

Gail's prayer group prayed for me. I was cleansed, shed tears, and the Holy Spirit touched my spirit, mind, and lips. I was being called to make Jesus Lord of my life. My world changed.[26]

Steps in Isaiah's Life

Isaiah's conversion about 2,740 years ago is a picture of a believer's salvation today. In the tabernacle in the wilderness, where the Jews worshipped while traveling through the wilderness, there was a bronze altar where animal sacrifices for sin occurred. The bronze altar was the first of seven pieces of furniture. It is interesting that all seven together were placed in the position of a cross. (Symbolism of the tabernacle is a study in itself.)

I believe that the seraph took the coal from this bronze altar because it represents the willing death of Jesus for our sins. The coal was placed on Isaiah's lips as a symbol of God's covenant with Israel and cleansing from sins.

By faith, Isaiah looked forward from his heart warming experience 740 years, to the death of Christ Jesus and appropriated salvation.

We, who believe today, look back in faith 2,000 years ago to Jerusalem where Jesus gave His life for our sins. When we see God's holiness, and our sinfulness, a coal from His altar has in some way cleansed our lives also.

Isaiah and You

Here are Isaiah's three steps that you can claim too:
1. Pray for an encounter with God. Jesus says, "Behold, I stand at the door, and knock: if any one hears my voice, and opens the door, I will come in and have fellowship with him" (Rev 3:20 KJV-MOD).

325

2. Realize the need to confess your sin. "For all have sinned and come short of the glory of God" (Rom 3:23 KJV). Use the Lord's Prayer to pray as a checklist for direction.[27]
3. God's calling for you, will be revealed. Jesus was choosing His disciples and said, "Follow Me and I will make you fishers of men" (Matt 4:19 KJV).

So now you know how Isaiah, you, and I have something in common.

The mirror of God's Word also shows us the best path and the way to wholeness, completeness.

I like taking time in the morning to read from a devotional like *Forward Day by Day* [28] one can then read the suggested scriptures. I also listen to speakers from Moody Bible Institute on KCIS Radio, especially in the morning. In-depth classes with Bible Study Fellowship, Women's Aglow International conferences, or *You Can Be Emotionally Free® Courses*,[29] for instance, will strengthen you on your exciting journey. The internet has some good Bible studies also. Sometimes I just read a special teaching book or biography as my devotional reading.

See you next time as we continue with Isaiah.

Children in Ancient Days Gave Prophetic Messages

We've been learning about the Prophet Isaiah as we dipped into his first six chapters. It was exciting to learn about Isaiah's changed life, and the preparation for his call to save the people of his own tribe of Judah. If you've had children, it was a special time when you picked out their names. Now days parents try to change the spelling of a common name so the child will stand out and be different. For instance: Diane, Dianne, Di, DiAnn.

Isaiah the prophet and his wife had two sons. These dedicated parents didn't simply name their children regular names, but each name had a prophetic meaning. Son number one was named *"Shear-Jashub"* meaning a remnant will return. When mother Isaiah wanted her son home for supper and she called, Shear-Jashub! the whole neighborhood got a message.

After the patriarch Jacob died, his twelve children became the twelve tribes of Israel (Gen 49). As is true for all of us in a fallen world, we exchange words of disagreement, fight with one another, and sometimes go to war even with our own families.

Isaiah's Lifetime

In Isaiah's lifetime beginning in 770 B.C., the twelve tribes had already divided into two groups: Judah (two tribes in the southern kingdom in Israel) and Israel (ten tribes the northern kingdom in Israel).

At this time, the good King Uzziah who ruled over Judah had died and son Ahaz was now on the throne in Jerusalem.

Now we have some sibling rivalry. King Pekah of Israel and King Rizin of Aram or Syria decided to fight the Assyian domination in the region. But King Ahaz of Judah refused to join the battle. In anger the two northern kings turned against the southern king, Ahaz.

Ahaz was comforted by Isaiah, with his son Shear-Jashup, and was told not to be afraid of Pekah and Rizin but to ignore them. Isaiah had a vision of the enemies as two smoldering stubs of firewood.

Unfortunately for Israel, the Assyrian king, Tiglath-Pileser came quickly against the two northern kings (2 Kings 17:24). Many Israelites were deported and people were brought from other lands to the towns of Samaria. Israel began to lose its power as a nation.

Through Shear-Jashub's name, the Lord let King Ahaz know that all of Judah will not be destroyed. A remnant will be saved and the nation will therefore be saved, ultimately (Isaiah10:21).

Second Son of Isaiah

God told Isaiah to prophesy and write it in a scroll that he and his wife would have a second son and should name him "*Maher-Shalal-Hash-Baz.*" The Hebrew meaning is "quick to the plunder" and "swift to the spoil" (Isa 8:1). Sounds like another battle brewing.

This sign is also given, "Before the boy knows how to say, 'My father' or 'My mother,' the wealth of Damascus and the plunder of Samaria will be carried off by Assyria" (Isa 8:4 KJV-MOD).

The Lord has let Ahaz know, through the birth and growth of this second son, that it would be about three years until his battle with the King of Assyria.

A Third Child Named

With all the battles that went on in the ancient world and that go on in our world today, a message of hope is needed. That must be the reason God put a prophetic picture of His Son Jesus right here in the midst of these battles to give them, and to give us, hope today.

Isaiah prophesied, "Therefore the Lord Himself shall give you a sign; Behold a virgin shall conceive, and bear a son, and shall call his name Immanuel" (Isa 7:14).

"For unto us a child is born, unto us a son is given: and the government shall be upon his shoulder: and his name shall be called Wonderful, Counselor, the mighty God, The everlasting Father, The Prince of Peace. Of the increase of his government and peace there shall be no end ..." (Isa 9:6-7 KJV).

Jesus' name in Hebrew is *Yeshu'ah* meaning salvation. His descriptive name *Immanuel* means God with us.

In Israel when mother Mary (*Miriam*) called her boy, *Yeshuah* to eat supper, the whole Jewish neighborhood knew His name meant salvation. Maybe she called Him Immanuel at times too, another great prophetic message.

Prophetic Signs

Isaiah's two sons were prophetic signs and biblical messages in history (Isa 8:18). Even more so this is true with God's Son! Think of it – Isaiah prophesied Immanuel's (Jesus') virgin birth hundreds of years before it happened (Isa 7:14)!

Father God gave His Son the name Immanuel meaning God with us. He also sent Gabriel, the archangel, to name Mary's baby, even before conception, Salvation or *Yeshuah*, and in English, Jesus (Matt 1:21, Luke 1:31).

God named his Son prophetically to let everyone know why Jesus came to earth. Jesus came to save us from our sins to deliver us from evil, to bring us into God's family, and to help us lead other sons and daughters into His eternal Kingdom.

Are you a sign and a symbol? What message do you carry or want to carry? Just follow the next steps God gives you.

More on Isaiah ahead.

Peace Far Beyond What the World Can Give You

In our last Isaiah study, it was revealed to King Ahaz that the powerful King of Assyria would invade the kingdom of Judah in three years. For comfort, Isaiah the prophet said that God had allowed Ahaz to ask Him for a sign. Out of fear, probably of making a mistake, Ahaz responded that he would not ask for a sign.

Then God gave Ahaz the best and greatest sign, which was a prophecy foretelling the coming Messiah.

Each year as you and I near Christmas, we can hear on radio or television Handel's Messiah as he put some of Isaiah's poetic prophecy to music, as well as the Apostle John's words in Revelation.

"For unto us a Child is born,
Unto us a Son is given:
And the government shall be
upon His shoulder.
And His name shall be called
Wonderful Counselor, The Mighty God,
The Everlasting Father, The Prince of Peace"
(Isa 9:6 KJV-MOD).

When writing these words to you, I enjoyed singing again this part of Handel's arrangement as I had done during my college years in church choirs.

This prose gives the fourfold name and attributes of the Child who in His adult years will be know by multitudes as The Messiah, born to reign over the throne of David in Jerusalem.

Four Titles of the Child

As a marriage and family counselor, I appreciate Jesus' attributes: **First** as Wonderful Counselor. My relationship with this most Wonderful Counselor, and through prayer and study of His words in Scripture, my counseling sessions are greatly informed. Great news for the believing counselor is that the Counselor lives in us!

A **second** title is The Mighty God. "Great in counsel and mighty in work; for Your eyes are open to the ways of the sons of men ..." (Jer 32:19 KJV-MOD). As the tribe of Judah finds, God will be mighty in battle for them.

His **third** title is The Everlasting Father. Jesus fathered us in our faith, He has been like a father or big brother to us. He and His Father are a lot alike, but He is not actually God the Father. He is God the Son.

The Child Jesus did not have His beginning at His birth, because He too is eternal and always has been. But He chose to be born in a human body to come to earth and give His life to save us.

Fourth He is The Prince of Peace. Peace on earth can only come from transformed human beings. *"Shalom, shalom, lo shalom,"* means "… peace, peace, there is no peace" (Jer 6:14 KJV-MOD).

In other words, we cannot create peace in natural ways, but with Christ in us, He can impart it to us supernaturally. We all should and do work for peace, but the only totally lasting peace comes from God, Father, Son, and Holy Spirit.

First and Second Advent

Isaiah's prophetic word goes ahead to the first **advent** of Jesus, 1 B.C. But it also goes much further, that is, to His **second** advent. That will be the coming climatic event in history.

Before Jesus' ascension He said, "Peace I leave with you, My peace I give to you: not as the world gives, give I unto you. Let not your heart be troubled, neither let it be afraid" (John 14:27 KJV-MOD).

Is your heart troubled by all the people and nations attacking one another not only in Bible history but in our present day? Sometimes I wonder, "Will it ever stop?"

Then I remember to take a few minutes to breathe deeply and let God's peace fill my soul. I know He is with me and all will be well.

You can do that too. Ask the Prince of Peace to fill your heart and soul with His sweet, everlasting peace. His *shalom.* All will be well for you, too.

With our LORD we have a great future ahead of us. Our King will come (Psalm 24:10).

Next column: How You Can Know God Is on Your Side.

How You Can Know God Is On Your Side

Why is the desire to know the future through occult ways luring to multitudes of people today and in millennia past? Some of the avenues for these activities are fortune telling through planets (astrology), cards, horoscopes, reading people's minds (clairvoyance), or being a medium talking to the dead (necromancy), to name a few.

Because I was raised in a Christian home, I did not get interested in occult activities, yet I did get close to the edge one day. During my college days, I'd drive over the causeway between my home in Tampa, Florida to St. Petersburg Beach.

On one such occasion, I noticed a family of Gypsies living by the side of the road. I thought it would be good to bring them some clothes.

My next trip I laid clothes on the back seat of my car. As I drove up to their little tented home, I asked the young people if they could use some clothes.

"Yes," they said, and came to my car for the items.

As I turned to leave they said, "Our grandma would be unhappy if you left without her telling your fortune."

I said, "Oh thank you, but I don't need to do that."

They said, "Oh please, she would be so disappointed."

Not to hurt their feelings, I went in to see her. She had the typical fortune telling story that, "I would marry a tall, dark, and handsome man." I left as fast as I could, satisfied that I had not hurt anyone's feelings.

By the way when I did marry, Dennis was 5 ft. 8, had a thick head of light brown hair, and blue eyes.

When I realized I was wrong. I did repent from putting myself in a compromising position. I wasn't wise enough at that time to say, "No thank you."

Back to Isaiah

In the study of the first ten chapters of Isaiah, we saw how the southern kingdom and the northern kingdom of Israel at this time in history were not in favor with God. In fact, in 2 Kings 17:23-24 we see that the ten tribes of Israel were taken away captive, by King Tiglath-Pileser of Assyria.

By chapters 8 and 9 of Isaiah, we find that the two tribes of the southern kingdom of Judah were being warned that Assyria was coming after them, too.

Through Isaiah the prophet, who spoke the true gift of prophecy, (1 Cor 12:7, 10a) he explained why God was allowing the enemy's kingdom to attack them. Here we can learn lessons today from what happened 2,750 years ago.

What Not to Do

The prophet Isaiah says, "When men tell you to consult mediums and spiritists, who whisper and mutter, should not a people inquire of their God? Why consult the dead on behalf of the living?" (Isa 8:19 NIV).

One of the worst spiritual sins is spiritism. Adolph Hitler is an example of a person who sought information through mediums. Not only was he inhumane, but also activities such as this can cause demonic possession. King Saul lost favor with God through the disobedience of inquiring from the witch of Endor (1 Sam 28).

The Law of God in the *Torah* has given warnings against the occult and consulting the dead (Deut 18:9-14, Leviticus 19:31).The so called dead are actually evil spirits masquerading as the dead.

Shakespeare said, "And oftentimes, to win us to our harm, The instruments of darkness tell us truths, Win us with honest trifles, to betray us In deepest consequence."[30]

More Sins

Other reasons that God judged His own covenant people were for creating images and idols to worship in place of God (Isa 10:10-11). This was breaking the first and second commandments: "You shall have no other gods before Me. You shall not make for yourself an idol ... You shall not bow down to them or worship them ..." (Exodus 20:3-5 KJV-MOD).

They also were depriving the poor from their rights and withholding justice from the oppressed of His people, making widows their prey and robbing the fatherless (Isa 10:2).

A Prayer of Repentance: "Dear Father God, if I have believed, studied, or practiced anything that is displeasing to You, or contrary to Your Word, I am truly sorry. I humbly repent. I want to follow You dear Lord. In Jesus' Name. Amen."

Next column: Isaiah and You Can Have a Well of Life Inside.

You Can Have a Well of Life Inside

As I study Isaiah's prophecies of human errors and wars, and as humanity ignores lessons learned from parents, teachers, pastors, rabbis, and priests, there are results. It's hard to read about mistakes of millennia past that continue on today.

Fortunately as we read along in Isaiah, we have respite with some happy scenes. Chapter 12 is one of those places, "A Hymn of Praise."

"And in that day you will say: 'O LORD, I will praise You; Though You were angry with me, Your anger is turned away and You comfort me'" (Isa 12:1 NKJV).

Yes, God has been angry with you and me at times in our lives. He is not a disinterested parent who doesn't care what we do. If we get involved with the occult and drugs, to name a few things He doesn't like, we separate ourselves from Him.

Even gossip and unforgiveness will make the Lord displeased. When you realize you've overstepped boundaries, you may feel your heart drop into your stomach as I have, and had to immediately stop and pray.

God is Salvation

Isaiah continues: "Behold, God is my salvation, I will trust and not be afraid; For *YAH [Yahweh]*, the LORD, is my strength and song; He also has become my salvation" (Isa 12:2 NKJV).

What does it mean for God to be your salvation? When you choose to walk with Him, He will take away your fears. He will give you strength when you are weak. He will give you a song in your heart. Life is so much better with God the Almighty in your life.

"He also has become my salvation. Therefore with joy you will draw water from the wells of salvation" (Isa 12:3b-4 NKJV).

The wells of salvation refer to the enjoyment of God's blessings through the Anointed One of David's house. They also point to the time when there will be a well of living water flowing out of the lives of believers in Jesus Christ (John 7:38).[31]

Woman at the Well

One day Jesus was tired of walking while on one of His missionary journeys. That afternoon He stopped and rested at a famous place in Samaria called Jacob's Well.

Soon a woman came to draw water. Jesus asked if she might give Him a drink. She chided him because He was a Jew and asked her, a lowly Samaritan woman for a drink.

She said, "Jews have no dealings with Samaritans. Jesus answered and said to her, if you knew the gift of God, and who it is that says to you, Give me to drink: you would have asked of Him, and He would have given you living water" (John 4:9b-10 KJV-MOD).

His water sounds better than Father Jacob's well, so she debates about which water is best.

Jesus explains that when a person drinks from Jacob's well he will thirst again. Yet, when a person drinks from the water Jesus gives, he or she will never thirst again. Not only that, the water within will spring up into everlasting life.

She Asks for a Drink

She finally says, "Sir, give me this water, that I thirst not, neither come here" (John 4:15 KJV-MOD).

He asks her to get her husband. She says she hasn't one. Jesus prophesies that she has had five husbands and the man she lives with is not her husband.

Amazed, she admits that He is right, and believes in Him as Messiah. She leaves and goes to the city to tell the people she has met the Messiah and that He knows all about her.

Through her testimony, the whole city meets at Jacob's well. Everyone chooses the spiritual drink of Everlasting Life from Jesus' well.

If you are tired of being thirsty for things that don't fully satisfy, cup your hands and lift them up and pray: "Fill my cup Lord Messiah. Quench the thirsting of my soul. Pour in Your eternal Life. Amen."

Next: Isaiah continues.

The Naked Truth and More

How did a legitimate prophet of ancient days get a serious message from God to an entire nation? There wasn't television, internet, iPods, Tweeter messaging. Nor was there YouTube to send video or photos, no e-mail, or radio to warn their world.

One of the greatest biblical discoveries today is the 2,000 year old Hebrew scroll of the book of Isaiah. Handwritten scrolls take a long time to write and production is slow. Yet ancient scroll discoveries make it possible for us to validate the prophet Isaiah's book today. He was born 2,770 years ago, or 770 B.C., and died 695 B.C. at age 75. His prophetic ministry lasted around 44 years. So his book was finished before his death.

But how did God direct leaders to relay His words in days past? They did write with quill pens on scrolls, but there were no printing presses until Gutenberg in A.D. 1440.[32]

Playing Charades

Still people were good at spreading news in ancient times if the message was dramatic enough.

Do you ever remember playing the game Charades? This is when an individual stands in front of a group to act out a book title, song, or famous war without speaking aloud. Basically Charades is pantomime. The movie *Gone with the Wind* would work. A child might pantomime, David and Goliath or Pinocchio.

In the first 39 chapters of Isaiah, there are numerous battles described. God would use a righteous man to warn a nation. Isaiah was chosen to warn Judah and others about coming battles so they would be prepared. Sometimes scores of years would go by before a prophesy would be fulfilled.

The group I was studying Isaiah with in 2011was Bible Study Fellowship. We were at that time reading chapters 15 through 20. I had studied parts of Isaiah before but not chapter by chapter through all sixty-six. What I saw in chapter 20 was surprising at first until I realized that God was guiding Isaiah to use a kind of charade for his message.

Naked and Barefoot

The Lord said to Isaiah, "Go and remove the sackcloth from your body and take your sandals off your feet. And he did so walking naked and barefoot" (Isa 20:2b NKJV). I hasten to say that he was not naked as we would use the term today.

"**Sackcloth** was a mourner's outer garment. **Naked** means without his outer garment, wearing only a simple tunic. **Three years:** 714-711 B.C."[33] A tunic is "akin to Heb *kuttoneth* coat. A simple slip-on garment made with or without sleeves and usually knee-length or longer, belted at the waist , and worn as an under or outer garment by men or women of ancient Greece or Rome."[34] I was relieved to learn this further information.

Isaiah was instructed to do this for three years! He was a walking sign or billboard. The pantomime, charade message was the best media of that day centuries ago. Yes, I think this news would get around by word of mouth and letter!

Here's what it meant: Isaiah was to be, a sign and a wonder against Egypt and Ethiopia (Isa 20:3). Isaiah prophesied, "So shall the King of Assyria lead away the Ethiopians as captives, young and old, naked and barefoot ... to the shame of Egypt" (Isa 20:4 NKJV).

Isaiah's Portraits of Christ

Isaiah's book describes Jesus as though he had met Him. In Isaiah 53 he calls Him Burden-bearer, Sin-bearer, Intercessor, Only Savior. Other places He is called Immanuel, Wonderful, Counselor, Mighty God, Prince of Peace, Divine Servant, Righteous King, Law-giver, Liberator. We can know the Lord in these ways too.

Do read and study Isaiah 53. "Messiah's Coming. This is the best-known prophecy of the Crucifixion in the Bible, and both Matthew and Peter quote from it. Writing eight centuries before Christ, Isaiah made incredibly accurate statements concerning the facts of the Crucifixion, but more importantly, he spoke of the purpose of the Cross."[35]

See you next time on Isaiah.

It Is a "Win Win" Situation with God

I was sitting with my friend, Carolyn Keogh, having a latte following Bible study. I asked her, "What seemed to impact you in our study of Isaiah in class tonight?"

She thought a moment, smiled, and said, "I liked the discussion about the resurrection; if I have already died when Christ comes for His people, I would be raised from the dead and taken home with Him. If I am alive when He comes, then without dying, I will be taken home to be with Him.

"Either way I look at it, there's a 'win, win' situation!"

I smiled back at her. "Hey, that's well put Carolyn."

"Well, I'll tell you what was especially interesting to me in our study," I said stirring my latte. "It's where the prophet Isaiah has the section of four chapters 24 through 27, right in the middle of his book. I never knew before, that these chapters have been called *The Small Apocalypse*. It's like a mini treatise of the book of Revelation. It gives us new information and confirmation for the last book of the Bible!"

Comparing Prophets

In comparing Isaiah's last-days treatise and the Apostle John's, we have Isaiah completing his book by the time of his death in 695 B.C. at age 75, and John who died about A.D. 90, having completed his five books by then. There is approximately 785 years between these two prophet's books in the Bible, and yet their apocalyptic concepts are compatible. That's amazing! That's God the Holy Spirit.

Reading these chapters in Isaiah is like putting a puzzle together. We students discovered a clue. Every time we read "in that day" there are several basic meanings:

- It speaks of the time when Christ returns.
- It lets us know that time has not happened yet.
- It shows us how wonderful and peaceful the world will be.

Ten Nations at War

Preceding this "little" book of Revelation, Isaiah 13–23 gives the reader a group of prophecies to ten nations. It included battles with Moab (central part of Jordan), Damascus, Israel (Ephraim), Cush (Ethiopia), Egypt, Babylon (Iraq), Edom (Dumah in Jordan), Arabia, Jerusalem, and Tyre (on the coast of Lebanon).

These wars were not my favorite Bible passages but they are the history of man's inhumanity to man.

Israel, for instance, has been conquered at least seven times. Two of those times were under cruel rulers you have heard of: Nebuchadnezzar King of Babylon and King Antiochus IV Epiphanes the Syrian Greek.

This is the reason why the Israelis are always discovering ancient artifacts. For instance, the oldest eastern gate was found underground at the base of the Mount of Olives. King Herod's coliseum was found buried near the Mediterranean Ocean! It is now excavated. I was privileged to see it before and after restoration.

In our present day, we have nuclear warfare that makes our potential battles even more frightening. North Korea and Iran are developing this kind of warfare. Then to the south of the United States we have the warfare of drugs being smuggled in to invade and destroy our youth, and their offspring.

Even the supposedly lesser drugs such as marijuana damage the brain. You can find images of brain damage on the Council of

Addictions of New York State's web site.[36] They have quoted information from *Change Your Brain, Change Your Life*[37] by Dr. Daniel Amen M.D., a neuroscientist.

Ways "People of The Book" follow the Lord

Isaiah 24:4, 5 sums up man's sin. I list God's remedies.
1. Study the Law of Moses for the Jews – The *Torah.* Study the Bible *Tanach* – 39 books. Keep the Ten Commandments – moral law.
2. Law of grace for Christians – confess sins, receive Jesus as Savior, Study the Bible – sixty-six books. Keep the Ten Commandments Jesus and Moses taught as a rule of life.

1. Jews: Keep God's ordinances: baptism, and *Bar Mitzvah* (male), *Bat Mitzvah* (female) for coming of age and parent's blessing,
Spring and Fall Festivals:
*   Passover meal (out of Egypt);
*   Unleavened Bread (bread for the journey–no yeast); and
*   First Fruits (miracle of the Red Sea crossing);
*   Pentecost (Moral Law given through Moses on Mr. Sinai);
*   Yom Terurah – New Year and Blowing of Trumpets, Harvest;
*   Yom Kippur - Day of Atonement (confessing sins and fasting one day for the year 24 hrs);
*   Sukkot or Feast of Tabernacles (reign of Messiah Jerusalem - for Sabbath rest for a millennia).

Some Jews celebrate *Hanukkah* in December – a reminder of the restoration of the Jerusalem temple after it was taken over by Antiochus Epiphanies the Syrian Greek, a type of Anti-messiah. The Jews won the temple back and God provided the sanctified oil for the Menorah for one day, to increase to last for eight days!

2. Christians have: Water Baptism; Holy Communion; Confirmation - (renouncing darkness –anointed with oil);
    *   Passover (Jesus' death on the cross);
    *   Unleavened Bread (Jesus' burial);
    *   First Fruits (Jesus' Resurrection) [Easter];
    *   Pentecost – (Empowerment - Confirmation).

Celebrating Jesus birth [Christmas] and Lent [40 days prayer and fasting] - these are followed by many but not all Christians.

Some celebrate the 3 Fall Festivals adding Christian concepts:

- Feast of Trumpets (rapture of believers);
- Day of Atonement (in Heaven with Jesus our Great High Priest);
- Feast of Tabernacles – (Return with Messiah Jesus to earth - bringing peace and millennial reign).

"So when His name is called, every knee will bow, in heaven, on earth, and below. And every tongue will confess "Jesus, the Anointed One, is Lord," to the glory of God our Father!" (Phil 2:10-11 VOICE).

Why not now? Bow now. And avoid the rush!

Next: Concluding with the book of Isaiah

The Holy Spirit Can Guide You Step by Step

In the early days of the nations of Judah and Israel, they had trouble getting involved with the negatives in the culture of their day. Overindulgence in wine and parties, also involvement with worshipping another God through idols, were two of the problems that caused them to make wrong decisions and lose favor with God.

God had to allow their bad judgment to lead them into alliances with nations who were under demonic leadership. The removal of God's presence would eventually cause Judah to come back to Him and repent. This happened over and over again.

Dangerous Territory

It reminds me of my childhood when I would make friends at school, or in my neighborhood, with a child who might innocently or purposefully lead me into wrong behavior. One time at the age of thirteen, a neighborhood acquaintance invited me to meet her older boyfriend. I didn't know he was a hypnotist. Guess who they picked for a demonstration?

It seemed innocent enough simply to hold my leg out straight for some minutes. People could touch to see how stiff it was. Yet, since I allowed someone to control my will, other than God, I had moved into dangerous territory. I did not know this was occult activity. God instructs Israel about this, "When you come into the land which the Lord your God is giving you, you shall not learn to follow the abominations of those nations" (Deut 18:9 NKJV). See also verses 10-14.

If you find that you've been led into something offensive to God, the best thing to do is to kneel, or bow in prayer, and ask God to forgive you. It was years later when I learned that the Bible warns us against submitting to hypnotic trances. At that moment, I asked God's forgiveness.

God was trying to deliver Judah and Israel from unholy warfare alliances with unbelieving nations (2 Cor 6:14). Their wrong behavior was blocking the very blessings and fellowship with God that they needed.

We need to remember that there are two kingdoms at war in this world, the Kingdom of light and the kingdom of darkness. As a teen I had never understood these two kingdoms. It would be a good sermon for a pastor to use once in a while!

The Kingdom of light is directed by our One, yet Triune God. The kingdom of darkness is directed by Lucifer (Satan), who was defeated when Jesus gave His life on the cross for our sins. Yet the battle between those two kingdoms will continue until the messianic reign of Christ.

Four Apocalypses

In my last column, I mentioned learning that the prophet Isaiah has four chapters, Isaiah 24 through 27, that have been called the Small Apocalypse. Apocalypse is, "One of the Jewish and Christian writings of 200 B.C. to A.D. 150 marked by pseudonymity, symbolic imagery, and the expectation of an imminent cosmic cataclysm in which God destroys the ruling powers of evil and raises the righteous to life in a messianic kingdom."[38]

These chapters can be summed up as follows:
- Impending judgment on the earth (Isa 24).
- Praise to God (Isa 25).
- A Song of Salvation (Isa 26).
- Take refuge from the coming judgment (Isa 27).

The book of Revelation has eight warfare or apocalyptic chapters: 8, 9, 12, 13, 14, 16, 17, and 18.

Four Woes Isaiah

We see that Isaiah also has four chapters on woes in the Bible, they are chapters 28 to 31. These four chapters are called the Book of Woes.
- Woe to Ephraim and Jerusalem.
- Woe to Jerusalem (Ariel is another name for Jerusalem).
- Woe to the rebellious children.
- Woe to those who go down to Egypt. – a type of the world
"Woe is an exclamation of grief, or alas, woe" in Heb. and Gr."[39]

Four Woes Revelation

The book of Revelation also has four woes.
- One woe is past, Revelation 9:12
- Second woe is past, Revelation 11:14
- Third woe comes quickly, Revelation 11:14
- Fourth, woe to the inhabitants of the earth, Revelation 12:12

Earlier I mentioned that the sixty-six chapters of Isaiah are a microcosm of the sixty-six books of the Bible.

This shows up well in the similarity of the apocalypse and the woe chapters in both Isaiah and Revelation.

Authors Isaiah and John were separated by 785 years. They weren't exactly reading one another's emails! I like this verse. "Your ears shall hear a word behind you, saying, 'This is the way, walk in it.' Whenever you turn to the right hand or whenever you turn to the left" (Isa 30:21 NKJV). How do we get to the place that we make right decisions, at least, most of the time?

It's through the *school of the Spirit* and our textbook, *the entire Bible*. By Prayer to God and using spiritual gifts we will *find inward direction*. Bible study helps you follow the right messages on the road of your lifelong journey. The Holy Spirit will guide you step by step.

Next is Chapter.7

Chapter 7

**Three Holidays Series
Help For the Journey, Aslan's Country, Losses
Breaking News: Temptation, Hezekiah's Healing Series
Conclusion: Romance and Poetry**

Rita Bennett, Author (photo above) – Rita, as widow, went back to university to obtain a Masters degree in counseling (2008). She was awarded a Doctor of Letters degree from Oral Roberts University in 2012 for her literary work, TBN television program hosting, CRA course curriculum, and *Beacon* newspaper column. *A New Look at the News*, her 13th book, shows us how to receive God's help for the journey.

Three Holidays
Thanks for All You Have Done for Me

Each Thanksgiving season you and I have a lot to be thankful for. Here's the list I have written. On November 21, 2010 in Edmonds, Washington we had our first winter snow. I saw really large white snowflakes coming down in sheets. I wondered whether I should go to church. Then I considered that my Honda has four-wheel drive, so I felt safe in venturing out.

My Thanksgiving List

After communion, I slipped out to meet a friend to drive to the book fair at the Country Village in Bothell.

As Carolyn Keogh and I drove up to Courtyard Hall there was just one parking space and it was right at the front door. It was so convenient for carrying our books, CDs, and supplies into the center. This was a seemingly small but in my viewpoint an important answer to prayer. Carolyn and I thanked God for this helpful gift.

October 4, I prayed with friends Herb and Trish Claflin for God's protection during his chemo shot the next day for a lung tumor and for release of pain. I shared Scripture to build his faith. After our prayer, we were all delightfully surprised when Herb reported that chronic pain from arthritis at the bottom of his spine was gone.

Trish gave me a miracle update later, "Herb's back pain left him following our prayer session and he remained that way for well over a year. It even stayed away when we took a 2,500 trip to southern California shortly before his death! The Lord banished that pain for him and we were both so very grateful."

October 10, on Sunday, I awoke with blurred vision in my right eye. When the Hem of His Garment prayer teams were gathered at St. Albans, I asked for prayer. Patty Timonen laid hands on both sides of my forehead and eyes and prayed for me. During the coffee hour a short time later I realize my eyes were normal. That healing has continued. I gave another prayer of thanksgiving near Thanksgiving Day.

Grateful, that I recorded a CD of 20 of my Christmas poems, *Christmas is All of This.* I had found the right male guest reader, Dr. Keith Oles, retired geologist professor, to join me in recording at the

Ford Video studio. The project was completed the week before Thanksgiving. This will be my organization's Christmas special. Full production took less than a month. I also added several brand new tasty limericks.

On November 9, I gave my *Christmas is All of This* CD to new friend, Ace, from Africa. This was to thank her for waiting with me at the hotel during a fundraiser gathering for Pilgrim Africa. She stayed with me until I saw some friends in the crowd. May the Ugandans, and friends, never give up the fight against poverty and malaria in order to save their people.

I'm thankful too for *The Edmonds Beacon* editors past and present, and the publisher: Al Hooper, Pat Ratliff, and Paul Archipley for inviting me to be Worship Columnist from January 2005 to February 2011. It's been an adventure with my local popular newspaper.

You might enjoy sharing, as I have with you, family thanks-givings on this special holiday. Some people like to do this between turkey dinner and dessert. I do not advise trying this when you first sit down to dinner!

How to Enter Heaven

My late sister-in-law, Kay Reed, had a spiritual dream before her death. She heard this question, "What is the key action to take when one reaches the entrance to Heaven?"

The answer she found was from Psalm 100, "Enter into His gates with thanksgiving, and into His courts with praise. Be thankful unto Him [God] and bless His Name" (Ps. 100:4 KJV-MOD).

It wasn't long before Kay made her final journey to enter the gates. I'm sure she went in with praise and thanksgiving! When we know our Lord personally, thanksgiving and praise to our triune God is a natural response.

Now is the best time to experience worship. Why wait?

One of my favorite praise songs is *My Tribute,* by Andraé Crouch:

"How can I say thanks,
for the things You have done for me?
Things so undeserved,
yet you gave to prove your love for me.
The voices of a million angels
could not express my gratitude.
All that I am and ever hope to be,

I owe it all to Thee."
The chorus begins: "To God be the glory …"

Happy Thanks-giving!

To hear the entire song, go to You Tube and listen to the incredible, coloratura soprano voice of Sissel and the Oslo Gospel Choir.[1] Or you may find the lyrics at http:www.lyricsty.com.[2]
Holidays continue next time.

The Christmas Story in Narrative

Joseph and Mary were betrothed (engaged) which in the Jewish culture was as binding as actual marriage. To break the betrothal one had to obtain a divorce. The relationship was not to be consummated until the marriage. It is believed that Mary was in her late teens and Joseph was somewhat older.

During the time of her engagement, the angel Gabriel came to her and said, "Hail, highly favored, the Lord is with you: blessed are you among women."

The next thing the angel said was wise, "Fear not!" His words of concern strengthened Mary for his next words.

Mary Chosen

"Mary you have found favor with God." She was possibly in tears with these words of affirmation.

Then Gabriel took the next step, news that would save the world!

"And, behold, you shall conceive in your womb, and bring forth a son, and shall call his name Jesus."

Here Mary has to think, "I'm only engaged to Joseph and how can I, a virgin, become pregnant? Who has ever heard of such a thing?"

The angel continues his message, "He shall be great, and shall be called the Son of the Highest …"

Mary asks, "How can this be, seeing I know not a man?"

Gabriel answers her, "The Holy Spirit shall come upon you, and the power of the Highest shall overshadow you: therefore also that holy one that shall be born of you shall be called the Son of God." [3]

The angel convinced Mary further by explaining that her cousin Elizabeth has conceived a son in her old age. What was amazing about this conception was that Elizabeth had been barren and beyond the natural age of childbearing. She was now six months pregnant.

"And Mary said, 'Behold the handmaid of the Lord; be it unto me according to your word.' Then the angel departed from her."

Mary hurried to the City of Judah and stayed with Elizabeth three months to assist her, and then returned home to Nazareth of Galilee. (All quotes are from Luke 1:28–40 KJV-MOD.)

Joseph is Convinced

When Mary saw Joseph next, she was three months pregnant but probably was not showing yet. Mary had a lot of explaining to do with Joseph. At first he thought he should divorce her quietly out of respect. But then the Angel of the Lord visited him in a dream and said, "Be not afraid to take to you Mary your wife [betrothed]: for that which is conceived in her is of the Holy Spirit" (Matt 1:20 KJV-MOD).

This calmed Joseph's fears but it did not calm the public who certainly talked about it a lot. In fact, Mary was in danger of being stoned to death! The battle and humiliation was raging for those six months. In her ninth month of pregnancy there was another challenge.

Caesar Augustus proclaimed, "All the world should be taxed" (Luke 2:1). Each man went to his own town. Joseph and Mary headed to Bethlehem of Judea. She rode sidesaddle on the donkey while Joseph walked beside her. The distance from Nazareth to Bethlehem is 70 miles and could have taken four or five days traveling with a pregnant woman.

Born in a Barn

When they arrived, hungry and tired, there was no place to stay. The town was packed. Mary was having severe birth pains. The Holy Spirit touched the innkeeper's heart with an idea, "Could the couple stay in the barn with the animals of his clients?"

Joseph was only too happy to say, "Yes."

The animals moved over for the new guests to make a place for the birth. The timing was divine because Mary's cries became louder. Joseph got water from the animal trough and rushed to Mary's side.

It was quite a cacophony: Mary's cries of pain, Joseph's sobs as he held her, the cows mooing, donkeys braying, and sheep baaing.

Eventually Joseph knelt before mother Mary to assist in the birth, reaching up to catch Jesus. Then the baby joined the chorus with His cries.

Joseph washed off the birth mucosa; the umbilical cord was cut and tied. Little Jesus was wrapped in some swaddling cloths, and Joseph bonded by looking into His eyes.

He gently handed Jesus to Mary. Her child nuzzled into her breast for his first drink of sweet milk. Comfort of a drink and arms of love greet the child. Joseph's arms around them make a trio of love.

The animals gather around as they see the glory settle on the scene.

The world has "The Answer" in human form. Will they listen? Will you and I?

The Savior of the world, the Messiah, the Son of God has arrived.

The New Year – Help for the Journey

I always experience a tingle of excitement when a new year is ready to begin. In December 2010 some of the possibilities for the next year showed up on my desk.

Presently they are Michael Drosnin's predictions in his *Bible Codes III* [4](His previous books were better), my study of Isaiah and its prophecies fulfilled and those yet to come, and evangelical author, Hal Lindsay's paper, *Revealing the future in Scripture*, and urging us all to live ready for that rapturous trumpet call.

Then there are the historic churches that help us each December to relive the first Advent when Jesus came from Heaven to earth for us, and to remind us that when we die, He (or an angel) will come for us. Basically, the New Year will be a walk of faith. "Your ears shall hear a word behind you, saying, 'This is the way, walk in it,' whenever you turn to the right hand or whenever you turn to the left" (Isa 30:21 KJV-MOD).

I wish it were as easy to do as it sounds. Yet the longer we walk with Jesus as our Shepherd, and study His messages left behind, the more capable we will be in hearing His voice. Every other predictive concept must agree with Him.

Scriptures for Our Journey

I also like some Scriptures to tuck in my pocket for the walk. Some of my favorites are: "... What does the Lord require of you, but to do justly, show mercy, and to walk humbly with your God" (Micah 6:8 KJV-MOD).

I've put this verse to music to help me remember it and its points. Of the three, humility perhaps needs to be worked on most of all. Humility is not to think of yourself more highly than you ought.

When learning to fly a Cessna 172, something I experienced is not to pull too far back on the stick as it puts the nose of the plane dangerously high. If this continues, the plane will begin to fall. Using this metaphor, you and I need to keep our nose down (Prov 16:18a). My late husband, Dennis, was a small plane pilot and his oldest son, Steve, was in the right seat when I was being checked out in taking off and landing.

The nose down illustration was one of Dennis' favorite flying metaphors.

God's Time Table

Another Scripture in my pocket is in Isaiah. "Remember the former things of old: for I am God, and ... there is none like Me. Declaring the end from the beginning, and from ancient times the things that are not yet done ..." (Isa 46:9-10 KJV).

When did God declare the end from the beginning? The first time was in Genesis, chapter 1 and 2:1-7. In addition to an outline of creation, it is an overview of things to come in the first seven thousand years of biblical history. (The seven days of creation are not meant to be a scientific treatise.) Another place is Leviticus 23 that gives us the entire picture of the biblical calendar events.

Our present church calendar was authored by Pope Gregory (Gregorian Calendar) and that tells us our coming New Year, after I wrote this, will be 2014.

However, our year from the Creator's Hebrew calendar is 5773. This shows us moving closer toward the year 6,000 than 2013 does. Both calendars are good but the second one gives us clarity of where we are on God's biblical timetable.[5]

Those who have studied the seven feasts of God, will remember that they also tell believers' entire history from Passover 3,500 B.C. – redemption (Exodus chapters 3-12) to Pentecost A.D. 33 – empowerment (Acts chapter 2); to *Sukkot*, fulfillment at a further unknown date – the millennial reign of Messiah (Lev 23:39-44, Rev chapters 19-22).[6]

The Word Is Armor

My concluding choice of scripture is: "'No weapon that is formed against you shall prosper; and every tongue that accuses you in judgment you will condemn. This is the heritage of the servants of the Lord, and their vindication is from Me,' declares the Lord" (Isa 54:17 NASB).

This present year you have probably experienced spiritual warfare. In my young adult years, I did not have much discernment and I was oblivious about spiritual battles. Fortunately I had a praying mother.

Last week I found myself worrying about a truncated conversation. Evaluating the situation, I realized that I had not been keeping up with my prayer time and Bible study. When I got back on my spiritual diet, my worries disappeared.

Each New Year, I encourage you to locate an inspiring Bible study so you will have divine guidance for your life and for those you love. Life is too short not to know The Book that is full of answers to your life's questions.

Happy New Life, my friends!

The Voyage to Aslan's Country

December 28th, 2010, I went to the Edmonds theater to see C.S. Lewis's third novel, *Voyage of the Dawn Treader*[7] in a movie format. The story begins when Edmund and Lucy had just arrived at their Uncle Harold's house at a country village in England. Their parents in were in America for several months.

Eustace did not like his cousins but since they were visitors he felt he would enjoy bullying them. In fact, he didn't like all four of the Pevensies – including Peter and Susan who fortunately were not with them.

Lucy and Edmund stole away to a room upstairs to speak privately to one another. They had been to Narnia twice before and liked to talk about their exciting adventures. Eustace barged in the room and said, "Oh there you are talking about that imaginary fairytale place Narnia. What a waste of time!"

"Come in Eustace. We were admiring the picture of the ship on the wall that looks like it is coming directly toward the observer."

Eustace said to Lucy, "What do you like about it?"

"It looks so real and inviting," said Lucy. "As I look at it, the waves seem to be coming out of the picture toward me. Oh, water just splashed in my face," she said.

Entering Narnia

From then on the water came into the room and soon they were swimming in an ocean. All three were able to surface to the top of the water. As they looked up they saw the same schooner that was in the picture. The front of the ship looked like the face and mouth of a dragon. Men were diving off the ship to come to them. Pretty soon Lucy felt someone put his arm under her. Men were throwing ropes down for them. Eustace was complaining as usual and said he wanted to go home. Edmund helped to rescue his younger cousin. Eventually they were all on deck.

The ship's owner, Caspian the boy-king of Narnia, greeted the three children. When Lucy recognized him from other voyages, she was so excited. They had so much to talk about but eventually Lucy sneezed. Caspian said, "Excuse me, I'm sorry. I will order some hot-spiced cider and give you some dry clothes to change into. Let me show you to your quarters.

They gathered back to visit and drink cider. A ship's mate brought the drinks and said, "Spiced cider for their Majesties." He addressed Edmund and Lucy that way because they, and Peter and Susan, had been kings and queens of Narnia years before in Narnia time.

Eustace burst out with, "Ooh get that creature, that rat away from me."

It was a mouse but he walked on his hind legs, and stood two feet high. A band of gold on his head held a long red feather. One hand was on the hilt of his small, sharp sword.

Edmund and Lucy recognized Reepicheep, the valiant talking beast. He was very cordial to the royalty who had joined them.

This evening began a battle between Reepicheep and Eustace. In fact, the talking mouse challenged the weakling English chap into several duels. Reepicheep, with the help of the hanging ropes, would fly through the air when Eustace would come after him with his much larger sword. In time, Reepicheep did a lot to help Eustace become a caring person.

Dragonish Thinking

In the next few days the Dawn Treader was passing an island that looked like a good place to have an adventure.

When they stopped, Eustace wandered off by himself and unbeknownst to him discovered a dragon's lair of jewels, diamonds, and gold. Even though he saw a cadaver lying on the ground, he still decided he would collect as much wealth as he could carry. As he did this and fell asleep, Eustace turned into the dragon himself. It took some time for him to discover it.

Dragonish thinking can lead one astray. In Eustace's desperation, Aslan the Lion, encountered him and helped to peel off several deep layers of dragon scales until the real boy could be seen again.

Aslan's Country

Many other adventures took place but the story ends, as it was time to return to the children's world.

Reepicheep was the only one who was allowed to go to Aslan's Country beyond the end of the world. He laid down his sword on the beach, got into his nut shaped coracle, and was lifted up on the 30-foot waterfall like wave, disappearing quickly.

"Aslan," said Lucy "When can we come back?"

He gently growled out the words, "Dearest you are getting too old for Narnia, you must get closer to your own world now."

Lucy sobbed, "The real reason we want to be in Narnia is to be with you, Aslan."

"I will be with you where ever you are. There you must learn to know me by another name."

He opened up a door in the sky. They felt a lion's mane and a kiss on their foreheads, and they were back home.

Metaphor's Speak

Many metaphors in the movie spoke to me, and also to my friend, Patricia.

I felt rather silly to have tears released when the children and Aslan were saying goodbye to Reepicheep who was joyfully leaving on his final voyage.

I was thinking about my big brother, Bill, Dr. Reed, retired cancer surgeon who was hit by a 2007 Toyota pickup truck in Tampa Christmas Eve, 2010 as he crossed the street. He never regained consciousness.

He was a great Christian leader. I miss our conversations about our Narnia, called Heaven, and our Aslan, called Jesus Christ. It hurts, but we will meet again.

Working Through Your Grief Step-By-Step

Tonight I received a phone call from a man who had recently seen a Trinity Broadcasting Network rerun of my late husband Dennis Bennett and me form twenty-five years ago.

Jack (pseudonym) said, "I'm trying to find my way after the recent loss of my wife. At times there is peace and at other times there is panic. Do you have any suggestions for overcoming grief?"

Most everyone who has lost a loved one, experiences these waves. I know I did when I first lost my husband, Dennis, over two decades ago. I learned to go with the waves and let them wash over me. They eventually got less and less.

Prayer Partners

Another thing I did was to have two Inner Healing Prayer Partners meet with me once a week for about eight times. I also journaled what I learned during these prayer sessions.

I also wrote down any significant dreams. Several times during that first year I had healing dreams in which I saw my spouse and I journaled them.

I have found that dreams about one's spouse in that first year are quite common.

Books on near-death experiences were very encouraging to me. I began to write down new Heaven experiences shared with me by individuals.

Eventually in 1996 my book *To Heaven and Back*[8] was published. It is out of print now, but my new book *Heaven Tours*[9] is still in print.

I also do grief work with those who contact me as a marriage and family counselor. Helping others is one of my motivational gifts. The seven-year Bible Study Fellowship program I attended was healing too.

Paul says in 2 Corinthians 1:3-4: "Blessed be God, even ... the Father of all mercies, and the God of all comfort; Who comforts us in all our tribulation, that we may be able to comfort them who are in any trouble, by the comfort wherewith we ourselves are comforted by God" (KJV-MOD).

It is good to get out of your house and exercise at a gym with other people. Sublimate your grief by getting in shape.

Loss of My Brother

On Christmas Day my sister, Georgia, phoned me from Florida to tell me the sad news. Our beloved older brother, Dr. Bill Reed M.D., S.D. was a patient in Tampa General Hospital.

Bill, and his lovely wife, Coppi, had gone to the Christmas Eve church service where they had great celebration. At 9:30 pm they had to walk across a wide street to their car. When they got half way across, a Toyota pick-up driven by a young man hit them at a fairly high speed.

They flew through the air and landed on their backs and heads on the cement. They were both knocked unconscious. A few people from the church were watching. Someone called 911.

A severe head injury when one is on a pacemaker and blood thinner is a disastrous combination. Of course, pedestrians are no match for a truck.

Coppi is petite and my brother is six feet tall. She is smaller and younger and physically recovered in several days yet has physical problems related to the accident.

Doctors said the only hope for Bill was brain surgery. During surgery a blood clot was removed and the wound was closed.

Through x-ray, the team of doctors saw that the right frontal lobe of the brain had been destroyed. The next day his brain bled some more. On his fourth day in the hospital, my brother died. Apparently, he never woke up from the accident.

I flew to Tampa, Florida for the funeral at St. John's Episcopal Church. The church was packed with about 500 people. It was comforting to sit next to his casket covered with the American flag from his six years in the Navy.

Healing Miracle

Those Coppi chose to speak included rehab counselor, Ralph Stinson. He said, "Dr. Reed was like a father to me. I loved him very much. When I was nineteen years old, my mother was diagnosed with cancer. Dr. Reed was her surgeon. When he operated, he saw that the cancer was too advanced. He sutured her up and said, 'There is nothing more man can do; it is totally up to God now. Only believers should remain in the room for the prayer of faith.'

"I stepped out because I was not a believer then," said Ralph. "My mother was healed that day and lived twenty more years!"

This testimony encouraged us all. I had brought Kleenex thinking I might cry at the funeral, but never did.

Instead it became a celebration with people breaking into applause from time to time.

I will especially miss talking or writing my dear brother Bill. We had such good rapport. But I know he is safe with his best Friend and Savior, Jesus Christ.

Breaking News
The Problem of Evil Acts and Temptation

Where did evil come from? Looking at biblical history that is about 6,000 years, we can see from God's viewpoint. In the beginning God created human beings and gave them free will to choose right or wrong.

"And God said, Let us make man in our image, after our likeness: and let them have dominion ..." (Gen 1:26a KJV).

Before the first child was born, the Tempter arrived on this beautiful blue planet Earth. He came to promote his kingdom. With the success he had that day, he never left the earth.

Why? Because this Tempter attacked God's reputation saying to the first couple, "Did God really say that? He was just trying to keep you ignorant. If you eat of the forbidden fruit, you won't die but you will be as gods ..." (Gen 3:4-5 paraphrased).

The temptation worked. The woman partook and then the man. In that moment, the dominion God had given humankind was taken over by God's archenemy, Lucifer, AKA Satan.

When Adam and Eve had their first son, Cain, they did not know that he would become a killer. They did not know that he would be so jealous of his younger brother, Abel, that he would kill him.

The only way Cain could be saved, and all people from then on, would be for the sinless Son of God to be the sacrifice for the sin of the whole human race. The Bible says that from that time on beginning with, Adam, Eve, and Cain, "All have sinned and fallen short of the glory of God" (Rom 3:23 KJV), See also Romans 5:12.

Four thousand years later, Jesus, Lamb of God, paid the price for Cain's sins and our sins by dying on a rugged cross in Jerusalem. He took the weight of the sins of the whole world on His shoulders. He regained the dominion of the world from Satan.

Dominion Regained

Those who choose to come into relationship with God's Son, enter back into righteous dominion of our world! They still fight the battle with sin, but the way has been made for them to be able to pray and confess their sins, and to become the righteous children of God. If they follow Him, they become more and more like their Savior and make an impact for good in the world.

The power to overcome evil has been given to every believer, but we must pray, study, and obey God's teachings to stay strong.

There is still a big problem. Since the invasion of evil, the Tempter is still here to deceive people into following him to build up his arsenal to destroy love, joy and peace on the earth. Satan ultimately lost the battle at Calvary, but won't give up on his failed plan to win the world.

In the News

The shooting in Tucson, Arizona on January 27, 2011 made me think of the battle of the two kingdoms.

The young man, Jared, had been deceived into thinking that he had the right to shoot a group of people he does not agree with or because he was angry with his university, parents, children, or women.

Where did he get this culture of death and the skull and crossbones altar where he worshiped? Is he mentally ill or possessed by demons?

Somehow he has chosen the side he is on. For Jared to be saved, he must turn to the One who died in his place, humbly repent, receive pardon and salvation.

I understand our United States Constitution gives us the right to bear arms to defend ourselves, but why don't we give a psychological test to those who buy guns? Can we learn from what is not working?

The sixth commandment of God's biblical constitution says, "You shall not murder" (Exodus 20:13 NIV). Let's get God and man's foundational laws synchronized.

Meanwhile let us make this world a better place, so that when we stand before God at the end of our life, we will have done our best to follow the example of our loving, healing, saving Lord.

Hezekiah Healing Series (Three Articles)
Hezekiah's Battles, Healing, and Fallibility – Part 1

Hezekiah was one of the better kings of Judah. He did quite a number of noteworthy acts that pleased God. He closed down the high places. You may wonder as I did, "What is a high place?"

They were "localities chosen as places of worship of … idols. The high places were features of Canaanite religion, and the conquering Israelites were commanded to destroy them when they entered Canaan … Israel came in contact with the high places of the Moabites before they entered the land … Being defiled by Canaanite fertility cults and other paganistic pollutions, the high places were often connected with licentiousness (Hos 4:11-14) and immorality (Jer 3:2). … The prophets denounced the high places … as Zion was the place to worship …"[10]

(Mount Zion is near the Temple Mount in Jerusalem and I found it is more like a low hillside today.)

Passover Celebrated

Hezekiah's regency was from 728 to 686 B.C. "As a godly king his first act was to purge, repair, and reopen the Temple, which had been neglected and polluted during the idolatrous reign of his weak father, Ahaz. …His great reformation was followed by the celebration of the Passover … to which not only all Judah was summoned but also the remnant of the ten tribes. … Hezekiah inherited the Assyrian menace from his father, who mortgaged the Judean Kingdom 'to the giant of the Semites.'"[11]

Assyria continued to pick away defeating Phoenicia, Moab, Philistia, and Edom. Then they came after Judah capturing Hezekiah's fortified cities. When the Assyrian king, Sennacherib, had played his "chess game" towards the heart of the capital of Jerusalem, from Lachish 27 miles away he sent a message to Hezekiah. He bragged about all the locations he had defeated and basically said it was futile to resist his army.

Hezekiah tried to stop the takeover of Jerusalem by stripping gold from the temple as payoff to Sennacherib, but it would not hold back this kingdom hungry enemy.

War of Words

The evil Assyrian field commander argued before Hezekiah and all the men rebuilding the Temple wall. He had written in the Hebrew language these words to battle the Jewish men's minds:

- "Do you think that *Yahveh* (God) will help you now because Hezekiah has removed all the high places, saying you must worship Him in Jerusalem?"
- "Why would *Yahveh* help you, when He is the One who sent me and my army against you?"
- "Don't you know that Hezekiah is a deceiver and is not telling you that God has let him down. He will not help you."

The questions from this satanic emissary, reminds me of the faith challenging questions that Satan used to battle Jesus. This age-old usurping enemy chose to attack Jesus when he was hungry at the end of His fasting and prayer of forty days and nights (Luke 4:1-15). Here are Satan's questions:

- "If you are the Son of God, command this stone that it be made bread."
- "And the devil said to Him, all this power I will give you, and the glory of them ... If you will worship me, all will be yours."
- "If you are the Son of God, cast yourself down from here." [It is believed this was referring to the pinnacle of the temple in Jerusalem].

What did Hezekiah do for victory about 705 B.C.? He went to the Holy Temple and opened the enemy's letter before the Lord and began to pray. The content and the results of that prayer were amazing!

What did Jesus do at His Great Temptation in the Judean Desert, around 2,000 years ago? He fought Satan directly from the Bible with three spiritual swords. Deuteronomy was the book of the Bible Jesus used when He defeated Satan's major attack! "It is written ..."

To learn more about Hezekiah's prayer, and Jesus Christ's answers to the Tempter, tune in next time.

Same time. Same place.

Hezekiah's Battles, Prayer, and Victory – Part 2

When we closed the story of Hezekiah, the King of Judah, last time, he and his leaders had been under attack. King Sennacherib of Assyria and his army field commander attempted various techniques on Hezekiah to make him give up the capital of Jerusalem. How serious is that, one might ask?

Why is Jerusalem such a desirable place to control? Many nations have taken it over in the past, and even today, many stand in line waiting for their chance. The main reason for this is that our Messiah Jesus will return to our broken world to bring us world peace and will do it reigning from the Temple Mount in Jerusalem. The Tempter, the one who brought chaos to the earth, does not want that.

Not to believe in Messiah's coming reign, one would have to delete a large portion of the Bible. The prophets Daniel, Isaiah, Jeremiah, the Psalms of David, Matthew, and Mark, all teach it.

Temptation

Last week I noted and paraphrased three charges of the Assyrian army captain against the King of Judah. Now I give the answers.

- "Do you think that *Yahveh* (God) will help you now because Hezekiah has removed all the high places, saying you must worship Him in Jerusalem?"
- Answer: This is a lie. Hezekiah obeyed God by removing the high places of idolatry and immorality. God was pleased.
- "Why would *Yahveh* help you, when He is the one who sent me and my Army against you?"
- Answer: Another lie. God, in this instance, did not send the Assyrian army against Judah.

- "Don't you know that Hezekiah is a deceiver and is not telling you that God has let him down. He will not help you."
- Answer: Another lie. King Hezekiah is not a deceiver but he is praying to God and listening to the prophet Isaiah for confirmation about his decisions.

Hezekiah Prays

It was the zero hour before King Hezekiah could lose Israel to the anti-God Assyrian king. But he made a wonderful decision; he took the threatening letter from his enemy asking for his surrender and headed for the altar at the temple in Jerusalem! He spread out the letter before God and began to pray.

"Oh LORD of hosts, God of Israel, who dwells between the cherubim, You are the God, even You alone, of all the kingdoms of the earth: You have made Heaven and earth.

"Incline Your ear, O LORD, and hear; open Your eyes, O LORD, and see: and hear all the words of Sennacherib, that he sent to reproach the living God.

"Of a truth, LORD, the kings of Assyria have laid waste all the nations, and their countries,

"And have cast their gods into the fire: for they were no gods, but the work of men's hands, wood and stone: therefore they have destroyed them.

"Now therefore, O LORD our God, save us from his hand, that all the kingdoms of the earth may know that You are the LORD, even You only" (Isa 37:16-20 KJV-MOD).

When the King of Judah spoke to the King of kings, he began with praise for the One true God who ultimately is in charge of all of earth's nations. He proclaimed God as Creator.

Then he shared the words of his enemy and God's enemy, and asked that God save Judah as a witness to His being the only Lord.

This is a good model for prayer. Have you ever received a threatening letter or email containing destructive, angry words?

If you have a church, you can lay it before the altar in prayer, or you can simply kneel at your bedside. You can then journal your prayer, date it, and see how God gives you further guidance.

Answer to Prayer

The prophet Isaiah is sent to Hezekiah with a word from the Lord, "For I [God] will defend this city to save it for My own sake, and for My servant David's sake" (Isa 37:35 KJV-MOD).

Following these words, "The angel of the LORD smote 185,000 in the camp of the Assyrians …" (Is. 37:36). One warring angel stopped the war. What a surprise ending!

Despite the battles and troubles on this earth also experienced in our present hour, we can pray for guidance for our leaders and us, and we can receive comfort from Scripture about the future for our earth.

Hezekiah's Illness, Prayer, and Miraculous Answer – Part 3

In the fourteenth year of his reign as King of Judah, at age 39, Hezekiah became seriously ill. The message came through Isaiah the prophet as a declaration, "Thus says the LORD, Set your house in order; for you shall die, and not live" (Isa 38:1b KJV-MOD).

Wow! God certainly gave Hezekiah fair warning. He even had time to make his will!

Until this prophecy, Hezekiah always agreed with Isaiah's instructions, but this time he sought a further answer. He would go to God directly, himself. He turned his face to the wall, and prayed this prayer:

"Remember now O LORD, I beseech You, how I have walked before You in truth and with a perfect heart, and have done what is good in Your sight. And Hezekiah wept sore" (Isa 38:3 KJV-MOD).

Hezekiah humbled himself, and repented (2 Chron 32:24-26). Then the LORD sent Isaiah to confirm that Hezekiah's prayer had been heard, and that he would have fifteen years added to his life, and be delivered from the King of Assyria.

"This is the only time [in the Bible] God ever told a man how long he would live. Just why He specified the time, and this much time, is not known; nevertheless, the prophecy was fulfilled to the letter. Hezekiah died a peaceful death after a reign of 29 years in year 686 B.C."[12]

God Gives a Sign

Isaiah said, "And this shall be a sign to you from the LORD, that the LORD will do this thing that He said: Behold I will bring again the shadow of the degrees, which is gone down on the sun dial of Ahaz, ten degrees backward. So the sun returned ten degrees, by which degrees it was gone down" (Isa 38:7-8 KJV-MOD).

For his healing confirmation, "Hezekiah chose the harder thing that the sun be turned backward 10 degrees instead of forward. By God's eternal law it always moves forward but here is a notable miracle of the sun being turned backward; or technically speaking, the earth revolving back 10 degrees from where it had come that day. There is no need to guess how this was done, by eclipse or some other act of nature, for then we begin to question the supernatural ..."[13]

You may want to read a psalm-like testimony Hezekiah wrote on the occasion of his healing (Isa 38:10-20).

At the end of this chapter is an old-fashioned remedy Isaiah had given King Hezekiah. This was like their medicine of the day. I believe God's supernatural healing and medicine created by man often go together to bring healing. An excellent book that confirms these two kinds of healings working together is *The Ultimate Voice* by Oral Roberts.[14]

"For Isaiah had said, Let them take a lump of figs, and lay it for a plaster upon the boil, and he shall recover" (Isa 38:21 KJV-MOD).

Hebrew Touch

As I read along in the Old Testament, it helps me to remember that it was originally written in Hebrew. Since Hezekiah, the Jewish king, was given fifteen more years to live, I looked in the syllabus, *The Hebrew Alphabet Course* to remind me of the spiritual meaning for letter fifteen of the alphabet.[15]

The Hebrew *samech* (our letter S) is shaped something like the ark in the Holy of Holies, with a square perimeter. So its spiritual meaning is God is my protector. "He surrounds me with a wall of fire" (Zech 2:5 paraphrase).

Perhaps Hezekiah had thought of this, as the Hebrew letter *samech* also means number fifteen. The Hebrew number system uses its alphabet for counting.

So we conclude, fifteen more years of life with God's presence and protection.

These facts also could have reminded him of Psalm 27:5-6, "For in the time of trouble He shall hide me in His pavilion: in the secret of His tabernacle shall He hide me ... Therefore will I offer in His tabernacle sacrifices of joy; I will sing, yes, I will sing praises to the LORD" (KJV-MOD).

Dear reader, if you need a touch of healing today, there are many such testimonies throughout the entire Bible. Reading them can build your faith and give you valuable steps to take on your journey to wholeness.

Romance and Spring farewell is next.

Romance, Poetry, Spring is in the Air

Usually on February fourteenth I'm already thinking of spring. It happened last February when I was at the QFC grocery store and walked by trays of yellow, magenta, and blue primroses. The price was luring at one dollar a posy in an individual black plastic container.

It picked up my spirit on a dark, rainy day, to see those flowers full of cheer. They seemed to be saying, "Don't be discouraged with those winter doldrums. I'm a witness that spring will soon be here."

I checked with friends, Betty had bought a primrose and it cheered her. Dr. Oles bought one to take to his beloved, Lee's, graveside.

Since it's hard to keep small plants upright, I shared how I had learned to bend a hanger into a "V-shape." I put one end into the plant's soil, and one end in the ground at the cemetery.

In the northwest we experience four seasons, which keeps us in a state of change. The foliage changes, our clothes change, our skin color may change, and our public utility bill changes, the sky changes, the water scenes change, and the beautiful Olympic Mountains change.

Last spring and summer I was vacationing and teaching in New Zealand. During my three weeks there, it was fall and winter again! I was curious about what this Down Under change would be like? I lost one and one-half days to get there and arrived in Seattle the same day I left New Zealand. Hopefully I returned wiser having walked upside down for several weeks!

Sometimes change for us is sorrowful and other times it brings us great joy. As with the seasons created for us, our lives are more interesting with change. Even the difficult times are part of the lessons we are sent here to learn.

At times in life I have thought, "I would like to live my life over and do everything better." But after a minute on that road of contemplation, I decide, "No, I want to live in the here and now and retain what memories and knowledge I have gained."

Romance and Valentines

In 2011, I was excited to receive a wedding invitation from Don Mulford, an ordained minister and friend in California. The past ten years had kept him busy fighting cancer until he won. His brother gave bone marrow twice; only with the second try was Don cancer free. Last summer he met a lovely woman at our Lynnwood *Emotionally Free*® *Seminar*. Sherry is just right for him. It wasn't long before they were happily married.

Many of you have given and received cards and gifts for Valentine's Day. I received a valentine from a faithful Edmonds Beacon reader. She began with, "God gave me this valentine to share with you, and your reader's if you like!" So here it is.

A Valentine's Gift of Love
Just a little Valentine, coming your way
In hopes a Love note will brighten your day!
You are loved by our Lord Jesus,
and you are loved by me,
His daily care and keeping, we can clearly see.
The Valley's can try us deeply,
the storm wind's violently blow,
But thru those tuff times, trials and tears,
our hearts know where to go.
For His promises prove true,
and His Word He does keep,
Though lesson's before us reach deep,
we know if we wait, obey,
Stay close, through all these storms He'll keep.

"Thank you for all the love you share in your column," Linda Danielson, Edmonds, 2-11-11.

That was so thoughtful, timely, and an encouraging gift from Linda, a faithful *Edmonds Beacon* reader. She had no idea this would be my concluding worship column, so she was prophetic in her writing!

I would soon find it out myself. This time of service to my hometown community was in a season of change. I had no idea, at that time, that my columns would become a 390 page book, *A New Look at the News*. So writing a weekly column and a book at the same time would not have worked. Now I find it was all a part of God's plan.

Here's another Valentine. It works for any time of the year.

A Valentine for Our Lord

Little Jesus did You know
That the star that shinned
To bring the Wisemen
Was created by You?

Jesus did You know
That being born to a
Jewish Mother, Miriam (Mary)
Made You a legitimate Jew?

Jesus did You know
that one star filled night
You named all the stars
when You were Home in Heaven?

Jesus did You know
that when you left Heaven
for the blue planet Earth below
there were tears in Father's eyes?

Jesus did You know
that when You died for earth's sins
it would hurt so awfully much,
But that You'd rejoice forever more?

Jesus did You know
that I'd be here to meet You
I'd fall in love with You
and spend eternity with You?

Yes, I know
that I was born for You
and that I soon realized
'You would never leave me
Nor forsake me.'
Yes, this I know..."
© 2011 by Rita Bennett

I hope you, my friends, will also receive these encouraging Valentines, for yourselves.

And you too were born to know God. Make Him your Forever Valentine.

My Testimony

New Eyes to See Through

It's "A New Look at the News"
And a new look at life
Forever changed my views
Took away trouble and strife.

The Healer made "All things new"
Was spiritually raised from dead
Born again eyes that can see
My spiritual hunger was fed.

No, my glasses are not scratched
It's not Rose Colored glasses
It is beyond all that
To Bible and Spirit-filled classes.

His L O V E is:
Life eternal
Omnipresent
Victorious and
Emotionally free®

I look through His eyes of love amazing
Eyes of Lord Jesus from Heaven above
Through eyes of love unconditional
His gentle eyes, tender as a Dove.

He changed my life, darkness to light
Gave me eyes of prophetic insight.
Ask, and He'll do the same for you
Giving you New Eyes to see through.

© 2013 by Rita Bennett
Luke 7:22 (KJV).

Thank you, to those who were "Rita's Beacon" Column readers, and those who have only joined us now for "A New Look at the News" book that has the updated and expanded version of those columns. Thank you one and all!

I hope you've found some Holy Spirit Bread crumbs on the way to feed and inspire you on your journey with me on our route 66.

In grateful fellowship,

Rita Bennett

Author's Postlude

Thank you for walking with me through my latest book, "A New Look at the News." As I was writing, I was reflecting on the Bible Studies I was involved in, or on the other hand, was responding to the Daily News I try to keep up with. That means you'll find articles that respond to the News happenings, and will often see my response through a Biblical perspective.

Often people will say, "I don't know what to pray about." A good idea would be as you read the newspaper to have a notebook and pen handy jotting down items that touch your heart. When you close the paper, take some time (even 10 minutes) to pray about those concerns that have been imprinted on your soul. You might even confess the sins of your national or state leaders, and pray that they will have a change of heart.

From there you might be led to some specific action. You might even want to write a Letter to the Editor with your ideas or concerns. Or you might like to Email a TV news program to respond to their request for Feedback.

Teaching Series

Throughout my book you will have found that within the 190 columns are 18 subjects grouped into individual study series. This was a "happening" as week-by-week my writing evolved. Ideas just flowed together in this order with no previous planning by me. What happened surprised me. These subjects like: *The Lord's Prayer Series*, *Series on Heaven*, or *Psalm 91 Series*, could be used for small group studies in your fellowship. You can dig in deeper to the biblical references, and add that to the group you are leading or co-leading.

Some older people who cannot get out to church could appreciate you teaching or reading to them. I remember my mother sitting with her Bible on her lap with no one to share Bible study with her. She never mentioned the need to me but looking back at that time I wish I had asked! If you read *My Personal Story Series* in chapter six part 1, that was before I had become a Bible study participant. I wish I had been able to fellowship with her around the Word and had shared some of the spiritual nuggets that I've been privileged to experience now. She was a dear Christian mother and one whom I'm sure prayed me into a greater dedication of my life.

Mother, Loretta Jesse Reed, is now in Heaven along with her lifelong mate, my dad, William Reed. I was fortunate to have believing parents. During their life time, my parents spent a lot of time together at church for worship, Bible teaching and fellowship.

Making More Sense

I do look at the news differently today than in the past. When the 9/11 Twin Towers attack occurred, Conrad, my son by marriage, phoned to see how I was and what I was doing.

I said, "I'm sitting here with my Bible reading the books of Joel and Revelation trying to find out what is going on."

Today the newspaper has more headlines that seem to be right out of the Bible. My goal for some years has been to study every book of the Bible, so naturally I gravitated to Daniel and Revelation some years ago. Though a lot of it is beyond me, it gives me a foundation to build upon.

Yet, even these two books, are making more sense to me today. To understand prophecy, I've found that the teacher, or minister who is a student of Hebrew will have clearer understanding to impart. That is true especially of these two eschatological, Hebraic, books of the Bible.

Thank you for keeping me company on this trip through many different topics, travels, and life studies.

Until we meet again, *maranatha*, my friend,

Rita Bennett

Expanded Table of Contents

Bibliography

Arterburn, Stephen, Fred Stoeker, and Mike Yorkey. *Every Man's Battle: Winning the War on Sexual Temptation* : One Victory at a Time. Colorado Springs, CO: WaterBrook, 2000.

Arthur, Kay. *Behold Jesus is Coming. Oregon*, Eugene: Harvest House, 1995.

Baker, Warren, Gen. ed. *The Complete Word Study Old Testament*, Chattanooga: AMG International, Inc.,1994.

Barrett, Marvin. *Death Trip*. New York, N.Y.: Lear, 1989.

Bennett, Dennis J. and Rita M. *The Holy Spirit and You – Guide to the Spirit-Filled Life*. Alachua: Bridge-Logos, 1971 – 2005.

Bennett, Dennis J. *Nine O'clock in the Morning*. Plainfield, NJ: Logos International, 1970.

Bennett, Rita M. *The Hebrew Alphabet Course. Spiritual Meanings for Judeo-Christian Biblical Teaching*. Edmonds, WA: Healing People Publishing House, 2002 – 2005, Hebrew Syllabus.

Bennett, Rita Marie. *Emotionally Free®Course Syllabi* (AKA *Prayer Counselors Study Guide*). Washington, Edmonds: Christian Renewal Association, Inc., 1980 – 2013.

Bennett, Rita, M.A., Litt.D, *Heaven Tours – Astonishing Journeys*. Alachua: Bridge–Logos, 2009.

Bennett, Rita, *To Heaven and Back: True Stories of Those Who Have Made the Journey*. Grand Rapids, MI: Zondervan Pub. House, 1997.

Bennett, Rita. *Treasures From An Oak Chest*. http://www.emotionallyfree.org/IBooks.html, 2012.

Bennett, Rita. *You Can Be Emotionally Free*. Alachua, FL: Bridge-Logos Publishing, 1981.

Brown, Dan. *The Da Vinci Code: A Novel*. New York: Doubleday, 2003

Burkett, Larry. *Business by the Book: The Complete Guide of Biblical Principles for the Workplace*. Nashville, TN: Thomas Nelson, 1998.

Church, Dr. J. R. *"Psalms 111-117 Have a Menorah Design!"* Oklahoma City, OK: Prophecy in the News, May 2010, p. 9.

Clarke, Adam, *Clark's Commentary: The Holy Bible*. Nashville: Abingdon, 1977.

Cox-Chapman, Mally. *The Case for Heaven*. New York: G.P. Putman's Sons, 1995.

Dalberg-Acton, John Emerich Edward. Lord Acton's Letter to Bishop Mandell Creighton [April 5, 1887]. *Bartlett's Familiar Quotations*. Boston: Little, Brown and Company, 1882 – 1980.

Davis, Rabbi Menachem, ed. *Tehillim Book of Psalms & Commentary* R' Hirsch. Brooklyn: Mesorah Publications, Ltd., 2001.

Douglas, J. D. *The New Bible Dictionary*. Grand Rapids, MI: Eerdmans, 1962.

Drosnin, Michael. *Bible Code III: Saving the World*. Worldmedia, 2010.

Dykes, John Bacchus. *The Hymnal*. New York, NY: The Church Hymnal Corporation, 1940.

Friesen, James G. *A Far Better Life: Spiritual and Psychological Insights from Jesus' Teaching*. Eugene, Or: Wipf & Stock, 2008.

Girdlestone, Robert Baker, White, Donald R., ed. *Synonyms of the Old Testament*, Grand Rapids: Baker, 1983.

Guilbert, Charles Mortimer. *The Book of Common Prayer*. New York: Oxford University Press, 1979.

Hayford, Jack W. *Spirit Filled Life: Student Bible*. Nashville, TN: Thomas Nelson, 2005.

Henry, Matthew. *Matthew Henry's Commentary in One Volume*. Michigan, Grand Rapids: Zondervan Publishing House, 1961.

Ilibagiza, Immaculée, and Steve Erwin. *Left to Tell: Discovering God amidst the Rwandan Holocaust*. Carlsbad, CA: Hay House, 2006.

Knopf, Alfred A. *The Holy Land, Knopf Guides*. New York, 1995.

Kohlenberger lll, John R.*The New NIV Interlinear Hebrew* – English Old Testament. Grand Rapids: Zondervan Publishing House - A Division of Harper Collins Publishers, 1979 - 1987.

Levitt, Zola. *The Seven Feasts of Israel*. Dallas, TX, 1979.

Lewis, C. S. *Perelandra*. New York: Macmillan, 1975.

Lewis, C. S. *That Hideous Strength*. New York: Macmillan, 1975.

Lewis, C. S. *The Great Divorce*. New York: Collier, 1984.

Lewis, C. S. *The Last Battle*. New York: Collier, 1970

Lewis, C. S., and Pauline Baynes. *The Chronicles of Narnia*. New York: HarperCollins, 1994.

Lewis, C.S., *Voyage of the Dawn Treader*, Collier Books, New York 1970.

Marshall D. Litt, Rev. Alfred. *The Interlinear Greek – Englilsh New Testament*. London, England: Samuel Bagster And Sons Limited, 1958 -1964.

Metaxas, Eric. *Amazing Grace William Wilberforce and the Heroic Campaign to End Slavery*. New York: Harper Collins, 2007.

Miles, Herbert Jackson. *Sexual Happiness in Marriage: A Christian Interpretation of Sexual Adjustment in Marriage*. Grand Rapids: Zondervan Pub. House,1982.

Morse, Melvin, and Paul Perry, *Transformed by the Light: The Powerful Effect of Near-death Experiences on People's Lives*. New York, NY: Villard/Random, 1992.

Reed, M.D., M.S., William Standish. Poetic *Thoughts Of Life and Hope – A Surgeon considers Healing and Christ*. www.xulonpress.com, 2009.

Roberts, Oral. *The Ultimate Voice – God's Still Small Voice*. Tulsa: Pengold Garrett & Assoc., 2008.

Rogers, Carl R. *On Becoming a Person*. New York: Houghton Mifflin Company, 1961 – 1995.

Rosen, Moishe. *Y'shua – the Jewish Way to Say Jesus*. Chicago: The Moody Bible Institute, 1982.

Schlessinger, Laura, and Stewart Vogel. *The Ten Commandments: The Significance of God's Laws in Everyday Life*. New York, NY: Cliff Street, 1998, p.182.

Schroeder, Gerald L. *The Science of God*. NY: Simon and Schuster, Inc., 1997.

Stern, David H. *Jewish New Testament Commentary: A Companion Volume to the Jewish New Testament*. Clarksville, MD: Jewish New Testament Publications, 1992.

Stern, David H. Complete Jewish Bible. Clarksville, MD: Jewish New Testament Publications, 1998.

Strong, L.L.D., James. *The New Strong's Exhaustive Concordance of the Bible*. Tennessee, Nashville: Thomas Nelson, 1984.

Swanson, Gerald C. *Statistics: A User Friendly Guide*. Edmonds, WA: GreyHeron, 2002.

Synan, Vinson. *The Century of the Holy Spirit: 100 Years of Pentecostal and Charismatic Renewal*, 1901-2001. Nashville: Thomas Nelson, 2001.

Tenney, Merrill C. *The Zondervan Pictorial Bible Dictionary*. Michigan: Grand Rapids: Zondervan Publishing House, 1963 – 1967.

Tennyson, Alfred (1809–1892), British poet. *Bartlett's Familiar Quotations*. Boston: Little, Brown and Company, 1937.

Trever, John C. *The Untold Story of Qumran*. Westwood, NJ: F.H. Revell, 1965.

Unger, Merrill F. Ph.D. *The New Unger's Bible Dictionary*, Chicago: Moody Bible Press, 1957.

Vaill, Peter B. *Learning as a Way of Being*. San Francisco: Jossey-Bass, 1996.

Van Impe, Jack. *TheJack Van Impe Prophecy Bible: King James Version*. Windsor, Canada: Jack Van Impe Ministries International, 1999.

Vine, W. E. Vine's, An Expository Dictionary of New Testament Words: Complete and Unabridged. Old Tappan, NJ: Revell, 1940 - 1966.

Reader's Write

Letters to the Editor: Resounding Vote for Rita Bennett

To the Editor: "I am pleased to see Rita Bennett's column appearing regularly in the Worship section of your newspaper. I know Rita personally, she had written many books, has given many seminars and, in her ministry, has traveled to many countries. Rita is well qualified to write for your newspaper. Thank you for "Rita's Beacon." Betty Bell. 2/3/05

Fan Mail for Rita Bennett

To the Editor: "Rita Bennett's column titled 'Innocent children at risk" (Feb. 10) was touching and deep.

"After tracing the history through the ages how innocent children have been the victims of tyrants and despots, her recent visit to the Children's Holocaust Memorial at *Yad Vashem Museum* in Jerusalem provides much food for thought and reflection.

"The vivid description of the thousands of candles lit in the midst of surrounding walls of mirrors, producing a sense of the vastness of the universe, points only to the fact that every single life that came into this world is precious in the sight of Our heavenly Father who will compensate ten times and more for all the wrongs that have been perpetrated through evil men by Jesus Christ our triumphant Savior and King." Alan Francis. 3/3/05

Lee Sheldon - neighbor
"Hi Rita, I think of you so often. Your articles in "The Beacon" are great. You are like (a) voice in the wilderness – going out with the message of Christ." Lee Sheldon, Teacher-Retired, Edmonds, WA 12/8/09

Joan Longstaff, Realtor
"I'm excited about the news of your column in the Edmonds Beacon. This is wonderful!" Joan 1/11/05

Al Hooper, Beacon Editor Emeritus Shares

"The Sparkling Jasper Wall." Nice job, Rita! You've hit your stride now. You might want to think about compiling your columns for a book publication at some point. And thanks for doing such a good job of meeting or beating your deadline." Al Hooper 6/8/05

"I should mention that one of your fans emailed us this week asking if your entire 'Heaven' series could be found on the Internet. I told him he could see the columns if he checked the archives every two weeks. His name is Fred. Anyway, you know you're developing an audience 'out there.'" From Al Hooper, editor 9/17/05

"Another fine, thorough piece it is. You certainly are a scholar of outstanding skills." Al Hooper 10/5/06

"Excellent! You've been doing the column long enough now that I think it's appropriate (and interesting to the readers) that you begin to share details about your background and challenges. The important thing is that every word you write is from the heart. Not many writers can do that." Al Hooper 1/25/07

"One of your best, Rita! Your scholarly studies are truly reflected here. At the same time you write from the heart, as always. On!" (Topic: "On Earth as it is in Heaven.") Al Hooper 8/16.07

"Another well written column! You've been a wonderful asset to the Beacon from the beginning, and you've always shown a real pro's respect for deadlines and guidelines. As a result you've built a loyal following for both yourself and the newspaper. My sincere thanks and appreciation go with you." Al Hooper, Editor Edmonds Beacon. Retired - 10/07/09

Lee Oles, Fine Artist
"Rita, I've read your book, "To Heaven and Back" every year. It brings Heaven closer to me. I've done this for the past 10 years. St. Alban's Church, 1/01/07 (15 years reading, before her journey Home.)

Rita's view of Heaven inspiring, Shirley Wilson

To the Editor: "I have been enjoying the series of columns by Rita Bennett on Heaven in your Worship Column, especially the most recent one (June 16) on Heaven's Jasper Wall. What a magnificent picture her words put into my mind, of Heaven being not only beautiful beyond our wildest imaginations, but spacious and powerful enough to accommodate all our needs for eternity.

"I was fortunate to be a member of the group that went with Rita on her first trip to Jerusalem in 1996. It was my first and only trip so far. Walking the streets that Jesus walked put me in awe of that holy city and brought His life on this earth a reality for me. The highlight of the trip was when we marched around the Old Jerusalem walls in our white robes, praying for God's chosen people and for peace in that land. Somehow we knew we were doing something truly significant and prophetic.

"Thank you for printing this series, and thank you Rita for all your research and thoughtful insights that are preparing us for our eternal home in Heaven." Shirley Wilson, Counselor 6/23/05

O'Driscoll Family
"Dear Rita, Mary, Dick and I loved your New Year's Beacon article! Thank you, thank you! Yea, Rita!" Shadie O'Driscoll, 1/3/10

Hipp Family
"Your articles make this hometown paper an extra delight to read!" Robin & Dave Hipp, 1/31/10

Bennett's Worship Column. "She is a widely traveled and highly educated writer and her knowledge and wisdom are undoubtedly touching hundreds of lives every week. A few weeks ago I began reading the intriguing story about Rita's early years as a young woman who would rather go to a beach party than a prayer meeting, and last week about her encounter with death and God's divine purpose in life.

"I'm so grateful for this wonderful column and especially Rita Bennett's transparency and willingness to share her fascinating personal story. It has touched me deeply and I want to thank the Beacon for giving us the privilege and benefit of this truly meaningful column." Sincerely, Dia Bock, Missionary 6/10/10

Pat Pierson, Graphic Artist

"Rita, you have a way of making the average reader —Christian and non-Christian—gently 'examine' themselves, and the things around them, in God's light. I don't ever want you to lose sight of that—it is a true gift of God." Patty Pierson, CRA Team Member, 9/6/06

Gaylord, Businessman
"Read your article in the Beacon.The topic was: 'Did Jesus marry Mary Magdalene?' Very good! Enlightening. Excellent. Compliments on your knowledge of the Bible.
You made my day!" Gaylord Sisk 6/12/06

Greenwood Family
"The Greenwood household loves Rita Bennett." From Carol Greenwood, Aglow leader. 8/9/05

Pat Ratliff, Editor
"I think your columns do a great job." Pat Ratliff Editor Edmonds Beacon, 1/19/10

"Interesting stuff Rita. Good article, thanks." Pat Ratliff, Editor, (Article for *Yom Kippur.*) 9/15/10.

Pastor Smith
"Rita, you are the perfect person to be writing this column in the Edmonds Beacon since you can talk both sides —bringing the Christian and Jew together. You're to the Christian what Dr. Daniel Lapin is to the Jew." Pastor Carl Smith. 1/23/05

finis

End Notes

Author's Prelude

[1] Schroeder, Gerald L. *The Science of God.* NY: Simon and Schuster, Inc., 1997.

[2] Bennett, Rita. *To Heaven & Back: True Stories of Those Who Have Made the Journey.* Grand Rapids, MI: Zondervan Pub. House, 1997.

[3] Lewis, C. S., and Pauline Baynes. *The Chronicles of Narnia,.* New York: HarperCollins, 1994.

Chapter One

[1] The 2004 Indian Ocean earthquake and Tsunami was an undersea mega-thrust earthquake that occurred at 00.58:53 UTC on Sunday, 26 December 2004, with an epicenter off the west coast of Sumatra Indonesia. (Wikipedia: The Free Encyclopedia. Wikimedia Foundation, Inc., 26 Dec. 2004. Web http://en.wikipedia.org/wiki/2004_indian_ocean_earthquake)

[2] Finis, Jennings Dake. *[Dake's] Annotated Reference Bible.* [S.l.]: Dake Bible Sales, 1963. Mt 2:18

[3] Hooper, Al ed. *Two Sisters Died of Med Overdose.* Mukilteo, WA: The Edmonds Beacon, Feb. 3, 2005, p.p. 1,5.

[4] Other special verses: Jesus promises a reward for kindness to children (Matt 10:42); declared that a childlike spirit is absolutely essential in religion (Matt 18:3-4); commands reception of (Mk 9:37); commanded that they should be fed spiritual food (John 21:15); also read Matthew 18:1-14, and much more.

[5] Dolan, David. "DDolan.com - Israel Update." *DDolan.com - Israel Update.* 1 Apr. 2005. Web. 24 Jan. 2013.

[6] Hekman, *"Second Treasure"* Message to Rita Bennett from Pastor Willem (Bill), D. Min., D.D.. 16 Feb. 2005. E-mail.

[7] Lapin, Rabbi Daniel. *Thought Tools.* Washington, Mercer Island: American Alliance of Jews and Christian's, circa 2005. (www.rabbidaniellapin.com)

[8] Barrett, Marvin, *Death Trip, Lear's,* Nov. 1989, p.119

[9] Bennett, Rita. *To Heaven & Back: True Stories of Those Who Have Made the Journey.* Grand Rapids, MI: Zondervan Pub. House, 1997.

[10] Kohlenberger lll, John R. *The New NIV Interlinear Hebrew – English Old Testament.* Grand Rapids: Zondervan Publishing House - A Division of Harper Collins Publishers, 1979 – 1987, Gen 1:1 "Berasheet berah Elohim et HaShamayim ..." p. 1.

[11] Girdlestone, Robert Baker, White, Donald R., ed. *Synonyms of the Old Testament,* Grand Rapids: Baker, 1983, p. 267.

[12] Moore, Thomas, *Come Ye Disconsolate,* Sacred Songs, 1816.

[13] Greely, Fr. Andrew. *Quotes by Andrew M. Greeley.* Web. © 2013 Goodreads inc. Web. http://www.goodreads.com/author/show/16639.Andrew_M_Greeley

[15] Schroeder, Gerald L. *The Science of God.* NY: Simon and Schuster, Inc., 1997, p. 23.

[15] Lewis, C. S., and Baynes, Pauline Baynes. *The Chronicles of Narnia.* New York: Harper Collins PublishersHarperCollinsPublishers, 2001.

[16] Lewis, C. S. *The Great Divorce,* New York: Macmillan, 1946.

[17] Knopf, Alfred A. *The Holy Land, Knopf Guides.* New York 1995, p. 244.

[18] Bennett, Rita, "Chapter 11" *To Heaven and& Back: True Stories of Those Who Have Made the Journey.* Grand Rapids, MI: Zondervan Pub. House, 1997. Available at http://emotionallyfree.org/IB-2H-B.html.

[19] Unger, Merrill F. "Apostle." *The New Unger's Bible Dictionary,* Chicago: Moody Press, 1957. p 88.

[20] Bennett, Rita. *Heaven Tours: Astonishing Journeys.* Alachua, FL: Bridge-Logos, 2009.

[21] Watson, Merla. Message to Rita Bennett. May 5, 2005. E-mail.

[22] Tenney, Merrill C., *The Zondervan Pictorial Bible Dictionary.* Zondervan Publishing House. Michigan: Grand Rapids. p. 782.

[23] Barrett, Marvin. *Death Trip.* New York, N.Y.: Lear, 1989. p.119.

[24] Cox-Chapman, Mally. *The Case for Heaven.* New York: G.P. Putman's Sons, 1995. p. 2.

[25] Morse, Melvin, and Paul Perry, Paul. *Transformed by the Light: The Powerful Effect of Near-death Experiences on People's Lives.* New York, NY: Villard/Random, 1992, p.18.

[26] Lapin, Rabbi Daniel. *Thought Tools.* Washington, Mercer Island: American Alliance of Jews and Christian's, circa 2005. (www.rabbidaniellapin.com)

[27] Dake, Finis Jennings (1963). *Dake's Annotated Reference Bible.* Atlanta, GA: Dake Bible Sales. p. 304.

[28] Unger, Merrill Frederick. "Smyrna." *The New Unger's Bible Dictionary.* Chicago: The Moody Bible Institute, 1957. p 1204.

[29] "In 1878 the German engineer, Carl Human, discovered in Pergamum, the great altar [of the idol] Zeus (believed by some to be Satan's seat Rev 2:13) now in East Berlin. *Ibid.* "Per'gamum" p. 986.

[30] *Ibid* "Antipas." p 83.

[31] Unger, Merrill F. "Balaam." *The New Unger's Bible Dictionary.* Chicago: Moody Press, 1957. p 139.

[32] Clarke, Adam, and Adam Clarke. *Clark's Commentary: The Holy Bible.* Nashville: Abingdon, 1977. pp. 981-981

[33] Van Impe, Jack. *TheJack Van Impe Prophecy Bible: King James Version.* Windsor, Canada: Jack Van Impe Ministries International, 1999, p. 19.

Chapter Two

[1] Lindberg, Christine A., Editor. *Oxford American Dictionary & Thesaurus.* Oxford University Press, Inc., New York: 2003.

[2] Henry, Matthew. *Matthew Henry's Commentary in One Volume.* Zondervan Publishing House. Michigan, Grand Rapids: 1961, pp. 1972-1973 Chapter 3.

[3] Dake, Finis Jennings, *Dake's Annotated Reference Bible.* Atlanta: Dake's Bible Sales, 1963, p. 288.

[4] Unger, Merrill F. "Sardis." *The New Unger's Bible Dictionary* Chicago: Moody Press, 1957, p. 1130.

[5] Unger, Merrill F. "Philadel'phia." *The New Unger's Bible Dictionary* Illinois, Chicago: Moody Press, 1957, pp. 999, 1000.

[6] Arthur, Kay. *Behold Jesus is Coming.* Oregon, Eugene: Harvest House, 1995, p.39.

[7] Porter, Catherine Toronto Star. *Men United for A Better Philadelphia.* Canada, Toronto: Cruickshank, John D, *The Toronto Star:* 1/8/2006. p. A6 Edition: MET.

[8] Webster, A Merriam. *Webster's New Collegiate Dictionary.* G. & C. Merriam Company: 1980. p. 853.

[9] Dake, Finis Jennings. *Dake's Annotated Reference Bible.* Georgia, Atlanta: Dake Bible Sales, 1963. p. 288, ref. note t.

[10] Guilbert, Charles Mortimer. *The Book of Common Prayer.* New York: Oxford University Press, for The Episcopal Church, 1979. p. 359.

[11] To understand Revelation 3:9, read David Stern's *Jewish New Testament Commentary,* page 796. To grasp this first century verse, and others, we must read them with early Christian and Jewish insight.

[12] Bennett, Rita. *To Heaven and Back.* Michigan, Grand Rapids: Zondervan, 1997, pp. 133 – 140.

[13] Seeger, Pete. *We Shall Overcome.* Columbia, 1963.

[14] Strong, L.L.D., James. "#3528." *The New Strong's Exhaustive Concordance of the Bible.* Tennessee, Nashville: Thomas Nelson, 1984, p.50.

[15] Swanson, Gerald C. *Statistics: A User Friendly Guide.* Edmonds, WA: GreyHeron, 2002.

[16] Ibid p1-2

[17] Church, Dr. J. R. "Psalms 111-117 Have a Menorah Design!" *Prophecy in the News.* May 2010: p.38.

[18] Synan, Vinson. *The Century of the Holy Spirit: 100 Years of Pentecostal and Charismatic Renewal, 1901-2001.* Nashville: Thomas Nelson, 2001, pp. 46 – 63.

[19] Bennett, Dennis J. *Nine O'clock in the Morning.* Plainfield, NJ: Logos International, 1970.

[20] Brown, Dan. *The Da Vinci Code: A Novel.* New York: Doubleday, 2003

[21] King, Karen. *Faded papyrus scrap refers to wife of Jesus.* Washington, Seattle: *The Seattle Times.,* 19 Sept. 2012, p. A12 News.

[22] Lindsay, Jay. "Harvard Journal: Jesus 'wife' Papyrus Unverified." *Grand Junction Colorado.* N.p., 21 Sept. 2012. Web. 02 Feb. 2013. http://www.gjfreepress.com/article/20120921/APA/1209210933.

[23] Bennett, Dennis J. *Nine O'clock in the Morning.* Plainfield, NJ: Logos International, 1970.

[24] Bennett, Rita Marie. *Emotionally Free®Course* Syllabi (aka *Prayer Counselors Study Guide*) (3 Levels now). Washington, Edmonds: Christian Renewal Association, Inc., 1980 – 2013. (www.EmotionallyFree.org)

[25] Vaill, Peter B. *Learning as a Way of Being.* San Francisco: Jossey-Bass, 1996, p. 121-149.

[26] Gorman, Christine, et. al`. "The Science of Anxiety" *Time* June 2002.

[27] Strong, James LL.D. "#3563." *The New Strong's Exhaustive Concordance of the Bible.* Nashville, Tenn.: Thomas Nelson Publishers, 1984, Greek Dictionary of N.T. p.50.

[28] Guilbert, Charles Mortimer. *The Book of Common Prayer.* New York, N.Y.: Oxford University Press, 1979, p. 358.

[29] Tennyson, Alfred (1809–1892), British poet. *Bartlett's Familiar Quotations.* Boston: Little, Brown and Company, 1937, p. 535 Ib. I. 414.

[30] Trever, John C. *The Untold Story of Qumran*. Westwood, NJ: F.H. Revell, 1965.

[31] I. TU, Janet, reporter. "Discovering the Dead Sea Scrolls; A Rare Window Into Biblical Times." The Seattle Times. Sunday, Sept. 17, 2006. pp. Local B1–B4.

[32] Noegel, Scott UW Professor. "Discovering the Dead Sea Scrolls; A Rare Window Into Biblical Times." The Seattle Times. Sunday, Sept. 17, 2006. p. Local B3.

[33] Laytner, Rabbi Anson Dir. Greater Seattle Chapter Jewish Committee. "Discovering the Dead Sea Scrolls; A Rare Window Into Biblical Times." The Seattle Times. Sunday, Sept. 17, 2006. p. Local B3.

Chapter Three

[1] *The Nativity Story*. Dir. Catherine Hardwicke. Prod. Wyck Godfrey and Marty Bowen. By Mike Rich. Perf. Keisha Castle-Hughes, Oscar Isaac, and Hiam Abbass. New Line Cinema, 2006. Film

[2] Gibson, David, and Michael McKinley. "CNN Presents." *After Jesus the First Christians*. Prod. Jody Gottlieb. CNN. 20 Dec. 2006 (first release). Television.

[3] Hayford, Jack W. *Spirit Filled Life: Student Bible*. Nashville, TN: Thomas Nelson, 2005.

[4] Guilbert, Charles Mortimer. *The Book of Common Prayer*. New York, N.Y.: Oxford University Press, 1979.

[5] Lewis, C. S. *The Last Battle*. New York: Collier, 1970. p184.

[6] Bennett, Rita. *You Can Be Emotionally Free*. Alachua, FL: Bridge-Logos Publishing, 1981.

[7] Lewis, C. S. *The Great Divorce*. New York: Collier, 1984.

[8] Bennett, Rita. *To Heaven & Back: True Stories of Those Who Have Made the Journey*. Grand Rapids, MI: Zondervan Pub. House, 1997

[9] Bennett, Rita. *Heaven Tours*. Florida, Alachua: Bridge-Logos, 2009.

[10] http://emotionallyfree.net/IB-2H-B.html and http://emotionallyfree.net/IB-HT.html

[11] See Ephesians 6:10-18; 2.John 8:32, 3; Isaiah 11:6, 4 (Greek, Commentary); 1 Peter 2:2-3; Psalm 139:13-14; Biblical historical record of the Scriptures is 3,500 years; Matthew 21:16; Ps. 8:2, 9; Matthew 18:14, 21:10; Isaiah 9:6; Acts 4:30.

[12] Bennett, Rita D.Litt. My next book will be: *The Lord's Prayer Heals,* with accompanying Syllabus. Check my website www. EmotionallyFree.org for more information.

[13] Bennett, Rita. *To Heaven & Back: True Stories of Those Who Have Made the Journey*. Grand Rapids, MI: Zondervan Pub. House, 1997 p 205.

[14] Kohlenberger lll, John R. *The New NIV Interlinear Hebrew – English Old Testament*. Grand Rapids: Zondervan Publishing House - A Division of Harper Collins Publishers, 1979 - 1987.

[15] Girdlestone, Robert Baker. *Synonyms of the Old Testament: Their Bearing on Christian Doctrine*. Grand Rapids, MI: Eerdmans, 1983. p 267.

[16] Baker, Mike. "With a tear, Billy Graham bids his wife farewell." The Seattle Times, June, 2007: p.1.

[17] Guilbert, Charles Mortimer. *The Book of Common Prayer*. New York, N.Y.: Oxford University Press, 1979. pp. 358, 359.

[18] Bennett, Rita. "Foreword: by Rev. Nelson E. Graham, M.A." *Heaven Tours: Astonishing Journeys* Alachua, FL: Bridge-Logos, 2009. pp. xiii – xvii.

[19] Sandra, Chambers. "Surprised by the Spirit." *Charisma Magazine*. 30 Apr. 2007. Web. 14 Feb. 2013. http://www.charismamag.com/site-archives/145-features/transformed-lives/2218-surprised-by-the-spirit.

[20] "Catholicseeking." : *St. Augustine of Hippo*. Web. 27 Mar. 2013. http://catholicseeking.blogspot.com/2012/08/st-augustine-of-hippo.html

[21] C. S. Lewis, The Great Divorce. New York: Macmillan Publishing Co., Inc., 1946, p.69.

[22] Bennett, Rita. *Heaven Tours: Astonishing Journeys*. Alachua, FL: Bridge-Logos, 2009.

[23] "LiveLeak.com - Nancy Pelosi On Fox News Sunday." *LiveLeak.com - Nancy Pelosi On Fox News Sunday*. 2007. Web. 25 Feb. 2013. http://www.liveleak.com/view?i=2f7_1191797202

[24] Strong, L.L.D., James. *The New Strong's Exhaustive Concordance of the Bible*. Tennessee, Nashville: Thomas Nelson, 1984.

[25] Burkett, Larry. *Business by the Book: The Complete Guide of Biblical Principles for the Workplace*. Nashville, TN: Thomas Nelson, 1998

[26] Lewis, C. S. *Perelandra*. New York: Macmillan, 1975.

[27] *Webster's New Collegiate Dictionary* defines evil as: (adj.) "morally bad or wrong conduct; wicked; harmfully wrong; disastrous; (noun): wickedness, sin. brings sorrow, distress or calamity." Springfield, Massachusetts, G & C Merriam Co., 1980. p.393.

[28] "September 11 Attacks." *Wikipedia*. Wikimedia Foundation, 21 Feb. 2013. Web. 25 Feb. 2013. <http://en.wikipedia.org/wiki/September_11_attacks>.

[29] *Webster's New Collegiate Dictionary* Springfield, Massachusetts, G & C Merriam Co., 1980. p. 341.

[30] Dykes, John Bacchus, writer. *The Hymnal*. New York, NY: The Church Hymnal Corporation, 1940. p. 345.

[31] Paradise is one of the descriptive biblical names of Heaven.

[32] Marshall D. Litt, Rev. Alfred. *The Interlinear Greek – Englilsh New Testament*. London, England: Samuel Bagster And Sons Limited, 1958 -1964

Chapter Four

[1] *Kenosis*. A term derived from the discussion as to the real meaning of Phil 2:6-7. "Who being in the form of God thought it not robbery to be equal with God: But emptied [*ekenosen*] Himself, taking the form of a servant, and was made in the likeness of men." (KJV–mod)

[2] Unger, Merrill Frederick, Ph.D. *The New Unger's Bible Dictionary*. "Mt. Hermon." Chicago: Moody Press, p. 554.

[3] Bennett, Rita. "Chapter 5" *To Heaven & Back: True Stories of Those Who Have Made the Journey*. Grand Rapids, MI: Zondervan Pub. House, 1997, p. 60.

[4] Stern, David H. "Amen." *Jewish New Testament Commentary: A Companion Volume to the Jewish New Testament*. Clarksville, MD: Jewish New Testament Publications, 1992, p. 26.

[5] Webster, Daniel. *Webster's New Collegiate Dictionary*. Massachusetts: G. & C. Merriam Company, 1980, p. 996.

[6] Stern, David H. "Amen." *Jewish New Testament Commentary: A Companion Volume to the Jewish New Testament*. Clarksville, MD: Jewish New Testament

Publications, 1992, p. 23.

[7] Douglas, J. D. *The New Bible Dictionary*. Grand Rapids, MI: Eerdmans, 1962. 694-95.

[8] Dake, Finis Jennings (1963). *Dake's Annotated Reference Bible*. Atlanta, GA: Dake Bible Sales. p. 4 NT.

[9] Vine, W. E. *Vine's An Expository Dictionary of New Testament Words: Complete and Unabridged*. Old Tappan, NJ: Revell, 1940 - 1966. p. 55.

[10] Stern, David H. " Matthew 5:5 *Jewish New Testament Commentary: A Companion Volume to the Jewish New Testament*. Clarksville, MD: Jewish New Testament Publications, 1992

[11] Ibid p. 23, 24.

[12] Bennett, Rita. *Heaven Tours: Astonishing Journeys*. "I Traveled at the Speed of Light," Alachua, FL: Bridge-Logos, 2009.

[13] Strong, James *The New Strong's Exhaustive Concordance of the Bible*. Nashville: Thomas Nelson, © 1984. p.p. 6663-6666.

[14] Vine, W. E. *Vine's Expository Dictionary of New Testament Words: Complete and Unabridged*. Westwood, NJ: Barbour, 1966. p. 298.

[15] Bennett, Dennis J., and Rita Bennett. *The Holy Spirit and You: A Study-guide to the Spirit-filled Life*. Plainfield, NJ: Logos International, 1971

[16] Blanchard, Rev. Richard, *Fill My Cup Lord*, Sacred Songs, 1964 Sheet Music.

[17] Hayford, Jack W. *Spirit-Filled Life: Student Bible*. Nashville: Thomas Nelson, 2005. Matthew 5:7.

[18] [18] Strong, James *The New Strong's Exhaustive Concordance of the Bible*. Nashville: Thomas Nelson, © 1984. p.p. 700-701.

[19] Vine, W. E. *Vine's Expository Dictionary of New Testament Words: Complete and Unabridged*. Westwood, NJ: Barbour, 1966. p. 206-7.

[20] Friesen, James G. *A Far Better Life: Spiritual and Psychological Insights from Jesus' Teaching*. Eugene, Or: Wipf & Stock, 2008. Print.

[21] *Ibid*, p. 29

[22] Bennett, Rita. *You Can Be Emotionally Free*. Alachua, FL: Bridge-Logos, 1982 - 2007.

[23] New Oxford American Dictionary, Oxford American Writer's Thesaurus, Apple Dictionary. Wikipedia, 2005.
http://en.wikipedia.org/wiki/Oxford_Dictionary_of_English

[24] American Psychiatric Association. *Desk Reference to the Diagnostic Criteria, Narcissistic Personality Disorder*. Washington, D.C., 2000, p.294.

[25] Bennett, Rita M. *The Hebrew Alphabet Course. Spiritual Meanings for Judeo-Christian Biblical Teaching*. Edmonds, WA: Healing People Publishing House, 2022 – 2005, Hebrew Syllabus p.p. 4 -1, 4 -2.

[26] Schlessinger, Dr. Laura, and Stewart Vogel. *The Ten Commandments: The Significance of God's Laws in Everyday Life*. New York, NY: Cliff Street, 1998, p.31.

[27] Webster, Daniel. *Webster's New World Dictionary*. Cleveland, OH: Pocket Books, 2003, p. 39.

[28] Unger, Merrill Frederick, Ph.D., D. (1988). *The New Unger's Bible Dictionary*. "God", Chicago: The Moody Bible Institute, p. 480.

[29] Schlessinger, Dr. Laura, and Stewart Vogel. *The Ten Commandments: The Significance of God's Laws in Everyday Life*. New York, NY: Cliff Street, 1998, p. 158.

[30] Bennett, Rita. *You Can Be Emotionally Free*. Alachua, FL: Bridge-Logos, 1982-2007.

[31] Schlessinger, Laura, and Stewart Vogel. *The Ten Commandments: The Significance of God's Laws in Everyday Life*. New York, NY: Cliff Street, 1998.p.182.

[32] Arterburn, Stephen, Fred Stoeker, and Mike Yorkey. *Every Man's Battle: Winning the War on Sexual Temptation : One Victory at a Time*. Colorado Springs, CO: WaterBrook, 2000, back cover.

[33] Miles, Herbert Jackson. *Sexual Happiness in Marriage: A Christian Interpretation of Sexual Adjustment in Marriage*. Grand Rapids: Zondervan Pub. House, 1982.

[34] Webster, Daniel. *Webster's New Collegiate Dictionary*. Springfield: G. & C. Merriam Co., 1980, p. 657.

[35] Schlessinger, Laura, and Stewart Vogel. *The Ten Commandments: The Significance of God's Laws in Everyday Life*. New York, NY: Cliff Street, 1998, p. 270.

Chapter Five

[1] Rogers, Carl R. *On Becoming a Person*. New York: Houghton Mifflin Company, 1961 – 1995, p.p. 47, 63.

[2] Strong, James. *The New Strong's Exhaustive Concordance of the Bible*. Nashville: Thomas Nelson, 1984, p.p. 75, # 5368 phileo; 7, #26 agape Greek Dictionary of N.T. For biblical examples of agape and phileo see: John 15:13, and John 21:15-17 (see Greek).

[3] Metaxas, Eric. *Amazing Grace William Wilberforce and the Heroic Campaign to End Slavery*. New York: Harper Collins, 2007.

[4] Ibid, p. 63.

[5] Ibid, p. 277.

[6] Dake, Finis Dake. *Dake's Annotated Reference Bible*. Atlanta: Dake Bible Sales, 1963, p.122, margin side bar – r.

[7] Rosen, Moishe. *Y'shua – the Jewish Way to Say Jesus*. Chicago: The Moody Bible Institute, 1982, p. 38,39 gives dates of Jesus being revealed as Messiah on the Mount of Olives as He rode the donkey (remembered as Palm Sunday today), and His following crucifixion.

[8] Bennett, Rita. "My Birthday Gift from Heaven." Rita's Reflections. CHRISTIAN RENEWAL ASSOCIATION INC., 2003. Web. 03 May 2013. http://emotionallyfree.com/RR-050213.html.

[9] Levitt, Zola. *The Seven Feasts of Israel*. [S.l.]: Author, 1979, p. 12.

[10] Ibid, p. 11.

[11] Levitt, Zola. *The Seven Feasts of Israel*. [S.l.]: Author, 1979, p.14.

[12] Guilbert, Charles Mortimer custodian. *The Book of Common Prayer*. 1979, p. 358 – 359 *The Nicene Creed*.

[13] Holman, Solaman. *Holman Christian Standard Bible*. Nashville: Holman Bible, 1999 – 2003.

[14] "Definition: Buckler." *Buckler*. Web. 13 Mar. 2013. http://dictionary.die.net/buckler

[15] Bennett, Rita. *You Can Be-- Emotionally Free*. Alachua: Bridge-Logos, 1982.

[16] New Oxford American Dictionary Online, n.d. April, 26, 2013.

[17] Dake, Finis Jennings. *Dake's Annotated Reference Bible*. Atlanta: Dake Bible Sales, 1963. p, 618, Summary of Psalms – General facts about the book of Psalms #3.

[18] Ibid. p. 591 side bar # r.

[19] Ibid, p. 591, side bars # r, #s.

[20] "Psalm 91 - Under the Shadow of the Almighty." *Psalm 91 - Under the Shadow of the Almighty*. N.p., n.d. Web. 13 Mar. 2013. http://www.bibleinsong.com/Song_Pages/Psalms/Psalm91/Psalm91.htm

[21] Dake, Finis Jennings. *Dake's Annotated Reference Bible*. Atlanta: Dake Bible Sales, 1963. p, 618, Summary of Psalms – Authors.

[22] "Psalm 91 - Under the Shadow of the Almighty." *Psalm 91 - Under the Shadow of the Almighty*. N.p., n.d. Web. 13 Mar. 2013.

[23] Tehillim, are from Feuer, Avrohom Chaim. *Tehillim*. Brooklyn, NY: Mesorah Publications, 1983, p. 260 notes.

[24] Ibid, p. 260, notes.

[25] Ibid. p. 260, notes (Radak).

[26] KJV is public domain.

[27] *Webster's New Collegiate Dictionary*. Springfield, MA: G. & C. Merriam, 1979.

[28] Reed, M.D., M.S., William Standish. *Poetic Thoughts Of Life and Hope – A Surgeon considers Healing and Christ*. www.xulonpress.com, 2009. For more information check with *Regent University Library Archives,* Virginia Beach, VA.

[29] "Alfred Tennyson, 1809-1892 - "Morte D'Arthur"" *Alfred Tennyson, 1809-1892 - "Morte D'Arthur"* Web. 13 Mar. 2013. http://library.sc.edu/spcoll/britlit/tenn/morte.html

[30] Lewis, C. S. *That Hideous Strength*. New York: Macmillan, 1975.

[31] "That Hideous Strength (Space Trilogy Series #3)." *Barnes & Noble*. Web. 13 Mar. 2013. http://www.barnesandnoble.com/w/that-hideous-strength-cs-lewis/1102934105?ean=9780743234924

[32] "Selah." *Wikipedia*. Wikimedia Foundation, 03 Apr. 2013. Web. 13 Mar. 2013. http://en.wikipedia.org/wiki/Selah

[33] Bennett, Rita. *You Can Be-- Emotionally Free*. Alachua: Bridge-Logos, 1982.

[34] Hayford, Jack W. *Spirit-Filled Life Bible*. Nashville:Thomas Nelson, 1991, p.217.

[35] Bennett, Rita. *Treasures From An Oak Chest*. http://www.emotionallyfree.org/IBooks.html, 2012. p. 86.

[36] Guilbert, Charles Mortimer. *The Book of Common Prayer,* New York: Oxford University Press, 1979, p.120.

[37] Davis, Rabbi Menachem, ed. *Tehillim,The Book of Psalms*. Brooklyn: Mesorah, 2001, p. 56, quote Rabbi Meiri.

[38] Ibid. p. 56.

[39] Bennett, Rita. *Heaven Tours: Astonishing Journeys*. Alachua, FL: Bridge-Logos, 2009, pp 68-70.

[40] Davis, Rabbi Menachem, ed. *Tehillim,The Book of Psalms*. Brooklyn: Mesorah, 2001, Psalm 26, p. 56.

[41] Ibid, Notes Rabbi Rashi, p.34, Psalm 17:3.

[42] Webster, Daniel. Webster's New Collegiate Dictionary. Springfield: G.&C. Merriam Co., 1980, p. 979.

[43] See www.EmotionallyFree.org

[44] Dalberg-Acton, John Emerich Edward. Lord Acton's Letter to Bishop Mandell Creighton [April 5, 1887]. *Bartlett's Familiar Quotations.* Boston: Little, Brown and Company, 1882 – 1980, p. 615.

[46] Stern, David H. *Complete Jewish Bible.* Clarksville: Jewish New Testament Publications, Inc., 1998, p.1597 Glossary.

[47] *The Bartlett's Familiar Quotations – William Shakespeare's "Macbeth" Banquo's quote, Act 1.* Boston: Little, Brown and Company, 1882 – 1980, p. 236.

[48] *Amplified Bible.* Grand Rapids: Zondervan Publishing House, 1965, p. 497 Solomon's wisdom.

Chapter Six Part 1

[1] Allen, Woody. "Cool Quotes Collection." *CoolQuotesCollection.com.* N.p., n.d. Web. 08 May 2013. http://coolquotescollection.com/Last/5.

[2] Davis, Rabbi Menachem, ed. *Tehillim Book of Psalms & Commentary R' Hirsch.* Brooklyn: Mesorah Publications, Ltd., 2001, p. 57.

[3] Ilibagiza, Immaculée, and Steve Erwin. *Left to Tell: Discovering God amidst the Rwandan Holocaust.* Carlsbad, CA: Hay House, 2006, p. 173.

[4] Bennett, Rita. *Heaven Tours – Astonishing Journeys.* Alachua, FL: Bridge-Logos, 2009, p. 78-79.

[5] Davis, Rabbi Menachem, ed. *Tehillim Book of Psalms & Commentary R' Hirsch.* Brooklyn: Mesorah Publications, Ltd., 2001, p. 57.

[6] Davis, Rabbi Menachem, ed. *Tehillim Book of Psalms & Commentary R' Hirsch.* Brooklyn: Mesorah Publications, Ltd., 2001, p. 57.

[7] Baker, Warren, Gen. ed. *The Complete Word Study Old Testament,* Chattanooga: AMG International, Inc.,1994, p. 1782. Ref Isaiah 54:8

[8] Davis, Rabbi Menachem, ed. *Tehillim Book of Psalms & Commentary R' Hirsch.* Brooklyn: Mesorah Publications, Ltd., 2001, p. 57, 58, *Ibn Ezra.*

[9] Kohlenberger lll, John R. *The New NIV Interlinear Hebrew – English Old Testament.* Grand Rapids: Zondervan Publishing House - A Division of Harper Collins Publishers, 1979 - 1987

[10] Bennett, Rita. *Heaven Tours – Astonishing Journeys.* Alachua: Bridge-Logos, 2009, p.1. Chapter One, *Starting the Journey.*

[11] Ilibagiza, Immaculée, and Steve Erwin. *Left to Tell: Discovering God amidst the Rwandan Holocaust.* Carlsbad, CA: Hay House, 2006, p. 173.

[12] D, Keith. "Lent." *Wikipedia.* Wikimedia Foundation, 24 Apr. 2013. Web. 08 May 2013. http://en.wikipedia.org/w/index.php?title=Lent.

[13] Cooper, Anderson, Arthur Brice, Elise Labott, Richard Roth, Chris Lawrence, and Steve Kastenbaum. *CNN.* Cable News Network, 16 Jan. 2010. Web. 08 May 2013.
http://www.cnn.com/2010/WORLD/americas/01/15/haiti.earthquake/index.html.

[14] Achenbach, Joel. "Chile Earthquake: The next Big One?" *Achenblog* -. N.p., 27 Feb. 2010. Web. 08 May 2013.
http://voices.washingtonpost.com/achenblog/2010/02/chile_earthquake_the_next_big.html.

[15] Fountain, Henry. "Chile Quake Similar to 2004 Indian Ocean Tremor." *Nation & World*. The Seattle Times, 27 Feb. 2010. Web. 09 May 2013. http://seattletimes.com/html/nationworld/2011212520_quakescience28.html.

[16] Sumida, Chiyomi, David Allen, and T. D. Flack. "Tsunami Warning Downgraded, Officials Warn of High Tidal Swells." *Daily Newsletter*. Stars and Stripes, 28 Feb. 2010. Web. 08 May 2013. http://www.stripes.com/news/tsunami-warning-downgraded-officials-warn-of-high-tidal-swells-1.99512

[17] Case, Wendy. "OKLAHOMA REPORTS 4.4 ON THE RICTOR SCALE." *Allvoices*. N.p., 27 Feb. 2010. Web. 08 May 2013. http://www.allvoices.com/contributed-news/5315948-oklahoma-reports-44-on-the-rictor-scale.

[18] Dake, Finis Jennings. *Dake's Annotated Reference Bible*. Atlanta: Dake's Bible Sales, 1963, p.421 1 Chronicles 1:19 side notes J.

[19] Bratcher, Dennis. "The Season of Lent." *The Season of Lent*. CRI / Voice, Institute, 25 Mar. 2013. Web. 13 May 2013. http://www.crivoice.org/cylent.html.

[20] Bennett, Rita. *Heaven Tours: Astonishing Journeys*. Alachua, FL: Bridge-Logos, 2009. pictures pp146, 150.

[21] Guilbert, Charles Mortimer. The Book of Common Prayer. New York: Oxford University Press,1979, p.363.

[22] "Peace Prayer of St. Francis of Assisi." *Peace Prayer of St. Francis of Assisi*. N.p., n.d. Web. 08 May 2013. http://www.americancatholic.org/Features/Francis/peaceprayer.asp.

[23] "Empowered21: Global Congress on Holy Spirit Empowerment in the 21st Century." *YouTube*. YouTube, 13 Oct. 2009. Web. 08 May 2013. http://www.youtube.com/watch?v=I2gDxp2lhrM.

[24] Bennett, Dennis, D.Div. "God's Strength for this Generation." *Charisma Magazine - Charismatic Renewal Turns 50*. April 2010: pp.55,56.

[25] Bennett, Dennis J. and Rita M. *The Holy Spirit and You – Guide to the Spirit-Filled Life*. Alachua: Bridge-Logos, 1971 – 2005.

[26] Guilbert, Charles Mortimer. The Book of Common Prayer. New York: Oxford University Press,1979, p.418.

[27] *Safe in the Arms of Jesus*, Fanny Crosby

Chapter Six Part 2

[1] Guilbert, Charles Mortimer. *The Book of Common Prayer*. New York: Oxford University Press, 1979, p. 370.

[2] Dake, Finis Jennings. *Dake's Annotated Reference Bible*. Atlanta: Dake's Bible Sales, 1963, p.872ß

[3] Fisher, Gary. "Increase of Knowledge and Travel" Lion of Judah Ministry Website. Year 2013 http://www.according2prophecy.org/42colleague.html

[4] Bennett, Dennis and Rita. *The Holy Spirit and You – a Guide to the Spirit-Filled life*. Alachua: Bridge-Logos, 1971 - 2005, p. 45. Warning about the psychic and occult.

[5] Dake, Finis Jennings. *Dake's Annotated Reference Bible*. Atlanta: Dake's Bible Sales, 1963, p.254, side bar notes Nos. 4, and 5. Hebrews 12:1–3.

[6] Strong, James. The New Strong's Exhaustive Concordance of the Bible. Nashville: Thomas Nelson, 1984, #4102, p.58 Greek *Pistis*.

[7] Bennett, Dennis and Rita. *The Holy Spirit and You.* Alachua: Bridge–Logos, 1971–2005, pp. 142–143.

[8] Dennis Bennett, *Nine O'clock in the Morning,* Alachua: Bridge-Logos, 1970, p.182-184.

[9] Strong, James. The New Strong's Exhaustive Concordance of the Bible. Nashville: Thomas Nelson, 1984, #3056, p.45 Greek.

[10] Ibid #4483 erco, 4487 rhema , p.63 Greek (the two words connect).

[11] Bennett, Rita. *To Heaven and Back.* Michigan, Grand Rapids: Zondervan, 1997

[12] Bennett, Rita. *Heaven Tours: Astonishing Journeys.* Alachua, FL: Bridge-Logos, 2009, pp. 81-83, illustrations in color p. 150.

[13] Bennett, Dennis and Rita. *The Holy Spirit and You.* Alachua: Bridge-Logos, 2005, p. 131.

[14] Ibid, p. 133.

[15] Church, J. R. *The Mystery of the Menorah ... and the Hebrew Alphabet.* Oklahoma: Prophecy Publications, 1993, Foreword.

[16] Ibid, p.1 Foreword.

[17] See www.moonconnection.com or www.israelnationalnews.com.

[18] Stern, David H. *Complete Jewish Bible.* Clarksville: Jewish New Testament Publications, Inc. 1998, p. 1601 Glossary.

[19] Thompson, Frank Charles. The New Chain-Reference Bible. Indianapolis: B.B. Kirkbride Bible Co.,Inc, 1957, *Levit* 23:39,42,43 KJV-MOD, p. 128.

[20] Scherman, Rabbi Nosson. *The Chumash.* Brooklyn: Mesorah Publications, Ltd., 1993.

[21] Ibid, p. 689.

[22] Guilbert, Charles Mortimer. *The Book of Common Prayer.* NewYork: Oxford University Press, 1979, p. 359.

[23] Christianity Today Gleanings." *Christianity Today Gleanings.* N.p., 12 Oct. 2010. Web. 24 May 2013.
<http://blog.christianitytoday.com/ctliveblog/archives/2010/10/chilean_miner_g.html>.

[24] Getting dates correct is hard even with good Bible references and commentaries, when we go back in history nearly three-thousand years. They didn't have computers back then!
I have updated Isaiah's birth date, and Uzziah's death date which was the date Isaiah's ministry would have begun. Isaiah was a Jewish prophet and it is believed by some Jewish Rabbi's that meant Isaiah would have had to be 30 years old for an acceptable time of ministry could begin. With this in place Isaiah was born in 770 B.C. and Uzziah died 740 B.C. = 30 years. Isaiah had his heart-warming experience as Uzziah was dying (Is 6:1a). He writes "In the year that Uzziah died, I saw the Lord ..." (Assisted by: Copyright © 2012 Answers Corporation. 12/1/12). As "Answers Corp." says about Isaiah's birth date: "Since the actual date is unknown all this is based on assumptions, but you have to start somewhere." I say "amen" to that. At any rate, the Rabbi's have perspectives I respect and that clarifies Judean History for us.

[25] *The Dead Sea Scrolls* Jerusalem, 1994, © Israel Antiquities Authority. To review

this subject, see the end of Chapter Two *"Dead Sea Scrolls, a Gift to all of us."*
[26] See chapter 6, part 1, My Personal Story).
[27] Bennett, Rita Litt.D. My next book will be: *The Lord's Prayer Heals,* with accompanying Syllabus. Check my website www. EmotionallyFree.org for more information.
[28] Gunn, Scott Exec, Dir. *Forward Day by Day* – Manual of Daily Bible reading and devotions. Cincinnati: Forward Movement, Email: orders@forwardmovement.org Vol. 79, No 2.
[29] www.EmotionallyFree.org
[30] Shakespeare, William, "Macbeth", Act 1 scene 3
[31] Hayford, Jack W. Exec. Ed. *Spirit Filled Life Bible for Students. Nashville, Thomas Nelson, 1995,* p. 858.
[32] "Printing Press." *Wikipedia.* Wikimedia Foundation, 29 Nov. 2010. Web. 29 Nov. 2010. http://en.wikipedia.org/wiki/Printing_Press.
[33] Hayford, Jack W. Exec. Ed. *Spirit-Filled Life Bible. Nashville: Thomas Nelson,* 1991, p. 987, footnote 20:2,3.
[34] Webster, A. Merriam. *Webster's New Collegiate Dictionary.* Springfield: G. & C. Merriam Company, 1980, p.1250.
[35] Hayford, Jack W., Exec. Ed. *Spirit-Filled Life Bible. Nashville:Thomas Nelson,* 1991, p. 1032 Notes: Kingdom Dynamics.
[36] http://www.canys.net/images/Page%209%20Mar%20and%20Men%20Illness.pdf posted on "Marijauna Is a Danger to Health and Safety." *Marijauna.* Council of Addictions of New York State, Web. 25 Apr. 2013. http://www.canys.net/marij.htm.
[37] Amen, Daniel G. *Change Your Brain Change Your Life.* New York: Three Rivers; Reprint Edition, 1999. p131. Print.
[38] Webster, A. Merriam. Webster's New *Collegiate Dictionary.* Springfield: G. & C. Merriam Company, 1980, p. 52.
[39] Strong, L.L.D., James. *The New Strong's Exhaustive Concordance of the Bible.* Tennessee, Nashville: Thomas Nelson, 1984, p. 53, #3759 Greek Ref.

Chapter Seven

[1] Crouch, Andraé. "Sissel & Oslo Gospel Choir- My Tribute (To God Be The Glory)." *YouTube.* YouTube, 20 Dec. 2006. Web. 01 May 2013. http://www.youtube.com/watch?v=xtenFJ6x75k.
[2] Crouch, Andraé. "My Tribute Lyrics." *Lyricsty.com.* Web. 01 May 2013. http://www.lyricsty.com/andrae-crouch-my-tribute-lyrics.html.
[3] Guilbert, Charles Mortimer. *The Book of Common Prayer.* New York: Oxford University Press. *The Nicene Creed* says, "For us and for our salvation: he [Jesus] came down from heaven: by the power of the Holy Spirit He became incarnate from the Virgin Mary, and was made man." p.358.
[4] Drosnin, Michael. *Bible Code III: Saving the World.* [United States]: Worldmedia, 2010. Print.
[5] http://www.chabad.org/calendar/1000year.asp?tdate=5/27/2013 When I wrote this note it was May 28, 2013, but on the Jewish Civil calendar it was Sivan 18, 5773.
[6] Church, J. R. *Daniel Reveals the Bloodline of the Antichrist.* Oklahoma City: Prophecy Publications, 2010, Book Back Cover. Dr. Church says, "Problems with

dating occurred because second-century rabbis removed 243 years from their calendars in order to cause Daniel's prophecy to line up with Rabbi Akiva's declaration that Bar Kokhba was the promised 'star' out of Jacob." Add those years back into the Hebrew year for a date closer to where we are now: 5773 + 243 = 6016. Bible history covers 7,000 years.

[7] Lewis, C.S., *Voyage of the Dawn Treader,* Collier Books, New York, 1970.

[8] Bennett, Rita LMFTA, *To Heaven and Back* – True Stories of Those Who Have Made the Journey. Edmonds, WA: CRA Publishing 98020, 1997 – 2013 reprints.

[9] Bennett, Rita, M.A., LITT.D, *Heaven Tours* – Astonishing Journeys. Alachua: Bridge–Logos, 2009.

[10] Unger, Merrill F. "High Place." *The New Unger's Bible Dictionary.* Chicago: Moody Press, 1957. p.569, 570).

[11] ibid, "Hezekiah." p. 566

[12] Dake. Finis Jennings. *Dake's Annotated Reference Bible.* Atlanta: Dake's Bible Sales, 1963, p. 709, Note P in margin.

[13] Ibid. p. 415, Hezekiah's sun dial, 2 Kings 20:9 note sidebar.

[14] Roberts, Oral. *The Ultimate Voice* – God's Still Small Voice. Tulsa: Pengold Garrett & Associates, 2008.

[15] Bennett, Rita. *The Hebrew Alphabet Course.* Edmonds: CRA Publisher, 2002, chapter 3.

22426322R00212

Made in the USA
Charleston, SC
21 September 2013